HOT ROD *Magazine*

The First 12 Issues

From the Editors of HOT ROD Magazine

MBI Publishing Company

First published in 1998 by MBI Publishing Company, 729 Prospect Avenue, PO Box 1, Osceola, WI 54020-0001 USA

MBI Publishing Company books are also available at discounts in bulk quantity for industrial or sales-promotional use. For details write to Special Sales Manager at Motorbooks International Wholesalers & Distributors, 729 Prospect Avenue, PO Box 1, Osceola, WI 54020-0001 USA.

Library of Congress Cataloging-in Publication Data Available
ISBN 0-7603-0638-9

On the front cover: On October 19, 1947, Eddie Hulse of Compton, California, raced Regg Schlemmer's Class C roadster at El Mirage Dry Lake. With an average speed of 130.65 mph, Hulse drove his way to a new Southern California Timing Association record and into American history as the cover subject of the premier issue of *Hot Rod* Magazine.

On the back cover: In 1948, Robert Petersen began a *Hot Rod* Magazine "to inform and entertain those interested in automobiles whose bodies and engines have been rebuilt in the quest for better performance and appearance." *Hot Rod Magazine: The First 12 Issues* celebrates the beginnings of the magazine that captured the imaginations of hot rodders across the United States fifty years ago and continues to hold it today.

Printed in the United States of America

Contents

Introduction

The end of World War II began a new era for the United States as tens of thousands of young men returned home filled with confidence after having taken on the world and won. Many of those men found fellow gearheads during their time in the service—guys from all over the country who shared their love of hot rods. When they returned to their garages, they had new ideas along with the time, money, and skills to work on them, and hot rodding began to boom across the country.

In 1947, Robert E. "Pete" Petersen was working as a publicist for Hollywood Publicity Associates, a firm hired to do publicity for the upcoming Hot Rod Exposition at the Los Angeles Armory. Bob saw a market and got together with Bob Lindsay to create *Hot Rod* magazine. The first issue was published in January 1948, and the new magazine was sold on the front steps of the Armory during the show. It was an immediate hit. While a few other magazines of the time covered racing, *Hot Rod* was the first to cover hot rodding, both on the track and the street.

Hot Rod's mission was clearly stated in the first lines of the first editorial: "*Hot Rod* is published to inform and entertain those interested in automobiles whose bodies and engines have been rebuilt in the quest for better performance and appearance." In the first few issues, it united hot rodders across the country and made them aware of each other's activities; an awareness that spurred the growth of a hobby and created an aftermarket industry that continued to grow.

Hot Rod magazine sparked some controversy at first, primarily because of its name. At the time, hot rodders were considered to be the worst form of juvenile delinquents, thanks to some sensationalized newspaper stories that generated by a critical media. Choosing *Hot Rod* as a title was a gutsy move on Petersen and Lindsay's part, but it worked. The magazine staff, along with the SCTA and later the NHRA, worked hard to change that juvenile delinquent image, and promote safe and socially acceptable hot rodding. Club profile magazine features showed hot rodders working with police and community leaders to promote safety. They proved that hot rodders were just a bunch of clean-cut kids who happened to like cars. Within a few years, hot rodders' public acceptance was beginning to change.

Part of *Hot Rod*'s success came from listening carefully to the reactions of the readers. In the second issue, while letters from readers panned the fiction story that appeared in issue one, they overwhelmingly requested more technical information on the cars shown in the issue. The editorial staff responded and in the course of its first year, the magazine changed from something that was more like a newsletter into a full-fledged national publication.

There were more than a few surprises during *Hot Rod*'s first twelve issues. Today, many of us tend to think of the dry lakes of Southern California as the birthplace of hot rodding. One look at these magazines proves that track roadster racing across the country on dirt tracks in Portland, St. Paul, and Indiana, as the focus of the publication. Certainly *Hot Rod*'s presence in Los Angeles guaranteed that Southern California would be the epicenter for hot rodding, but initially dirt track racing was the hot bed of hot rod action back in 1948.

Hot Rod also helped create phenomenal growth in the automotive aftermarket industry. While small companies had been producing speed equipment since the 1920s, they generally had regional clientele. Furthermore, they carried parts that were primarily for racing. The companies that advertised in *Hot Rod* quickly found that they had customers nationwide. The first issue had a few dozen ads, all with Los Angeles-area addresses. But by the end of 1954, *Hot Rod* had more than 70 advertisers from all over the country, many with full-page displays and sophisticated approaches to their new-found audience.

Hot Rod was the foundation for Petersen Publishing, which later became (and still is) one of the largest automotive publishers in the world. Perhaps Bob Petersen's most important legacy to hot rodders, though, was the creation of the Petersen Automotive Museum in Los Angeles in connection with the County of Los Angeles Museum System. By itself, it's worth a trip to the West coast.

Bob Petersen didn't accomplish all this by himself. The magazine's list of editors and staffers reads like a "Who's Who of Hot Rodding." Wally Parks was the first full-time editor of Hot Rod and was instrumental in creating the National Hot Rod Association in 1951. Tom Medley gave us a lot of laughs with Stroker McGurk and his insight into hot rodding culture. Tex Smith has been an automotive publishing constant since the 1950s, and names like Eric Rickman, Bob D'Olivo, Ray Brock, Jim McFarland, Racer Brown, Bill Burke, Gray Baskerville, John Dianna, Don Francisco, and many others are familiar to us all.

Hot Rod, like the sport it covers, has changed and grown over the years. These first 12 issues show us the beginning of an industry and the birth of a national phenomenon that would influence the automotive industry in the United States and worldwide. But more important than that, they also show us our roots: who we are and where we came from. When you pick up this book, read the stories. Look closely at the photos. Scrutinize the cars. Remember the faces. You'll see just what hot rodding is all about—ingenuity, speed, freedom, creativity, individuality, and fun with cars and trucks. Some things never change, even after 50 years.

Steve Hendrickson
Senior Editor, Rodder's Digest Magazine

VOLUME 1

January—December 1948

HOT ROD *Magazine*

VOL. 1, NO. 1 ★ ★ ★ PRICE 25c   WORLD'S MOST COMPLETE HOT ROD COVERAGE   JANUARY 1948

HOT ROD OF THE MONTH

Sitting in the driver's seat is Eddie Hulse, who, a few moments after this picture was taken, drove number 668, to set a new SCTA record for Class C roadsters. Hulse, a native Californian, nosed out Randy Shinn, a long-time top honor holder for the RC Class. Shinn's old record was 129.40 in a channeled Mercury T.

Keeping the Car Out Front by George Riley—Page 10

Editor's Column

Hot rod is published to inform and entertain those interested in automobiles whose bodies and engines have been rebuilt in the quest for better performance and appearance.

In this publication readers will find a chance to air their views, ask questions (and get the answers), read about racing and timing meets and automobile shows, see the latest in engine and body designs, enjoy entertaining fiction and see engine parts displayed with what we call "the feminine touch."

Getting off to a good start, HRM wants the readers to meet Regg Schlemmer, owner and builder of our cover car. Some of our readers may know him already. Others will recognize his picture. Everyone will want to read about the roadster of which Regg is proud. Our feature story appears on page 5.

The center page (12 & 13) carries 16 pictures of hot rodders and their cars. These shots were taken at the tracks, the dry lakes, in garages, wherever the roadsters and streamliners are to be found. Readers will spot many familiar names and faces there.

A special spot has been devoted to an unusual picture and story about a fuel pump. The photo has been given a touch of leg art, which we feel our readers won't mind. This feature is on page 15.

George Riley, one of the fathers of hot rods as they are known today, gives us a better understanding of the problems of a race mechanic with his article, "KEEPING THE CAR OUT FRONT." This is the same Mr. R. who designed and built the famous two-port and four-port Riley racing heads.

Richard Lane Bernstein has written a laugh-filled story, *Someone To Understand Me*, which begins on page 6. In the past, Bernstein has been noted as editor of the Los Angeles City College magazine, *POINT*.

From page 21 to the inside back cover are results and standings from the tracks and dry lakes where the hot rods do their stuff.

HRM aims to please its readers. Let us know of your likes and dislikes and we'll do our utmost to comply with them.

Look for HRM every month. Copies will be on sale in many parts shops and garages as well as through club representatives. If your club has no representative for the publication, ask your club secretary to contact us.

HRM may be purchased by yearly subscription.

ED.

(P.S.—Interesting news and photos from our readers throughout the world will be welcomed.)

HOT ROD MAGAZINE

HOT ROD *Magazine*

TABLE OF CONTENTS

HRM—Published Monthly

Associate Editors ....Robert R. Lindsay
Robert E. Petersen

Advertising ....Richard Sobotka

Staff Photographer ....Lee Blaisdell

Assistant Photographer ....Gordon Forslund

Cartoons ....Donald Miller

Distribution ....Hugh Gilbert

Reporters...Anthony Grantelli, John Lelis

HOT ROD MAGAZINE
112 South La Brea
Los Angeles 34, California

$3.00 Per Year

Please send me HRM for one year beginning with the .... issue.

Name ....

Street Address ....

City ...., Zone ...., State ....

(Check one)　　Cash ☐　　　　Check ☐　　　　Money Order ☐

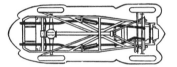

JANUARY 1948

On October 19 the last official Southern California Timing Association meet was held at El Mirage Dry Lake. As could be expected of the final meet of the season, the turnout was good and entries were in top running order. The crowd numbered about four thousand. Spectators and entrants alike were keyed to the importance of the meet. They hoped for some new and surprising hot rods to turn out and for some old records to be shattered. In neither case ere they disappointed.

SCTA NEWCOMER

The man of the hour was a relative newcomer to the SCTA and to The Gaters, the club which he represented. He was Regg Schlemmer, whose class C roadster, number 668, smashed past records with its initial competitive run at the lakes. The car stepped out ahead of all others in its class to lay a new average of 136.05 mph. Eddie Hulse of Compton, California, piloted 668 to that mark.

Behind the record of this car are 20 years engine experience and six weeks of relentless day and night work on the part of owner-builder Schlemmer. The roadster checked in at El Mirage with Mercury engine, Navarro Heads, Evans Manifold and a Smith Cam and running 3.27-1 gears. For ignition he is running two four-cylinder Wico mags. 668's body is 27 "T" channeled over a special built tubular frame. Body work on the car, done by El Slaven, is a job of which any body man would be proud.

Regg's car is built up with a gear box and quick-change locked rear end as he plans to enter it in track competition at a later date.

Schlemmer came west from his birthplace, Louisville, Kentucky, some twenty-five years ago. At the age of thirteen he started to putter around with automobile engines, buying old cars to experiment with and even finding time to repair his neighbors' autos. He completed his schooling at Muir in Pasadena, California.

Although new to the SCTA, Regg has had previous experience in record breaking. Last year, while taking to the waterways, he entered the "Patsy Dee," a Class F runabout, in the five mile competitive and the mile straightaway walking away with a new speed record of 43 mph. This was done with a V-8 "85" engine.

In the near future Regg Schlemmer will open his new speed shop at the corner of Wright and Imperial Road in South Gate, California, where he will build both boat and auto engines for speed enthusiasts.

MARRIED BETWEEN RACES

Back in 1933, while running cars at Muroc Dry Lake, Regg drove a Winfield flathead, number 21, clocking 117 mph. This was the third fastest time run in his class at Muroc. In '33, of course, there were no classes as they are known today. Cars were classified in the ninety to one hundred mile an hour group, the one hundred to one-ten group and the one-ten to unlimited group. Regg was entered in the later class.

It was in that same year that he took time out from his racing activities to marry a young California girl named Dolores. "We had to squeeze the marriage in between a couple of Regg's races," claims Mrs. Schlemmer. Today they are the proud parents of three children; an eleven-year-old boy and two daughters, aged six and eight.

Regg's fans will not be particularly surprised if next year he enters a V-8 roadster in the Bendix races . . . . and WINS! Regg, however, denies that he will. "I like airplanes, but the Mrs. doesn't want me to get into flying. Therefore, I won't."

Following his El Mirage victory dozens of spectators and drivers alike swarmed around Schlemmer and number

REGG SCHLEMMER

All of this just goes to show that you never know what will happen when a new car clears the starting line and speeds down the measured strip.

HRM is happy to be able to introduce Regg Schlemmer to its readers in this issue.

Under the Hood

668 to congratulate the new record holder and to get a good look at his mechanical masterpiece. The roadster is one of the smoothest looking cars running on the lakes today. It has a rounded grille extending from the front of the hood and the body has been completely smoothed out with all cracks and ridges filled in. The entire underside is encased in a belly pan.

During all of the excitement which ensued the timing of this car, Schlemmer wore one of the widest grins on record . . . . the smile of a man who can be proud of his own accomplishment. Asked about his hobbies and outside sports, Regg retorted, "I'm strictly an engine man. They are by business, my hobby and my sport."

*ABBREVIATIONS IN COMMON US WIT HOT ROD FANS

SCTA—Southern California Timing Association
CRA — California Roadster Assn.
ASC —   American Sports Car
R—roadster
S—streamliner (any car not conforming to contour of stock roadster body)

Classes for dry lakes entrants—SCTA
A—0-150 cubic inches
B—150-250 cubic inches
C—250-350 cubic inches
D—350 and over.

11

Somehow he didn't want to kiss her, he wanted to get the car started and get home where he could think by himself.

Someone to Understand Me____ *by Richard Lane Bernstein*

It was the talk of the town. Jerry Conners could see people laughing at him everytime he parked his hot rod and went s o m e w h e r e. Everybody thought that his engagement to Eve Bogardus was some sort of a gag. He could see their faces when he told them.

Curly Winthrop was the first to hear it. He could still vision that bewildered look on Curly's tomato red kisser. "You must be kidding, Jerry. You're the lady killer in this town. You're for somebody like Myra Cummings, who has as many curves as Bobby Feller can pitch. Eve looks like the result of an unhappy marriage and her figure is just like a washboard. It's a gag, isn't

it, Jerry? Women are wise about facts and figures. A girl with a good figure soon learns the facts."

A gag to get engaged to a girl like Eve. A woman who appealed to him. Then he had met Byron Foster at the Speed Show. He watched Foster almost choke on his bridgework when he told him the news. "Eve Bogardus! Not the tiny one with the glasses that make her look like an owl. Surely April Fool's Day isn't here again so soon, Conners."

Come to think of it, Eve wasn't beautiful, but her face was different. It had a serene look. Calm. Peaceful. Then when he walked into the snack shop he'd seen Corky Rogers munching

on a burger. Corky beamed, "Eve and you. Say, that's a scream."

It had all started at the Toppers Dance at the Ridgeway Club. The gang was there and he took Myrna Cummings. Myra was sort of an eyeful. She liked to talk and she continually peppered him with conversation while they were dancing.

"So when I got on the bus the conductor said, 'You're fare", and I said to him, 'You're not so hot yourself'. Myra laughed at her own joke. He had known Myra a long time. They had been all over together. Weenie bakes. Shows. He got so that he knew which way the breeze would blow her hair when they took a ride in his car. Or what she would say when he told her about his roadster.

Then came the tag dance. Myra slipped out of his arms and another girl whirled him out on the dance floor. She wasn't a good looking girl. Just ordinary with big, wide blue eyes. Orchid blue eyes that seemed to fascinate him. He gazed at her eyes and they made him feel funny. They were sad looking. Deep, like a crystal ball. He was ashamed of looking into them too much. He felt as if he were looking inside her. He heard her talking. Her voice was low and yet sounded like the ripples of a waterfall. Cool words. Refreshing. He could feel her in his arms and yet it was as if she were floating.

"I've seen you around," the girl said softly. "You're Jerry Conners. One of my girl friends told me."

"And who are you?" he asked innocently.

"Eve Bogardus. This is such a nice dance. I like dancing and music and laughing."

And so they stood there talking about little things, everyday things. He was standing there holding her in his arms not noticing that it was intermission.

"Am I interrupting something? Is this a private game or can anybody play?" It was Myra. Her tone was sarcastic. It seemed as if she were speaking from faraway.

"Oh, I'm sorry," said Jerry, "Eve Bogardus, this is Myra Cummings. We were just getting acquainted, Myra."

"Keep it up. You're doing okay," Myra smiled. "By the way, if you want me I'll be dancing with Cary Jones. Be careful, Eve, he bites."

Somehow or other, there was something about her. He took her to the fights. He even told Spike Bradley about her. Spike was his boss. Spike had been in the garage business for years. Jerry worked there as a mechanic. He liked the job, mostly because Spike was such a character. He was a dumpy little guy built like a fireplug with soulful brown eyes and a baldpate that looked like the back of a retreating mule.

"Sure, Myra gets sore at the dance. Gals are like that. Reminds me of a dance I went to. I used to be quite a gay dog, very hep on the repartee. No babe could outtalk me. One girl was sitting surrounded by a score of admirers. Her beauty was beyond description. When the music started I walked up to her. 'Pardon me, Miss, may I have this dance?' Then she said, 'I'm sorry, but I never dance with children.' I grinned back, 'Oh pardon me, I didn't know your condition'."

Spike was like that. Always there with a story to illustrate a point. But when he brought Eve around Spike wasn't too enthusiastic.

"She's okay, but I seen a lot better. To hear you rave, I'd think that you need glasses."

When he sat with her on her front porch he felt as if he couldn't stand it any more. He'd show them. He'd get their goats. He kept thinking about Wendy. Wendy was the girl that he met at the beach. She was a pretty blonde. Somehow he'd stop seeing her when he met Verna. Verna was a redhead with green eyes that had done absolutely nothing to him compared with Eve's blue orchid ones.

Then he figured out the solution. He would invite her home to meet the folks. They understood him. They would know what there was about Eve that made him fall for her. Sure, she was a funny kind of girl. She would sit and listen to all he had to say. She would smile when he told her about his days as a kid. The time he beat up Harry Connelly for swiping his lunch. The time that he and Larry Corbett stole watermelons at Mr. Jones' when they spent their vacation in the country. About how sore he got when his Mother washed the white shirt he had cribbed all the answers to the math questions on during final exams. Eve's eyes always twinkled with understanding.

His Mother was pretty happy to hear that he was bringing a girl home for dinner. Especially Eve. He had talked so much about her. She wanted to see her. She had seen Myra and liked her and she was curious to see this girl who had bowled over her boy and made him stop going with Myra.

The dinner party was about as successful as a panhandler in a police station. Eve sat there through dinner, toying with the food in her plate and talking about as much as a blues singer with laryngitis. Pop asked her questions, which she answered with a plain "Yes" or "No". Mom was friendly, too, but it was apparent that Eve wasn't going over too well. Jerry started to kid around and cover up, but no dice. The smiles were gone. Eve had erased their smiles as if their faces were blackboards. No, his eyes hadn't been playing tricks on him.

They didn't like Eve. He was surprised. Yet, what had he expected? The world looked dreary. He needed someone to understand him. The world was full of "theys" laughing at him. After dinner he went into the kitchen. Mom was in there washing the dishes.

"Jerry, Dad and I know you and we were kind of surprised to meet this girl you've been going around with. This Eve. She isn't the right one for you. She's too quiet. You like the outside too much. You are always around peppy things. Interesting things, like working on your car. I'll bet her idea of excitement is curling up with a book."

Pop had the same verdict and Jerry

was puzzled when he and Eve left the house. Maybe he was on a foul ball. Yet she understood him. She listened to all he had to say. Was that the wrong idea?

"Let's go for a ride," he suggested.

Eve nodded, "Let's."

Jerry watched his car eat up the black asphalt highway like a lion chewing up some licorice. His mind wandered like a stray dog. He thought about Breezy. Breezy was his buddy in the Tank Corps. Breezy had a philosophy about women. He didn't like girls. All they wanted to do, he kept telling Jerry, was hook some guy, then quit their jobs so they could sit around the house and eat all day. Breezy believed that a guy chased a girl until she caught him.

He looked sideways at Eve. Her hair was flowing in the wind like a floating cape. It was a mousy brown. She was watching the road. She seemed to enjoy the ride like a little girl frolicking over a game.

When they got to the top of Heaven's Ridge, he parked alongside a bunch of other cars. Below, etched in a maze of white lights and vari-colored neon, was the city. The lights looked like pinpoints in the darkness.

"Just think, Eve, behind each of those lights are people doing all kinds of things. People living and tasting life. Life if a great thing. I learned that in the service. You really won't suspect how important and swell being alive and breathing is until you come close to wearing a wooden overcoat." His voice was low and hoarse. He looked strange in the glimmer of the stars. His blonde hair looked silvery and his gray eyes looked colorless.

"I like it up here," Eve replied, "It's high and away from everybody. When I was a kid I used to like to come home and find the house empty. When I was by myself I was curiously alive. I always thought about understanding. If I could find somebody that I could understand and who would understand me."

Jerry looked over at her. "You're a funny kid," he said.

Somehow he didn't want to kiss her. He wanted to get the car out of there and get home where he could think by himself.

That night he tossed in his sleep. He dreamed about the time when he was a little kid visiting his grandmother and his big brother, and his cousin went out on dates and he had to stay home. He felt hurt that time because he didn't have a girl. But no one understood. He had no one to talk to. Then he remembered his first girl. Bonnie. They had met at a birthday party. She was a redhead. He liked red hair. It was like flame. He used to tell her

(Continued on Page 18)

DICK VINEYARD'S "LITTLE BEAUTY"
Top Flight CRA Track Job

BILL BURKE'S "SWEET SIXTEEN"
(Wally Parks driving SCTA record holder)

KEEPING THE CAR OUT FRONT

by
GEORGE RILEY
Builder of Record Holder Race Engines and Equipment

Experienced racing mechanics generally agree that the small, apparently unimportant details which are frequently overlooked cause the largest percentage of racing failures.

Upon the driver's return to the pit, immediately following an event, the top racing mechanic asks the oil pressure on both turn and straightaway, checks on oil and water temperature and wants to know if there was any unusual noise or roughness of the engine. Spark plugs are inspected to check carburetor mixture and if heat range of plug is correct. Evidence of extreme temperature may be noted when porcelain shows very brown or burned, or by electrodes partially melted across the spark gap. The latter should be examined with a magnifying glass. Too rich a fuel mixture will show soot on end of plug. Too much oil coming up will show by oiliness on end of porcelain. When using alcohol fuel an extremely rich carburetor mixture will show as a very wet plug end. Faulty ignition or a fouled plug may be indicated by the gap between electrodes showing black or dirty. A properly firing plug will be clean and bright between electrodes.

The mechanic checks with driver as to tachometer reading to determine whether or not gear ratio is correct. Experienced mechanics watch carefully while the car is on the track in an effort to arrive at correct gear ratio.

Mechanics know that tires and wheels are of utmost importance as no car can be expected to perform properly without traction. Both mechanics and track officials watch closely for oil or water leaks as many serious accidents are caused by oil or water on the tracks.

During competition good mechanics, even in a short race, give signals to the driver and receive signals from him. In a longer race signals from the pit showing the lap, the position, the lap time, etc., are of utmost importance for team work is absolutely essential for success in racing.

As early as possible following each race the race mechanic checks not only the engine but every part of the chassis: steering, spindles, axles, wheels, tires, tubes, hubs, shocks, brakes, wheel alignment, balance, fuel and oil tanks, the valves and lines. He also checks the air pump when used or the fuel pump. He looks for cracks which may develop in the frame or for loose cross members, makes sure the foot throttle is working properly, being particular to see that the return spring closes the throttles rapidly and fully to the stop. The carburetor float bowls should be drained and a small amount of fuel flushed through to remove sediment.

The rear end assembly must have plenty of attention as the power developed by modern racing engines is perhaps three times the amount used in highway driving.

A top racing mechanic who keeps a car under a winning driver is a competent, studious person and is entitled to and receives the respect of his competitors who know well the effort required to keep a car out front.

LAUGHS....
FROM HERE AND THERE

A woman trying to maneuver her sedan out of a parking space banged into the car ahead, then into the car behind, and finally, pulling into the street, struck a passing delivery truck. A policeman who had been watching, approached her:

"Let's see your license," he demanded.

"Don't be silly, officer," she said archly, "who's give me a license?"

Montreal Star

* * *

A prominent member and officer of a Southern California hot rod group was invited to visit the home of a British author who was doing an article on hot rods and their drivers. The visit took our friend to Pasadena where he looked forward to learning a great deal about British cars and engines. As this young man was very interested in everything mechanical, he could hardly wait to hear what his host had to say about the foreign autos.

Upon arrival at the author's home, the young man received a friendly welcome, a cup of tea and a generous share of conversation about California's "lovely weather." Minutes and hours rolled by, and in no way could our friend turn the conversation to British automobiles.

"Certainly I understand the principle, Joe . . . but isn't this overdoing it just a bit?"

Finally, when the roadster enthusiast was about to leave in utter disgust, the author's wife ventured to ask, "Would you care to see our Cheetah run?"

Remembering that a Cheetah is an English car built along the same lines as our Chevrolet, our friend thought, 'Well, now, this is more like it.'

"Of course!" he replied.

"Good," said the hostess. "Just follow me."

She led the visitor through the back door into the yard, where she switched on the yard lights. "There!" she said.

There, before the astounded gaze of the young man, was the cheetah . . . a type of hunting leopard from India.

HOT ROD SMASHUP

When you're reading in the paper
That a fellow cut a caper
With a hopped-up cut-down Ford of '29
You'd better think about it
And perhaps you ought to doubt it
Or you may mislay the blame along the line
Now the caption says it's "hopped-up"
That's because the engine's propped up
To prevent its falling out into the road
There's the line that reads "it's speedy"
That's the truth, bud. Yes, indeedy!
It made thirty miles per hour . . . without a load
And when it says the car is cut-down
Then the writers hit a rut down
At the local office of the Star Gazette
For the body's strictly stock
No more cut down than a clock
And I'll lay you odds on that for any bet
But the part that brings a gripe
Is where reporters add the tripe
That the "hot rod" driver thought he as so bold
When the car was really "junk"
And the driver just a punk
Only seventeen or eighteen summers old
Someday you'll read the story
Of the hot rods in their glory
When they're legal and accepted in their place
By then you'll have forgotten
All the items that were rotten (I mean written)
By the "hopped up" news reporters who've lost face.

"You say we're going to the lakes? That's swell. Then I won't have to change my clothes'

Tom Beatty turned up at El Mirage Dry Lake with four Stromberg carbs on a GMC blower.

Even the drivers pitch in to "ready" this track job for qualifying at Gardena, California. Owner Phil Weiand (striped shirt) looks on.

Chauncey Crist in his midget Class AS which turned 117.49 at the final SCTA lake meet of the season.

Phil Remington in the cockpit of his consistently fast Class BS. Phil, a member of The Low Flyers, prides himself on his car's beautiful body work.

Johnson-Caruthers lake entry now holds BS record of 136.39. Shown here is Doug Caruthers getting his wheel balance checked.

Homer Farnum waiting at the starting line to try out his boat engine in Manuel Ayulo's chassis.

Something unusual in roadster front ends is seen here in this '40 Studebaker setup mounted on a V-8 A.

Pat Flaherty receives pit crew's congratulations after clocking a fast qualifying time at Huntington Beach Speedway in California. The car runs a four-barrelled rocker arm setup on a '25 T body.

JANUARY 1948

18

Dick Craft gets a push at the lakes starting line. He showed up sporting a goatee to match his announcement, "Avak is here."

Arnold Birner, president of the Mojave Timing Association, checks the plugs on his model B-4 cyl. belly tank. Arnold plans to convert to an alcohol-burning setup next season.

CRA's Dick Rathman brought his track job to this Russetta Timing meet at El Mirage. Here he is clocking 126 plus.

Andy Linden, No. 5, tries to pass Troy Ruttman the hard way during night racing at Bonnelli Stadium in Saugus, California.

Manuel Ayulo's garage buzzes with activity as CRA mechanics and drivers soup up for the next race. Manuel's car is on the left, Jack McGrath's on the right.

At Russetta Timing meet Don Brown's '36 coupe clocked a surprising 115.97 as is—fenders and all. Don is on the right.

Almer Vess at the wheel of his Class AS. He was a guest entrant in SCTA's last '47 meet.

Al Palamidas of the Northern California Roadster Racing Association shows off his '25 T V-8 in Oakland, California.

HOT ROD MAGAZINE

First Annual Hot Rod Exposition

Long regarded as a screwball diversion for a lot of reckless kids with more nerve than brains, the building and racing of hot rods has finally come to be recognized as a major sport in this area.

Realizing that there is more to the sport than just an outlet for a bunch of young buckos to blow off steam, the public has finally accepted this activity, as sponsored and conducted by the Southern California Timing Association as a healthful, beneficial avocation for thousands of motor car enthusiasts.

Taking the veil of semi-secrecy off their operations, the S.C.T.A. is sponsoring a unique and colorful Exposition at the National Guard Armory in January when the best designed and engineered cars belonging to Association members will be placed on public display.

In the conviction that the benefits and advantages, which accrue to scientific knowledge through the time trials conducted by the Association, are of such import that they may be proclaimed generally, the S.C.T.A. membership agreed to stage the Exposition.

There will be at least 30 Association cars on exhibit at the show strategically spaced among display booths for industrial exhibitors in the automotive field. The list of exhibitors includes not only specialty equipment manufacturers in the Los Angeles area but many other automotive firms of national reputation whose officers believe that the hot rod sport should be supported as a contribution to automotive advancement.

The Exposition is being staged primarily as a public relations project for the Association and secondly as a contribution to the current safety campaign being conducted in Los Angeles to put a halt to reckless driving and the use of unsafe motor vehicles.

Throwing the full support of the Association's 700 members behind this campaign, the S.C.T.A. officers believe that they can show the younger element of the community that fast cars can be safely built and safely operated.

The rules of operation and the code of conduct observed by the S.C.T.A. will be made known to the people attending the Exposition and it is hoped that through this direct contact with youthful car operators the gospel of safety may be effectively spread.

The Los Angeles Police Department, through its traffic education unit, will participate in the Exposition, showing sound movies on traffic regulations and safe driving. The safety Department of the Southern California Automobile Club has also been invited to participate.

The Exposition itself will offer many unusual attractions aside from the technical exhibits. A program of entertainment will be presented each night with stage and screen luminaries who are hot rod enthusiasts participating in the festivities.

One of the principal attractions of the show, and a feature which is expected to attract news-reel, television and national magazine and press cover-

(Continued on Page 17, Col. 2)

SOME OF THE CARS TO BE ON DISPLAY AT THE HOT ROD SHOW

JANUARY 1948

PARTS WITH APPEAL

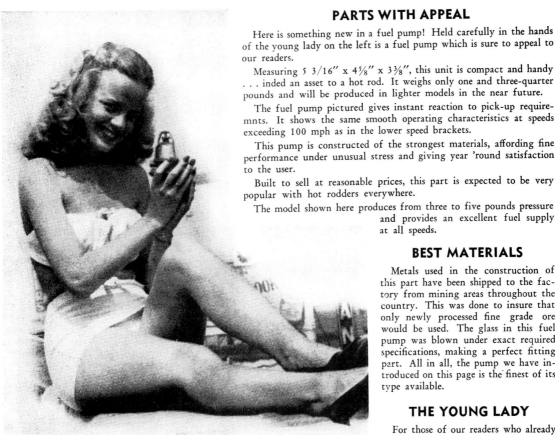

Here is something new in a fuel pump! Held carefully in the hands of the young lady on the left is a fuel pump which is sure to appeal to our readers.

Measuring 5 3/16″ x 4⅝″ x 3⅜″, this unit is compact and handy . . . inded an asset to a hot rod. It weighs only one and three-quarter pounds and will be produced in lighter models in the near future.

The fuel pump pictured gives instant reaction to pick-up requiremnts. It shows the same smooth operating characteristics at speeds exceeding 100 mph as in the lower speed brackets.

This pump is constructed of the strongest materials, affording fine performance under unusual stress and giving year 'round satisfaction to the user.

Built to sell at reasonable prices, this part is expected to be very popular with hot rodders everywhere.

The model shown here produces from three to five pounds pressure and provides an excellent fuel supply at all speeds.

BEST MATERIALS

Metals used in the construction of this part have been shipped to the factory from mining areas throughout the country. This was done to insure that only newly processed fine grade ore would be used. The glass in this fuel pump was blown under exact required specifications, making a perfect fitting part. All in all, the pump we have introduced on this page is the finest of its type available.

THE YOUNG LADY

For those of our readers who already have a fuel pump, here are a few important facts about the rest of the picture.

Posing with the fuel pump is nineteen-year-old Jane Norred, a Patricia Stevens model. Every bit as well-proportioned as the engine part she holds, Miss Norred hails from Culver City, California. Aside from modeling, she works as a stenographer at a local motion picture studio.

Miss Norred was born in Fort Worth, Texas, and moved west with her family in 1943. She is a graduate of Alexander Hamilton High School in Los Angeles.

Looking to the future, she hopes to become one of the nation's top photographic models. Beyond her working amitions, she looks forward to marriage and a home in her adopted state, California. Of her "dream man" she says, "He must be tall, dark, not necessarily handsome, have a fine sense of humor and enjoy most of the things I do."

Miss Norred's favorite sports are horseback riding, ice skating and tennis.

She loves to dance, enjoys movies, hot rods, hot dogs, phonograph records and beach parties. Although interested in hot rods, Miss Norred confesses an ignorance of their working parts. When handed the fuel pump she was to pose with, she revealingly asked, "What is it?" (We are still explaining.)

This Is the C. R. A.

by Dorothy Sloan

The California Roadster Association was fathered by Babe Ouse. It's birthplace was the garage at Babe's home where he gathered together a group of fellows, all interested in the amateur racing game. Most of the boys had run at the lakes. Babe had set a lake record in a Marmon. The hobby was an expensive one; so, in the interest of racing and to help get the speed-happy boys off the streets, Babe, along with Bill Dehler and Emmett Malloy, encouraged the building of the track at Gardena. Babe then called the first group together to form an association for the protection of the boys. C. R. A. as the first hot rod racing organization on the Pacific Coast after the war.

The charter members of that first meeting included Babe, Johnny Walker, Gordy Reid, Chuck Leighton and his partner, Paul Cantarano, Don Freeland, Johnny McManama, Walt Bowen, Rudy Ramos and a few others. Present-day meetings call for a large hall to accommodate the attendance.

Babe conducted the meetings until elections were held when Johnny Walker was voted in as the first president. At the next election Babe was voted in as president and since then he has done a fine job of looking out for the interest of the boys.

The first race of the C. R. A. was run on Labor Day, 1946, at the completed Gardena track. At that time it was a half-mile dirt track. The drivers had only one day to practice before the race and many of the 50 cars that participated had never before been on a track. Wally Pancratz was the day's winner.

By the third race 95 cars had been listed with the C.R.A. and about 85 of them were on hand to qualify.

The main consideration of the organization has been and will continue to be the safety of the drivers. Cars must fulfill all specifications before they are allowed on the track. Each new car is checked thoroughly by at least two of the members of the technical committee. Each driver must prove his age to be 21 or over and have a clean bill of health from a physician.

C.R.A. worked out their own system for the payoff to assure a fair deal to everyone.

In a year's time the association has paid out approximately $180,000 in prize money and had given the racing world a large number of top race drivers. A great many of the hot rot drivers have gone on to make names for themselves in big cars, midgets and stock cars where their fearless, hard, close driving has given the old timers something to think about. Several of the fellows have already been invited to run on the Indianapolis track next year. This, of course, is about the height of any race driver's ambition. The names of the hot rod drivers are becoming as well known as De Palma, Rex Mays or any of the other big names in racing. However, be they big shots or little, the C.R.A. makes no discrimination between them when it comes to upholding the rules. Manuel Ayulo and Troy Ruttman have both felt the whip of a thirty day suspension for tract infractions.

Mechanically the cars have gone as far in a year's time as the drivers, and the old type street job with self starters and license plates still attached is now extinct from the tracks. The cars on the C.R.A. tracks today are strictly track jobs and could not be run on the streets. They have only in-an-out gears, doing away with a clutch. They must be pushed or towed to get them started because starters, flywheels, and unnecessary machinery are all eliminated to cut down weight. The cars are towed to the tracks on trailers. In recent months drivers have been competing for trophies to be presented at the end of the season. These are for best looking car and best looking pit crew, which has encouraged the boys to bring out some beautiful jobs.

The C.R.A.'s track jobs are not only beautiful outside but are superior examples of mechanical workmanship. Some of the owners have over $3,000 tied up in their cars an the least you could buy one for would be about $1500. Going under the much publicized name of Hot Rods has been somewhat of a handicap in that the public has been slow to realize that these rods are not convertible to street jobs. Many people still confuse them with the "junks" responsible for so many accidents on the streets. The C.R.A. is building up a good reputation and gradually overcoming the prejudice and is now encouraged, not only by the public but by the city and state police for the help it has been in letting drivers work off their speed legitimately.

The C.R.A. has also won over the city fathers of Pasadena and has held races several times at the Rose Bowl. It was there they held their National Championship race to which organizations all over the United States were invited. The boys have also been invited to the Orange Bowl at San Bernardino, a dirt track, making a particularly thrilling show. They recently held a benefit show there for the Shrine Club Chilren's Hospital Fund. Along with weekly races at Bonelli and Huntington Beach Speedways they have had spot shows at Gardena and out of town tracks, including Bakersfield and Fresno. This has given the boys enough racing to make it profitable so that they could devote their full time to the game.

Many of the boys who own their own cars also do their own machine work. Jack McGrath, crowned King of the Hot Rods when he won the Pacific Coast Championship last year, is a good example. He is not only a superior driver but an excellent mechanic. Jack is also making a name for himself in big car racing, having won six main events to date.

Troy Ruttman, long a favorite of hot rod fans, is as well known to the midget crowd and recently went to Langhorn to compete in the National Midget Championship race. Troy ran second fastest qualifying time and was well up in the running when motor trouble put him out.

Andy Linden has been specializing in stock car racing and is doing all right for himself, too.

These are only a few of the boys that had their start in Hot Rod competition and branched out. The list includes many names well known in the other fields such as Gordy Reid, Ed Korgan, Manuel Ayulo, Doug Groves and Bill Steves, just to mention a few. As the

In Memoriam

"CHICO"

Pet, Friend and Mascot
of HRM,
who died Dec. 1, 1947

Mr. and Mrs. Houlette are doing a series of sketches of hot rod streamliners for Ford Times. They are from Disney studios.

———

Bob Tattersfield has a new blower in the development stage which he has run on a Ford truck with very fine performance.

———

A new cam, not reground, but completely custom made will soon be in production by Bill Spaulding.

———

We hear that Phil Weiand will soon announce a new and improved line of heads and manifolds.

CRA

boys branch out others come up in the ranks to take their places and show their skill by breaking records. Pat Flaherty, Roy Prosser, Colby Scroggin, Jim Rathman and Dick Vineyard are just a few of the boys that are out to prove that the best driving hasn't been done yet.

Of course, there are the old-timers like Slim Mathis and Ed Barnett, who know their way around in anything with wheels but prefer hot rods. Both of these fellows have placed consistently high in main events and Slim has been winning trophy dashes regularly. They have generally helped put many a newcomer on the right track with advice on driving an dmechanics.

Hot rod racing has given the boys a healthy outlet not only for their speed but for their skill and inventiveness. Street racing is no longer of interest to them. The California Roadster Association is justly proud of the part it has played in encouraging interest in fair play and sportsmanship and providing the stimulus for the advancement of the racing profession.

The S.C.T.A. has a special committee working on a system of lights for warning drivers of hazards on the timing strip during speed runs. This system, similar to that used at Salt Lake, would speed up the meets considerably.

———

In Florida some of the roadster enthusiasts are holding time trials on Daytona Beach and charging spectators two dollars per head.

———

Joe Rathman is using the new Kinmont brake on his track roadster. It has been used successfully on Indianapolis cars and looks like it might be the coming thing for hot rods.

HOT ROD EXPOSITION

(*Continued from Page 14*)

age, will be the actual transformation of a 1932 roadster into a dazzling, chrome-plated hot rod during the progress of the show.

Skillful planning and timing is required to accomplish this renovating process but the team of experts in charge of the project assert they will have the car ready to be given away as door prize.

No expense is being spared to make this show a class production. The booths of uniform construction will be made of velour of various colors, the lighting will be both overhead and indirect and the booth arrangement will be such to provide maximum spectator interest for each exhibitor.

Dates of the Exposition are Jan. 23, 24 and 25. Hollywood Associates, Inc. are in charge of arrangements. They may be reached by telephone at RI 9937 and RI 9064 or by writing National Guard Armory, 700 Exposition Blvd., Los Angeles 7, Calif.

"Why is Jones pacing up and down like that?"

"He's awfully worried about his wife, poor chap."

"Why, what's she got?"

"The car."

Gosport

Hot rod drivers in the Los Angeles area were up in arms over the way local newspapers wrote up a five-way accident in which a roadster driver lost his life. The only way the reader could tell the wreck was not the roadster's fault was by reading far into the story where it explained that a woman stopped her car and a truck, unable to stop, swerved around her and turned over on the youth's car. Driver George Hyder deserved a better break.

SOMEONE TO UNDERSTAND ME

(Continued from Page 7)

that he liked to put his hands over her red hair to warm them.

The dream wandered to his operation. The time the doctors operated on him. Acute appendicitis. In the hospital there was a guy in the next bed to him. The fellow was named Ryan. He was a talkative man with a gift for blarney.

"Hospitals make you realize how swell it is to be outside all ship shape. Some guys say 'I'm Irish and proud of it' . . . me, I'm Scotch and fond of it. Me, when I get out of here I'm getting me a beautiful doll. Women are something. I think they're here to stay. Me, I recommend them highly."

After the hospital he dreamed of college. He met Byron Fowler in college. By was his pal. In a way he had felt sort of brotherly to Byron. They read books together in the library. They even went out for football together. By was the quarterback and Jerry was the halfback. Every once in awhile they'd go on a trip up to the mountains. They'd fish and sleep under the trees beneath a blanket of leaves. Jerry had studied engineering. He liked the campus and the profs and all the routine. Then the dream replayed the war. Byron had joined the Infantry but Jerry had enlisted in the Tank Corps. Like he told Byron, "It's better than walking."

They wrote and talked about tomorrow. Patten kept moving like scurrying wildfire. The tanks rubbed out enemy replacements, rumbling on. All the guys would sit around and talk about the weenie bakes, the beach, funny little incidents. It kind of brought back a bit of home and some laughs.

Patten couldn't be stopped and the whole U. S. Army seemed like a big motor clicking on all cylinders. The whole war machine pasted the Nazis and after V-E Day came V-J Day. Everybody was saying goodbye and soon Jerry was sent to a separation center.

When he got home, he noticed that the home town hadn't stood still. It had grown. Where there were once vacant lots, there were now stores and buildings. He stayed home a few days taking it easy and then went down to the garage. He wanted to see Spike.

"You look good, kid. Your buddy, Byron, was in the other day."

They talked and then Byron came over to the house and there was Myra and music and laughter. And he was building a rod with a Merc motor. Suddenly he heard the alarm ring. It was morning and he realized that he had been dreaming all the time. He remembered last night and he grinned slackly.

That Sunday he called up Eve and asked her to go to the beach. She said okay and he picked her up. She had on

a playsuit. As they drove down to the beach he watched her quizzically.

They walked down to Muscle Beach and sat there. Eve took off her playsuit. There was a bathing suit underneath. She looked thin and milky white. He stretched out on the sand and fell asleep.

He was awakened by the sound of laughter. He looked up, blinking his eyes. Myra was sitting there with some other guy. She was in a black bathing suit that looked like it had been made out of half of a handkerchief. 'It was probably legal or they wouldn't have sold it to her', Jerry mused. He noticed the difference between Eve and Myra.

"Long time no see, Jerry. You becoming a hermit? Why don't you bring Eve around and let the gang see her?" Myra was smiling. "Oh yeah, I guess I better get back to my Emily Post. I didn't introduce you. This is Johnny Keston. Johnny, this is Jerry Conners. And this is his fiancee, Eve Bogardus."

"Pleased to meetcha." Jerry glanced at Myra, "See you around."

After they left, Jerry got to thinking. He had been away from the gang. That was because they didn't understand about him and Eve. It had been better to keep to himself with Eve. Then there were no laughs. No gags or giggling.

He was going to talk to Byron tomorrow. By would give him some good advice. By knew the score. All the answers. He hadn't seen much of By since he was going with Eve. He seemed to keep to himself. It was strange. They had been close pals. Like two of the three musketeers. All for one and one for all.

He went over to Byron's place after work. It was a nice little apartment. Strictly from Esquire. Pictures on the wall. Pipes in a handcarved pipe rack. An ivory radio sitting on a desk table. Small kitchenette. It was just what he expected of Byron. He sort of fitted into a place like this. Jerry felt that he knew Byron like a book.

"Hi, Jerry," Byron greeted, sitting in an easy chair." Make yourself at home. You kind of surprised me. From what I hear you're pretty busy with a romance. I haven't seen you for quite awhile."

Byron Foster had quiet brown eyes and a trim mustache. His hair was a curly brown and he had a perpetual smile on his face, as if he were constantly laughing at the world. By seldom combed his hair and was continually making jokes about it, something about combing it with an eggbeater. He was seldom without a pipe in his hand.

"What's new, By? How's it been going?" Jerry wasn't too sure about how he was going to bring up the subject of Eve and him. He didn't want to sound like a dope about it. Like a character who would write a letter to a lovelorn columnist. He hadn't been able to figure out how he started going with Eve. It seemed like it just happened. First thing he knew he was engaged. He was not in a happy state. Sure, Eve understood him. But he couldn't figure her out. She hadn't gone over with anybody. She liked solitude and sad movies and classical music.

Foster shook his head, "Same old stuff. Following the crowd. Been kind of busy lately, getting set for the next time trials. How's everything down at the garage?"

"Same gang of characters. Spike is a lot of laughs, too. Somebody ought to write a book about that place. All kinds of characters coming in all day. Charlie Anderson, who says he likes to go window shopping with his wife because he can bring home so many windows. Screwball. Georgie Shaw still plays the ponies. One horse of his is still running. It was scared to finish by itself yesterday, afraid of the dark." Jerry watched Byron's face wreath in laconic chuckles.

"You look a little troubled, Jerry, kind of under the weather. Anything I can do?"

The time had come. Jerry breathed deeply, "Well, Byron, I could stand a bit of advice. You see, I'm engaged to Eve Bogardus. I think you know her. Well, everybody thinks we're a mismatch and after my Mom and Dad nixed her, I started to wonder. Then I began to notice things myself. Before I met Eve I used to be right in the middle of the crowd. Parties. Meetings. Dances. With Eve lately, we're all by ourselves. She don't talk or laugh or even kid. She kind of dreams. There is a faraway look in those shiny blue orchid eyes. When I saw Myra at the beach I kind of felt that maybe we could get together again. Call me fickle, but that's what I felt when I saw her. But Eve was there. We were engaged and I felt ashamed of my thoughts. After all, Eve was dependent on me. No other guy's given her a tumble like I have. Here's the 64 buck question, By. Do you think I should break our engagement?"

Foster puffed on his pipe, the smoke

(Continued on Page 20)

I have a car.
It never runs out of gas.
It never skids.
It never gets a puncture.
It never gets overheated.
It has never got me into a collision or accident of any kind since I got it.
How I wish I could start it..
Quaker Campus

spiraled to the ceiling in a bluish haze. "Listen, Jerry, I'm not a guy that can tell people what to do. I make mistakes myself. I'm human. I have two hands . . . two legs . . . two arms . . . a heart. I'm no Solomon, but since you're asking me this way, I'm going to give you my opinion. It's just an opinion. Take it or leave it. Eve Bogardus is not for you. Everybody is talking about it all over town. It's the wrong partner. You can't dance through life with the wrong partner. You're the type of guy that likes to be with people. You like to kibitz with a gang of friends at after-show snacks. Eve is no Myra Cummings. She has a strange way about her. Do you see, Jerry? Do you get my drift?"

Here it was, the straw that broke the camel's back. His best pal was giving him the goods on the level. That about made it unanimous. He was glad that he wasn't head over heels in love. Just a touch of infatuation probably. He thought back about all the steers that Byron Foster had given him. Not a bum steer in the bunch. By had helped him build his first rod. Given his tips on jobs. Gotten him dates. By had called the signals that had made him score touchdowns and become a football hero.

"Yeah, I get the pitch," Jerry said, dismally. "That about makes it unanimous."

Foster chuckled, "To coin an adage, one man's dream girl is another's nightmare."

Jerry smiled weakly. "Very funny. As humorous as a broken back."

It took him a couple of days to get up enough nerve to tell her. He had wrung it through his mind as if it were an article of clothing going through a wringer. He wondered if this Keston guy had cut him out completely with Myra. He pondered the extent of his turmoil and the amount of l'amour he had for Eve. These thoughts made a shambles of his mind, cluttering it like a disordered room.

He kept watching the squares on the sidewalk and kicked a can, that bounced tinnily into the gutter. As he got closer to her house, he felt as if a clammy hand were clutching his stomach. Some people, he thought, have no worries. It was guys like himself that finished with one problem and leaped into another. His existence was one conveyor belt of woes.

He kept rehearsing his speech in his mind. He would be here and she would be there. Jerry knew that things would not work out that way. Something would be out of place. It always was.

Then he saw the apartment house and he forced himself forward reluctantly. He wished it was over and he was back home in bed. Jerry opened the front door of the apartment house, eyed the foyer rapidly, then walked over to the elevator. The car was on the main floor. He opened the cage door, stepped in, let it squeak shut and pressed the buzzer. Third floor. The elevator jolted to a stop at the third floor. Jerry opened the door, mechanically ambled out. He walked down the green carpet as if it were the last mile. There it was. 306. Now . . . the buzzer. His hand rose toward the little pushbutton. His palm was sweaty. Brrr.

Clatter, clatter. Eve's high heels. Tidying up the room probably. It seemed like an eternity before she came to the door.

Orchid blue eyes staring at him, "Hello, Jerry, haven't seen you for a few days. Won't you come in?"

He sat on the lavender lounge and she was close to him. The lounge was close to the color of her eyes . . . yet different. Nothing matched those eyes.

"What's on your mind, Jerry. You look troubled?" It was that low voice that sent chills up his spine.

He stared at her. Somehow he couldn't get his mouth to open so words would spill out.

"Well," Eve's voice shook him out of it.

"I've been busy the last few days. Had a lot on my mind."

"I can imagine." He detected a hint of sarcasm in her voice, but ignored it. It was odd, how strange she suddenly seemed to him. He eyed her curiously as if he were seeing her for the first time.

"Sometimes the days seem too short for me. The hours seem to race by. I'm working on my car."

"What exactly do you have on your mind? You could have phoned, but maybe you didn't have a nickel?"

There was no sense sitting there like a 24-carat dope. Jerry decided to get it off his chest fast and then get out. It would be better that way.

"Okay, Eve. I've been thinking a lot the last few days. About us. You and I, you see, we're a problem." He looked at her blankly.

"Are we?"

"Yeah, you see I'm a funny guy. I always have been. I like people to be nice to me. I like things to run smoothly. No rush, no hurry, just leisurely. I found that I enjoy life more that way. I always hoped that I'd find someone who understood. Someone who would listen to what I had to say. I figured that maybe that's what romance would be like." He stopped, wet his lip with the tip of his tongue.

She didn't say anything. She seemed nervous and the blue orchid eyes seemed a little feverish. There was an unnatural look in them.

"I met you and you were understanding. But somehow I drifted away from my pals and my crowd. My life seemed to be draining of all the fun that was in it. Pretty soon there was just the two of us by ourselves. Then I realized that I was only infatuated with you and that it wasn't the real thing at all. We're wrong for each other."

Her low voice was beating like a drum. The words were pulselike. "I suppose you want to call it quits. I expected it. I could see it in your eyes. That questioning look."

"It's better this way. Eve. Better now that later."

"If that's the way you want it. Here's you're ring." She sobbed a little. It was a funny kind of sobbing, something like you'd see in the movies.

He slammed the door and went out.

Eve Bogardus got up from the divan and walked over to the closet, "You can come out now, darling," she called.

The closet door opened and out stepped—Byron Foster.

(The End)

CRA, RESULTS OF RECENT RACES

BONELLI STADIUM, SAUGUS, CALIFORNIA, Oct. 19

(1/3 MILE—PAVED—AFTERNOON RACE)
(Fastest qualifying time turned in by Slim Mathis—19.03)

Place	Driver		Time
TROPHY DASH			
1.—Slim Mathis		3 laps	58.43
2.—Pat Flaherty			
FIRST HEAT			
1.—Harry Stockman		6	2:00.03
2.—Jim Davis			
3.—Bud Van Mannen			
SECOND HEAT			
1.—Jack Bayliss		6	1:58.68
2.—Archie Tipton			
3.—Bob Lindsey			
THIRD HEAT			
1.—Colby Scroggins		6	1:57.85
2.—Lou Figaro			
3.—Bob Cross			

FOURTH HEAT			
1.—Jim Rathman		6	1:57.46
2.—Slim Mathis			
3.—Pat Flaherty			
AUSTRALIAN PURSUIT			
1.—Joe James		6	2:09.60
2.—Corvy Tulieo			
SEMI FINAL			
(Stopped on the Eleventh Lap due to water on the track. Standings at that time)			
1.—Harry Stockman			
2.—Ed Ball			
3.—Steve Dusich			
FINAL			
1.—Colby Scroggins		30	10:11.30
2.—Pat Flaherty			
3.—Lou Figaro			

BONELLI STADIUM, SAUGUS, OCTOBER 26

(PAVED — 1/3 MILE)
(Fastest qualifying time turned—Slim Mathis: 19.23.)

TROPHY DASH			
1.—Slim Mathis		3 laps	58.53
2.—Pat Flaherty			
FIRST HEAT			
1.—Roy Prosser		6	2:01.53
2.—Colby Scroggins			
3.—Bud Van Mannen			
SECOND HEAT			
1.—Jack Baylis		6	1:59.43
2.—Yam Oka			
3.—Chuck Leighton			
THIRD HEAT*			
1.—Archie Tipton		6	
2.—Bob Cross			
3.—Jim Rathman			

FOURTH HEAT			
1.—Bud Gregory		6	1:59.71
2.—Ed Ball			
3.—Pat Flaherty			
AUSTRALIAN PURSUIT			
1.—Walt James		6	2:02.09
Dan Tracy			
SEMI-MAIN			
1.—Colby Scroggins		15	5:02.37
2.—Roy Prosser			
3.—Bud Van Mannen			
MAIN			
1.—Jim Rathman		30	9:55.53
2.—Wayne Tipton			
3.—Pat Flaherty			

*This race was stopped without a finish when Bob Cross and Archie Tipton cracked up on the North end of the track. Above are the lineups at the time of the smashup. Cross's car overturned, however, he walked away from the wreck under his own power. A few minutes later Bob ran a mock race "just to get into the feel of it again."

HUNTINGTON BEACH SPEEDWAY, NOVEMBER 2

(1/5 MILE)
(Qualifying time 15:06 by Slim Mathis)

TROPHY DASH			
1.—Slim Mathis		3 laps	45.92
Jim Rathman			
FIRST HEAT			
1.—Jay Frank		6	1:34.79
2.—Lou Figaro			
3.—Jim Davies			
SECOND HEAT			
1.—Dan Tracy		6	1:37.40
2.—Puffy Puffer			
3.—Walt James			
THIRD HEAT			
1.—Don Baylis		6	1:33.65
2.—Wayne Tipton			
3.—Jim Rathman			

FOURTH HEAT			
1.—Bud Gregory		6	1:31.41
2.—Yam Oka			(new record)
3.—Dick Vineyard			
AUSTRALIAN PURSUIT			
1.—Joe James		6	1:40.27
2.—Jim Rigsby			
3.—Ed Corgan			
B MAIN			
1.—Ed Barnett		25	6:34.53
2.—Wayne Tipton			
3.—Jim Davies			
A MAIN			
1.—Slim Mathis		25	6:47.63
2.—Dick Vineyard			
3.—Dan Tracy			
RUNOFF			
1.—Wayne Tipton		6	1:36.07
2.—Slim Mathis			
3.—Dick Vineyard			

HUNTINGTON BEACH SPEEDWAY, NOVEMBER 9

(A new qualifying record was set by Slim Mathis: 14.86; Old Time—14.92.)

TROPHY DASH			
1.—Slim Mathis		3 laps	45:46
2.—Bud Van Mannen			
FIRST HEAT			
1.—Jim Rigsby		6	1:34.76
2.—Bob Lindsey			
3.—Colby Scroggins			
SECOND HEAT			
1.—Jim Davies		6	1:33.43
2.—Roy Prosser			
3.—Don Freeland			
THIRD HEAT			
1.—Yam Oka		6	1:31.51
2.—Pat Flaherty			
3.—Bud Gregory			

FOURTH HEAT			
1.—Dick Vineyard		6	1:32.56
2.—Lou Figaro			
3.—Jim Rathman			
AUSTRALIAN PURSUIT			
1.—Joe James		6	1:39.60
2.—Puffy Puffer			
3.—Archie Tipton			
B MAIN			
1.—Colby Scroggins		25	6:53.86
2.—Bob Lindsey			
3.—Jim Rigsby			
A MAIN			
1.—Roy Prosser		25	6:31.45
2.—Jack Baylis			
3.—Dick Vineyard			
RUNOFF			
1.—Colby Scroggins		5	1:18.82
2.—Jack Baylis			
3.—Bob Lindsey			

ASC, RESULTS OF RECENT RACES

CULVER CITY SPEEDWAY, Oct. 19

(PAVED 1/5 MILE)

AFTERNOON RACE

Fastest qualifying time was turned in by Bill Steves, who ran 14.34.

TROPHY DASH
1.—Bill Steves — 3 laps — 39.55
2.—Mickey Davis

FIRST HEAT
1.—A. A. Knight — 6 — 1:56.81
2.—Chet Stafford
3.—Bill La Roy

SECOND HEAT
1.—Tom Wiley — 6 — 1:52.51
2.—Bob Rozzano
3.—Jess Pompa

THIRD HEAT
1.—Chuck Burnett — 6 — 2:05.03
2.—Len Shreenan
3.—No Car

FOURTH HEAT
1.—Pat Patrick — 6 — 1:29.58
2.—George Seegar
3.—Bruce Emmons

AUSTRALIAN PURSUIT
1.—Curtis Hayes — 8 — 2:38.31
2.—Jack Hill
3.—No Car

SEMI FINAL
1.—A. A. Knight — 15 — 3:49.83
2.—Tom Wiley
3.—Jess Pompa

MAIN
1.—Bill Steves — 25 — 6:26.12
2.—Mickey Davis
3.—Len Shreenan

An ASC record was broken at this meet when Pat Patrick set a new six lap mark of 1:29.58 in the Fourth Heat, topping the past record by .12.

CULVER CITY SPEEDWAY, Nov. 2

(This race was run with an open centered figure eight course. Fastest qualifying time — 31.07 — set by Bruce Emmons.)

TROPHY DASH
1.—Mickey Davis — 3 laps — 1:34.61
2.—Bruce Emmons

FIRST HEAT
1.—Chet Stafford — 6 — 3:45.77
3.—A. A. Knight

SECOND HEAT
1.—Bill Steves — 6 — 3:13.63
2.—Bruce Emmons
3.—Kenny Vorce

THIRD HEAT
1.—Pat Patrick — 6 — 3:22.39
2.—Rod Parker
3.—Len Shreenan

FOURTH HEAT
1.—Frank Danielson — 6 — 3:18.04
2.—Chuck Burness
3.—Bernie Parks

B MAIN
1.—Bill Steves — 20 — 9:54.52
2.—A. A. Knight

A MAIN
1.—Chuck Burness — 20 — 11:12.14
2.—Mickey Davis
3.—Len Shreenen

RUNOFF
1.—Bill Steves — 10 — 5:11.10
2.—Micgey Davis
3.—Chuck Burness

BONELLI STADIUM, SAUGUS, Nov. 15

(A new qualifying record was set by Slim Mathis: 14:86)

TROPHY DASH
1.—George Seegar — 3 laps — 1:04.00
2.—Bob Rozzano

FIRST HEAT
1.—Chet Stafford — 6 — 2:12.35
2.—Dan Marruffo
3.—A. A. Knight

SECOND HEAT
1.—Hook Klein — 6 — 2:32.41
2.—John Mark
3.—Don Bailey

THIRD HEAT
1.—Pat Patrick — 6 — 2:05.05
2.—Frank Danielson
3.—Chuck Burness

FOURTH HEAT
1.—Bill Steves — 6 — 2:02.03
2.—George Seegar
3.—Tom Wiley

SEMI-MAIN
(Called in Eight Lap due to accident on track.)
1.—Chet Stafford
2.—John Mark
3.—Curtis Hayes

MAIN
1.—R. C. Morton — 30 — 10:05.12
2.—Pat Patrick
3.—Mickey Davis

S. C. T. A. POINTS STANDING - 1947 *Season*

<table>
<tr><td colspan="4">CLUB'S POINTS</td><td colspan="4">INDIVIDUAL'S POINTS</td></tr>
<tr><td></td><td>Previous</td><td>Oct. 19</td><td>Total</td><td></td><td>Previous</td><td>Oct. 19</td><td>Total</td></tr>
<tr><td>Lancers</td><td>212</td><td>33</td><td>245</td><td>Doug Hartelt</td><td>60</td><td>12</td><td>72</td></tr>
<tr><td>Road Runners</td><td>177</td><td>67</td><td>244</td><td>Dietrich-Thomas</td><td>60</td><td>12</td><td>72</td></tr>
<tr><td>Low Flyers</td><td>116</td><td>27</td><td>143</td><td>Randy Shinn</td><td>49</td><td>11</td><td>60</td></tr>
<tr><td>Gophers</td><td>113</td><td>16</td><td>129</td><td>Jack Calori</td><td>48</td><td>8</td><td>56</td></tr>
<tr><td>Gaters</td><td>67</td><td>32</td><td>99</td><td>Bill Burke</td><td>35</td><td>17</td><td>52</td></tr>
<tr><td>Gear Grinders</td><td>44</td><td>13</td><td>57</td><td>Bob Riese</td><td>37</td><td>9</td><td>46</td></tr>
<tr><td>Stokers</td><td>46</td><td>N</td><td>46</td><td>Jim Palm</td><td>43</td><td>—</td><td>43</td></tr>
<tr><td>So. Calif. Roadster</td><td>20</td><td>13</td><td>33</td><td>Frank Coon</td><td>34</td><td>6</td><td>40</td></tr>
<tr><td>Albata</td><td>27</td><td>6</td><td>33</td><td>Jack Mickelson</td><td>34</td><td>5</td><td>39</td></tr>
<tr><td>Dolphins</td><td>14</td><td>14</td><td>28</td><td>Tom Beatty</td><td>39</td><td>—</td><td>39</td></tr>
<tr><td>Mobilers</td><td>25</td><td>N</td><td>25</td><td>Johnny Johnson</td><td>38</td><td>—</td><td>38</td></tr>
<tr><td>San Diego Roadster</td><td>18</td><td>4</td><td>22</td><td>Stuart Hilborn</td><td>19</td><td>11</td><td>30</td></tr>
<tr><td>Pasadena Roadster</td><td>12</td><td>1</td><td>13</td><td>Bert Letner</td><td>29</td><td>—</td><td>29</td></tr>
<tr><td>Clutchers</td><td>9</td><td>3</td><td>12</td><td>James Culbert</td><td>20</td><td>8</td><td>28</td></tr>
<tr><td>Throttlers</td><td>N</td><td>12</td><td>12</td><td>Spurgin-Giovanine</td><td>18</td><td>6</td><td>24</td></tr>
<tr><td>Strokers</td><td>11</td><td>N</td><td>11</td><td>Lee & Geo. Wise</td><td>24</td><td>—</td><td>24</td></tr>
<tr><td>Wheelers</td><td>7</td><td>N</td><td>7</td><td>Ludvig Solberg</td><td>23</td><td>—</td><td>23</td></tr>
<tr><td>Cal. Roadster</td><td>4</td><td>N</td><td>4</td><td>Nelson Taylor</td><td>13</td><td>9</td><td>22</td></tr>
<tr><td>Hornets</td><td>4</td><td>N</td><td>4</td><td>Burleigh Dolph</td><td>21</td><td>—</td><td>21</td></tr>
<tr><td>Sidewinders</td><td>4</td><td>N</td><td>4</td><td>Ed Stewart</td><td>16</td><td>4</td><td>20</td></tr>
<tr><td></td><td></td><td></td><td></td><td>Robert Drew</td><td>19</td><td>—</td><td>19</td></tr>
<tr><td></td><td></td><td></td><td></td><td>Johnson-Caruthers</td><td>—</td><td>17</td><td>17</td></tr>
<tr><td></td><td></td><td></td><td></td><td>Regg Schlemmer</td><td>—</td><td>17</td><td>17</td></tr>
<tr><td></td><td></td><td></td><td></td><td>Dick Kraft</td><td>16</td><td>—</td><td>16</td></tr>
<tr><td></td><td></td><td></td><td></td><td>Arnold Birner</td><td>0</td><td>19</td><td>12</td></tr>
</table>

S. C. T. A. TIME TRIALS - - - RESULTS

October 19, 1947

1	*668—Regg Schlemmer	136.05	mph.	Gaters	17
2	1—Randy Shinn	131.77		Road Runners	11
3	115—Akton Miller	125.69		Road Runners	10
4	147—Nelson Taylor	125.34		Gophers	9
5	12—Jack Calori	124.82		Lancers	8
6	500—Chuck Daigh	123.62		Dolphins	7
7	25—Frank Coon	123.45		Low Flyers	6
7	75—Harold Warnock	123.45		Lancers	6
7	77—Bob Syks	123.45		Lancers	6
8	161—Jack Mickelson	123.28		Gophers	5
9	480—Ed Stewart	123.11		San Diego Rd.	4
10	36—R. L. Shinn	122.95		Road Runners	3
10	666—Chuck Hossfeld	122.95		Gaters	3
11	23—Jack McGrath	122.78		Gophers	2
12	55—Blackie Gold	122.11		Pasadena Rd.	1
12	74—Coshow Brothers	122.11		Lancers	1

*—New Class Recordd: 136.57, 135.54. 136.05 Average.

CLASS "B" ROADSTERS —

1	60—Doug Hartelt	125.34	mph.	Lancers	12
2	5—Stuart Hilborn	123.11		Low Flyers	11
3	110—Harvey Haller	122.11		Road Runners	10
4	51—Bob Riese	121.45		Gear Grinders	9
5	264—James Culbert	120.00		Southern California Rd.	8
6	487—Bill Slawson	119.20		Dolphins	7
7	87—Giovanine Spurgin	118.89		Albata	6
8	277—K. P. Yenawine	118.73		Southern California Rd.	5
9	361—Byron Froelich	118.42		Gear Grinders	4
10	616—Donald Jensen	11747.		Clutchers	3

CLASS "C" STREAMLINERS—

1	* 16—Bill Burke	139.10	mph.	Road Runners	17

*—New Class Record' 139.96, 138.46. 139.21 Average.

CLASS "B" STREAMLINERS—

1	27—Arnold Birner	134.73	mph.	Throttlers	12
2	* 6—Johnson - Caruthers	134.52		Road Runners	16
3	19—Phil Remington	128.02		Low Flyers	10

*—New Class Record 13412, 138.67. 139.39 Average.

CLASS "D" STREAMLINERS—

1	657—Dietrich - Thomas	139.31	mph.	Gaters	12

HOT ROD MAGAZINE

SOUTHERN CALIFORNIA TIMING ASSOCIATION INC.

Announces

The First Annual

Automotive Equipment Display

and

Hot Rod Exposition

JAN. 23rd - 24th - 25th

At The National Guard Armory - - - Exposition Park
Los Angeles

Drive Carefully . . . Save A Life

HOT ROD *Magazine*

VOL. 1, No. 2 ⁕ ⁕ ⁕ PRICE 25c   WORLD'S MOST COMPLETE HOT ROD COVERAGE   FEBRUARY, 1948

Overhead Valves **by Wayne—Page 10**   31

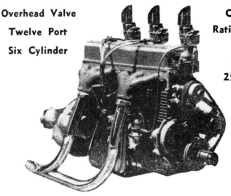

Editor's Column

Readers will find the February issue jam-packed with interesting reading and dozens of photos. Our incoming mail indicated that the followers and drivers of hot rods particularly enjoy lots of pictures . . . and that's just what we are supplying.

A new feature, which is something you can contribute to, is "IT'S IN THE BAG," which appears on page 4. It is composed of many of the interesting letters our readers have sent us. If you have a gripe or a praise about hot rods in general or about HRM, drop a line to "IT'S IN THE BAG" today!

The feature car of the month is Keith Landrigan's La Salle roadster which appears on the cover. Other shots of the car are on page 5 along with a detailed story of the roadster and its owner.

From WAYNE comes a clarification of the soup-up possibilities of a Chevy engine. His article, "OVERHEAD VALVES," is on page 10.

Robert Snyder of San Francisco, California, captured a sensational motion picture sequence with a 16mm. camera at the Oakland New Year's Day race. Story and pictures of the action appear on pages 6 and 7.

On page 16 is the first of 12 enlightening articles on fuel and carburetion. These were contributed by William Gieseke and are well worth the reading time.

The center page once again carries a full spread of sixteen shots of the hot rods and their owners, drivers and fans.

Whether you live in California or out of state, look over our list of dealers on page 22. If you are interested in handling HRM in your shop or store, drop us a line stating so. We'll welcome your representation.

Once again we're happy to present a full page photo of "Parts With Appeal." Turn to page 15 to see the latest development in dual equipment.

Once again we'd like to remind you . . . send us photos and news of your club's or individual hot rod activities.

If you've never seen a jet car, you'll get an eyeful on page 23. Don't miss it, for this may be the hot rod of the future.

A word of congratulation to the Southern California Timing Association, Inc., on the presentation of the First Annual Hot Rod Exposition and Automotive Equipment Display in Los Angeles.

Be sure you don't miss an issue of Hot Rod Magazine. Send us your subscription order today.—ED.

HOT ROD *Magazine*

TABLE OF CONTENTS

HRM—Published Monthly

Associate Editors ....Robert R. Lindsay
Robert E. Petersen

Advertising Manager ....Richard Sabotka

Advertising Representatives ....Fred Eggers, Hal Larson,
Fred Humphrey, Gordon Wheeler

Staff Photographer ....Lee Blaisdell

Cartoons and Humor ....Tom Medley

Distribution ....Hugh Gilbert

Reporters...Anthony Grantelli, John Lelis
Robert Williams, Glenn Glendening

HOT ROD MAGAZINE
112 South La Brea
Los Angeles 36, California

$3.00 Per Year

Please send me HRM for one year beginning with the .... issue.

Name ....

Street Address ....

City ...., Zone ...., State ....

(Check one) Cash ☐ Check ☐ Money Order ☐

It's in the Bag...

Dear Sir:

Congratulations on your first issue of Hot Rod Magazine. I am happy to see a publication covering this field which is far more than just a hobby in Southern California. In fact, the development of fast cars in this state, by non-professionals, is a major endeavor.

I also agree with your editorial stand on a recent accident involving a rebuilt car. Most of the fellows are far better car handlers due to the training they have given themselves. It is a shame that the general public, including newspaper reporters, immediately cry "Hot Rod Driver!" whenever they see an accident.

If half of the drivers on the road today could react to an emergency with the alertness of our roadster pushers, there would be just half as many accidents.

William E. Orr
1601 W. Victory Blvd.
Burbank, Calif.

• • •

Dear Sir:

I have read the January edition of Hot Rod Magazine and find no other as even competition. Yes, way out here in Chicago a few of the boys are Hot Rod jockeys and builders though nothing like L.A. . . . Since they got Soldier's Field for one of the tracks it is getting very popular.

I would like to subscribe to this Hot Rod Magazine. I am sure it is the best buy for the money.

Fuji Yonehara
1233 No. La Salle
Chicago, Ill.

• • •

Hot Rod Magazine:

Please send me HRM for one year beginning with the February issue.

William Jas. Foley—I.B.I.
Arabian Division
Dhahran, Saudi Arabia

Dear Sirs:

Enclosed you will find a money order for $3.00 for one year's subscription to your magazine. Let me congratulate you on your first issue, it really was fine. . . . I would like to add a few suggestions if you don't mind. Your magazine seems to be of a technical nature, and in my opinion you should stow the fiction setup. Maybe you could mention something about the pro's and con's of different intake manifolds, H. C. heads, magnetos, high speed ignition systems, etc.

I also might add that the West Coast isn't the only section of the country that has public opinion against "Roadsters," and by making your magazine a technical issue you could sell a lot of people. Wish you luck in future issues.

Donald E. Miegio
Hurricane HRRA
Chicago, Illinois

Readers will note that HRM carries no fiction "setup" in this issue.—ED.

• • •

Editors:

. . . The magazine is tops and a pleasure to sell so we are getting them out to all the fellows we can. Keep up the good work and it will be a great success.

Ben and Mary Sanders
3100 San Pablo Ave.
Oakland, Calif.

• • •

Dear Sir:

Enclosed find my check for a year's subscription to Hot Rod Magazine, starting with Volume I, No. 1. I ran across my first copy of "Hot Rod" in the Tattersfield office on a recent trip to Los Angeles, and I believe you have a very promising publication which should be welcomed enthusiastically by roadster fans and drivers alike the country over . . .

Robert M. Snyder
470 Castro Street
San Francisco, Calif.

• • •

Dear Sir:

. . . . I purchased your first issue at the one-hundred-lap roadster race on the ⅝ mile dirt track in Oakland, California on New Year's Day purely out of curiosity. Upon looking at the magazine I found it to be the best publication on roadsters and hot rods I have ever seen, bar none.

I like very much the many pictures in your magazine. Hoping they remain as plentiful in future issues— I remain

E. R. LEIBFRITZ,
25 Hernandez
Los Gatos, Calif.

Sirs:

I was rather hurt to see that my partner's name (Bill Van Noy) was not mentioned in your informative article ASC's, Results of Recent Races (HRM Jan. 1, 1948). It should have appeared in the Nov 2 race, at Culver City Speedway, where Bill placed 3rd in the 1st main and 4th in the runoff.

Also, congratulations on your first issue of HRM. We have been in need of a publication of this sort for a long time.

CARL REDCHER,
604 North Harding,
Montebello, Calif.

To be sure HRM erred in omitting the name of Driver Bill Van Noy from the Nov. 2 results. Van Noy placed third in the First Main event in his V-8, number 999. Apologies to Bill and reader Carl Redcher.—ED.

(Continued on Next Page)

Hot Rod of the Month

Combining a heavy engine with light running gear, Keith Landrigan's sleek blue D class roadster turns in fine performance records both in time trials and on the highway.

The engine is a 1938 La Salle, ported, relieved and bored to .155 which is .030 over Cadillac bore. Special built

La Salle V-8

1 7/8 sodium filled exhaust valves are used with a Winfield full race cam. Heads made by Arco are milled .040 and filled.

CARBURETION

For carburetion a stock manifold is used with the single carburetor mount blocked and two new mounts welded one at each end. A. A. 25 Stromberg carburetors with double floats fit on the mounts. Keith built his own distributor with parts from a 1933 La Salle and special heavy duty points. Flywheel and other parts are chopped

The 1932 roadster body is channeled to decrease the weight and the whole engine is electronically balanced.

TRANSMISSION

Power is transmitted to the 3.54 gears in the 1934 Ford differential by a 1941 Cadillac stearing wheel shift transmission. Front axel and stearing assembly are from a 1942 Ford.

Gabriel airplane type shock absorbers provide easy riding. A belly-pan extends from the firewall to the rear. Door handles are removed, doors are welded shut and all body creases are filled in. A panel covers the rear where the gas tank normally is, the tank being placed in the trunk.

Mufflers are incased in the ends of the large dual pipes that extend from the headers. Dash instruments fit in a chrome box on the stearing column with a full leather crash pad extending around the cowl and doors. Seats are about six inches high to compensate for the channeling. For running at the lakes, the custom windshield slips easily out of its brackets.

Keith has found that running 600-16 tires on the front instead of the usual 500-15 gives better riding performance. On the rear 700-16's are best for his 3.54 gear ratio. The braking system is full hydraulic.

TIMED 115.83

Last July Keith timed his car at the Lakes turning 115.83. He is hoping to better that time next season by changing gear ratio and tire sizes. On the highway, gas mileage varies between 13 and 17 miles per gallon.

Although born in Michigan, Keith has spent most of his twenty-seven years in California. In 1939 he built several T Fords, timing them at the Lakes as a member of the Flyers Club, which is now the Pasadena Roadster Club.

UNCLE SAM CALLS

Then came the war. Keith enlisted in the Navy and served four years as an Aviation Mechanic, with 32 months overseas on the Carriers Essex, Lexington, and Yorktown. He had plenty of opportunity to put to use the skills acquired while hopping up roadsters.

After his discharge from the Navy he started collecting parts for his La Salle B, financed by the U. S. Navy. Seems that there just wasn't any place to spend paychecks on a carrier.

THE ROMANTIC ANGLE

As for mechanical help, there was plenty of that. Betty, his girl friend, turned out to be a very fine wrench holder with a special knack for finding

Padded Interior

those hard to locate parts. The two worked steadily for ten months before the car was completed. Shortly after the roadster was finished they were married, using the car for a long honeymoon trip.

Keith works for the Crown Motor Rebuilding & Sales Company as a salesman. In his off hours he serves as vice-president of the Pasadena Roadster Club.

Another full time job is coming along for Keith. In February the Landrigans are expecting a new addition to the family. Says Keith: "My youngster will have the only full race La Salle baby carriage in town."

---

* **ABBREVIATIONS IN COMMON USE WITH HOT ROD FANS**
SCTA—Southern California Timing Association
CRA — California Roadster Assn.
ASC —   American Sports Car
NCRRA —   Northern California Roadster Racing Association
R—roadster
S—streamliner (any car not conforming to contour of stock roadster body)
Classes for dry lakes entrants—SCTA
A—0-183 cubic inches
B—183-250 cubic inches
C—250-350 cubic inches
D—350 and over.

(Continued from Opposite Page)

Hot Rod Magazine:

Wisconsin will be represented at last in the hot rods. Tom Friedman, Hank Geiser and myself are building the one and only "Badger" car. It will be a track job.

We are negotiating for the mile and

1/4 mile dirt tracks here in Milwaukee to run the rods on. We're also working against the old headache of some young punks in "junkers" giving the hot rods a bad name.

> Glenn Glendening
> 686 Oak Park Court
> Milwaukee, Wisc.

Dear Sir:

We received the magazines you sent us and are completely sold out. The boys seem to like the magazine very much.

> Anthony Granatelli
> Grancor Automotive Specialists
> 5652 N. Broadway
> Chicago, Ill.

A. S. C.

January 18th

Trophy dash
1. Bill Steves
2. Bill LaRoy

Semi final
1. Bob Stanclift
2. Bud Hetzler
3. Bruce McClaire
4. Warren Gerdes

Final
1. Bill Steves
2. Bill Patrick
3. Mickey Davis
4. Chuck Burness

New Year's Day Race at Oakland, Calif.   NCRRA

QUALIFYING TIME OF 23.64 ON THE 5/8 MILE TRACK SET BY GENE TESSIEN

TROPHY DASH, 4 LAPS	
1—Joe Valente	1:46.55
2—Elisian	
B RACE, 15 LAPS	
1—Al Germolis	7:16.30
2—Jack Smyers	
3—Tommy Cheek	
MAIN EVENT, 100 LAPS	
1—Lemoine Frey	46:06.10
2—Joe Valente	
3—Jim Heath	

This race was run on a slippery track due to the drizzly New Year's Day weather in Oakland. Jim Rathman, guest entrant from Los Angeles, was the first car of the featured 100-lap main event to get out of control. This can be partly accountable to the weather and partly to the fact that Jim is not used to driving on a high-banked track such as that at the Oakland Stadium.

On the opposite page appears a series of pictures taken during the 7-way accident which caused a restart of the main event. These pictures were shot by Robert Snyder, a fan in the grandstand, who enlarged them to this size from their original 16mm. frames.

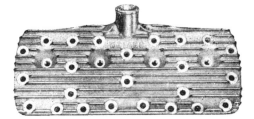

On the first lap of the main event 100 lapper at Oakland Stadium, Jim Rathman, a guest entrant from Los Angeles, starts to spin and is struck on the left side by Bob Sweikert, in a light blue roadster. At the same time Bob Machin, president of the NCRRA, comes up from behind, hitting Sweikert.

Now Pettit passes high, Sweiket is sliding sideways, Rathman is straightened out and Machin is locked into the mixup. The rest of the field is starting to close in.

Bob Machin's hood can be seen flying off in this shot. Corbin has almost completed his first roll. Rathman is clear at the left. Bob Kelleher in No. 70 (white hood), tries to avoid the crackup and swerves to the high side, just left of Corbin.

Corbin's car has come to rest after 1½ rolls broadside. Kelleher is seen near the left traveling backwards. Rathman is against the left wall (third car). Corbin's roadster is upside down.

Ed Corbin rushes up from the rear and in trying to pass the pileup his car rides over the right rear wheel of Sweikert's roadster. He (Corbin) begins to go into a roll. That's Pettit, Salt Lake champ, going high.

The field is scattering in all directions to avoid the collision. Corbin is halfway through the first roll. Pettit is high and clear, and by this time Rathman is clear.

Now Corbin is going into the first half of his second roll. Bob Kelleher is shown towards the left beginning to spin on the slippery track. Rathman is far left. Sweikert's roadster has skidded to a stop in the background.

Kelleher's car (No. 70) has come to a stop facing the opposite direction. 10X, the visiting champion from Salt Lake City, passes the camera safely. Directly behind him is Rathman, the first man to get into trouble in the race. Other drivers leave their cars to help the overturned Corbin. After his car was lifted Corbin walked away from the accident with a tremendous round of applause from the crowd.

WILLIT BROWN'S MERCURY-POWERED MODIFIED
Formerly owned by the late Danny Sakai

JIM RATHMAN'S CRA ENTRY
25T V-8

OVERHEAD VALVES

What has happened to the many fellows who were so successful with the four barrel rocker arm jobs? Frontenacs, Rajos, Gerbers, Cragars, Rileys, and all the rest.

There are still a few running, and good too; and doesn't the four barrel Chevvie still hold the top lakes' time? Have the rest of the rocker arm experts retired as the four barrel equipment disappeared or are they on the "bent-eight" band wagon?

Just in case you agree with me that the rocker boxes are worth working on, let's check the specifications of the Chevrolet Six. Bore and stroke combinations are ideal, especially for those who prefer a "square" engine. Here are the stock engine dimensions and a few of the combinations that can be worked out.

STOCK ENGINES

	Bore	Stroke	Displacement
Chev.: "Std."	3 1/2	3 3/4	216.5 cu. in.
Chev.: "Hi-Torque"	3 9/16	3 15/16	235.0 cu. in.

COMBINATIONS

	Bore	Stroke	Displacement
Hi-Torque Bloc & std. crank	3 9/16	3 3/4	225.0 cu. in.
Hi-Torque Bored 1/16 over	3 5/8	3 15/16	244.0 cu. in.
Hi-Torque Bored 1/8 over	3 11/16	3 15/16	255.0 cu. in.
Std. Bored & sleeved 1/4 over	3 3/4	3 3/4	248.5 cu. in.

The Hi-torque is Chevrolet's optional "big" engine—for passenger car and truck use. Nearly all parts are interchangeable with the Standard engine, 1937 thru 1947. The crankshafts are identical except for the 3/16 difference in stroke. The standard cam can not be used with the Hi-torque crank but the Hi-torque cam can be used in either engine. The Hi-torque bloc is 3/32 in. taller, due to the extra stroke, otherwise all parts are interchangeable.

The next logical question is: will it stay together? This engine has one of the highest bearing area to displacement ratios now being made. Ask a few Chevvie owners, particularly truck operators how many miles they have on their "lower ends." With the right babbitt and proper clearances, this large bearing area pays off.

Clearance is important! The large diameter crank needs a proportionately greater clearance. At least .0035 on the rods and .003 on the mains, and the bearings are there to stay. We learned about clearances the hard way, but since then we are turning these engines up to critical piston speeds (4,000 ft. per min.) and have not lost a bearing at r.p.m.'s of 6,000 with the Hi-torque

crank and 6,500 with the Standard.

Oiling System: Don't let the "splash" system scare you. With enough clearance on the bearings the stock oil spray tubes and rod scoops will do the job. However, a pressure system is easy to install. There is a 1/2 inch oil channel full length of the bloc with 1/4 inch leads to the main bearing oil grooves.

Drill the crank and re-babbitt the rods and you have a pressure system. This is important: the oil groove in the main is not big enough for a pressure system. The easiest way to enlarge this oil passage is by grooving the crank journal to match the groove in the bearing. Cut this groove at least 1/16 inch deep and 3/16 inch wide. You won't worry about "notch fatigue" in the crank after seeing the size of the journal and besides have you seen an "Offie" crank lately?

The cylinder head can be improved by polishing the three Siamese intake ports. The stock valve actuating mechanism will do the job, but get your cam reground by someone who specializes on Chevvies. A substantial increase in compression can only be obtained by welding in the combustion chamber. Drill

(*Continued on Page* 23)

EVANS *Speed and Power Equipment*

Engineered for best performance for all 24 stud Ford V-8 and Mercury engines. Smoother engine performance with more economy, power and acceleration.

Evans Makes the Best Dual Model A & B Manifold

This car using *Evans* manifold set a new S. C. T. A. roadster record of 136.05 ⟫▶
The National Hot Rod Race won by Manuel Ayulo using *Evans* Equipment

Look for this car at Hot Rod Auto Show.

24 Studs Only

The *Evans* Cylinder Heads are made of the best aluminum, heat treated. Extra heavy wall thickness is maintained over the combustion chamber area. *Evans* Heads are designed to carry maximum amount of water. Built to eliminate any restriction to the flow of gas with maximum compression ratio.

SEE YOUR DEALERS

Phone WHittier 422-387

2667 WHITTIER BLVD.   WHITTIER, CALIFORNIA

Laughs

FROM HERE AND THERE

By Tom Medley

Does she know much about cars?

No, she thinks you cool the engine by stripping the gears!

* * *

"Boy, think of those Spaniards going 3,000 miles on a galleon!"

"Aw, forget it, yuh can't believe all ya hear about them foreign cars!"

* * *

"Talk about power, my roadster can't be stopped on the hills!"

"Yes, mine was like that too, 'till I fixed the brakes!"

* * *

"Miss, you were doing 60 MPH."

"Oh, isn't that splendid. I only learned to drive yesterday!"

* * *

A Garage man was called out on the highway to fix a stalled car. Upon arriving he lifted the hood, hit the engine one blow with his hammer and the car started. When presented with the bill for $50.00, the motorist demanded an itemized account. So the garage man presented him the following statement:

One blow with the hammer .. $1.00

Knowing what to hit $49.00

A Top! And ruin the lines of my car?

A Miss in the car is worth two in the engine!

* * *

There was plain and fancy cussing coming from a parked roadster, when the policeman approached and wanted to know what was going on.

"Some so and so stole my steering gear," complained the slightly woozy driver.

"You just quiet down and get out of that turtle deck and get up here in the front seat where you belong!"

Most of us have had occasion to be driving a little too fast when we've seen a police car or motorcycle coming towards us from the opposite direction. Naturally, after spotting the official vehicle, we've slowed down to a legal speed and cruised on by. Without a chance to make an accurate speedometer check the policeman could only gauge our speed by guesswork, not true enough to warrant a citation. Therefore, we've slipped by without a ticket. Today something new has arrived on the scene. HRM passes this along as a tip to all motorists.

With the coming of jet propulsion, supersonic speeds, television and the split atom there is another amazing instrument of science—radar. Today radar, the same radar with which we spotted enemy planes during World War II, the same radar with which fliers now avoid mountain crashes, is being tested as means of plotting the speeds of ground-traveling vehicles. These tests are being performed at present by the Los Angeles Traffic Bureau. The complete outfit can be rigged to a prowl car or motorcycle. Most important is the fact that it makes no difference whether the vehicle being checked is approaching, leaving or passing the radar unit.

If the experiments prove successful (and it looks as though they will) speed violators had better watch their step! There will be little chance of "getting away with" excessive speeds on streets and highways patroled by the watchful eye of radar.

I think I've solved the ticket problem

Len Knolhoff in his 25T Ford 6 at Carrell Speedway in Gardena, California. Len's roadster runs Winfield heads and manifold.

This is the Bill Burke-Lodes co-entry belly tank. The shot of the small bore engine V-8 streamliner was taken at an S.C.T.A. lakes meet.

R. B. "Dick" Robinson's car races in the eastern track circuits and is one of the outstanding cars there. Dick owns a speed shop in Akron, Ohio.

Jack McGrath is presented with a trophy for his CRA driving skill at the Gardena track . . . a trophy and that ain't all!

Burleigh Dolph's No. 444 is a rear engine '42 Mercury. Seen here at El Mirage, this car has timed 129.31 at an S.C.T.A. meet.

Wayne Frankfurter and Bob Garlick of the Santa Monica, California, Almegas, have a little flywheel trouble while at a lakes meet. With some help from several friends, the boys had the car running within an hour.

Ed Stewart (right) and Nellie Taylor in Stewart's '32 roadster. Ed is a member of the San Diego Roadster Club and is boy who turns out those San Diego dropped axles.

This tail job runs in the streamliner class. Thatcher Darwin in the seat waits with John Cannon for the starter's signal. Both are members of the Hollywood Throttlers Club.

Art McCormick, his wife Ellena, and son Gary, are shown at the turnout for Hot Rod Exposition display cars. This meeting was held at the new Lincoln-Mercury plant in Los Angeles.

At the Firestone Blvd. Motordrome, ASC President Tony Coldewey (wearing sweater), and Secretary Chuck Burness (right) pose with Driver Grant Lambert and Owner Lawrence Mueller.

Taken at 6:30 in the morning, this shot reflects the enthusiasm with which Californians and out-of-staters turn out for timing meets held by the S.C.T..A Shown here is part of an estimated 10,000 person crowd.

Doane Spencer of the Glendale Stokers received his first place trophy in a roadster beauty contest held by the Pasadena Roadster Club at the Rose Bowl.

CRA's Chuck Leighton dropped a cam follower in warm-up laps at Carrell Speedway. Fast working crew members had the track job in shape again in time to be in the time trials.

Jim Lindsley (Gear Grinders), just after he stroked it through the traps for a time of 123.23. This was clocked at a Russetta Timing Meet.

Two of the NCRRA drivers mix it up during a race at the Highway 99 Stadium near Modesto, California. Here's mud in your eyes, fellows!

Bill Roberts, of the Van Nuys Roadmasters, runs Riley rocker arm heads on this 1937 Ford V-8 engine.

BELL AUTO PARTS

Featuring the FINEST IN RACING EQUIPMENT

for Roadsters - Boats and Race Cars

Send for our free
illustrated catalog

ROY RICHTER

3633 E. GAGE AVE.

BELL, CALIF.　　　　　　**KImball 5728**

Parts with appeal

 →

Pictured at the right is Norma Maxine "Mac" Hammitt, who wants road-ster fans to get acquainted with the latest in dual equipment.

According to the manufacturer of the manifold shown, "It gives added power to your engine by a more perfect distribution of fuel mixture. The ports are designed so as to give an alternate firing action, thus equalizing the charge between two carburetors and giving a simulated four carburetor effect. The firing action assures a constant acceleration from idling to peak RPM, eliminating flat spots." But enough of this technical talk . . .

Miss Hammitt, who made an able model fo our "Parts With Appeal" page, is a native of Portland, Oregon. She was born there in 1927. (Let's see, now . . . that makes her about twenty-one). A graduate of Alexander Hamil-ton High School in Los Angeles, she works as a junior stenographer. She hopes to one day become a professional model for magazine and poster art work.

Among her likes she lists dancing, ice skating, bowling ("I bowled a mean 99 the first time I tried."), the snow and the beach.

Her dislikes include people who munch on popcorn during movies, women who wear big hats during movies, and having to get up early in the morning.

Norma's idea of an ideal man is that "he must be tall, handsome, plus a good dancer. Also, he must know how to cook as I haven't learned yet my-self."

Miss Hammitt hopes that someday she'll realize her ambition to make a parachute jump, but she doubts that she'd have the nerve if offered the chance.

Incidentally, fellows, the gal has a boyfriend already . . . an apprentice to a local optician. An optician, eh? Hmmm, maybe HER eyes are bother-ing him.

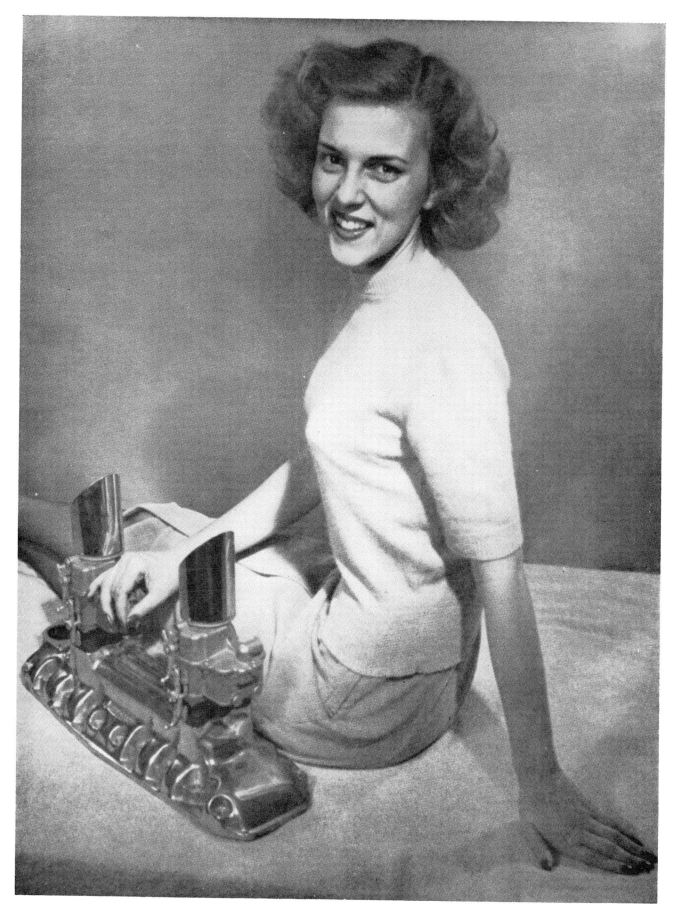

Norma Hammitt with a Dual Manifold

CARBURETION

by William Giezeke

Combustion—Potential and Kinetic Energy

Combustion or burning, in a chemical sense, signifies the combination of one or more elements, accompanied in all cases by the liberation of heat. The heat produced may be considered as the result of a chemical reaction which converts the potential (stored up) energy in the fuel into heat, which in turn may be utilized inside a closed cylinder and converted, in part, into kinetic energy (energy of motion). Energy may be transferred and transformed in many ways, but it is never created or destroyed.

Elements of Combustion

Oxygen — Oxygen (O/2), which is essential to combustion, is present in the air to the extent of approximately 20 percent. The remaining 80 percent is chiefly nitrogen, a very inert gas which does not enter chemically into the process of combustion. Oxygen, a very active gas, will combine with a great number of elements and compounds, and in each instance the amount of heat liberated will depend on the chemical nature of the substance involved. Hydrogen and carbon alone or in any of their various combinations produce large quantities of heat when burned and constitute our most important fuels for the production of heat and power.

Hydrogen—Hydrogen (H) is a very light and inflammable gas. When mixed with air and ignited it combines with oxygen to form the oxide H_2O, or water. The combustion of pure hydrogen is a very rapid process which, if confined, may produce a very high pressure.

Carbon—Carbon (C) is a solid existing in three forms: The familiar carbon present in soot or lampblack, graphite, and the diamond. Although differing in physical properties, these are all pure carbon, and under proper conditions one form may be converted into another without any change in chemical structure. At a very high temperature, carbon will pass from the solid into the

vapor state. Carbon in its natural state does not exist as a liquid. When ignited in a plentiful supply of air or oxygen, carbon burns with a clear flame to form carbon dioxide (CO_2), an inactive and harmless gas. However, when the supply of oxygen is insufficient (rich mixture), a certain quantity of carbon monoxide (CO) will also be produced. Carbon monoxide is a poisonous gas which may cause death when present in the air to the extent of only 4 parts in 10,000 (0.04 of 1 percent) by volume. The gas is colorless and odorless, and thus gives practically no warning of its presence.

Hyrdocarbons (CH group) — As fuels, hydrogen and carbon are seldom available in their natural state, but occur in combination with each other, forming compounds known as hydrocarbons (CH group). There are many thousands of these compounds in existence, and all are classified as fuels. These hydrocarbons are present in large quantities in coal and petroleum, occurring as solids, liquids, and gases.

Crude Petroleum

Due to the abundance of crude petroleum and because of the various products which may be extracted therefrom, it has become our most important source of hydrocarbon compounds for internal-combustion engine fuels and lubricants. Although crude samples from different fields usually vary in composition, all crudes are made up of a great number of hydrocarbon compounds arranged in groups, the paraffin series being the most common in the United States. The chemical nature of petroleum is so complex that complete analysis is seldom attempted, but by distillation the crude may be separated into fractions in order to produce the desired commercial products, including gasoline and lubricating oil.

Gasoline—Boiling Range—Gasoline is a blend or mixture of hydrocarbon liquids ranging in boiling point from approximately 90 degrees F. to 425 degrees F. There is no exact limit established for this mixture range. Because of this latitude in boiling point and in various other characteristics, it is impossible to list the detailed specifications of gasoline. Any sample must be subjected to a number of tests before its exact properties may be determined. Only after such testing can a gasoline be pronounced satisfactory for use as a fuel in a particular type of internal-combustion engine.

Methods of Producing Gasoline

Of the many methods employed for producing gasoline, three are of sufficient importance to warrant a brief description of the apparatus and procedure involved. These are the fractional distillation process, the cracking process, and the absorption process.

Fractional Distillation — The fractional distillation process was the first to be developed and produces what is known as a straight-run gasoline. In this process the crude is heated to a moderate temperature in a retort to vaporize progressively the various hydrocarbon liquids. The lighter and more volatile compounds are first vaporized, followed in order by those of higher boiling points. These vapors are then led through condensers which return them to the liquid state. By proper regulation of the vaporization and condensation, the hydrocarbons may be separated into various grades of gasoline, fuel oil, lubricating oil, etc., although further treatment and purification are often necessary. The fractional distillation process is accomplished at atmospheric pressure, and during the process no effort is made to change the chemical nature of any of the fractions.

Cracking Process—The cracking process is employed principally as a means of increasing the yield of gasoline from a given amount of crude. Very often petroleum fractions which are neither suitable for gasoline nor lubricating oil may be cracked, thus obtaining a considerable quantity of gasoline. The cracking process is a form of destructive distillation in which the crude of a portion of it is placed in a sealed retort and subjected to a high temperature and high pressure. These conditions serve to break up the chemical arrangement of the heavy hydrocarbon molecules and partially convert the heavier products into a cracked gasoline. The fuel thus produced is often superior to many grades of straight-run gasoline in anti-knock value but requires thorough refining to make it suitable for storage. The reason for this is that the cracked hydrocarbons, which are chemically the olefins and diolefins, produce gum on aging. Some types of cracked gasoline may be stabilized or inhibited from gum formation by the addition of a small quantity of a suitable anti-catalyst. A high percentage of the total

(Continued on Page 18)

gasoline production at present is the result of the cracking process.

Absorption Process—Extracting gasoline from certain compounds present in natural gas produces a fuel of comparatively high volatility, known as casing head or natural gasoline. The most common method of extracting gasoline from natural gas is the absorption process. This is accomplished by forcing natural gas through a heavy oil which absorbs the liquid content of the gas. The oil is then distilled to reclaim the light fraction, which is gasoline. If properly blended with a straight-run or cracked gasoline, it is quite satisfactory as an engine fuel.

Special Fuels

Alcohol and Benzol — Although the petroleum fractions known as gasoline have been employed almost exclusively for internal combustion engine fuels, other liquid fuels have also been investigated and used to some extent. Ethyl (grain) alcohol (C_2H_5OH) and benzol (C_6H_6) appear to be preferred at present.

Ethyl and Methyl Alcohol—In the alcohol group the ethyl and the methyl alcohols are the most useful as fuel for internal combustion engines and of the two, ethyl alcohol has the best fuel properties. Ethyl alcohol, known as grain alcohol, differs from benzol and gasoline in that it is not strictly a hydrocarbon, but contains a large proportion of oxygen. Alcohol is safe to handle due to its low volatility and nonexplosibility under ordinary conditions. Due to its miscibility with water, fires may be extinguished with water. Less carbon is formed in engines burning fuel containing over 35 percent alcohol. The heat of combustion is about 13,000 British thermal units per pound as compared with 18,000 for benzol and 20,000 for gasoline. However, alcohol will withstand much higher compression pressure than gasoline without detonation, so the added power due to increased compression may more than offset the loss of heat energy available.

Straight Alcohol—Straight alcohol is not suitable for ordinary engines. Its vapor pressure is only one-fourth that of gasoline while its heat of vaporization is three times that of gasoline. Thus, it would be difficult, if not impossible to start an ordinary engine by straight alcohol.

The difficulty may be overcome by adding ether, priming the cylinders, or using special blends for starting. Also, pure alcohol in general tends to produce preignition in engines with high cylinder wall temperature. This tendency can be reduced by the addition of water.

Ethyl Alcohol—Ethyl Alcohol (C_2H_5OH) is a compound of hydrogen, carbon, and oxygen which may be prepared from any organic compound such as grain, starch and sugar. As an engine fuel its chief virtue is that it will withstand a high compression pressure, which in turn promotes clean and efficient engine operation. The particular disadvantages of alcohol as compared with gasoline are its low heat value, low vapor pressure, and a pronounced affinity for water.

Benzol—Benzol (C_6H_6) is a hydrocarbon compound obtained from coal. It may be compressed to a high degree, but it has a low specific heat value, slow burning rate, sooty, high freezing point, and greater cost, and the available supply would be urgently required by other industries in case of military emergency. It has been successfully blended with gasoline as an anti-knock compound, but, as such, it is inferior to such anti-knock compounds as tetraethyl lead, iso-octane, and iso-pentane.

Volatility of Liquid Fuels

Since liquid fuels are generally used for internal combustion engines, they must always be converted into a vapor state before combustion occurs. This property of a liquid, which enables it to change readily into a vapor, is known as "volatility," a characteristic which may be determined by a distillation test and vapor pressure test.

Distillation Test—In the distillation test, the gasoline is heated and vaporized at a constant rate. The boiling temperatures are recorded as the various percentages of fuel are recovered. These percentages determine the volatility range between the initial and end boiling points of the fuel under test. The distillation apparatus is shown in *fig. 1*.

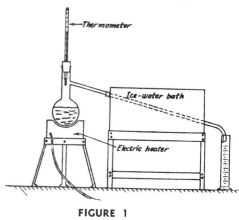

FIGURE 1

Vapor Pressure Test—The vapor pressure test is accomplished by sealing a sample of the fuel in a bomb equipped with a pressure gage. The apparatus is then immersed in a constant temperature bath, and the indicated pressure is noted. The higher the corrected vapor pressure obtained from the fuel under test, the more susceptible it is to vapor locking. The apparatus used for this test is illustrated in *figure 2*.

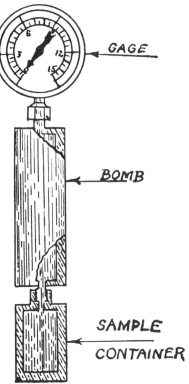

FIGURE 2

Volatility (*Cold Starting*)—The volatility of a fuel is quite important in determining whether or not an engine may be started when cold. In this connection, it is well to know that gasoline is not combustible in its liquid form, principally because the molecules of the liquid will not readily mix with the oxygen of the air. Gasoline vapor, however, unites quite readily with oxygen, resulting in very rapid combustion. From this it is evident that an engine fuel should be sufficiently volatile to form combustible vapor at low atmospheric temperatures.

Vapor Lock—On the other hand, excessively volatile gasolines are very troublesome, because they promote a condition known as "vapor lock." This condition is due to vapor formation in the fuel lines which restricts the liquid flow, resulting in a lean mixture and the possibility of engine failure.

Freedom from Vapor Lock—A compromise between the two extremes in volatility of gasolines is generally at-

(*Continued on Page 20*)

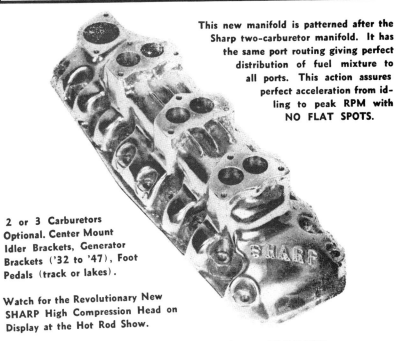

tained, permitting satisfactory starting characteristics, and at the same time probable freedom from vapor lock under all conditions. For present aircraft engine fuels a maximum vapor pressure of about 7 pounds, with 10 perecent distilled at 140 degrees F. to 160 degrees F., is satisfactory. The 90 percent point should not exceed 300 degrees F., and approximately 250 degrees F. is ideal.

For present automotive fuels a maximum vapor pressure of 10 lbs. (winter fuels) or 8 lbs. (summer fuels) is permissable, with 10 percent distilled at 110 degrees F. Maximum; 50 percent, 257 degrees F. maximum; 90 percent, 356 degrees F. maximum.

Purity

It is important that the finished gasoline, after refining, be as free from foreign substances as possible. The elimination of gum, sulphur and corrosive sulphur compounds is particularly desirable especially in aircraft gasolines. The apparatus as shown in *figure 3* for

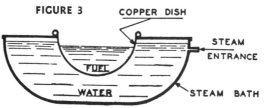

FIGURE 3   COPPER DISH
STEAM ENTRANCE
FUEL
WATER   STEAM BATH

testing the gasoline for gum and corrosion consists of a spun copper dish and a steam bath. After evaporating a certain amount of gasoline placed in the copper dish a gray, black or amber discoloration deposited on the inside surface indicates the presence of gum and/or corrosive sulphur which condemns the sample.

Water and Sediment—Even though all precautions are observed in storing and handling gasoline, it is not uncommon to discover a small amount of water and sediment in a fuel system. The sediment is usually retained in the strainers located at various points in the fuel system, and this it not generally considered a source of great danger. The water, however, presents a rather serious problem since it drops to the bottom of the fuel tank and may then be circulated freely through the fuel system. A small quantity of water will flow with the gasoline through the carburetor jets and not be especially harmful. However, an excessive quantity of water upon reaching the carburetor will effectively displace the gasoline passing through the jets and restrict the flow of fuel which may result in engine failure.

Water Segregators — Efficient water segregators can be installed and there will be little danger of water actually

being pumped into the jets. However, under certain conditions of temperature and humidity, condensation of moisture occurs on the inner surfaces of the fuel tanks. Since the amount of such condensation is proportionate to the unfilled volume of the tank (air space), it is obvious that the practice of servicing a tank immediately after use will do much to eliminate this hazard.

Water Test—Whenever water is believed to be present in a fuel system, a small quantity of gasoline may be drained from the lowest point of the system and tested with water-test paper. This paper is coated with a compound which is soluble in water but is not affected by gasoline. A strip of the paper is immersed vertically in the container so that it touches the bottom. If the water is present, the coating will be removed from the lower portion of the strip, thus indicating the amount of water. This simple test will prove conclusively whether or not a real danger exists, and is well worth the time and efforts required.

Purity—The qualities previously discussed of heat energy and volatility have been qualities directly and immediately affecting performance. The qualities generally described under the heading of purity are those which prevent some undesirable constituent in the gasoline, or formed in the gasoline before it is used, from detracting from the desired performance.

Purity of Gasoline—Gasoline as received from the vendor should be free from water and sediment of any kind and every care should be taken in its storage and handling to prevent the introduction of water or any other substance into it. This prohibition applies also to air, which should not be introduced into the gasoline by means of leaking suction lines to pumps, in pump handling of gasoline, or by exposing gasoline stored in small tanks or drums

CARBURETION

(Continued from Page 20)

to violent temperature such as are set up by direct exposure to sun and rain. Gasoline storage containers, unless hermetically sealed, tend to breathe out vapor when heated and breathe in air when cooled.

Gasoline, as received from the vendor, should contain a minimum of sulphur and its compounds, which are common impurities in petroleum in the ground. Gasoline suitable for aviation should not contain gum, formed as a result of its exposure to heat in its distillation, or contain hydrocarbons which in storage will tend to produce gum as a matter of time or exposure to the normal temperatures encountered in storage.

(Additional copies may be obtained by writing SOLV-X CHEMICAL CO., "Manufacturing Chemists for the Jobbing Trade," 3608 Roselawn Ave., Glendale 8, Calif., CHurchill 9-3533. Members American Chemical Society; Society of Automotive Engineers. Copyright 1946 (Permission of reprint reserved).

Classified Advertisements

RUSSETTA TIMING ASSOCIATION

Ray Ingram, President

AWARDS for 1947

Ray Schlegel Perpetual Trophy

to

Jim Palm, Doug Hartelt

Fastest Roadster Award

Jim Palm, Doug Hartelt, 130.05 mph

2nd ....Bert Letner, Nellie Taylor

3rd ....Jack Nicholson

Fastest Coupe Award

Don Brown
116.59 mph, 115.97 mph average

Fastest Modified Award
Joe Butler, 119.21 mph

Fastest Streamliner Award
Bill Burke, 142 plus mph

Dealers . . . . .
HOT ROD MAGAZINE

LOS ANGELES LOCALE

HOT ROD MAGAZINE, 1008 North Fairfax, Hollywood 46,
or write HRM, 112 South La Brea, L.A. 36.

COLLEGE BOOK STORE, 3474 University, Los Angeles 7.

COPPER BOWL, 1801 Glendale Blvd., L.A. 26.

LEWIE SHELL'S SERVICE, 11726 Wilshire Blvd., L.A. 25.

TOMMY IKKANDA, 2060 Sawtelle Blvd., L.A. 26.

PHIL WEIAND, 2733 San Fernando Rd., L.A. 41.

RUSSELL TIRE CO., 2101 San Fernando Rd., L.A. 41.

SOUTHERN CALIFORNIA

PAT'S SERVICE, 9641 Venice Blvd., Culver City.

NAVARRO RACING EQUIPMENT, 718 South Verdugo, Glendale.

SO-CAL SPEED SHOP, 1104 South Victory, Burbank.

BELL AUTO PARTS, 3633 East Gage Avenue, Bell.

BLAIR'S AUTO PARTS, 826 Arroyo Parkway, Pasadena.

DOUGLASS MUFFLER SHOP, 1916 West Valley Blvd., Alhambra.

SPEEDWAY AUTO PARTS, 1001 East Pacific Coast Highway.

J. A. DOLPH, Box 402, Barstow.

CENTRAL AND NORTHERN CALIFORNIA

BEN SANDERS, 3100 San Pablo Avenue, Oakland 8.

C. P. HUNT AUTO SUPPLY, 2406 Webster Street, Oakland.

HUBBARD AUTO PARTS CO., 2901 Telegraph, Oakland.

MOLANDER'S SPEED SHOP, 730 Van Ness Avenue, San Francsico.

GUS RUDELBACH, c/o Mantica Auto Parts, Mantica.

JAMES R. MOONJEAN, 751-17th Street, Merced.

BUCK'S AUTO PARTS, 16th and R, Merced.

F. L. MAGNIS, Route 5, Box 323, Modesto.

LAWRENCE LEONG, 1405 K Street, Bakersfield.

STEVE'S AUTOMOTIVE SERVICE, South Highway 99, Tulare.

BOB INGRAM, Ben Maddox Way and 1st North, Visalia.

JIM COLE'S BODY SHOP, 4245 Belmont, Fresno.

HUNTER DRUG STORE, 127 East Yosemite Avenue, Madera.

BOB MOHR, Box 204, California Polytechnic, San Luis Obispo.

BOB'S SPEED EQUIPMENT, Mission and De La Vina, Santa Barbara.

MIKE & ROY'S SERVICE, 197 East Jackson Street, San Jose.

DANNY'S HOT DOG STAND, 508 Pacific Avenue, Santa Cruz.

FRANK LIPSCOMBY, 1150 Garner Street, Salinas.

MARCUS AUTO SUPPLY, 12th and J Street, Sacramento.

JACK GENTRY, 3701 23rd Street, Del Paso Heights.

OUT OF STATE

NEVADA: MC CAUGHEY MOTORS, 515 Virginia Street, Reno.

UTAH: JOHNNY'S FORD SHOP, 47 West 4th South, Salt Lake City.

UTAH: DICK TRIBE, 3230 Washington Blvd., Ogden.

ILLINOIS: GRANCOR AUTOMOTIVE SPECIALISTS, 5058 N. Broadway, Chicago 40.

MICHIGAN: ROBERT WILLIAMS, 1021 Lapeer Street, Flint 3.

OHIO: AKRON SPEED SHOP, 1904 South Main Street, Akron.

CHATTER

Sharp is casting a new head, larger than any other hot rod head we know of. The new job includes incorporated water manifold in the head, features greater thickness than heads used in the past on V-8's. It uses stock long studs. Any socket wrench will fit without rubbing or cutting the cooling fins. This will be on display at the Hot Rod Exposition.

* * *

The SCTA is in the voting stage on the suggested idea of having two-day time trials at the lakes this coming season.

* * *

The ASC, Inc., has leased the old Don Mar track near Downey, California, where they expect to put on many a thrilling show in the coming race season. The group has renamed the track the Firestone Blvd. Motordrome, planning that the new title will locate as well as name the stadium. ASC plans to run a two or three-way circuit between The Motordrome, Roscoe Ranch and, perhaps, one other spot in the 1948 season.

* * *

In 1895 Levassor, a French motorist, raced a "horseless carriage" from Paris to Bordeaux at an average speed of 15 miles an hour.

Los Angeles Daily News

●

●

From the looks of the above photo one might be led to think that the "boys" from Mars have finally arrived. However, such is not the case. Clad in an asbestos suit to avoid the hot power unit of the vehicle shown, is Bob Yeakel, one of the six builders of this jet propelled auto.

The design and building of this unit was directed by Gale Kelly, a machinist. Others who helped to build the unit are Jim Muntz, race driver, Bob Spaid, Paul Bennett, Jim Vickers and Yeakel.

The jet car was first tried out at Rosamond Dry Lake, near Lancaster, California, last year. With the throttle open only a fraction the unit cruised at 30 MPH. The car is started on propane liquid. The car got so hot during its initial test runs that the driver had to swing his legs away from the power unit.

At 100 MPH an automobile developes 15 pounds of thrust per square inch. In comparison, the jet car developes around 350 per inch.

The power unit itself is a fifteen foot tube, which has only two moving parts. Both of these parts are in the intake valve in the head of the tube.

As crude as the unit appears, its cost ran around $10,000. Other than the power tube, the unit consists of chassis, conventional stearing apparatus, four wheels, brakes and a bucket seat for the driver.

The car was built at Yeakel's garage on South Vermont Avenue in Los Angeles.

OVERHEAD VALVES

(Continued from Page 10)

and tap the spark plug holes for 14 MM plugs in order to take advantage of the wider heat ranges available.

The possibilities of this engine have proven out so well that a number of engine specialists have designed and are now manufacturing a complete line of racing equipment to complement this rugged crank and bloc assembly. Plan to inspect the Chevrolet Six displays when you attend the first annual Hot Rod Show.

NEW OFFICERS

December 27, 1947
SCTA

Akton Miller ....President
Bozzy Willis ....Vice-president
Mel Leighton ....Treasurer
Wally Parks ....Business manager
Thatcher Darwin ....Recording secretary

December 10, 1947
CRA

Johnny Lucas ....President
Jack Baylis ....Vice-president
Tom Sloane ....Secretary

BOARD OF DIRECTORS

Del Baxter, Ralph Ruttman, Don Blair, Babe Ouse, also the above named officers

ASC
President
Tony Coldewey
Vice President
Everett Haskins
Sec.-Treas.
Chuck Burness

Starter	**Steward**
Jim Sheridan	Howard Seymour
Pit Manager	**Timer**
H. M. Robinson	Howard Gibbs

"Please!" Join the MARCH OF DIMES

JANUARY 15-30

FIGHT INFANTILE PARALYSIS

THE NATIONAL FOUNDATION FOR INFANTILE PARALYSIS

FRANKLIN D. ROOSEVELT, FOUNDER

HOT ROD *Magazine*

. 1, No. 3 * * * PRICE 25c   WORLD'S MOST COMPLETE HOT ROD COVERAGE   MARCH, 1948

Choosing a Cam by Weber—Page 10

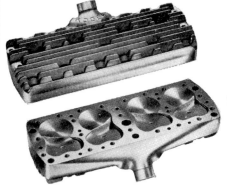

Editor's Column

For the month of March HRM comes forth with a new bag of entertainment written, photographed, drawn especially for the hot rod followers the world over.

HOT ROD OF THE MONTH features Don Blair's track job, No. 57. The story, on page 5, is supplemented with the able photographic material of Lee Blaisdell, recently made official photographer for the S.C.T.A., Inc.

Southern California has yet to come forth with it's annual winter-spring rain showers, so race drivers and fans are still able to have a go at it now and then. On page 6 are the results of three recent races held by the up-and-coming American Sports Cars, Inc.

Something new for HMR are the story and pictures of hot rod history featured on page 7. If readers find this material enjoyable, there'll be more to come in future issues.

Pictures reprinted with this story are from the collection of George Riley. We will confine our interests to the 1930-35 period in this issue.

Gus Maanum, favorite artist with the hot rod enthusiasts of the west, has drawn a beautiful original of Jack Calori's lakes roadster. This has been reprinted for our readers on page 9 of this issue.

Fellows assembling or working on a hot rod will find much to interest them in Harry Weber's article "Choosing a Cam," which appears on page 10.

W. I. "Bill" Gieseke continues his series of articles with "Leaded Fuels" on page 16. In this issue Gieseke also outlines the rest of the series, which will include invaluable material on compression ratio, porting, relieving, trouble shooting, etc.

A recap of the recent Hot Rod Exposition in Los Angeles appears on page 23 of HRM.

Want to buy a hot rod? Want to sell one? Want to trade one? Try our classified ad section which is on page 21 of this issue. You'll find it the most economical way to do your advertising. At our low price of 25c per line YOU CAN'T MISS!

Due to our increasing circulation, this will probably be the last issue of HRM in which we can run a list of our dealers in California. If you buy your copy of the magazine from a dealer, be sure to jot down his address so you'll have it next month. Readers unable to find a dealer in their area are asked to write HRM for information along this line.

Continue to write us those swell letters and we'll continue to print the most interesting ones. Until next issue, so long!—ED.

HOT ROD *Magazine*

TABLE OF CONTENTS

HRM—Published Monthly

Associate Editors ....Robert R. Lindsay
Robert E. Petersen

Advertising Manager ....Richard Sabotka

Staff Photographer ....Lee Blaisdell

Cartoons and Humor ....Tom Medley

Reporters.................................Anthony Grantelli, John Lelis
Robert Williams, Glenn Glendening
Richard K. Martin

HOT ROD MAGAZINE
112 South La Brea
Los Angeles 36, California

$3.00 Per Year

Please send me HRM for one year beginning with the .... issue.

Name ....

Street Address ....

City ...., Zone ...., State ....

(Check one)   Cash ☐   Check ☐   Money Order ☐

Its in the Bag . . .

Gentlemen:

I enjoyed reading your February issue of Hot Rod. I found the text interesting and the photographs eye-arresting. I'm sorry that I missed your first issue so will you please start a subscription rolling to the above address starting with the January issue.

Lt. Col. NED T. NORRIS
Fort Leavenworth, Kansas

. . .

Dear Sirs:

. . . Have recently arrived in Chicago from California and want to keep in touch with the recent and future developments in roadster material. Find HRM an ideal way of keeping posted as there isn't much roadster interest back here as yet.

Good luck on your fine publication. There's been a great need for your magazine for years.

L. NEWTON
c/o Institute of Design
Chicago 10, Ill.

. . .

Dear Sir:

This is the only magazine that I have ever run accross that is so complete.

This is what the public needs to read so they can distinguish a true hot rod from the typical squirrels that show off on our crowded highways today.

. . . . Wishing you luck in your future issues.

GERRY K. HINCH
Eureka, Calif.

. . .

Dear Editors:

Congratulations on your first two editions of Hot Rod Magazine. I was surprised to see the coverage of Oakland's New Year's Day Race, especially the pictures. I would like to have the address of Robert Snyder who took those pictures. I would like a set of those shots.

The name of the driver who flipped was Red Corbin, instead of Ed Corbin.

Again I extend my best wishes for the future of the best racing publication I have seen to date, with no exceptions.

C. H. (Red) CORBIN
Richmond, Calif.

OOOPS! Red Corbin it is! . . . and who should know better than the driver himself? Apologies to Mr. C. for the mistake and congratulations on the quick thinking which saved him from serious harm on New Year's Day. Mr. Snyder Lives at 470 Castro Street in San Francisco. However, HRM has the negative strip of the action mentioned. We are forwarding same to Mr. Corbin that he might print a set for posterity. Incidentally, Mr. Snyder mistakenly listed Driver Corbin's name as Ed in the information he sent with the pictures. Closer investigation showed that Corbin's name did not appear on the New Year's Day program.—ED.

. . .

Gentlemen:

I find your magazine very informative, particularly the photographs. We get very little photographic material on roadsters here.

W. C. BUCK
Denver, Colorado.

HRM hopes to supply photographic material, along with informative editorials, to ALL of the spots which up until now have had little linkage with the hot rod centers of the world.—ED.

. . .

Gentlemen:

Congratulations on the first issue of your very fine magazine.

Here in the east, we are a little slow getting started on hot rods, but this summer we expect to see some of the boys get going on the half mile tracks.

I have written a couple of your advertisers with the intention of handling their lines here in New England. If you have Barker's address, I would appreciate it if you would send it to me. He is the manufacturer of the Barker mag and dry sump oil pump, so I am very anxious to get his address...

ED STONE
New England Auto Racing Equipment
Belmont 78, Mass.

Barker's address is 2100 Diamond, in Burbank, California.—ED.

. . .

Dear Sirs:

. . . A friend in Berkley sent me the January issue . . . Really thought it was great. In the year I've been away from Southern California there sure have been many changes, especially in the times that have been clocked.

There are very few roadsters here but the number seems to be on the increase.

You have a good mag. . . . I will be looking forward to receiving my first issue.

T. E. AUSTIN
Waimanalo
Oahu, Territory of Hawaii

(Continued on Page 14)

Hot Rod of the Month

Don Blair's 27 T not only ranks with the best track jobs in the California Roadster Association but recently clocked 124.88 mph at a Russetta timing meet. The 1946 Mercury engine has a quarter inch stroke with a 3 5/16 inch bore. It runs Weiand Heads and Manifold, Potvin Ignition, Harman Cam and is balanced throughout.

Being a track job, number 57, also known as "The Hot Dog", features the in-out gear box and quick-change spooled rear end. Blair uses regulation safety hubs to insure wheels against breakage. The T body rides on an A frame. Safety innovations include the aircraft type bucket seat and safety belt, hydraulic brakes and gas cut-off valve.

On February 1st of this year when Blair set the Russetta time of 124.88 "57" was running straight gas.

Don was born in Los Angeles twenty-six years ago. A graduate of Lincoln High school, he continued his studies at Pasadena Junior College (now Pasadena City College) and Frank Wiggin's Trade School in Los Angeles. When he was fourteen or fifteen Don began to

putter around with cars and engines. Since that time he has owned about fifty cars. Blair began going to the lakes when he was twenty, his first lakes job being an A pickup. This car originally timed 98 mph. Don boosted this speed to 108 before selling the car.

In 1942 he drove his modified, "The Goat", at 130.81. Don returned to the lakes with this car in 1945 when he timed 135. This was while running his roots blower engine.

Don, until recently a member of The Gophers, is now in the Pasadena Roadster Club. He is one of the original members of the C.R.A.

In June of 1947 Don first began running "57" with Bud Van Mannen as his driver. Don and driver Van Mannen evidently hold little regard for the usual run of racing superstitions . . . number 57 is painted a bright green, a color supposedly unlucky on race tracks and courses.

In our cover shot Don's roadster is shown with treaded tires. It had recently been run at the dry lakes where good tires are an essential. On asphalt

Interior shows in-out gear box, gas shut-off valve, bucket seat.

tracks, however, he uses the conventional smooth "tread" which gives better traction for that surface. Owner-builder Don Blair operates an auto parts shop in Pasadena, California. HRM is happy to have introduced his "57" as our first track "Hot Rod of the Month".

Blair's '46 Mercury engine performs equally well on tracks and day lakes

FIRESTONE BLVD. MOTORDROME, NORWALK, CALIFORNIA, FEB. 1st

TROPHY DASH   Time :57.18   3 laps
1.—Grant Lambert
2.—Mickey Davis

FIRST HEAT   No Time   5 laps
1.—Dan Marruffo
2.—Bob Stanclift
3.—Don Brown

SECOND HEAT   5 laps
1.—Bob Rozzano
2.—Gene Carpenter
3.—Len Shreenan

THIRD HEAT   5 laps
1.—George Seeger
2.—Ed Papac
3.—Chuck Burness

FOURTH HEAT   5 laps
1.—Bruce Emmons
2.—Pat Patrick
3.—Grant Lambert

SEMI-MAIN   Time 4:25.20   12 laps
1.—Bob Rozzano
2.—Len Shreenan
3.—Bob Stanclift
4.—Dan Marruffo
5.—John Mark

MAIN EVENT   Time 8:02.12   25 laps
1.—Bruce McClaire
2.—Grant Lamber
3.—George Seeger
4.—Bruce Emmons
5.—Don Bailey

FIRESTONE BLVD. MOTORDROME, FEB. 8th

TROPHY DASH   Time :58.27   3 laps
1.—Bill LaRoy
2.—Grant Lamber

FIRST HEAT   5 laps
1.—Bob Stanclift
2.—John Mark
3.—George Berry

SECOND HEAT   5 laps
1.—Dead heat for 1st between Ed Papac and Dan Marruffo
3.—Bob Rozzano

THIRD HEAT   5 laps
1.—Gene Carpenter
2.—Buck Knight
3.—Pat Patrick

FOURTH HEAT   5 laps
1.—Chuck Burness
2.—Mickey Davis
3.—Grant Lambert

SEMI-MAIN   Time 4:27.32   12 laps
1.—Dan Marruffo
2.—John Mark
3.—Bob Rozzano
4.—Bob Stanclift
5.—Gene Carpenter

MAIN EVENT   Time 8:07.00   25 laps
1.—Chuck Burness
2.—Bruce McClaire
3.—George Seeger
4.—Grant Lambert
5.—Bill La Roy

FIRESTONE BLVD. MOTORDROME, FEB. 15th

TROPHY DASH   Time 58.74   3 laps
1.—Grant Lambert
2.—Chuck Burness

FIRST HEAT   5 laps
1.—Curtis Hayes
2.—Harry Pribble
3.—George Berry

SECOND HEAT   5 laps
1.—Bruce McClair
2.—Bill Steves
3.—Gene Carpenter

THIRD HEAT   5 laps
1.—A. A. Knight
2.—John Mark
3.—Bill Steves

FOURTH HEAT
1.—Chuck Burness
2.—Pat Patrick
3.—A. A. Knight

MATCH RACE, 3 laps, between a midget and a roadster
1.—Chuck Burness (roadster) 56.38 A new record 2.5 sec. faster than old record.
2.—Hal Minyard (midget)

SEMI MAIN   12 laps   Time 3:49.17
1.—Bill Steves
2.—Gene Carpenter
3.—Bob Stancliff

MAIN EVENT   25 laps   6:47.02 . . . a new track record
The finish on this race was protested and remains unsettled at this printing.
1.—Bill Steves
2.—Bill La Roy
3.—Chuck Burness

HIS CAR WAS HOT
By HOWARD BITTNER

(Reprinted from "Throttle" Magazine)

All kinds of stuff, and a winfield "pot";

No doubt about it, his car was hot!

He could peel in high, when others could not

No doubt about it, his car was hot!
Solid panel, fastened by lock,

When asked what he had; he'd say "strictly-stock".

But we all knew that that was rot,

'Cause we all knew, that his car was hot!

He even got tickets, as tickets go;

But not for speeding; for flying so low!

He'd "gow out" in low, cause his car was hot,

And still be "peeling", eighty feet from the spot,

Winding his motor, pipes that "blubber",

Crackling mufflers, and the scream of rubber!

Tight in second, the same in low,

No doubt about it, his car would go,

Meshing of gears, to him, was an art,

In a race with him, you were "chopped" from the start.

He'd "speed shift" to second, and "snap" it in high,

His car was hot, and that's no lie!

But all things must start, and all things must end,

Iron will give, and steel will bend.

He got his, on a Saturday night.

He was feeling good, and his motor was tight.

He really shouldn't have tried to pass,

But he "dropped" in second, and gave it the gas.

Head-lights were shining in his face,

For once he was going to lose a race!

Even then, he could have turned back,

But his car was hot, so he wouldn't slack.

A deafening crash, that was heard for miles,

And two fast cars were worthless piles.

A whisp of smoke from his motor came,

And soon his car was a sheet of flame,

It had turned over twice, and burnt on the spot,

No doubt about it, his car was hot!

Hot Rod History

Readers have written to HRM asking that we tell something of the history of hot rods. Knowing that hod rod racing and timing have been California sports for some time, we have come up with this story, these pictures and a hope for more to come. In this issue we will confine our interests to the 1930-35 period, during which hot rod lakes meets were first held under a central organization.

Many, many hot rod drivers, builders and fans had been making trips to Muroc Dry Lake in the hopes of finding there others of their kind who were interested in the construction and performance of amateur speed jobs. Sometimes these trips were successful, a large crowd would be there to hold races and compare engines and parts. At other times, and usually more often, there would be no one or so few that it would prove impracticable to hold a race.

In the year 1931 hot rod builders and drivers in Southern California received letters inviting them to a meeting held for the purpose of organizing their automotive interests. This meeting was held in East Los Angeles in the early Spring of that year. The Gilmore Oil Company, through the efforts of George Riley and others, had consented to sponsor amateur races at the dry lakes IF hot rodders could come to an agreement about rules and regulations.

An agreement was reached and on March 25, 1931, the first organized group met at Muroc to try their skills. These early meets attracted crowds nearly as large as those seen at the lakes today, sometimes as many as ten thousand. Rules provided that cars would be raced in these classes:

Model T Rajos
Model T Flatheads

Model T Chevies & Frontenacs
Model A Overhead Valves
Model A Flatheads

1st and 2nd Place winners were eligible for open competition with winners from other clases. No superchargers were allowed. Heads or pans were removed to check the qualifications of the cars. With a pace car to set the running start, drivers were away at about fifty miles per hour, reaching a maximum speed by the time they started through the timing device. Some of these early races were timed by stopwatch, others by Purdy's Electrical Timer. Any car that jumped the start would be given a one hundred foot penalty at the re-start. No wildcat warmups were allowed. Cars returned to the start at 40 mph. The entry fee was one dollar. This period in hot rod history brought forth coupe times of 85 to 100 mph. One truck pickup clocked 100 mph.

Ike Trone receives 1st place trophy from Gilmore representative Beezmeyer as George Riley looks on. This car ran a Riley head in the race at Muroc, April 19, 1931.

Spectators look under the hood of this '29 roadster as Driver Machettie awaits the next race. This car, with its chrome hood & running board light, was one of the best looking roadsters of that period.

Kenny Harman (hand in pocket) smiles at the camera as Pete Dinger (sitting in car) and George Riley ready the Ford for the next event. The smiling lad at right is George Riley, Jr.

Driver Pete & Kenny Harman get ready to run as Rex Welch (hand in under-hood) makes a last minute engine check.

JOHNNY McCOY IN HIS FULL BELLY-PAN '32 MERCURY

Class C Roadster

JACK CALORI'S MERCURY-POWERED ROADSTER
S.C.T.A. Time — 128.38

Choosing a Cam

By Weber

Picking the correct cam is not easy, even for a seasoned veteran of the racing world. Every car owner has his ideas on how the perfect cam should be ground and each grinder employs a different type of grind. Here are a few suggestions that are good to have in mind when making a selection.

One of the first considerations is the body type of the car in which the cam will be used. Coupes, lake roadsters, track roadsters, streamliners and sedans each have combinations proven to be the best for their purpose. Every grinder has his own methods of classifying cams, but all grinds fit into about four basic groups.

For coupes and sedans the best suited cams are the R or semi-race type. This cam is ground with a slower action than the roadster or streamliner cams. Power and acceleration are increased without hindering idling or low speed operation. A fast action F1 or full-race cam used in a coupe should accelerate faster, but will make the idling rough and noisey.

The 252° race cam or F1 is a faster action cam ideal for track roadsters, lake roadsters and for coupes where the driver desires to sacrifice the smoother action of a slow-action cam for increased acceleration. This very popular grind is best suited for rapid acceleration in the lower gears.

For high gear and top speed efficiency the 266° F2 or full-race cam is recommended. Lake roadsters and streamliners can use the full-race with best results.

The most radical grind is the 272° F3 or super-race. Not too often used, these cams are developed for streamliners where the body is light and the engine is performing at high speeds. When contemplating the purchase of a radical cam it is best to first talk it over with the manufacturer as this type gives top performance ONLY with a correct combination. Also for engines that have been stroked or de-stroked the manufacturer should build a cam to suit the engine.

How a specially ground cam increases engine speed can best be explained by first clarifying its purpose. The cam lifts the valves and lets the gases in and out of the combustion chambers. Engine efficiency is increased by opening and closing the valves more rapidly, by keeping the valves at the wide open point is long as possible and by increasing duration of opening to the point just before the volumetric efficiency of the engine starts to drop. The greater the duration, the more radical the cam.

Valve openings and closings for a complete engine cycle with an F1 or semi-race are as follows: Intake opens before top dead center at 22°, intake closes after bottom center at 62°, exhaust opens before bottom center at 66° and exhaust closes after top center at 18°.

When purchasing a used cam, check the end for identifying marks. Most grinders stamp their names and type of grind for identification. Further information may be obtained from the manufacturer.

A grinder can furnish the buyer a ready ground cam or can grind a stock cam to the owner's specifications. It is best to start with a new one . . . used cams are sometimes so worn that a good grind is impossible. New bearings should also be inserted to provide an even surface and to prevent loss of main bearing oil pressure.

After installation of the cam there are other engine changes recommended to assure proper performance. Lincoln Zephyr valve springs should be used to assure complete closing of the valves at high engine speeds. The valves should be lengthened or adjustable tappets

(Continued on Page 14)

Laughs

FROM HERE AND THERE
By Tom Medley

Recent reports from the authorities show that 75% of the accidents in autos are due to drivers hugging too close to the curves.

* * *

Perfection will be reached when the automobiles can be made fool-in-the-other car proof.

* * *

"Why is your roadster painted blue on one side and red on the other?"

"It is a great scheme; you should hear the witnesses contradicting each other."

* * *

Traffic Cop. "Now miss, what gear were you in at the time of the accident?"

Demure Miss, "Oh, I had on brown skirt, nylons and a pink sweater!!!!"

* * *

It is a funny woman who can spot a blonde hair on your coat but can't see a pair of garage doors.

* * *

Judge, "Why did you run down this pedestrian in broad daylight on a straight stretch of road?"

Driver, "Your Honor, my windshield was almost totally obscured with safety stickers."

* * *

Hell, for garage mechanics, will be a land of abundant grease and no steering wheel to wipe their hands on.

Sure, you qualified at 135 mph.—but they don't think the public will believe it.

Woman driver, "I wasn't going 40 miles per hour, not 20 miles or 10 miles per hour, in fact I was almost stopped. Judge, "I had better stop this or you will be backing into something—$25.00.

* * *

Cop, "Use your noodle, use your noodle".

Lady, "My goodness! where is it? I have pushed and pulled everything in the car."

* * *

How far do you get on a gallon? "All depends on what is in the gallon!"

1st auto mechanic, "Which do you prefer, leather or fabric upholstery?"

2nd mechanic, "I like fabrics, leather is too hard to wipe your hands on."

* * *

What is the best thing to do when your brakes give out?

Hit something CHEAP!!!!!

* * *

"It's absurd for this man to charge us $10.00 for towing us 4 miles."

"That's all right, he's earning it. I have my brakes on!!!"

* * *

1934 chevrolet sedan, a good running car, completely refinished, *this one won't last long*, only $145.00.

* * *

He who stops to look each way will drive his car another day.

But he who speeds across the STOP will land in some morticians shop.

* * *

Cop, "Who was driving when this accident happened?"

Drunk, "No one, we were all sitting in the back seat."

* * *

In Los Angeles a man is run over every 5 minutes—what a man!!!!!

McGurk says he's damned tired of going around 'em.

1. Bob Cross at the wheel of Yam Oka's '25 T Ford Cyclone 4 does a spectacular filp during the C.R.A. race October 26 at Bonelli Stadium, Saugus, California. Bob wasn't injured.
Photo by Ted Tanner.

2. The new Tattersfield four carburetor manifold is displayed by one of its designers, Frank Baron.

3. A member of the Long Beach Dolphins, Chuck Daigh timed 123.96 at S.C.T.A. lakes meet with his '29 roadster. His '41 Mercury engine is built with Navarro heads and manifold.

4. This sleek '25 T belongs to Bill Van Noy who is starting his second season as a member of the A.S.C. Wico dual magnetos are used on the full race '40 block.

5. Driving into the pits is Bob Gregg in Richard Martins O.R.-R.A. championship roadster. The '27's V-8 engine has a Harmon cam, Spaulding ignition, Offenhauser heads and manifold.

6. Of radical design, Bob Hoeppner's rear-engine Mercury streamliner is being built without a frame, employing flush riveted aircraft type construction.

7. Meb Healy's Chevy 6 powered Austin roadster, equipped with a Nash 6 ignition that sparked two plugs on each cylinder.

8. An innovation in race tracks was introduced at the Culver City Speedway in 1947 when this figure 8 course was opened.

66

9. Driver Johnny Gorman and Owner Bill Exner in the Hi Points car of the Roadster Racing Association of Washington. The roadster is bored and stroked with Meyer's heads, McCullough blower, and Winfield cam.

10. Charlie, who "assists" the starters at C.R.A. races, shows the crowd what he found under the hood of a fast roadster.
Photo by Bob Dayton.

11. From Chicago comes this picture of A. T. Thompson Jr's. '34 Ford coupe with a '41 Mercury motor.

12. Handsome Ollie DePew with his '32 V8 coupe that clocked 115.80 at a recent Russetta lakes meet.

13. Driver Lemoine Frey and owner Al Dickman with the trophys they have won in N.C.R.R.A. competition.

14. A close-up of Bobbie Fritch's Ford 6 engine with Winfield head and manifold running dry sump.

15. Jack Morgan in his '34 Ford roadster ready to go through the traps. Jack's car has a Navarro manifold and Meyers heads.

Photo by Dave Smith.
16. In a C.R.A. race at Gardena, car 10, driven by Don Freeland, blew a hose causing him to spin and Jim Rathman to slide on top of him. Jack McGrath got around safely.

used to compensate for the shorter cam lobes. The stock fiber cam gear should be replaced with a metal gear to prevent the increased pressure of the Zephyr springs from causing breakage.

Raising compression and increasing carburetion efficiency will help to make a cam do its best where peak performance is desired.

A cam also brings about changes in gear ratios and tire sizes by increasing the RPM. The more radical the cam, the lower the gear ratios or the smaller the tires.

All these details are important for the grinder's skill is wasted unless the cam is chosen with care and engine modifications are effected.

IT'S IN THE BAG— continued

HRM:

I bought both copies of HRM at the Roadster Show (S.C.T.A.'s Hot Rod Exposition in Los Angeles) . . . and enjoyed both immensely, hence my request for the two subscriptions placed hereby. There were some beautiful little jobs at the show, but I still like my '33 roadster as well as anything I saw there and immediately changed my mind about selling it . . .

Dick Rasmussen, for whom my second subscription is intended, is also and old lakes boy. He originated around Alhambra and Monterey Park but is now a sterling minion of the law, working out of the Red Bluff office of the California State Highway Patrol, and I know he will enjoy his first two copies of HRM as much as I did and will join me in anticipating the succeeding ones.

Would love to see some early (1925 or so and susequent) Dry Lakes pictures and commentaries . . . some of us were going pretty fast before Henry brought out the V8, or even the Model A.

Congratulations and my wish for your success . . .

ANDREW A. DAVIS
Beverly Hills, California

Upon the suggestion of Mr. Davis, we looked into the past of hot rod history in California, coming up with the photos and information shown in this issue of HRM. This data centers around the 1930-35 era, when hot rod lakes meets were first held under any type of central organization, at this time under the sponsorship of the Gilmore Oil Company. Delving into this period in hot rod history, brought forth stories of Model T's that timed upwards of 115 MPH. (This information remains unconfirmed to date.) However, facts do prove that hot rods are not a thing of this generation alone. Further articles along this line are anticipated for the future. Readers who have information and photographs of early lakes meets are asked to contact HRM editors at our new main office, 7164 Melrose Avenue in Los Angeles.—ED. (Cont. on Page 20)

Parts with appeal

For those interested in things mechanical, Patti Frank displays a high compression head for late model Fords and Mercurys.

The water outlet on top of the head is flanged to keep the hose secure and the fins assure maximum heat dissipation while adding to the overall beauty. Chambers have sufficient clearance to allow for oversized valves and the heads fit all late model engines without alterations. Shaping of the chamber to conform to the outline of a stock gasket prevents clogging of gas from valve to cylinder, giving maximum passage, avoiding hot spots and assuring a smooth, even flow of fuel. Heavily constructed of heat treated aluminum, having a tensile strength of 36,000 pounds, this head comes in compression ratios of 7.75, 8.25 and 8.75 with special ratios upon request.

For those NOT interested in things mechanical, Miss Frank's biography should make interesting reading.

Almost a native Californian, Patti came to Hollywood from Mansfield, Ohio, in 1941. A graduate of Hollywood High School, she now attends Los Angeles City College. Drama and art are her main subjects. Between classes she finds time to do junior miss and bathing suit modeling for the Mary Webb Davis Agency.

Patti not only poses for bathing suit advertisements, she actually enjoys swimming. Volleyball and horseback riding are her two other favorite sports, and yes, she is also a roaring roadster fan.

As to her career, she intends to be a housewife. Until that time her modeling and dramatic work will keep her busy.

Blonde, beautiful and nineteen years old, Patti is still single. She does have a boy friend though. He attends Compton Junior College, spending his spare time playing football and working on his Ford.

In conclusion, let us say—Patti Frank is not only a girl with a head on her shoulders, but with one in her hand besides.

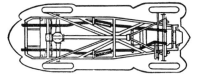

Patti Frank with a High Compression Head

LEADED FUELS

by William Gieseke

LEADED FUELS
FACTS CONCERNING LEADED HYDROCARBON FUELS

TETHRAETHYL LEAD. — It is made by aloying together equimolar parts of lead and sodium. This requires 90 percent lead and 10 percent sodium by weight. The alloy is crushed into granules and heated in an autoclave with ethyl chloride. About 85 percent is recovered as tetraethyl lead and sodium chloride. This is then steam-distilled to separate the tetraethyl lead. Ethyl fluid, in addition to tetraethyl lead and a trace of dye, contains sufficient ethylene dibromide to convert the lead to lead bromide, which is volatile at exhaust temperatures and so passes out of the engine with the exhaust gases. Without the use of ethylene dibromide, the lead would be deposited in the engine as lead oxide, which, in addition to building up a deposit, would cause considerable corrosion. Lead bromide at high temperature is also an extraordinarily highly corrosive compound.

LEAD SUSCEPTIBILITY. — Tetraethyl lead has a greater effect on raising the antiknock value of one fuel than another; or expressed in a different way, the lead-susceptibility of different fuels varies. In all cases, however, any given increment of lead added raises the antiknock value a greater amount than any succeeding increment. The Air Corps does not permit the addition of more than 6 milliliters per gallon, as any amount in excess of this has very little effect on the antiknock value, whereas it increases enormously corrosion and spark plug trouble. The addition of more lead than is required to eliminate detonation has the effect of decreasing the power slightly and increasing the temperature of the exhaust gases.

OCTANE RATING

"Octane rating" is a term universally used to designate the antiknock value of the fuel mixture in an engine cylinder. Modern aircraft engines of high power output have been possible principally as a result of the blending of fuels of high octane rating. The use of such fuels has permitted increases in compression ratio and manifold pressure with resultant improvement in engine power and efficiency. However, it must be remembered that even the high octane fuels will detonate under severe operating conditions, or if certain engine controls are improperly operated.

FLAME PROPAGATION (Travel). —In this connection it is necessary to consider briefly the nature of combustion in an engine cylinder of high power output. Figure 1 indicates the

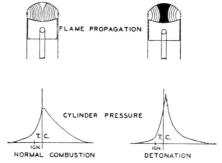

FLAME PROPAGATION

CYLINDER PRESSURE

NORMAL COMBUSTION — DETONATION

flame propagation and pressure produced in a cylinder during normal combustion and also during detonation. Both of these conditions may be produced in the same engine by operating it with a fuel containing satisfactory antiknock properties, and then again with a fuel of inadequate antiknock properties.

A study of the combustion chamber during normal combustion illustrates how the burning of the charge originates at the spark-plug electrodes (dual ignition) and travels progressively toward the center of the combustion head, meeting at the approximate center of the combustion chamber. The pressure curve reveals that the pressure rise is quite regular, although rapid, reaching a peak value at piston top center or slightly thereafter. A fairly high pressure is then maintained throughout the power stroke, and thus the engine is capable of developing its rated horsepower. The power output is related to the mean effective pressure; however, with detonation, serious danger to engine parts will result from abnormally high peak cylinder pressure.

DETONATION — 'AUTO'matic IGNITION.—When detonation occurs, the flame travel is of a somewhat different character. Combustion of the charge is initiated, and for a certain distance the rate of flame propagation is quite normal until possibly four-fifths of the charge is burning. However, at this point a marked change takes place. The combustion accelerates with such rapidity that the remaining charge is burned almost instantaneously, resulting in an unusually rapid pressure rise. The pressure curve ascends to a very high peak and then quickly drops to a lower value, remaining comparatively low throughout the balance of the power stroke. Thus, when detonation occurs, the mean effective pressure and consequent power output are substantially reduced. At the same time the engine is subjected to a series of mechanical shocks. If detonation is permitted to continue, the shocks will become violent and probably terminate in sudden and complete engine failure.

KNOCK VALUE — MINIMUM AND MAXIMUM FLAME TRAVEL. The change in the rate of burning known as detonation is a chemical phenomenon and depends in large measure on the type of hydrocarbons in the gasoline. Detonation is a change in the rate of burning of the fuel charge. In normal combustion without detonation, the flame of combustion measured from the spark plug, travels out across the combustion chamber at the rate of 25 to 75 lineal feet per second. When detonation occurs, the rate of movement of the flame is increased to approximately 4,000 or 5,000 feet per second and frequently traverses the combustion chamber several times during one firing. This tremendous increase in the speed of burning is accompanied by extremely

(Continued on Page 18)

THIS IS THE NCRRA —by NILS LILJEDAHL

The Northern California Roadster Racing Association was formed and incorporated in September of 1946, in the basement meeting place of the East Bay Auto Club.

Bob Machin, Clyde Miller, Bob McLean, and Dick Sabotka, who worked organizing enough fellows with hopped up roadsters to stage a race, had finally persuaded the owners of Oakland Stadium to try a roadster race. The first N.C.R.R.A. sanctioned race was held at Oakland Stadium, October 11, 1946. A crowd of 6,000 cheering fans watched their first post war roadster race. Five more post season races were run in 1946.

Those first roadsters were mostly street jobs with windshields and lights removed. A few were pre-war track jobs that had been gathering dust while their owners had been to the far corners of the earth. By the start of the 1947 season, they had developed into full fledged racing cars, with locked rear ends, gear boxes, safety belts, and all the other mechanical features of a racing machine.

Safety is the first consideration of these roaring racers. Strict rules and regulations govern the building and racing of these roadsters. Each car is carefully inspected before being allowed in competition. The rules and regulations of the N.C.R.R.A. were carefully garnered from the "Bible" of all racing, the A. A. A. Compulsory insurance covers every man in the pits of every race. This insurance, which until recently was not available to the racing profession, is carried by Lloyd's of London. There have been no fatalities among drivers, pitmen or spectators at the ninety odd races sanctioned by N.C.R.R.A. since its beginning, and only a few minor injuries.

Roadster racing is not entirely new in Northern California, having been started back in 1933 by Bay Cities Roadster Racing Assn. The members of this Roadster Association were the nucleus that formed the present B.C.R.A. Midget Association. Freddie Agabashian, 1946 and 47 champion of B.C.R.A. and also finishing eighth in the "500" mile Indianapolis race last year, started his racing in roadsters.

George Pacheco, N. C. R. R. A. Champion for 1947, and Al Neves, both pre-war roadster men have been offered rides in other types of cars but both prefer the roadsters.

Starting the 1947 season in April with two or three races a week, they were soon racing five nights a week. They even raced a double header one Sunday, with an afternoon show in Sacramento and traveled 80 miles to put on a night show in Modesto that same day. This they feel sure has never been done by any other racing association. The same cars and drivers participated in both races. Racing to an estimated 300,000 fans in 1947 the roaring roadsters feel they are definitly a part of the thrilling sport of Auto Racing.

(The End)

FUEL—continued

high local temperatures and tremendous increases in maximum pressure. The expansion of the burning gases with normal combustion presses the head of the piston firmly down through the cylinder bore without excessive shock. The tremendously increased pressure of detonation exerted in such a short space of time gives a heavy shock load to the walls of the combustion chamber and the piston head. The piston cannot move rapidly enough to escape the full force of the blow.

AUDIBLE KNOCK.—This pressure effect is sufficient in the short time in which it occurs to spring the walls of the combustion chamber in moderatively heavy detonation. It is this shock to the combustion chamber that is heard in the case of audible knock noted frequently in the automobile engine. If other sounds can be filtered out, the knock is equally audible in the aircraft engine, but it generally is necessary to depend upon instruments rather than the ear to detect detonating combustion in an aircraft engine. De-

tonation is accompanied by temperature rise, since the heat cannot be dissipated as an energy thrust to the piston or through the cooling system at the cylinder head. Therefore, an increase in cylinder head temperatures is measurable when detonation occurs.

DETONATION SUPPRESSORS.— Fuels inherenty less prone to detonate can be selected. Having made the best selection of hydrocarbons inclined inherently to burn without detonation, this tendency may be improved by detonation suppressors such as tetraethyl lead. Other materials are desirable somewhat for this purpose but are less effective or more expensive than tetraethyl lead. In the selection of the best hydrocarbons the blends of fuel are selected which have the most desirable characteristics. For instance, a synthetic blend known as iso-octane is now being used extensively to increase the antiknock qualitites of high-grade gasolines. Iso-octane permits the development of higher antiknock qualities of gasolines

(Continued on Page 19)

without increasing undesirable characteristics such as vapor lock. After securing the most desirable blends the fuel may be brought to the required standard of antiknock rating by doping or by the addition of small amounts of tetraethyl lead ranging from $\frac{1}{4}$ to 4 cubic centimeters per gallon, the amount depending on its effectiveness on the particular type of fuel which is being doped.

FACTORS CONTROLLING DETONATION

Since it is most important that detonation be avoided in the operation of aircraft and automobile engines, it is well to consider the principal factors which contribute to this condition. The antiknock value of the fuel, spark setting, cylinder temperature, induced charge temperature, mixture of carburetion and intake manifold pressure are the most important factors and will be discussed briefly. Many other factors of technical interest could also be included, but these given have the greatest significance for the engine operator.

PROPER FUEL SELECTION.—Both the power output and the reliability of a power plant depend to a great extent on the use of a fuel of high antiknock value or high octane rating. The substitution of an inferior fuel, while

The operation of a high-output engine at full power usually requires a very rich mixture in order to avoid overheating and detonation. Therefore, excessive leaning of the mixture when operating a high manifold pressure is considered a most dangerous practice. However, when the manifold pressure is reduced to the value recommended for continuous cruising, it is often advisable to lean the mixture slightly in order to lower the fuel consumption.

OCTANE RATING - REFERENCE FUELS.—In order to be able to express the antiknock characteristics of a gasoline in accurate numbers, reference is made to the octane rating of the fuel. The octane number system is based on a comparison of any fuel with certain mixtures of iso-octane and normal heptane. Iso-octane has a very high antiknock value, whereas, heptane detonates readily in an engine cylinder. A mixture of these two liquids will possess an intermediate value, depending on the relative percentage of each of the liquids in the mixture.

LABORATORY EVALUATION FOR ANTIKNOCK

KNOCK TESTING. — The knock testing of fuels must be done by a means which is simple, rapid, and in-

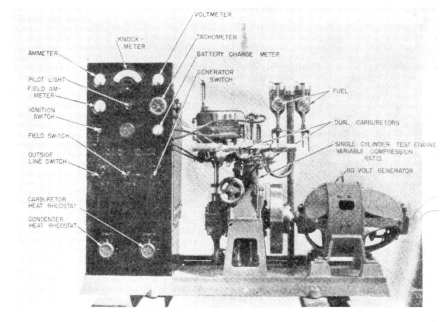

permissable in certain emergencies, is attended by serious danger of detonation unless the engine is operated at reduced throttle. The cylinder temperature and the charge temperature are, within certain limits, under control of the operator, and neither reading should be permitted to exceed the maximum value specified for a particular engine.

PROPER MIXTURE RATIO.-With reference to mixture ratio and manifold pressure, it is evident that there is a definite relation between these two factors under conditions of detonation.

expensive, as well as giving reproducible results. Due to the marked effect on knock of engine variables, these must be controlled carefully. The most accurately reproducible means of testing is by changing rapidly from the fuel being tested to a standardized fuel before any of the engine conditions have time to change. Thus there is need of a special engine for knock test purposes. This again necessitates the fixing of engine conditions which will give knock ratings in as close agreement as possible with the average of those obtained on all

(Continued on Page 22)

S.C.T.A.'s COMING SEASON

Members of the Southern California Timing Association, Inc., sponsors of the world's safest automotive speed trials, are looking forward with enthusiasm to what is expected to be the hottest season of competition in its active history. Through revising and streamlining their competition rules they are hopeful of stimulating added interest among their varied classes and it is anticipated that many new and radical types and designs of cars and engines will make their appearances.

To make the small 'A' Class more attractive the engine displacement maximum has been raised from 150 to 183 cubic inches, and qualification speeds for points eligibility have been lowered to 90 miles per hour in the Roadster class and 100 m.p.h. in the Streamliner class.

Total points available in each of the eight classes have been raised from twelve to the first twenty fastest cars. This will give runners-up who have formerly had little chance of finishing in the points a renewed interest in their enthusiastic efforts to move their respective clubs to the top of the season's association standings.

Many of the S.C.T.A. member clubs are eagerly grooming their cars and equipment with the primary intent of capturing from the Lancers Club, last season's champions, the coveted title of "The World's Fastest Roadster Club". The Lancers have won the title for two consecutive seasons and also have every intention of holding onto it through 1948.

In order to accomodate the hundreds of members who run their cars at each meet, S.C.T.A. has inaugurated a new system of two-day meets which will allow for official runs on both Saturday and Sunday. Car owners may take their qualifying time runs on either or both days at their own option. This new plan is expected to make the sport more interesting to all participants by eliminating long waiting periods between runs and allowing for more leisurely association between members while at the lakes.

With new classes, more points awards, more trophies and scores of amazingly radically designed cars in the running this should be a season well worth watching. With any kind of favorable course conditions, the speeds that may be attained will undoubtedly be raised even above some of the present existing remarkable record times.

IT'S IN THE BAG— Continued

Dear Sirs:

. . . The February issue was the first issue I looked over and I enjoyed the pictures and articles very much especially the one entitled "Overhead Valves." However, those fellows interested in building up a straight six with a rocker box should look over a G.M.C. truck engine. The G.M.C. is quite similiar to a Chevy except that it has insert mains and rods. Most of the other parts are interchangeable for the same year and G.M.C. engines hook up OK with Chevy gear boxes.

BRUCE W. SCHLIESMAYER
Long Beach 13, Calif.
Thanks for your letter Mr. Schliesmayer! HRM welcomes such information and comments thereon.—ED.

Dear Sirs:

I was pleased to see that my present to my husband in Arabia, a subscription to your fine magazine, rated a mention in your mag. Many thanks to your cartoonist for the accompanying picture. (Who ever heard of a camel with outside exhaust pipes?)

A magazine like yours will be a priceless possession in Arabia. Good things are hard to find over there.

MRS. WM. J. FOLEY
Oakland 2, Calif.

We hesitate to ask "who ever heard
*of a camel with exhaust pipes . . .
PERIOD!?"—ED.*

Classified Advertisements

Dear Sirs:

. . . It's a fine thing that someone had the forsight to see the necessity for a magazine of its type. It will bring to light the corrected viewpoint of many who are much too slowly realizing why a fellow fools around with cars to such an extent.

I'm building a road job and lakes car combined. I have completed the front and rear end and part of the mill so far. I am undecided on a body type because of my engine type.

I have a 176 cu. in. Chevy 4 with a single overhead cam of my own design. I have also planned on using a vane or roots type blower with the combination.

How far up in the various classes will this shove me, and will there be any advantage in running in one class or the other considering above combination?

Thanks for your trouble.

F. DOUGLAS SHAUL
Oakland 10, Calif.

Under new S.C.T.A. classes Mr. Shaul's 176 cubic inches would fall into the extended Class A, which was recently changed from 0-150 to 0-183 cubic inches. The use of the blower will move him up one class to Class B, which if from 183-250 cubic inches. As to body type (streamliner or roadster), there is a difference of about 10 miles per hour between Class B Roadsters and Class B Streamliners. Naturally, it is up to the individual to choose his body type once he is acquainted with these facts.—ED.

* * *

Dear Sirs:

I had the pleasure of looking over one of your first issues last night and enjoyed it very much . . .

I am a member of the Roadster Racing Association of Oregon, Inc. The year 1947 just past ended our first year of track racing with some fine results in a short space of time. Possibly, one of these coming days RRAO will MAKE an issue of Hot Rod Mag. with a scoop of some kind. Never can tell! OK? . . .

R. B. WINTERS
Portland 6, Oregon

RRAO's top points car appears on Page 12 of this issue.—ED.

* * *

Gentlemen:

Thank you for your first number of Hot Rod Magazine . . . It is a fine magazine and is what the racing world needs.

DICK BROWN
Dick Brown & Company
Auto Racing Equipment
Albany 6, New York

* * *

Editors:

Enjoyed your initial issue. Keep up the good work and much luck in the new venture.

G. ROKUTANI
Motor Repair Service
St. Paul 4, Minn.

FUEL—continued

types of multi-cylinder engines. Some authorities contend that fuels also should be final tested and rated on full-scale engines to guard against discrepancies which sometimes occur between laboratory and field results.

CFR TEST ENGINE.—Knock tests are run on special engines which usually are of the single-cylinder type having variable compression on which the speed is maintained constant by means of a suitable loaded generator similar to that in figure 2. The jacket temperature, spark advance, air-fuel ratio, throttle setting, and compression ratio are readily adjustable. Two separate fuel chambers and carburetors are provided, with a rapid means of changing from the fuel being tested to the standard reference. From the foregoing, it is evident that any rating obtained will be under certain specified test conditions which may not be obtained always in the field. This explains the reason for full-scale testing to substantiate results obtained in the laboratory.

Experience has shown that different fuels react very differently to changes in the condition and method of test. Therefore, fuels rated as equal under one condition and method may vary widely under other conditions and methods. In other words, under actual conditions, knock tendency of a fuel may vary enormously in different engines and even in the same engine under different operating conditions.

CORRELATED STANDARD. — However, some means of measurement of the fuel's ability to resist specified temperatures and pressures under controlled conditions are necessary in order to furnish a means of selection of gasolines for engines having given compression ratio, supercharging pressures, speeds, etc. By having a unit of measurement of the fuel's resistance to certain severe conditions, then by checking it in the engine under actual operating conditions a correlated standard may be established.

Additional copies may be obtained by sending 25c per copy to SOLV-X CHEMICAL COMPANY, "Manufacturing Chemists for the Jobbing Trade", 3608 Roselawn Ave., CHurchill 9-3533, Glendale 8, California.—Copyright 1946 (Permission to reprint reserved).

HOT ROD EXPOSITION

The First Annual Hot Rod Exposition, sponsored by the Southern California Timing Association, Inc., drew a record three-day crowd of 55,000 people at the Los Angeles National Guard Armory in January.

Public opinion of the sport of building and driving hot rods was changed from one of criticism and condemnation to one of praise and admiration as press and public officials viewed the mechanical masterpieces.

Fifty of the Association members' finest cars, stressing safety, engineering and mechanical innovation, displayed more clearly than any written word the sound, constructive side of roadster building and dry lake time trials.

Los Angeles Police and Fire Departments, the U. S. Army and the National Guard participated in the show with motion pictures and displays.

During the three days of the show a small group of roadster experts converted a dilapidated '32 Ford into a sleek hot rod, complete with every mechanical improvement. Prospective car builders learned first-hand that a true hot rod is not just a car minus fenders but a precision-built automobile, which embodies all of the latest safety features. On the final night of the show this car was given as a door prize to Nelson C. Morris of Long Beach, California.

On the third evening of the show trophies were presented to S.C.T.A. members for the 1947 dry lakes season. Winner of the coveted Art Tilden Sportsmanship Trophy was Boswell Willis of San Diego, California.

Participants, news representatives, public officials and spectators alike agreed that the First Annual Hot Rod Exposition was a complete success.

Bozzy Willis, left, and Otto Crocker (wearing cap) demonstrate to the public how the S.C.T.A. operates their dry lake time trials. This scale miniature graphically illustrates how a hot rod is timed.

"Miss Streamliner", 20th Century-Fox Starlet Colleen Townsend, congratulates Lou Baney (right of announcer) on the unprecedented speed with which he and his selected crew constructed the prize roadster.

Pictured is part of the record crowd that jammed the Armory for a glimpse at California's finest roadsters and streamliners.

The largest exhibit in the show was the Ford Dealers' Booth, which featured Regg Schlemmer's record-holding Class C Roadster.

The give-away roadster in an early stage of construction is fitted with a new disc-type safety brake.

Miss Townsend poses for photographers shortly after construction is completed on the roadster built during the show.

SHARP
SPEED EQUIPMENT

6225 Wilmington Avenue　　　**LOgan 5-1329**　　　**Los Angeles, Calif.**

THE NEW SHARP HIGH COMPRESSION HEAD

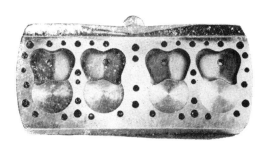

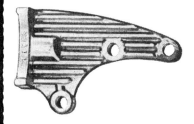

The new Sharp head gives maximum efficiency in acceleration as well as top speed. The Combustion Chamber is designed to allow adequate breathing at any R.P.M. The water capacity of the head is almost double over the stock heads. Two directional flow ribs over each cylinder assures even cooling, the extra width acting as a water manifold to eliminate steam pockets, thus reducing heat and giving more efficiency. The metal used in the heads is of the highest alloy obtainable. Each head is heat treated to eliminate corrosion and warping as well as increasing the tensile strength of the material. The heads are tested under 45 lbs. water pressure for leaks. **Compression ratios 8.75 to 10-1.**

37 (21 STUD) BRACKET
This bracket for 37-21 stud blocks only.

32 TO 36 BRACKET
The 32 to 36 Bracket is made to allow the use of a low manifold on early model blocks with no extra belts or brackets.

THE SHARP TRIPLET
This new manifold is patterned after the **Sharp Dual Manifold,** having the same port routing, thus giving perfect distribution to all ports. This action assures perfect acceleration from idling to peak R.P.M. with **no flat spots.**

HOT ROD *Magazine*

VOL. 1, No. 4 ✵ ✵ ✵ PRICE 25c   WORLD'S MOST COMPLETE HOT ROD COVERAGE   APRIL, 1948

Dynamometer Testing by Harmon—See Page 10

SHARP SPEED EQUIPMENT

6225 Wilmington Avenue   LOgan 5-1329   Los Angeles, Calif.

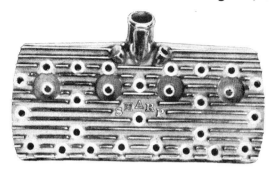

The new Sharp head gives maximum efficiency in acceleration as well as top speed. The Combustion Chamber is designed to allow adequate breathing at any R.P.M. The water capacity of the head is almost double over the stock heads. Two directional flow ribs over each cylinder assures even cooling, the extra width acting as a water manifold to eliminate steam pockets, thus reducing heat and giving more efficiency. The metal used in the heads is of the highest alloy obtainable. Each head is heat treated to eliminate corrosion and warping as well as increasing the tensile strength of the material. The heads are tested under 45 lbs. water pressure for leaks. Compression ratios 8.75 to 10-1.

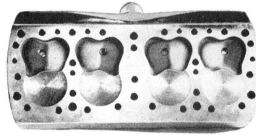

THE SHARP TRIPLET

This new manifold is patterned after the **Sharp Dual Manifold**, having the same port routing, thus giving perfect distribution to all ports. This action assures perfect acceleration from idling to peak R.P.M. with **no flat spots**.

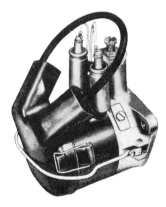

Editor's Column

Spring is here. At least so says the calendar. Hot rod drivers and owners are starting to make the final tuneups and adjustments needed to run their cars for the '48 season. This year promises to be the biggest the rods have ever known, with new racing and timing groups cropping up throughout the country. On page six readers will find the latest dope on the nation's racing and timing organizations as well as tips on manufacturers' new products.

Stuart Hilborn's Streamliner (Class B, S.C.T.A.) is the Hot Rod of the Month for April. The black-coated speed job piled up points in S.C.T.A. last year for the Santa Monica Low Flyers Club, of which Hilborn is a member.

On page 8, HRM presents another Gus Maanum drawing, this time Spider Webb's modified track hot rod. The car ran at Southern Speedway in 1936. (Incidentally, we wish to remind our readers, Gus's drawings may be purchased —only $1.00 for a set of 16—all suitable for framing. Write to either HRM or Mr. Maanum at the address given in his ad, page 22 in this issue.)

Kenny Harmon lends us his knowledge of the dynamometer with his story, "Dynamometer Testing" which is on page 10.

Many requests have been received from our readers asking that we print S.C.T.A. rules and C.R.A. specifications. S.C.T.A.'s rules are on pages 22 and 23 of this issue. The information on the C.R.A. is on page 20.

"Parts With Appeal" is sure to interest those readers who are looking for an ignition. This "part" features curly blond hair . . . 'er, that is, the latest thing in . . . what we mean is, ah . . . anyway, turn to page 15. You're bound to be entertained.

German hot rods take a bow in this issue with a picture and letter on page 21. This car, which goes in excess of 125 mph, is in the 2 liter class in Germany. (That's about 122 cubic inches here.)

Tom Medley, our able cartoonist and general "funnyman," initiates his comic strip, "Stroker McGurk," in this issue. Any similarity to any of the "lakes" boys is purely intentional.

Readers have written asking that we begin a "Questions and Answers" Column. HRM will be glad to oblige. Send us your questions and we'll promise to dig up the info you need.

Continue to send in your snapshots and news items. It's the best way to let the rest of the country's hot rod enthusiasts know what' going on in your part of the nation. —Ed.

HOT ROD Magazine

TABLE OF CONTENTS

HRM—Published Monthly

Associate Editors .... Robert R. Lindsay
Robert E. Petersen

Advertising Manager .... Richard Sabotka
Staff Photographer .... Lee Blaisdell
Cartoons and Humor .... Tom Medley
Reporters .... Anthony Granatelli, John Lelis
Robert Williams, Glenn Glendening
Dick Robinson, Richard K. Martin
Arthur Elliot

HOT ROD MAGAZINE $3.00 Per Year

Subscription Dept.
7164 Melrose Avenue
Hollywood 46, California

Please send me HRM for one year beginning with the .... issue.

Name ....

Street Address ....

City .... , Zone .... , State ....

(Check one)   Cash ☐   Check ☐   Money Order ☐

It's in the Bag . . .

FEBRUARY
From the "Parts with Appeal" picture (right) reader Eddie Haynes
of Pasadena sketched the drawing at left.—ED.

Hot Rod Magazine:

. . . I am certainly glad someone has finally put out a magazine on hot rods worth reading. I hope you have a great deal of luck with your new venture.
BOB JONES
Salt Lake City, Utah

*　*　*

To the Staff of HRM:

We wish to congratulate you for your splendid magazine and the fine job you are doing in publishing it. May the future of Hot Rod Magazine be successful in the coming years.
RICHARD J. BUTLER,
Secretary
Mojave Timing Association
Los Angeles, California

Gentlemen:

. . . So that my file of copies will be completed I would appreciate it if you would begin it with the January 1948 issue . . . and let it run for a full two years to December 1949. Good luck!
LAWRENCE ERNST
Mount Rainier, Maryland

*　*　*

Dear Sirs:

Picked up your mag on my last visit to your "land of sunshine". I think the mag is GREAT! . . .

Regardless of what you may hear . . . there are rods in Wisconsin.
BOB HANSEN
Racine, Wisconsin.

Dear Sirs:

I am writing this letter to inform you of the wonderful response we have had from the ads run in Hot Rod Magazine. In view of the fact that your magazine has been in operation such a short time we feel that it has done a wonderful job in advertising as well as coverage of many states . . .

To show that we are entirely sold on HRM we are taking and ad for 12 months starting with the next issue.
AL SHARP
Sharp Speed Equipment
Los Angeles, California.

*　*　*

Gentlemen:

I've been receiving your HRM ever since it came out in January, and think it is one of the best books put out on information of the hot rod.

I especially like the articles you've been putting out the last two months . . . like "Overhead Valves" and "Choosing a Cam." Congratulations on the excellent work you are doing.
HENRY FELTMAN
West Los Angeles, Calif.

*　*　*

Gentlemen:

An ex-Throttler of Hollywood would like to receive your magazine, having seen it at Kansas City at a Roadster Association meeting.

Last year (and '46) I ran a Kurtis V8-60 midget in the Northwest (Washington & Oregon) and was runner up for the championship, also was president of the Washington Midget Racing Association, Inc.

. . . The Army takes most of my time but so far I've helped them (Midwest Roadster Association) write the constitutional and bylaws, but haven't had time to build up a rig yet. Would like to come back to the "land of sunshine" and pick up a chassis and channelled job to run here.
Lt. Col. TEX ROBERTS
Fort Leavenworth, Kansas

Hot Rod Magazine's
NEW PHONE NUMBER IS
WEbster 3-4433

Hot Rod of the Month

An old-timer at the lakes, Stuart Hilborn's jet black B class streamliner still ranks high in point standings.

The engine first ran in a roadster in 1940, turning a record time of 124 mph. Desiring to raise his speed, Stuart bought a chassis and some parts from Bill Worth and constructed his present speedster. First timed in 1942, a speed of 134 mph was reached. That speed has since been raised to 139.96, placing the car high in S.C.T.A. point standings.

Stuart has been developing the same engine, a 1934 Ford, for the last eight years. He has constantly improved it and hopes to improve it even more in the future. At one lakes' meet a rod went through the block, shattering a 4x8-inch hole in the side of the engine. He salvaged the pieces, welded them together and welded that piece into the hole. Performance was not altered.

Eddie Miller designed and built the manifold which employs four carburetors, 3 Stromberg E's and one Stromberg Double E. The purpose of the double-throated carburetor is to provide a more equal fuel distribution. One and two cylinders fire one behind the other, the overlap of the cam keeping both valves open at the same time. Each throat of the carburetor feeds one cylinder, giving the effect of a five-carburetor fuel system. Ed also ground the custom cam, not with the usual elaborate grinder but with a grindstone and a file.

Heads are milled and filled; the mag is a Centilla. A special oil pump constructed of two stock units cut in two and welded together brings the oil pressure up to 90 pounds.

Hilborn sometimes uses a fuel injection system which he has designed and built. This injection system is different from most in that there is a constant flow without a metering pump, the throttle being connected to the fuel pump. With this equipment, an unofficial time of 136 mph was reached.

The chassis is a combination of Ford and Chevrolet parts. Front axle is a '37 Ford faired with wood and canvas and the rear end is from an A Ford with 3.27 gears. More efficient springing is brought about by turning the '32 Ford housings upside down and placing them on opposite sides so that the spring rides to the rear of the axle. The brakes are hydraulic, steering is by Franklin with an aircraft steering wheel. Large 5.25-17 Indianapolis-type tires are necessary on the front as well as on the rear to keep the nose from scraping the ground in the event of a blowout. Discs inside and outside of the wheels cut wind-resistance and add to the overall appearance of the car.

Stuart Hilborn, a native of Canada, has lived in California for the past 20 years .During the war he served in the Army Air Corps as an aerial gunnery instructor. At present he is working in the experimental lab of the General Paint Company. His spare time is taken up developing an overhead rocker arm setup for V8's. Stuart claims the head, with 8 intake and 8 exhaust valves utilizing compression ratios of from 8-1 to 14-1, operates with no loss of volumetric efficiency.

If plans for manufacture of the new

Top view of the cockpit stresses simplicity of design.

heads do not interfere, Hilborn hopes to run his car for its ninth successive season and crack the evasive "ground-sonic curtain" speed of 140 mph.

The engine when uncovered discloses Stuart Hilborn's fuel injection manifold on the under side of the hood.

CHATTER & MANUFACTURER NEWS

Ohio Speedway Association and Ohio Raceways, Inc. plan to run the hot rods at Berea, Ohio; Dover, Ohio; Sharon, Pennsylvania; Jefferson, Ohio; Akron, Ohio, and possibly at Can field, Ohio, during the coming race season. The sport seems to be catching on throughout the New England area as well as the rest of the nation.

Oregon Roadster Racing Association, Inc. plans to trek on a "gypsy" tour to Long Beach in the State of Washington where they will time their cars on the beach. According to information received, this will be the first time the roadsters have been timed in the Northwest.

Tex Roberts, former president of the Washington Midget Racing Association, Inc., is up for prexyship of the newly formed Midwest Roadster Racing Association.

S.C.T.A., Inc. has okeyed the proposed two-day time trials to be held at the dry lakes this coming season. The Association plans to use a new two-way phone system which will eliminate drivers having to stop at the finish line to get their times. Drivers will return directly to the starting point where an operator will have their times for them. At the same time, S.C.T.A. plans to inaugurate a "safe, stop and go" lighting system similar to that used by railroads and, more recently, race tracks. Their first meet will probably be held towards the latter part of April.

Russetta Timing Association (Southern California locale) plans to incorporate in the near future. Its over two hundred active members recently elected officers for the 1948 season. Their new President is Nelson Taylor. Bob Corbett is Vice President, Richard Egleston, Secretary, and C. E. Camp is the new Treasurer.

The group plans its first '48 timing meet for the early part of April. It will be a one-day meet, and they will practice their newly-written safety rules: crash helmets, fire extinguishers, etc.

Hot rod racing fans will be interested in the formation of the California Hot Rods, Inc., a newly formed track outfit. Headed by Johnny Lucas, the group boasts such well known drivers and owners as Wayne and Archie Tipton Jim Rathman, Pat Flaherty, Bud Van Mannen, Dan Tracy, Dick Vineyard, Bob Lindsey, Phil Weiand, and others. Good luck to the CHR!

New equipment is in order for the 1948 racing and timing season. In accord with this, HRM brings you the advance notes on things to come:
Electric & Carburetor Engineering Co. announced several new speed items. First on their list is the Tattersfield-Baron Speed Unit, which consists of a 4 carburetor manifold, special heads and pistons. The company also anonunces their new manifold for V8-60. This unit has several innovations which include rerouting of exhaust heat to give a cooler running motor. From the same manu-

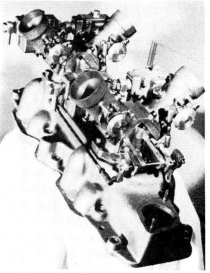

New adjustable carburetor makes its debut.

facturer comes a new manifold for the Ford 6, adjustable for two or three carburetor operation.

Norden Machine Works will soon present a new carburetor, which can be used as an up, down or side draft, with the float bowl always remaining in the same position. This unit (pictured here) can be used on Offies as well as Fords. This is unique in that the setup is interchangable from side to down draft operation, etc. There is a minimum of working parts and a simplified adjusting screw. Jets can be easily changed for different types of fuels.

Eddie Meyer Engineering has introduced a new low manifold for V8's and Mercurys. The unit, which falls into a lower price field for speed manifolds, is patterned after the one originally used in the record-breaking boat engine of The Invader. There is a side bracket for generator, making the complete unit as compact as possible.

SPIDER WEBB IN ACTION AT SOUTHERN ASCOT SPEEDWAY IN 1936

Powered by Fronty T

WALTER ROSE IN HIS '27 T ROADSTER
Supercharged V-8 Cord, running Winfield cam.

DYNAMOMETER TESTING

By KENNETH HARMON

The advantages of dynamometer testing have been known for about 200 years. James Watt, who was a successful engine manufacturer as well as inventor, devised the first dynamometer. It was a crude affair being similar to a windlass and was used to determine the amount of work a horse could do. The horse was used on tread mills in those days to supply power, so the prospective purchaser of Watt's engines wanted to know how many horses the engine was equivalent to.

The modern dynamometer bears little resemblance to its forebearer, the prony brake, with its wooden friction blocks. These brakes were limited in speed and power handling capacity and could be run for only short periods. The modern eddy current electronic controlled dynamometer can be run for weeks continuously.

Dynamometers are primarly torque indicating devices. The force required to hold the engine at some desired speed is reflected in a torque arm.. The tip of the torque arm can be considered equal to the radius of a windlass drum. Watt found that a horse could lift the *equivalent* of 33,000 lbs one ft. in one minute, hence the formula; one HP equals 33,000 ft. lbs. per minute. To simplify calculations, a drum 33 ft. in circumference could be used or an arm with a radius of 63" (approximately). As a long arm is inconvenient, some simple fraction of the 63" arm radius is commonly used; usually 1/5, 1/4 or 1/3. Our own dynamometer has a 1/5 arm, that is 12.605 inches long. We have only to multiply R.P.M. times the scale reading and divide by 5,000. The actual formula is: H.P. equals:

$$\frac{\text{arm length} \times 2\pi \times RPM \times \text{scale reading}}{33,000}$$

Attempting to develop or tune an engine without a dynamometer is time consuming and not too conclusive. True, most records have been set without the aid of a dynamometer. But equal or *better* performance could have been had in a fraction of the time. Checks on running compression, spark plugs, mixture, spark setting, best fuel combination can be made in a matter of minutes. It can be safely said that, "Three days on the dynamometer is worth three years at the Lakes". One V8 engine brought into our shop developed 147 H.P. as originally set up. Three days later it was pulling 185 H.P. Within a week it was pulling 193 H.P. This engine was equipped with the usual advertised equipment. Nothing was special. Maximum gains were made by changing the cam, compression ratio and fuel. It would have been impossible to have improved the same job a like amount at the "Lakes" in months. The variables one usually encounters; wind with you, wind against you, hot day, cold day, humidity up, humidity down, can foul up any minor change beyond recognition. The minor changes when added together account for about 90% of the improvement. Most changes can be made on the dynamometer in a few minutes.

Advantages: Knowing at what RPM your engine develops its maximum power is *very* important. One can select the best gear ratio and tire size easily, especially for lakes meets. Other advantages are; no waiting in the line-up to check a change (the wind also may change). No dust, no waiting for three or four weeks for another *try* and having to drive 300 miles.

The day of guessing horse power and talking horse power is about over. Tuning a job by the feel in the seat of your pants is not very accurate. Will the jobs in the future turning in the fastest time be tuned on a dyno? We think so. Will some builders poohpooh the dynamometer? We think so. But they had better stand back out of the draft!

Laughs

FROM HERE AND THERE

By TOM MEDLEY

A big Indian chief came speeding down the highway in a brand new Cadillac. A traffic cop hailed him to the curb.

Cop: "O.K.; that's going to cost you fifty dollars!"

Chief: "Ugh; you takum hundred dollars. Me coming back same way."

* * *

A young miss was selling Hot Rod magazines one day, but all the boys wanted to take Liberty's.

* * *

"—XX★O/X★O!!!—ALL I WANT TO DO IS TIME MY CAR!"

* * *

"I hardly know what to do with my week-end."

"Have you tried wearing a hat on it?"

Repentent He: "Sweetheart, I've bought some things for the one I love best. I bet you can't guess what they are."

Unhappy Girl: "A dual manifold and a new set of pistons."

* * *

A rodney and his girl were driving along a lonely road when the babe broke the silence. "Stroker, dear," she purred sweetly, "Can you drive with one hand?"

"Yes, honey," he cooed in anticipation.

"Then," said the lovely one, "you'd better wipe your nose. It's running."

A pretty girl eyed a youth invitingly half a dozen times; then, finally, said: "Hello, Handsome!"

"Don't bother me, Babe," he retorted. "Hot Rods are my weakness."

* * *

"Here's your receipt sir," said the taxi driver as he handed his fare his change.

· "Oh," exclaimed the passenger "did I buy the car?"

STROKER McGURK

Chuck Abbott of the Glendale Sidewinders compares his roadster (clocked 118 plus) with Cobb's 400-mph record holder at last year's Bonneville Salt Flats.

Bob Ruffi's 1940 S.C.T.A. championship streamliner. This car clocked 143-mph one way. The '25 Chev 4 ran a B crank, T pistons, 3 port Olds head.

(Left to right) Vic Edelbrock ('32 V8), Tom Spaulding (A-V8) and Clint Seccombe (A-Cad 16) crossing the starting line in a race held at Harper Dry Lake, 1940.

"The Blue Flame," owned by the Wymore Brothers, runs Meyer Heads and Manifold, Winfield Cam and 4 Winfield Carbs. The car set an S.C.T.A. time of 112.64-mph.

Driver Gene Tessien of the N.C.R.R.A. in Dick Hubbard's track roadster at the 1947 National Championship Race. (Pasadena Rose Bowl). The car is Weiand equipped.

Tony Capana and his driver at an S.C.T.A. meet. The long hood houses a Marmon V-16. Its best S.C.T.A. time—145.38-mph in 1946.

This unusual looking rig belongs to Jim Taylor of Oklahoma City, Oklahoma. The frame is 2½ inch chrome alloy tubing, '46 Merc block, 3 5/16 inch bore, Edelbrock Heads and Manifold, Winfield Cam, Kurten Ignition.

"Kong" Jackson's 236 cu. in. V8 clocked 110.42-mph at Harper Dry Lake in 1941. It ran Weiand Manifold and Winfield Cam.

Close-up of Bob Hays' Cragar which timed 112-mph in 1941 with Winfield Carbs and Cam.

From Bill Brumbach of Chicago comes this picture of a '32 B track job. It has a '41 Merc engine, special cam and chopped fly-wheel. The car is shown with a coupe body used for winter.

In 1937 William Richards clocked 104.4-mph with this '32 Ford V8 at Muroc Dry Lake. The car ran a Bosch Coil.

This "station wagon" pickup owned by Seymour Meadows was one of the featured cars in S.C.T.A.'s Hot Rod Show. The car has an Evans Manifold and Edelbrock Heads.

Owner Pat O'Neil and Driver Vern Slankard pose with their track roadster at Bonelli Stadium in Saugus, California. It runs a '46 Merc, 3 5/16", 3/8 stroke, Navarro Heads and Manifold.

Ed Korgan in Bill Burke's first belly tank. The streamliner (S.C.T.A.) set a mark of 131.96 on July 7 of 1946 with Korgan at the helm.

Snapped at an S.C.T.A. meet is Alan Hall's Alexander exhaust overhead B Streamliner. The manifold is Edelbrock, the cam Engle. Clocked 117.03-mph.

Yam Oka and his channelled '32 V8. It clocked 119 in 1946 at an S.C.T.A. El Mirage meet, with E & S Heads, Edelbrock Manifold and Winfield Cam.

Parts With Appeal

▶▶▶

Miss Noreen Mortensen (at right) is looking over a new type custom distributor built for Fords and Mercurys.

Constructed of special heat-treated aluminum, the igniter base will stand the great amount of heat generated by a high speed engine. Lock-type manual control simplifies adjustments that must be made so often during time trials. This distributor has been turned as high at 8000 RPM in low and 9000 RPM free engine. Of interest to the "chrome and polish" enthusiasts is the shiny black finish, which is sure to attract attention. That is, if Miss Mortensen doesn't attract it all.

Blonde, blue eyed Noreen, a native Californian, was born in Los Angeles. The daughter of a traveling . . . . engineer, her schooling was acquired at schools in 42 of our 48 states.

Teaching the rhumba is Noreen's profession and also her favorite recreation. Between lessons she models for magazine art.

Strenuous sports that appeal to her are horseback riding, swimming and boating.

While shooting this picture of Miss Mortensen we brought up the usual subject of fast roadsters . . . . expecting to show off a slight bit. In no time at all we were deeply engrossed in a conversation about boats, a subject Noreen "just happens" to know all about.

And that's all of April's Parts With Appeal.

P.S. . . . Wat's a jib?

KONG

ENGINEERING

MERCURY
   FORD 85
      FORD 60
         FORD 6

Price
$55.00
Plus Tax

INTRODUCING

A completely NEW AND DIFFERENT Ignition. This is not a "RE-BUILT" Ignition, but has been designed on the drawing board, cast and machined to the finished product. Featuring Dual HI-SPEED Points, WINFIELD 4-LOBE Breaker Cam, which is mounted on a DOUBLE ROW BALL BEARING. Full manual control (LOCK TYPE). The CAM Dwell is 89% or 74 degrees at 6500 RPM.

SPECIAL IGNITIONS MADE ON REQUEST
FORD AND MERCURY ENGINES CUSTOM BUILT
COMPLETE LINE OF WINFIELD CAMS

Dealers and Builders—Write for Information

Charles "Kong" Jackson   342 "E" Chevy Chase Dr.
                              Glendale, Calif.

Noreen Mortensen with A Distributor

FUELS AND CARBURETION SYSTEMS

by W. I. "Bill" Gieseke

FUEL

(Continued from March Issue)

SPARK SETTING. — During the knock testing the spark setting used is that for maximum power. This is for the following reasons: (1) It simulates actual operation; (2) it decreases variations due to air-fuel ratio; (3) it decreases the effect of slight changes in spark setting.

AIR-FUEL RATIO. — The air-fuel ratio is in all cases adjusted to that setting which gives maximum knock, and this is for the following reasons: (1) It is definite and can be reproduced; (2) it is practical because it lies within the range of ordinary operation of engines.

The various other engine conditions, such as revolutions per minute, jacket temperature, and mixture temperature, are fixed at different values by the different standard test methods, either for convenience or in order to obtain results which correlate with multicylinder engine performance. It is for this reason that a fuel may be rated differently by the various methods.

METHOD OF TESTING. — Upon determination of the desired test method the engine is adjusted, then started and warmed up. It is first operated on reference fuel, the octane rating of which has been selected according to the estimated characteristics of the fuel being tested. As soon as the important factors are stabilized, the control valves are adjusted so that the engine will operate on the fuel being tested. If the knock meter indicates a higher rating, the head temperature increases, and the engine speed falls off, the octane rating of the fuel being tested is lower than the reference fuel. If, however, the performance is the same on both fuels, then the rating is the same. The margin or rating above the reference fuel may be estimated by creating a slightly more severe operating condition of the engine.

REFERENCE FUEL.—In developing the reference fuel, certain stable blends are used, with perhaps the addition of a small amount of tetraethyl lead to obtain the desired rating. As mentioned previously, iso-octane is highly resistant to knock, while normal heptane is

susceptible to it. If the fuel being tested reacts similar to a reference fuel which has been matched with 87-percent octane it will have an 87-percent octane rating, if 75 percent, a 75-octane rating, etc.

The technical definition of octane rating is as follows:

Octane rating is the percentage of iso-octane in a mixture of iso-octane and normal heptane required to match the performance of the fuel being tested in a special test engine under controlled conditions.

For general use it could be stated that it is a rating of the antiknock qualities of a gasoline.

OCTANE RATING. — The octane rating of a fuel required by a given engine will be determined mainly by the compression ratio and the supercharger ratio. The efficiency of the cooling system also will be a determining factor. If the system is not arranged properly to give efficient cooling, a higher octane-rated fuel than normally is required should be used in order to reduce the possibility of detonation.

CAREFUL BLENDING AND ADDITIVES.—Efforts are constantly being made to increase the octane rating of all gasolines by careful blending of the hydrocarbons and also by adding small quantities of ethyl fluid, which contains tetraethyl lead, ethylene dibromide, and aniline dye. The tetraethyl lead in the ethyl fluid is a heavy liquid containing lead, which has been found to be highly effective in suppressing detonation. In some fuels the addition of 3 cubic centimeters per gallon results in an increase from ten to eighteen points in octane rating. Some difficulties, such as spark plug fouling and corrosion of certain engine parts, have been encountered as a result of the use of "leaded" fuels, but these objections are rather insignificant when compared with the results obtained from the higher octane number of the ethylized fuel.

ISO - OCTANE, ISO - PENTANE, TRI-METHYL-PENTANE. — Modern high octane aircraft engine fuels contain a high percentage of iso-octane in addition to the gasoline and ethyl fluid. The iso-octane is a chemically prepared compound (tri-methyl-pentane) having a high volatility and a 100 octane rating. Small amounts of iso-pentane (bimethyl-propane) may also be added to the fuel to increase further its octane rating and volatility.

DETONATION AND PREIGNITION.—It is necessary to differentiate

between detonation and pre-ignition. During certain conditions of engine operation a phenomenon occurs which, while often confused with detonation, is properly known as preignition or auto-ignition. Preignition is generally attributed to overheating of such parts as spark plug electrodes, exhaust valves, carbon deposits, etc., to such a high degree that the charge is ignited before the spark occurs at the spark plug electrodes. In such cases an engine may continue to operate after the ignition system is turned off, until the fuel supply in the carburetor is exhausted. Special care must be exercised in stopping many high output engines in order to eliminate this condition.

BACKFIRING.—Backfiring is not to be confused with kickback, which is merely a tendency to reverse the direction of rotation when starting the engine and is caused by a highly advanced ignition timing or preignition. A backfire is caused by slow flame propagation resulting from a lean mixture, so that the charge is still burning when the cycle is completed (end of exhaust stroke). As the intake valve opens to admit the fresh charge to the cylinder, it is immediately ignited by the residual flame of the previous cycle. The flame travels back through the induction system burning all the combustible charge, and often will ignite any accumulation of gasoline near the carburetor.

PRECAUTIONS IN HANDLING ETHYL FLUID

Direct contact of concentrated ethyl fluid on the skin should be avoided. The lead content of ethylized fuels after mixing is not sufficient to produce poisoning by contact with the skin under normal conditions of use, but extreme caution should be taken to avoid breathing the vapors as the lead content of ethyl fluid is volatile and

(Continued on Page 18)

(Continued from Page 16)

the fumes very poisonous. Rubber gloves should be worn while handling the concentrated fluid to avoid any possibility of contact with the skin. The fluid must be poured carefully to avoid splashing and should be handled outdoors whenever possible to avoid the possibility of a concentration of toxic vapor.

ANTIDOTE.—If the fluid comes in contact with the skin, the area should be washed immediately with gasoline or kerosene, followed by Fels-Naphtha soap and water. It the fluid is spilled on the clothing, the garment should be removed immediately and the affected area of the skin cleansed as specified above. The garment on which the fluid has been spilled should be washed in gasoline or naphtha and dried thoroughly.

CAUTION. — Ethylized gasoline should be used only as an engine fuel. It never should be used as a cleaning agent or for other miscellaneous purposes, such as camp stoves, lamps, etc.

CARBURETION SYSTEMS

GENERAL.—The common explanation of the four-stroke cycle principle of internal combustion engine operation usually begins by stating that "the intake valve opens, and the piston moves outward, drawing a combustible charge into the cylinder". It will be observed that although a description of engine operation might begin at any point in the cycle, the logical procedure is to begin with the suction stroke. Such an order is quite proper, since the induction of the fuel charge directly affects the remaining operations in the cycle. Engine speed, power, and efficiency are regulated principally by the quantity and nature of the charge drawn in through the induction system; in fact, all operations which follow may be considered as resulting from the suction stroke. Thus, the induction of the fuel and air is a fundamental operation which must be clearly understood in order to obtain a complete understanding of an internal combustion engine.

The study of carburetion deals with many of the laws of chemistry, hydraulics, heat, and other branches of science. It is necessary, therefore, to point out certain established laws and principles which are applied to the operation of carburetion systems.

CARBURETION PRINCIPLES— The conventional engine may be classified as a form of heat engine in which the burning process occurs inside a closed cylinder. Although an engine is often said to develop power, strictly speaking, an engine is merely a mechanism for converting one form of energy into another. In the gasoline engine, for example, heat which is one form of energy is partially converted into mechanical work. The necessary heat is produced by burning suitable fuels, and the heat liberated is utilized to cause expansion and pressure; thus, the original heat energy performs useful work.

COMBUSTION—Combustion is the result of the rapid combination of certain elements with oxygen (O) ordinarily obtained from the atmosphere. For example, hydrogen (H) may be burned in air or oxygen in a manner represented by the following formula: $H_2 + O = H_2O$. It will be observed that after the chemical reaction has taken place an entirely new substance is formed having no resemblance to the original elements. In this case the product formed is water. In the same manner carbon (C) will combine with oxygen, but in this reaction two different products may result, depending on the amount of oxygen present. In a plentiful supply of oxygen, carbon will combine as follows: $C + O_2 = CO_2$ (carbon dioxide). However, when the oxygen supply is limited, as is often the case in an engine cylinder, the formula will be: $C + O = CO$ (carbon monoxide). Both of these gases are often present in the exhaust of an engine, their relative proportions depending on the mixture ratio.

COMBUSTION FROM HYDROCARBONS — Compounds containing hydrogen and carbon such as gasoline, benzene, acetylene, etc., react with oxygen in a similar manner. For example, a hydrocarbon known as heptane (C_7H_{16}), when burned in a correct amount of oxygen, yields carbon dioxide and water of: $C_7H_{16} + 11(O_2) = 7CO_2 + 8H_2O$. Under normal conditions both the water and carbon dioxide are absorbed as individual gases into the atmosphere. However, if suitable condensers are installed the water may be recovered. The above reaction assumes that the correct amount of air is present, but this condition of a perfect mixture is generally not obtained and often is not desirable. Lean mixtures permit the formation of a large amount of carbon dioxide, whereas a rich mixture increases the percentage of carbon monoxide in the exhaust gases. From this it can readily be shown that there is a definite relation between the fuel-air ratio, or mixture strength, and the composition of the exhaust gases. (This will be mentioned later in connection with the measure of mixture ratios in a subsequent article.)

* * *

To be continued next issue.

C. R. A. SPECIFICATIONS
Limitations and Restrictions For the Track

ROADSTER
Engine

1. Engine Limitations—No overhead cams, 300 cu. in. unblown, 183 cu. in. blown. American stock production block.

2. Carburetors—No limitations.

3. Exhaust Pipes—Extend past the driver seat and safe distance from fuel system.

Chassis

1. Chassis and Body Type—Standard size, stock, roadster body unaltered in contour. Pickups must have a reinforced guard extending at least six inches below the bottom of the bed, or the bed must not extend past rear wheels any further than stock roadster body. All car bodies at rear must not be less than 17" or more than 26" from ground at bottom. All cars must have rear bumpers to within 17" to 23" of the ground. Pickup beds must be a minimum of 3½ ft. in length and must extend not more than 20 inches past the center of rear axle. All cars must have adequate bumpers to prevent under-running. Doors may be cut away on driver's side only.

2. Weight—Not less than 1200 lbs. nor more than 2600 lbs. Each car must have weight certificate.

3. Wheel Base—Not less than 99 inches; maximum of 115 inches.

4. Thread—Minimum of 50 inches; maximum of 58 inches.

5. Wheels—Maximum of 20 inches; minimum of 15 inches.

6. Steering Wheel—All cars must be equipped with flexible steel spider-type wheels placed so that driver has easy entrance and exit and can handle car without interference.

7. Steering Assembly — Tie rods must be reinforced or a truck tie rod used. No welds will be allowed on pit-arms unless approved by Technical Committee. No brazing allowed on steering. Gear box location optional.

8. Fenders and Braces—All Fenders and Braces must be removed.

9. Bumpers — Stock Bumpers will not be permitted. Only bumpers of steel or tubing to protect radiators and engines and arc welding or bolted to frame, which must not extend forward of front wheels. Rear bumpers must not extend beyond frame more than three inches. There shall be no sharp corners.

10. Glass—No glass shall be allowed for windshields — only a soft, pliable windbreak such as Pyrolin shall be used.

11. Headlights and Tail Lights — Must be removed or recessed. Tail lights must be taped.

(Continued on Page 21)

Mexican Screen Star Sara Blanco (standing) is greeted by Train of Industry Official Mike Lawrence, Ellen Koller (Queen of the Train) and Director Eddie J. Dupuy. Plans are to include a hot rod along with speed equipment displays when the train circles the nation.

Classified Advertisements

12. Doors — Must be securely fastened or welded.

13. Safety Belts—Each car entered must have regulation safety belt securely bolted to frame.

14. Ignition Switch—Each car must have a cut-off switch within easy reach of driver.

15. Fuel Line—Shut-off valve within easy reach of driver on all cars.

16. Clutch — All cars must be equipped with a positive neutral and pass the Technical Committee's approval.

17. Brakes — All cars must be equipped with a suitable braking device and pass inspection.

18. Locked Rear Ends—Optional.

19. Tires — No factory built mudgrip or Knobbies will be permitted.

20. No four-wheel drives shall be allowed.

21. All cars must have double-acting shocks on all four wheels.

22. All cars must be equipped with fireproof, metal firewall between driver and engine compartment.

23. All cars must be equipped with full hood and radiator shells, securely fastened to body or frame.

24. All exterior accessories must be removed from car.

25. All cars must have a catch tank on the radiator overflow of at least one gallon capacity. Tank must be securely fastened to car.

26. All cars must have identification number at least 12" high on both sides of car.

27. Rules—Board of Directors will inspect and register each car by appointment at least 24 hours before race time. All cars must be inspected by Technical Committee prior to qualifying time.

HRM recently received the above picture and this letter reprinted here. We feel it will be of great interest to our readers. (Note the engine size.)

Gentlemen:

I noticed your very new hot rod magazine, and as I thought you might wish to show a very "warm" German hot rod, now going into production, I am enclosing a photo of it.

The BMW-Veritas is being developed by a group of former BMW (Bavarian Motor Works) men and was found by well-known European drivers to be the fastest thing without supercharger in its class of 2 liters (122 cu. in.).

It's a 6-cylinder, with two overhead cam shafts, chain driven so far, but will eventually be changed to cam shaft drive. Three carburetors; no special fuels used.

The job has all four wheels independently suspended, torsion bar springs system (twist rod). The weight should not exceed 550 kg. Revolution:: 6000 pm. Road clearance: 150 mm. It has four speeds and the teeth-rod or direct gear steering system which is popular in Germany.

George L. Glaser

Southern California Timing Association, Inc.
1948 COMPETITION RULES

1. RACING DATES: The racing dates will be determined by the Board of Representatives. The time trials will be held on two consecutive days with qualifying runs for all classes starting Saturday A.M. and ending Sunday P.M.

2. RACING COURSE: The electrically timed racing course will be a measured distance of 1320 feet (one quarter mile) and the approaching run will be as long as is safely necessary. The timing device will be approved by the Board of Representatives.

3. STARTING PROCEDURE: The time trials shall commence at 6 A.M., or as early as clear visibility permits, subject to decision of the Contest Board. At the time of starting the meet, the identity of the last car in line will be recorded and all first runs will be completed to that point. These shall be referred to as the Initial First Runs. After that time, cars in the first and second run lines will be run alternately. The same procedure will be followed on the second and third runs. These methods will apply to both Saturday and Sunday running. The meet shall be deemed official upon completion of the Initial First Runs on Sunday.

4. DEFINITION of CLASSES: Classes shall be divided into Roadsters and Streamliners, with four classes in each as follows:
'A' Class, 0 to 183 cubic inches engine displacement; 'B' class, 183 to 250 cubic inches; 'C' class, 250 to 350 cubic inches; and 'D' class, 350 and over.

Engines equipped with superchargers or added double-overhead camshafts will automatically advance into the next higher engine size class of competition. No car will run in other than it's designated engine class.

(a) Roadsters: Cars competing in the Roadster classes must be equipped with an American Production Roadster body of unaltered height, width, and profile. Streamlining, except tarpaulins, may be added only to the chassis of the car. Engines must be of American Automotive Production manufacture (at least 500 must have been made of this particular item to be classed as production manufacture). Pickups may be run as roadsters provided the cargo bed is 36 inches or more in length and standard width and height. Tarp covers will not be permitted on pickup beds. Minimum wheelbase permissable in the Roadster classes is 95 inches.

(b) Streamliners: Cars competing in the Streamliner classes may have any type of body not allowable in the Roaster classes, except stock bodies, coupes, or sedans. Engines must be American Automotive Production manufacture. Minimum wheelbase allowed in the Streamliner Classes is 85 inches.

5. PROTESTS and PENALTIES: Any car in competition may be protested against by any club for a protest fee of $15.00. The car will be inspected by the Contest Board and one (1) member of the protesting club. In the event that the protested car is found to be acceptable the car owner shall receive the protest fee. If the car is not acceptable the entry will be disqualified and the fee will be refunded to the protesting club. Any member found wilfully violating any cubic-inch regulation shall be cause for the forfeiting of all personal points and all points his Club may have earned at that particular meet.

6. TRIAL RUNS: Each car entered shall be entitled to two Time Trial runs, and to qualify for a third run the following class speeds must be exceeded:

'A' Roadster	90 mph.
'B' "	110 "
'C' "	115 "
'D' "	120 "
'A' Streamliner	100 "
'B' "	120 "
'C' "	125 "
'D' "	130 "

7. POINT AWARDS: Points shall be awarded for the first twenty fastest cars in each class, provided that the above class speeds are exceeded. Points awarded for qualifying times will be as follows:

First Fastest Car	200	points
Second	190	"
Third	180	"
Fourth	170	"
Fifth	160	"
Sixth	150	"
Seventh	140	"
Eighth	130	"
Ninth	120	"
Tenth	110	"
Eleventh	100	"
Twelfth	90	"
Thirteenth	80	"
Fourteenth	70	"
Fifteenth	60	"
Sixteenth	50	"
Seventeenth	40	"
Eighteenth	30	"
Nineteenth	20	"
Twentieth	10	"

Duplicate points will be awarded in case of ties to winning clubs as to winning entrants.

No points will be awarded to entrants who are disqualified for infraction of rules at any time during any race meet.

8. OFFICIAL RECORDS: There shall be one Official Record for each of the eight classes of competition. 100 points will be awarded for new records established. However, only the final existing record established in any class at any one meet will be eligible for points awards. All record-breaking cars will be subject to inspection by the Contest Board for cubic-inch displacements.

9. RECORD RUNS: Any car which in qualifying exceeds the speed of the existing record in it's class shall be entitled to make a two-way run for record. Original qualifying times will

not be included in record runs. Two runs must be made in opposite directions on the course within a total elapsed time of fifteen minutes.

Record runs may be made after the initial first runs on either day.

10. COMPETITION: A member may enter more than one car at a meet, provided they are legally his property, and may receive points for each car but these cannot be combined for a total. No engine or chassis will be allowed to run under more than one entry or in more than one class at any one meet.

Points awarded to joint-entries will be figured as a team and not divided between or awarded to either of the entrants. In case of inter-club transfers of members, club points will remain with the club to which the members belonged at the time they were won.

11. TROPHIES: Standard trophies will be awarded for the first three fastest Roadsters and Streamliners in each class, provided the speeds attained are eligible for points awards. Exclusive S.C.T.A. Trophies will be awarded to the season's five highest points winners in each competition class and to the season's highest points winning club. S.C.T.A. Trophies will be awarded for new records set during a season and held at the end of the same season.

12. PRESENTATION of AWARDS: Presentation of awards won by individuals or clubs shall be determined by the Board of S.C.T.A. Representatives.

13. ELIGIBILITY: No person will be allowed to participate in racing events sponsored by this Association unless he is a member in good standing with no financial obligations to the Association outstanding. No one will be allowed to compete who has not been a bona-fide member of his current club, and the S.C.T.A., for a period of at least thirty days prior to the date of the racing event.

14. GUESTS: A limited number of guest entry blanks may be issued to desirable non-association members residing outside a three hundred mile radius of Los Angeles proper. These shall not however, be eligible for competition trophies, points, or Hospital Fund benefits. There will be no post entries.

15. CREDENTIALS: Each driver of a competition car must present his Motor Vehicle Operators License and his S.C.T.A. Membership Card on the starting line before being permitted to participate in any Association event.

16. MINORS: All drivers under twenty-one years of age must have their Parents or Guardians NOTARIZED consent on file with the Association Secretary's office.

17. CAR OCCUPANTS: Only one person will be allowed in cars taking part in any Association event.

18. GOGGLES: All drivers must wear approved type windproof goggles while running their cars on the course.

19. TEMPERANCE: Any participant in an Association event who shows signs of intoxication will be immediately disqualified from taking part in that event and the matter will be referred to the Contest Board and the Board of Representatives for possible further action.

20. FORFEIT of FEES: Owners of cars disqualified for any reason will forfeit their entry fees. Also, owners who enter cars for the time trials but fail to be on hand when the trials are run will forfeit their entry fees.

TECHNICAL REGULATIONS

T-1. INSPECTION: Each car must satisfactorily pass the inspection of the Technical Committee before it will be allowed to participate in any Association Event.

T-2. NUMBERS: All entrants in competition must have their correct assigned numbers plainly visible on both sides of the car. Numbers assigned by the clubs are permanent through the season. Numerals must be twelve inches high with a six inch letter designating the cubic-inch class entered.

T-3. FIRE EXTINGUISHERS: Each car entered in the time trials must be equipped with a suitable, loaded, fire extinguisher attached within easy reach of the driver while on the course.

T-4. WINDSHIELDS and HEAD-LIGHTS: No glass windshields will be permitted. Non-shatterable windscreens of lucite, plexiglass, or other transparent plastics are permissable. Glass head-light lenses are permissable providing they are suitably taped.

T-5. TARPAULINS: Tarps may be used to cover the open cockpit on stock body cars, but they must be securely fastened and arranged and fitted so that they do not cover the steering wheel and/or restrict or limit the driver's use of controls. They must be so constructed that the driver can easily get into or out of the car without having to undo snaps, fasteners, or zippers.

T-6. EXHAUST SYSTEMS: All cars must be equipped with exhaust collectors or stacks which must be installed in such a way that the exhaust cannot stir up dust from the course, and so that it is directed past or away from the driver, fuel tank, and tires.

T-7. HOODS: All cars must be equipped with metal engine-hoods extending from the firewall to a firmly attached radiator shell and across the top to the beginning of the vertical hood sides. Vertical hood side-panels may be omitted. All hoods must be securely fastened in place.

T-8. FLOORBOARDS: All cars must be equipped with either floorboards or belly-pans. Floorboards must be well fitted and securely fastened in place with no unnecessary holes left open.

T-9. BELLYPANS: Metal bellypans are permitted, but they must be provided with suitable vents or drainage holes located so as to prevent fuel or oil from collecting in the pan. No bellypans made of canvas, wood, or other inflammable material are permitted.

T-10. FIREWALLS: All cars must be equipped with full firewalls to provide an effective seal between engine and driver. Firewalls must extend down and meet floorboards or bellypans. All unnecessary holes must be suitably sealed, including areas around pedals and steering column.

T-11. MISCELLANEOUS. All tires, brakes, steering mechanism, welding, and construction methods, as well as controls and equipment are subject to inspection by the Technical Committee. Any car may be barred from the course at their discretion.

T-12. APPEALS: Any ruling by a member of the Technical Committee may be appealed to the Contest Board and the Board's decision in all cases will be final.

T-12. STARTER. The Official Starter may bar a car from the course by refusing to start it, even though the car may have passed the inspection of the Technical Committee. The Starter does not however, have the authority to reverse a decision made by the Contest Board.

TATTERSFIELD - *Baron* *Racing Equipment*

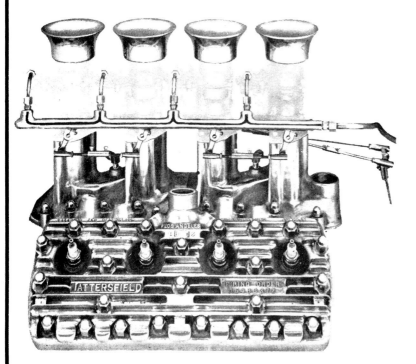

—NEW—
→ **4 Carburetor Manifold**
→ **Special Heads**
→ **Special Pistons**

A combination designed for every speed range.

If it's a record you want, install a Tattersfield - Baron Speed unit today.

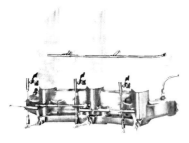

—FORD 6—
This manifold is designed to use 2 or 3 carburetors more efficiently than with only 1 carburetor.

—FORD 60—
Illustrated is the new Ford 60 manifold with many new added features—Adds more dynamic power to your 60 midget.

—FORD "A"—
This manifold can be purchased in either single or dual carburetion.

→ **Many other types of Manifolds are available for your truck or passenger car.**

→ **Write today for information regarding dual Carburetion on your own car.**

Manifold Division

ELECTRIC & CARBURETOR ENG. CO.

2321-23 E. 8th St.,   Los Angeles 21, California

HOT ROD
Magazine

Bert Letner in the Elco Twin

MAY, 1948 103 **25c**

SHARP SPEED EQUIPMENT

6225 Wilmington Avenue   **LOgan 5-1329**   **Los Angeles, Calif.**

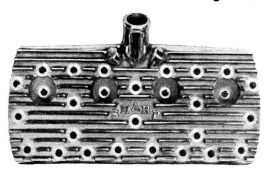

THE SHARP TRIPLET

This new manifold is patterned ofter the **Sharp Dual Manifold**, having the same port routing, thus giving perfect distribution to all ports. This action assures perfect acceleration from idling to peak R.P.M. with **no flat spots.**

The new Sharp head gives maximum efficiency in acceleration as well as top speed. The Combustion Chamber is designed to allow adequate breathing at any R.P.M. The water capacity of the head is almost double over the stock heads. Two directional flow ribs over each cylinder assures even cooling, the extra width acting as a water manifold to eliminate steam pockets, thus reducing heat and giving more efficiency. The metal used in the heads is of the highest alloy obtainable. Each head is heat treated to eliminate corrosion and warping as well as increasing the tensile strength of the material. The heads are tested under 45 lbs. water pressure for leaks. **Compression ratios 8.75 to 10-1.**

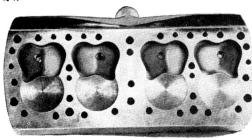

It's in the Bag . . .

Dear Sir:

I find your magazine very interesting although the racing we do up here is with dog teams.

. . . I would like to send my congratulations on a very fine magazine.

Carl B. Smith
Fairbanks, Alaska

Gentlemen:

. . . How many of the boys remember the late George White who opened the Bell Auto Parts back in 1927? I believe I am the first customer George had. George was a "regular guy". The boys would hang around there, borrow his tools, lose half of them and George would never say a word. We knew when Sunday came for George would have a clean shave and put on a clean pair of coveralls. The hot rods then were T Fords. My brother "Corky" had a four-cylinder Buick in his T and Bill Taylor had an Overland in his. I know that Roscoe Turner remembers those two cars.

All the luck in the world to HRM, keep up the good work.

ROD QUISENBERRY
Los Angeles, California

* * *

Hot Rod Magazine:

. . . I have personally admired your magazine's features, pictures, and news, and know your organization has plenty of hard work . . . to tackle the speed problem.

I hope to be in a position to give some old records of S.C.T.A. or even earlier, say 1934-5-6 roadster speeds at dry lakes meets. I know such information would make interesting reading to our modern day audience when you consider in 1934 a model B Ford, 1932 roadster body, clocked 119 mph. at Muroc Timing Association Meet! . . .

BOZZY WILLIS
San Diego, California.

* * *

Dear Sir:

The magazine is going over great with not only the roadster boys but everyone else, too . . .

I thought I would ask you, if I send some pictures and information about some of the hot rods here would you print it in the magazine? If so—when we send the pictures do you want the negatives or the prints? . . .

DUKE SHERRIFF
Phoenix, Arizona.

The prints will work fine.—ED

Editor:

. . . I am in the NCRRA and have yet too see a better, more explanatory magazine than HRM . . .

LEE "BUD" COFFEE
Oakland, California.

* * *

I got a copy of your HOT ROD MAGAZINE from a friend in Los Angeles. I was very much impressed by that you had in it. I had never seen it before or any other magazine like it here in Northern California.

LEO JURI
Palo Alto, Calif.

* * *

Dear Sir:

I would appreciate it if you would put this poem in the Hot Rod Magazine . . . I am writing this poem about Troy Ruttman as you can plainly see.

Will be waiting to hear from you!!!!!

Celeste McLure
Ventura, Calif.

P.S. I sure hope that Troy sees this!!!!!!

Well, he can't miss it here!!!!!!—ED.

TROY AND HIS HOTROD

Look at that guy go, "Oh Boy,"
I'm not sure but I think it's Troy.
Oh, what a thrill,
Just look at him peel.
Move over boy let's make room,
Here comes Ruttman with a great big boom.
Listen to that rubber scream,
And look at Leadfoot's face beam.
He may be tall and a lanky header,
But don't kid yourself, he's even better.
They call him Leadfoot, I guess you know why,
That kid's going places as he whizzes by.
I guess I'll close now, the race is near its end,
Oh, look out Troy you're coming to a bend.
I think the races are really a thrill,
Oh, Oh, He's now taking a spill.
They turn the car over and out Troy jumps,
Not a scratch, not a bruise, not even a bump!

—by Celeste McLure

Editor's Column

For the May issue HRM boasts stories, pictures and news from points throughout the nation. Racing has started up along the West Coast from Los Angeles north to Portland. At the same time, race announcements have been received from the Pecos Valley Racing Association (Roswell, New Mexico) and Mutual Racing (Indiana), telling of their opening races.

S.C.T.A.'s first 1948 meet (a two-day event) is set for April 24 and 25. Results and pictures from this event and the first Russetta Timing Meet will be printed in the June issue.

The Hot Rod of the Month is Bert Letner's roadster, popular at both lakes and track events.

Readers have requested more "Hot Rod History." A story with photos appears on page 20 of the May issue. We wish to thank Lee Chapel of Oakland, Calif., for his help on this story.

Mel Dudley, of the Mutual Racing Association, is also due a vote of thanks for his cooperation on the story of Mutual, which will be found on page 21.

Another Maanum drawing, this of Arnold Birner's lakes entry, is reproduced on page 9.

Stroker McGurk is shown in action on the track this month.

'Rusty' Accornero gives us his outlook on "rubber" with his article, "Tires For Speed." Story is on page 11.

Apologies to Vern Slankard of the California Hot Rods for overlooking his ownership of car no. 26 in April's Autosnaps. Vern is co-owner of the roadster as well as its able driver.

Regulations of the newly reorganized Russetta Timing Association are on page 22, along with results of Mojave Timing's recent dry lakes time trials.

Look for a bigger and better Hot Rod Magazine in June. Indianapolis will be represented in that issue. Be sure you have your copy. Subscribe today!

Keep those letters and snapshots coming in.—ED.

HOT ROD Magazine

WORLD'S MOST COMPLETE HOT ROD COVERAGE

TABLE OF CONTENTS

Hot Rod Magazine, U. S. Copyright 1948 by the Hot Rod Publishing Company, 112 South La Brea, Los Angeles, Calif.
SUBSCRIPTION PRICE: $3.00 per year throughout the world.

HRM—Published Monthly

Associate Editors .... Robert R. Lindsay
Robert E. Petersen
Advertising Manager .... Richard Sabotka
Photography .... Lee Blaisdell, Alan Dean, Paul Shaeffer, Don Mohr
Cartoons and Humor .... Tom Medley
Reporters .... Anthony Granatelli, John Lelis
Robert Williams, Glenn Glendening
Dick Robinson, Richard K. Martin
Arthur Elliot

Bert Letner's red-and-white roadster doubles as a lakes and track job.

The engine was first clocked in 1946 turning a fast 120.96 mph in a heavy, full belly pan '32 Ford roadster. Later, in 1947, the engine was clocked in the present chassis, turning consistently fast times. Its best C Class time at an S.C.T.A. meet was 125.87. Russetta time was a little faster with 126.86 average for two directions. The car attained the top record speed for the Pacific Timing Association with a time of 130:05.

Now, the same roadster, with a few modifications, has taken to the track and is rapidly stacking up a new ream of laurels. In one of its first appearances at Carrell Speedway, Calif., the car was the fastest qualifier, coming within 5/100's of the track record. The Elco Twin held the lead in the main event only to blow a tire in the 17th lap. At Culver City Speedway,

two Stromberg 97 carburetors.

The most unusual feature of the car is its twin spark plug arrangement. Designed by Bert Letner and Ted Evans, the heads are named Elco Twins—a combination of the designers' names. The unique heads employ two spark plugs in each cylinder, giving the engine a total of 16 spark plugs. The principle of the twin plugs in each cylinder is to provide a maximum of flash in the combustion chamber to ignite the charge more rapidly and burn the gasses more completely.

Spark is sent to the plugs by a converted 1 GK 400 Autolite Ignition. This distributor is the type used on an early model Nash 6.

Better cooling is achieved by water-manifolding. Stock water pumps are removed and a ½-inch geared marine pump is installed in the bottom left side of the radiator. This pump lifts the coolant from the radiator and sends

Dash and interior feature an in-out gear box, fuel hand pump, centered steering mechanism.

course, fully hydraulic for maximum safety.

This roadster is the result of many years of experience in the racing field. Bert first became interested in speed back in the model T era. In 1936 he and Ted Evans had a dual-ignition Cragar entered in the modified T roadster races at Southern Ascot Speedway. For the last eighteen years he has been building all types of cars and at present has five roadsters under construction in his garage.

A member of the Roadrunners Club, Bert is also on the Board of Directors of the California Roadster Association.

Letner is a family man . . . and the family is definitely hot-rod-minded. Bert's wife is an avid roadster fan, and his son, Danny, is at present building up a full-race Mercury.

In the coming season Bert hopes to win new honors with his Elco Twin . . . that is, if he can break away from the spark plug salesmen long enough to do so.

Close-up view of the Elco Twin's unusual "double plug" arrangement.

the following week, the car broke the qualifying record, the 10-lap record, and placed first in the 8-lap main event run-off.

Bert designed and built the car in his own shop, the Modern Auto Works in Hynes, California. Working with him were Ted Evans and Art Lamey. Art drove the car on its initial lakes runs and will probably drive it again at the lakes this year. Fred Luce has been at the wheel for several races. Now veteran hot rod chauffeur Troy Ruttman, who has driven the car in several races in the past, will take over as regular driver.

Well-balanced construction makes for easy handling.

The dry sump power plant is a '40 Mercury bored .125 over with .125 stroke. Cam was ground by Smith and the manifold is a Sharp Dual, mounting

it through the block by way of six pipes entering under the exhaust ports.

Body of the car is a '25 T Ford channelled over a T Ford frame. Battery and transmission are accessible through the turtle-back. A pressure-type gas tank is used to speed the flow of fluid. The driver sits in an upholstered aircraft-type seat with a belt for safety.

For quick gear changes, necessary when driving on varied-length tracks, a Cook Cyclone differential with a range of 209 to 822 is used with an in-out gear box. The front end is suspended with the spring in front of the dropped axle. Franklin standard 6-to-1 steering mechanism is used. Bert has 500-16 tires on the front and 700-16 on the rear. On the tracks he uses slicks and on the lakes, the conventional tread tires. Braking is, of

Under the turtle back Bert carries his battery. Quick-change rear end gives greater gear range on tracks and lakes.

Laughs

FROM HERE AND THERE

By TOM MEDLEY

Many a man who is a five-ton truck at the office is nothing but a trailer at home.

* * *

Pictures are better than words. Think how utterly flat and inexpressive the word "crumpled" was until fenders were invented.

* * *

"Say, Jerry, I got a new job over at Honest Johns!"

"What doing?"

"Painting whiskers on Fords."

"Huh!"

"Yea; making them look like *Lincolns*."

* * *

And from the depths of the sedan
   there came a muffled curse,
He was trying to fold a road map,
Same as it was at first.

* * *

An old yokel saw a motor car for the first time in his life. It came dashing up the main street and disappeared in a cloud of dust.

"Well," said the yokel, "the horses must ha'bin going a good speed when they got loose from the carriage."

* * *

Cop: "How do you know the guy who stole your roadster was a professional?"

Owner: "Cause no amateur could have started it."

"WE HAVEN'T THE HEART TO TELL HIM."

According to some automobile manufacturers, the shortest distance between two points is a straight eight.

* * *

Sign at a busy small town filling station:

"Automobiles washed—one dollar."

"Austins dunked—50 cents."

* * *

"How long did it take your wife to learn to drive?"

"It will be ten years in September."

An arm protruding from the side of a car ahead apparently can signify any of the following things:

The motorist is: 1, knocking off ashes; 2, going to turn to the left; 3, warning a small boy to shut up; 4, going to turn to the right; 5, pointing to the scenery; 6, going to back up; 7, feeling for rain; 8, telling the wife he is sure the front door is locked; 9, hailing a friend in passing car; 10, going to stop.

STROKER McGURK

BOB SOUTHLAND'S TRACK ROADSTER
FORMER A.S.C. PRESIDENT "TAKES OFF" AT CULVER CITY SPEEDWAY

Photo by Don Mohr.

ARNOLD BIRNER'S LAKES MODIFIED
Riley Four-Port clocked at 126.93 M.P.H.

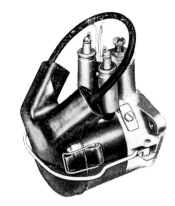

TIRES FOR SPEED
_____ By "RUSTY" ACCORNERO

Racing and timing enthusiasts are looking more and more towards those factors which go towards making an automobile safe. Possibly the foremost feature in the safety of a fast-moving vehicle is the tires on which it runs. There are numerous factors to be considered before choosing the "rubber" which will carry one of those cars through its speedy paces.

In this article we will divide our interests into two categories, race tires and timing tires.

Race Tires

Sizes used on racing-type hot rods vary. Generally, the drivers prefer to use 7.00x16's on the rear and 5.00 or 5.50x16's on the front wheels. Next in popularity are 7.00x15's and 5.50 x15's.

The next point to be considered is the air pressure. On asphalt tracks drivers seem to prefer the following combinations: 18-20# on the front tires and 15-18# on the rears. These pressures and tire sizes differ, with the characteristics of the cars and the tracks on which they are running.

The race will build up the pressure of the tires; so, the driver must strike a medium in choosing his pressures. (A little lower than desirable at the beginning of the race and a little higher towards the end). In choosing air pressures the following things must be considered: increased air pressure will increase the life of the tire, at the same time increasing the "skid" characteristics; too low a pressure will cause the tires to "run flat," cords will pop out, leaving no body to the tire and resulting in blowouts. The larger the track, the rougher on the tires.

For track jobs it is recommended not to use any tire in which the casing is beginning to show. If such tires are used they will soon begin to tear, and usually the entire tread will rip away. It is practically impossible to use synthetic tires for track racing. This has the same effect as running on tires which have casing showing through. When track racing of hot rods rose in popularity in 1946, some of the drivers used recaps, but this practice soon proved impractical. At present most drivers will settle for nothing less than new tires on the tracks. A new tire, when run on a half-mile asphalt track, will be good for the "heat" and the "main" event in which it qualifies. Many drivers find it inadvisable to use one set, especially the right rear's, for longer than that.

Lakes Tires

On the lakes the drivers prefer sizes from 7.00x16's-5.50x16's to 7.00x16's. At the lakes as well as on the tracks the most popular and practical tires are 4-plys. Most hot rod enthusiasts know that there are definite advantages in running large rears and small fronts. The larger the rears, the greater the length of ground covered by each revolution of the engine. This applies up to the point where too much is asked of the car's engine, whereupon it will be overloaded and run even slower than with a smaller sized tire. The fronts are preferably small because smaller tires afford a greater control of steering. The combinations on the rears vary with the engine and body types, the gear ratios, etc. Each driver must experiment to find the most favorable tire sizes for his car. The duration of lakes tires is indefinite as long as they are not otherwise mistreated.

Lakes drivers usually find that pressures around 30# afford the best traction on the lake bed.

This information should help beginning racing and timing entrants in choosing the tires, pressures, etc. they will wish to run. Be sure the tires you use are safe. Without safe tires, even an expert driver can run into dangerous trouble.

Mickey Chiachi's channelled '39 Merc. The car set a Russetta time of 111 mph. running '41 Merc. engine, Edelbrock Heads, Evans Manifold and Winfield Cam. Body work by Barris.

Wayne Tipton's track roadster gets a check-up in the pits at Bonelli Stadium, Saugus. Wayne is a member of CHR's Board of Directors.

From Seattle, Washington, comes this shot of Bill Exner's track job. The roadster runs McCullough Blower, Meyers Heads.

The Spalding Brothers' well-known "Carpet Sweeper" streamliner.. This unusual job clocked 126 mph. at its peak.

A typical starting line-up at an S.C.T.A. lakes meet. Starting stand may be seen in rear.

Several Caddies run at the dry lakes. Here is a Cad V-12 in a channelled Ford body.

Singer Martha Tilton presents Jack McGrath with a prize at Carrell Speedway. The prize, a driver's helmet for winning the trophy dash.

The "long and short" of hot rod racing. Slim Mathis and Roy Prosser standing by Elmer's Muffler Special during a CRA night race.

114

This shot of a Crager engine proves that the old-line speed engines are still popular amongst hot rod builders.

Jack McGrath spins and Jim Rathman (#16), trying to avoid a crash, skids into his roadster. This happened during a race at the Pasadena Rose Bowl.

April 24th and 25th thousands of spectators will again witness an excellent S.C.T.A. timing meet. The meet will be held at El Mirage Dry Lakes as was the one pictured here.

Gene Dupertius' custom built hot rod is mounted on a '40 Merc frame. The outside body is wood-constructed. Engine is full-race '40 Merc. Grille is from a late Dodge.

Herman Jordan of Chicago runs this roadster on Midwest tracks. The car has Model B Murphy Overheads, Von Esser Cam, Thomas Manifold. Herman is prexy of the Rolling Roadsters.

The camera's eye caught this fine action at Gardena, Calif. Leroy Nooks, running CRA, loses his left rear wheel. (Upper right).

This sleek streamliner was run at the lakes by Tommy Lee. With an Offenhauser engine it clocked 130 mph.

A starting line-up at Seattle shows Kenny Imus' roadster (26), T. & M. Motors entry (42) and Dick Berger's job (60) getting ready for the "go."

Ellen Koller with a Dropped Axle

Photo by Alan Dean

Parts With Appeal

Miss Ellen Koller gets into the "swing" of things with the latest in dropped axles.

The axle, made from a stock Ford axle, is stretched and bent at the ends. At the same time it is reinforced to provide maximum strength for extreme driving conditions. Chrome is added to enhance the overall appearance of the car. The purpose of the dropped axle is to lower the center of gravity of the automobile, providing for more efficient steering.

Now, let's drop the parts and consider the appeal.

The appeal is 5'5" Ellen Koller, a native Californian . . . born in Mount Claire, New Jersey. Ellen came west at the early age of seventeen months.

Miss Koller models for top-flight magazine and billboard art. Her favorite sports include swimming, boating, badminton and hiking.

She has recently received bids from several motion picture studios. At present, however, she prefers to stay with her modeling career.

She admits that she does not know much about hot rods, but shows a definite interest in them.

Little did the manufacturer of this "part with appeal" suspect that he would one day find it under these circumstances.

A WINNER!

For All V-8
Fords — 1938 To
Present Models

ITS THE
NEW FREIMAN

UNIVERSAL TYPE **DUAL MANIFOLD**

WITH FREIMAN FLUTED STACKS

Revolutionary! The Freiman Dual Manifold is the result of months of experimental engineering and development. You'll enjoy the greater efficiency this manifold guarantees to give to your V-8 motor. Easily installed — all fittings furnished. New design. Fluted carburetor stacks at slight extra cost.

GUARANTEED UNCONDITIONALLY TO GIVE YOU
- More power
- Faster starting and pickup
- Increased mileage
- Smoother operation — less engine wear.

ASK YOUR DEALER!

FREIMAN MANUFACTURING CO.
1302 E. SLAUSON AVE., LOS ANGELES 11, CALIFORNIA

POTVIN AUTOMOTIVE
—— New Location ——
700 N. Los Angeles St., Anaheim, Calif.
EVANS SPEED & POWER EQUIPMENT
DUAL IGNITIONS
Phone Anaheim 6454

CLARKE EXHAUST HEADER CO.

Most Popular Header Today

'32-'34 V-8 Header with muffler takeoff and easily removed racing plug. Airplane jig-built.

Also Model A-B, Ford '60' - two types
Ford 6 - two types
Ford 85 - two types

Chevrolet Lowering Blocks

6612 E. SAN LUIS   COMPTON, CALIF.
Metcalf 3-3541

---

*"Peak Performance for All Engines
Thru Chemistry"*

SOLV-EX *Chemical Co.*

3608 ROSELAWN AVE. ■ GLENDALE 8, CALIF.
CHurchill 9-3533

1. SOLV-X Chemical Tune-Up
2. HI-TORQUE Add Oil
3. SOLV-O-LUBE Fuel Additive
4. CHEM-O-LUBE Fuel Additive

★ ★ ★

RACING FUEL ★ DOPES ★ ADDITIVES

Try our special blends . . .
RACING FUEL #104 (up to 9.5 to 1)
RACING FUEL #105 (9.5 to 14-1)

METHANOL-BENZOL—80-91-100 OCTANE

Special Distributor

VALVOLINE OIL S.A.E. 10 to 70

W. I. "BILL" GIESEKE

MEMBER

Society of Automotive Engineers, American Chemical Society, Motor Vehicle Engineering Society, Trailblazers, and American Society of Lubrication Engineers

---

WEIAND

IT'S BEEN LIKE THIS EVER SINCE I INSTALLED THIS "WEIAND" EQUIPMENT!

POWER and RACING EQUIPMENT

Ford '60' — Studebaker — Mercury

See Your Dealers

2733 San Fernando Road   CApitol 0668

Los Angeles 41, Calif.

CARBURETION

W. I. 'BILL' GIESEKE

(Continued from April issue.)

PHYSICS OF CARBURETION.—The carburetion system of an internal-combustion engine deals with the movement of fluids (liquids and gases) through various passages and orifices according to certain well-defined principles. Liquids have a fairly constant volume and density, but gases will expand and contract under the influence of pressure variations. For example, a certain volume of air at sea level is approximately twice as heavy as an equal volume at 20,000 feet altitude. It must be remembered in connection with gases that it is important to know weight or mass of flow in addition to volume. Since it is generally impractical to weigh gases, it is common practice to measure the pressure which they exert by the use of suitable instruments. If pressure is known, the quantity (mass) of a gas in a given volume can be easily determined.

BAROMETRIC (ATMOSPHERIC) PRESSURE—The weight of the earth's atmosphere causes it to exert a pressure on all objects and in all directions.

At sea level this pressure is approximately 14.7 pounds per square inch, or since a mercurial barometer is often used to measure this pressure it may be expressed as a pressure capable of supporting a mercury column 29.92 inches in height. Pressures are very commonly given in pounds per square inch or inches of mercury. For practical purposes the conversion ratio between these two expressions may be considered as one to two (14.7 to 29.92). Thus a manifold pressure of 28 inches of mercury corresponds to about 14 pounds per square inch.

MEASURING PRESSURE-*Negative, Positive* and *Absolute.*—In measuring pressures, confusion is often caused by the fact that in some cases it is necessary to know only the extent of a pressure above or below atmospheric rather than the actual total value. For example, the statement is made that a fuel pump generates a pressure of 3 pounds per square inch in the fuel lines, and the gage connected to the system registers 3 pounds. Actually, the total or absolute pressure in the line at sea level is 14.7 pounds plus 3 pounds or 17.7 pounds per square inch. It must

be remembered that an absolute pressure includes the atmospheric pressure, whereas a relative pressure is based on the assumption that atmospheric pressure is zero. Bourdon tube instruments such as fuel-pressure gages, steam gages, etc., and many other instruments indicate relative or differential pressure.

Further confusion is encountered when it is necessary to measure pressure below atmospheric, often erroneously called negative pressures. Actually, these subatmospheric indications are positive in value. A perfect vacuum exerts a zero pressure, and all pressures above this figure are inherently positive. For a clear understanding of pressure and pressure variations in carburetion systems, it is important that recognition be given these facts.

VELOCITY AND DIFFERENTIAL PRESSURE—Since carburetion involves the movement of fluids at various velocities, consideration of the relation between velocity and pressure is also essential. The principal factor to be observed in this connection is the fact that fluids in motion will undergo pressure changes in a manner inversely related to speed or velocity. That is, as the speed of a moving column is increased, there will occur a decrease in the pressure exerted by the fluid. The application of this principle is utilized in many devices such as atomizers, spray guns of many types, water injectors for steam boilers, and in carburetor equipment. The venturi tube (fig.)

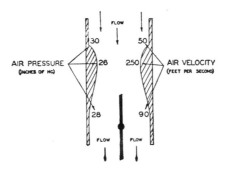

furnishes an excellent example of the relation between pressure and velocity in a moving column of air. An inspection of the shape of venturi tube reveals that since the cross sectional area is

reduced at the throat, the velocity at this point must be correspondingly higher. Because of this high velocity, the pressure in the throat of the tube will be lowered. In carburetor operation, the pressure drop (often improperly termed a negative pressure) existing at the venturi throat may be utilized in inducing liquid flow toward this point, so that correct mixing of fuel and air is accomplished. Various methods of utilizing this principle may be employed in carburetors of different designs, but in all cases the laws of fluid pressure and velocity are applied in some manner.

PRESSURE VARIATION — The subject of carburetion is intimately associated with the properties and behavior of the atmosphere which furnishes the necessary oxygen for combustion. As previously stated, the atmospheric pressure at sea level is 14.7 pounds per square inch, with minor variations according to weather conditions. This pressure is of great significance, because one of the most important factors in regulating engine power output is the weight (or mass) of air which may be taken into the cylinders in a given time period. A decrease in power when operating an engine at altitudes above sea level is obvious, for even though the proper volume of air is induced the mass of air consumed will be lower. At the same time, the mixture ratio will generally become rich as a result of the reduced air density.

MANUFACTURER'S NEWS

A new helmet is being designed by
Jerome Manufacturing Co. of Los Angeles. This headpiece is expected to meet
all requirements for racing and timing
associations. It is to be fabricated of
laminated fiber glass and plastic. They
will be painted instead of leather covered. The manufacturer claims they will
withstand more punishment than any
other helmet on the market. There will
be leather straps and the helmet will be
lined with soft felt. Expect to see them
on the retail market during the month
of May. The front visor will be optional. Retail price is estimated at $25.

Weber Tool Co. announces a new
high compression head for Studebakers.
The aluminum head has a tensile
strength of approximately 35,000 lbs.
per square inch. Weber says the head is
made in compression ratios of 8, 8.25,
8.75 to one. Special ratios may be secured upon request.

Thomas Mfg. Co. of Lynwood, Calif.,
will soon have a new magnesium crank
on the market. They are for V-8 and
Merc in any desired stroke. The crank
will take standard Ford inserts for the
rods. The unit weighs about 30 lbs.,
which is considerably lighter than a
stock crank.

* * *

Rusetta Timing Association
May 2 — June 25 — July 25
Aug. 15 — Sept. 12 — Oct. 10
Nov. 7 (If weather permits.)
Later dates by Assn. option if weather
permits.

* * *

MOJAVE TIMING RESULTS . . .
April 18, 1948 . . . Rosamond
Dry Lake, Calif.

The lake bed was fairly dry but became slippery after a few hours of timing. The course was then moved over
to a fresh spot. There were an estimated
1,000 spectators and 80-90 entries.

A CLASS—0-230 cubic inches.
B CLASS—230-201 cubic inches.
C CLASS—291; unlimited.
CLASS A MODIFIED, 119 mph. Entry: Larson-
Cleveland.
CLASS B MODIFIED, 129 mph. Entry: Bobby
Shield (4-cylinder Ford).
CLASS B ROADSTER, 125 mph. Entry: Bill Bart-
let.

Johnnie Fameralo in the driver's seat of a model A Winfield Flathead job. It clocked 112 mph in April of 1931.

This Chevy 4 (Tornado Head) held lakes record of 111.11 mph until 1941 when Bob Ruffi beat that time.

(Photos Courtesy Lee Chapel)

Hot Rod History

Fifteen years ago hot rod activities centered around Muroc Dry Lake, California. This site is now used as an experimental base for army aircraft.

Programs from those races feature the names of many of today's well-known hot rod experts: Riley, Winfield, Frank McGurk, Weiand, Cannon, Pete Clark, and others.

Engines used included many Chevs, Rajos, Frontenacs, Winfields, Millers, Cragars, Rileys, etc.

Here are a few of the times set at the meet of September 17, 1933:

Driver	Time	Motor Type
Pete Clark	114.65	Riley 4 port
Frank Lyons	117.64	Riley 4 port
Regg Schlemmer	113.21	Winfield Flathead

These same programs carried a page called "Muroc Dry Lakes News," giving many of the recent developments among the enthusiasts. From one of these pages news items are reprinted. Remember when? . . .

"The Main Event with the stock roadster bodies should show some fast times and close competition today. Pres Lodwick is running his roadster with a new Riley four-port with Joe Mozzetti driving. Joe has won first place in the last three races he has driven. He also holds the qualifying time record of 118.43 m.p.h. made July 10, 1932.

Pete Clark, who operates the Uptown Garage out on Tenth and Western, changes over to this event with a Riley four-port. Pete, in the last few races, has been nosed out by Joe, so it will be interesting to see how these two boys do in this event.

"The two McDowell jobs, one owned by Les Coan and Paul Straub, No. 5 which took third place in this event and No. 8, owned and driven by Jack Chrisman, should be considerably faster than they were at the last races. These two cars clocked within less than one mile per hour of each other.

"The outstanding flat head car is the Winfield job owned and driven by A. McDonald who holds the course record for both this type of body and for a flat head motor of 108.10 m.p.h. made at the last race. He has won first place in the stock roadster body class the last two or three races. Willie Utzman, who runs No. 52, a flat head at Ascot, will have one of his 'simple set ups', as he calls them, for this event. If any one can make a flat head go, Willie should be able to. Bill Worth, who hasn't had a car at the Lakes for some time, hopes to have his Winfield tuned up for today. Bill, too, knows how to make flat heads run.

"Last but not least is the Schofield driven by Duke Hallock, who always has a very fast car and has been driving here for several years.

"In the Modified body class, the outstanding entry is No. 6, the Neal-Hi Halfhill entry since Joe Mozzetti and Pete Clark are running stock bodies. This is a single spark Riley of the older type and they challenge any single spark Riley except the new four-port to a race for a side bet. They clocked 107.14 at the last races. There will be a number of new entries in this event that have not been turned in at this time so nothing can be said of them.

"The Muroc Racing Association wishes to thank George White of the Bell Auto Parts Exchange and 'Morrie' Morris of Dunhams for the splendid way they have assisted us in staging these races. We also wish to thank our many cup and merchandise donors for the part they have played in making these races a success."

Next month HRM will print a story on one of the first hot rod speed shops. Any information our readers can supply concerning the early developments in hot rod racing and timing will be welcomed.

Chapel at the wheel of a 1924 Chevy 4. In 1929 this job set a lakes mark of 103 mph, running a 3 port Olds head.

An old picture of a Model T Rajo from the early Muroc races.

MUTUAL RACING ASSOCIATION

(This information furnished through Melvin Dudley, former secretary-treasurer of Mutual.)

In 1939 the Mutual Association was formed at a track in Muncie, Indiana. Most of their events are run on ¼ and ⅓ mile tracks. Their programs are similar to the big-car races: 10-lap eliminations and 25-lap feature events. The Mutual will run four nights weekly during this season. Their tracks will include Fort Wayne, Anderson, Mt. Lawn, and Dayton, Ohio. Mutual has a working agreement with the Hurricane Hot Rod Club of Chicago and the Triangle of Dayton so that their drivers and cars may compete with each other. Mutual's first meet of this year was held April 4 at Salem, Indiana. One entry was from St. Paul, Minnesota.

Safety rules are definite and well enforced. Most of the cars are built on Model A frames with T bodies. (26T, if the builders can find them.) The builders let themselves go on their motors. Ford V-8, Mercury, Ford 6, Hudson, Chevrolet, and Champion are the most popular types.

Below are exerpts from MRA's 1948 RULES & REGULATIONS:

No. 7-11, a Chevy 6 owned by Maurice Mutersbaugh of Newcastle, Indiana. Shown here being unloaded at Mt. Lawn near Newcastle, Indiana.

MECHANICAL REGULATIONS

Motors must be of American-made stock design as sold in passenger cars. No commercial motors allowed; this includes station wagons. No special racing motors will be permitted to compete. No overhead valves may be used on blocks designed for flat-heads. No superchargers may be used unless they are standard equipment for that block. Motors with overhead valves as standard equipment may be used but no special rocker-arms may be installed.

Any other changes may be made such as special flat-heads, over-size valves, increased carburetion, etc. All cars must have a de-clutching device. Gear boxes will be permitted.

Bodies must be on and of stock roadster or coupe design. Only roadster bodies of Austin or Bantom permitted. Front and rear bumpers may be constructed but must be designed so there is no danger to other cars in case of contact. Bodies must not be narrowed or shortened. The only cutting of the body permitted is that part necessary to give elbow room at the door. Bottom and hangers may be cut in order to lower body on the chassis.

Bodies and motors and chassis are inter-changeable one make to another so long as they come under the above requirements.

There is no limit to wheelbase as long as the tread is not under 56″ nor over 61″. Dual wheels will not be permitted.

No car shall have wheels smaller than stock wheels, 15″ in diameter. Each car must have suitable and safe brakes at least on the rear wheels, in good working order.

Exhaust pipes must be extended so as to clear the inflammable parts of the car and must not direct the exhaust to the surface of the track.

All cars must be equipped with suitable radiator overflow (catch) tank when racing on hard-surface tracks.

All cars must be in good mechanical condition subject to the approval of the Board of Directors. (As to condition and safety.)

In case a coupe body is used, the space back of the seat may be filled in so long as no other changes are made. (Except those covered by the rules.)

PIT RULES

Each owner and driver is responsible for conduct in his pit. Drinking of intoxicating liquor will not be tolerated.

There shall be no fighting at the track. Anyone starting a fight will be subject to thirty (30) days' penalty from racing in the Mutual Racing Association. The penalty carries for car, driver and pit crew. However, no one shall be suspended without a hearing before the Board of Directors.

RE-STARTS

Any car spinning out on the first turn will call for a re-start. Any one car causing a re-start the second time in one event shall take the last position in that event.

In case a race is stopped due to accident, congestion of the track or track conditions, the last lap completed by the field shall be the number of laps run, and placement for the re-start will be according to the positions on that lap. The race shall be re-started if there is more than five laps to run. If there is less than five laps, it is called a race.

SAFETY

All drivers must wear an approved type crash helmet. Under no circumstances will a football or any type army helmet be permitted.

All drivers must wear shatterproof goggles while on the track.

Under no circumstances will women be permitted on the track unless approved by the Board.

Jim Morrison at Muncie, Indiana, in No. 39, a Ford 5 owned by Walt Straber of Indianapolis. The body is from an old Essex.

Drivers signal a false start during a Mutual heat race. (Note dirt track.) No. 10 (below), a Ford 6, built by Dan Walls of Columbus, Indiana.

Russeletta Timing Association Rules
RULES FOR CAR CLASSIFICATIONS

COUPE:	Car must have stock fenders. May be cut or channeled, but not both.
SUPER COUPE: COUPE UNLIMITED**:	Fenders not required. May have reduced frontal area. May be cut, channeled, or belly panned.
ROADSTER:	Fenders not required. Body must be on top of the frame. Frontal area not reduced. No belly pan.
SUPER ROADSTER: ROADSTER UNLIMITED**:	May have reduced frontal area, may be channeled, and may have a belly pan.
STREAMLINERS:	No limitations other than motor.
STREAMLINERS UNLIMITED:	Limitations: Supercharged or over 300 cu. in.

** Any car having less than 300 cubic inches displacement.
Supercharged moves up one class in body class. Over 300 cu. in. engine runs unlimited. D.O.'s run unlimited.

SAFETY REGULATIONS RUSSETTA TIMING

1. All entries must have at least half hoods.
2. All entries must have a windshield or driver wear goggles.
3. Headlights must be removed or taped.
4. All entries must have a fire wall.
5. Exhausts must protude past the fire wall.
6. All entries must be equipped with a fire extinguisher.
7. All turtle decks must be secured.
8. All entries must have good brakes.
9. Tarps must clear stearing wheel at least four inches.
10. Hoods opening from the front must be secured.
11. All entries equipped with springs must have shock absorbers.
12. Running gear will be thoroughly checked and must be passed.
13. All entries must have belly pans or floor boards.
14. Radiator hoses must have clamps, radiators must have caps.
15. Intoxicated persons will not be allowed to drive.
16. Decisions of the safety committee will be final on all points governing the running of cars.
17. Crash helmets.

*   *   *

"Hello, old top; new car?"
"No! Old car, new top!"

Classified Advertisements

RACE RESULTS

CRA

CARRELL SPEEDWAY, 1/2-mile, April 4, 1948. Gardena, Calif.
Trophy Dash (3 laps)—1, Roy Prosser; 2, Frank McGurk. 1:08.05.
1st Heat (6 laps)—1, Bill Anderson; 2, Dempsey Wilson; 3, Ed Korgan. 2:32.79.
2nd Heat (6 laps)—1, Puffy Puffer; 2, Ed Barnett; 3, Jim Rigsby. 2:24.58.
3rd Heat (6 laps)—1, Yam Oka; 2, Jay Frank; 3, Slim Mathis. 2:20.72.
4th Heat (6 laps)—1, Leroy Nooks; 2, Roy Prosser; 3, Don Freeland. 2:18.65.
Semi-Main (15 laps)—1, Dempsey Wilson; 2, Jim Rigsby; 3, Puffy Puffer. 6:09.62.
Main (25 laps)—1, Jay Frank; 2, Lou Figaro; 3, Don Freeland. 9:07.12.

CULVER CITY SPEEDWAY, April 11, 1948. 1/2-mile Road Race.
Trophy Dash (3 laps)—1, Don Freeland; 2, Manuel Ayulo. 1:60.09.
1st Heat (6 laps)—1, Chuck Leighton; 2, Jimmy Davies; 3, Ken Stanberry. 3:50.03.
2nd Heat (6 laps)—1, Dick Hughes; 2, Yam Oka; 3, Puffy Puffer. 3:80.01.
3rd Heat (6 laps)—1, Jay Frank; 2, Manuel Ayulo; 3, Troy Ruttman. 3:60.04.
4th Heat (6 laps)—1, Gordy Reid; 2, Jack McGrath. 3:03.39.
Semi-Main (26 laps)—1, Troy Ruttman; 2, Jay Frank; 3, Manuel Ayulo. 13:10.55.
Main (25 laps)—1, Don Freeland; 2, Yam Oka; 3, Lou Figaro. 12:50.58.
Run-off (10 laps)—1, Troy Ruttman; 2, Yam Oka; 3, Lou Figaro. 5:00.43.

CARRELL SPEEDWAY, Gardena, Calif., April 18, 1948; 1/2-mile.
Trophy Dash (3 laps)—1, Lou Figaro; 2, Frank McGurk. 1:08.18.
1st Heat (6 laps)—1, Harry Stockman; 2, Red Amic; 3, Bob Williams. 2:27.30.
2nd Heat (6 laps)—1, Dempsey Wilson; 2, Chuck Leighton; 3, Jim Rigsby. 2:22.50.
3rd Heat (6 laps)—1, Puffy Puffer; 2, Jay Frank; 3, Bruce Blair. 2:20.70.
4th Heat (6 laps)—1, Don Freeland; 2, Leroy Nooks; 3, Jimmy Davies. 2:17.25.
Semi Main (15 laps)—1, Dempsey Wilson; 2, Harry Stockman; 3, Jim Rigsby. 5:54.90.
Main (25 laps)—1, Jim Davies; 2, Yam Oka; 3, Don Freeland, 9:15.10.

CHR

LAS VEGAS, Last Frontier Sportsdrome, 1/5 mile-banked, April 4, 1948.
Fastest qualifying time, :13:84, set by Jim Rathman.
Trophy Dash (3 laps)—1, Jim Rathman; 2, Stan Kross. :42.34.
1st Heat (6 laps)—1, Grant Caspar; 2, Gordon Cox; 3, Dick Benninger. 1:38.86.
2nd Heat (6 laps)—1, Bud Gregory; 2, Dan Tracy; 3, Bud Van Mannen. 1:26.55.
3rd Heat (6 laps)—1, Ed Ball; 2, Wayne Tipton; 3, Pat Flaherty. 1:25.78.
4th Heat (6 laps)—1, Fred Ryness; 2, Jim Rathman; 3, Stan Kross. 1:25.55.
Semi-Main (15 laps)—1, Bud Gregory; 2, Bud Van Mannen; 3, Dan Tracy. 4:57.99.
Main (30 laps)—1, Ed Ball; 2, Colby Scroggins; 3, Jim Rathman. 7:11.97.

CHR — Cont.

BONELLI STADIUM, Saugus, Calif. 1/3 mile, April 11, 1948.
Fastest qualifying time, :19.04, set by Jim Rathman.
Trophy Dash (3 laps)—1, Jim Rathman; 2, Pat Flaherty. :58.91.
1st Heat (6 laps)—1, Vern Slankard; 2, Steve Dusich; 3, Lyle Dickey. 2:01.55.
2nd Heat (6 laps)—1, Bud Gregory; 2, Mackey Davis; 3, Stan Kross. 4:01.32.
3rd Heat (6 laps)—1, Archie Tipton; 2, Colby Scroggins; 3, Jim Rathman. 1:57.52.
4th Heat (6 laps)—1, Pat Flaherty; 2, Bob Lindsey; 3, Fred Ryness. 1:57.56.
A "pie" race was held wherein the drivers stopped their cars on the back stretch, ran across the field, picked up pies. The first to finish his pie won the race. Don Nichelson was the winner.
Semi-Main (25 laps)—1, Jim Rathman; 2, Colby Scroggins; 3, Bob Cross. 8:14.92.
Main (25 laps)—1, Pat Flaherty; 2, Bob Lindsey; 3, Wayne Tipton. 8:34.71.
Run-off (10 laps)—1, Jim Rathman; 2, Colby Scroggins; 3, Pat Flaherty. 3:01.24.

RRAO (Oregon)

PORTLAND, 5/8-mile paved, April 11, 1948. (This was the first RRAO race of the season. It drew nearly 8,000 spectators.)
Fastest qualifying time, :25.24, set by Bob Gregg. This was a new track record; however, Gregg's spindle arm broke and he was unable to get back into the show until the last heat.
Trophy Dash—1, Len Sutton; 2, Jim Martin; 3, Dick Boubel.
1st Heat—1, Len Sutton; 2, Jim Martin; 3, Gordy Youngstrom.
2nd Heat—1, Leo Wahl; 2, Dick Doubel; 3, Darmond Moore.
3rd Heat—1, Andy Wilson; 2, Max Humm; 3, Dave Ware.
4th Heat—1, Bob Gregg; 2, Don Miller; 3, Bob Marco (Hudson).
Semi-Main—7, Arman Millen (Chev); 2, Bill Wade (Chev); 3, Don Crockett.
Main—7, Bob Gregg; 2, Len Sutton; 3, Dick Doubel.

PVRA (Pecas Valley Racing Association)

ROSWELL SPEEDWAY, Roswell, New Mexico, March 26, 1948, 1/2 mile.
Helmet Dash (4 laps)—71, Earl Emmons.
2nd Heat (6 laps)—1, Gale Napp; 2, Art Lambert.
3rd Heat (6 laps)—1, Earl Emmons; 2, Earl Farris.
Semi-Main (15 laps)—1, Art Lambert; 2, Gale Napp.
Main (20 laps)—1, Earl Emmons; 2, Gale Napp.

TATTERSFIELD — *Baron*   *Racing Equipment*

High Type Risers

● **NEW** ●

→ **4 Carburetor Manifold**
→ **Special High Compression Cylinder Heads**
→ **Special Pistons**
→ **Venturi Type Stacks**
→ **Large Cast Gas Lines**

2 ADVANTAGES

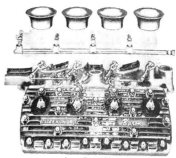

Low Type Risers

MULTIPLE VENTURI SYSTEM

A Tattersfield-Baron four carburetor manifold has eight venturi tubes. On a Ford V8 and Mercury installation, for example, this means one venturi tube for each cylinder insuring the absolute packing of every cylinder with a power-loaded charge of combustible gas. This multiple venturi construction, by reducing the demand on each tube, produces even mix‘ure with plenty of air and thus gives greater power and speed.

ISOLATION OF GASES

With ordinary manifolds there is often a tendency for one cylinder to "rob" another. This cannot happen with a TATTERSFIELD-BARON manifold. Provision has been made for individual distr bution of gases to each cylinder, with complete partitioning to prevent any possibility of "theft" or over-lap. The net result is the packing of each cylinder with a uniform and complete charge of fuel.

For thrilling new economy or speed install a

TATTERSFIELD-BARON FOUR CARBURETOR manifold on your Ford or Mercury

A COMBINATION DESIGNED FOR EVERY SPEED RANGE

IF IT'S A RECORD YOU WANT, INSTALL A TATTERSFIELD-BARON SPEED UNIT TODAY

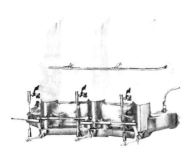

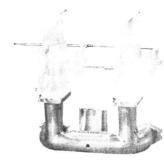

—FORD 6—
This manifold is designed to use 2 or 3 carburetors more efficiently than with only 1 carburetor.

—FORD 60—
Illustrated is the new Ford 60 manifold with many new added features—Adds more dynamic power to your 60 midget.

—FORD "A"—
This manifold can be purchased in either single or dual carburetion.

→ **Many other types of Manifolds are available for your truck or passenger car.**

→ **Write today for information regarding dual Carburetion on your own car.**

Manifold Division

ELECTRIC & CARBURETOR ENG. CO.

2321-23 E. 8th St.,   TR. 4863   **Los Angeles 21, California**

HOT ROD
Magazine

25c

Iskenderian in his T Roadster   JUNE, 1948   25c

SHARP SPEED EQUIPMENT

6225 Wilmington Avenue   **LOgan 5-1329**   **Los Angeles, Calif.**

Sharp High Compression Head

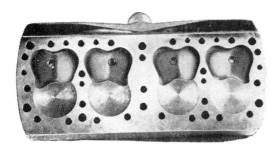

THE

SHARP

TRIPLET

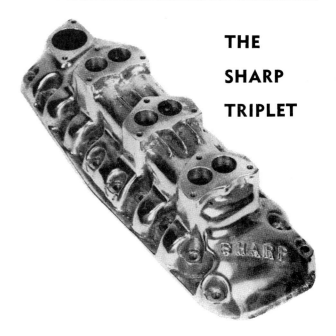

The new Sharp head gives maximum efficiency in acceleration as well as top speed. The Combustion Chamber is designed to allow adequate breathing at any R.P.M. The water capacity of the head is almost double over the stock heads. Two directional flow ribs over each cylinder assures even cooling, the extra width acting as a water manifold to eliminate steam pockets, thus reducing heat and giving more efficiency. The metal used in the heads is of the highest alloy obtainable. Each head is heat treated to eliminate corrosion and warping as well as increasing the tensile strength of the material. The heads are tested under 45 lbs. water pressure for leaks. **Compression ratios 8.75 to 10-1.**

★

SHARP cams for tracks, lakes and road.

This new manifold is patterned after the **Sharp Dual Manifold**, having the same port routing, thus giving perfect distribution to all ports. This action assures perfect acceleration from idling to peak R.P.M. with **no flat spots.**

SEE YOUR DEALER Or Write For Information

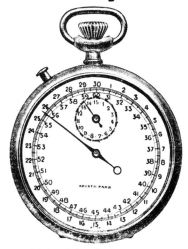

It's in the Bag . . .

Hot Rod Magazine:

. . . Here is my check for $3.00 to start me off—with the March issue, please, if you are not sold out on it.

When I get things a little more organized, I hope to be able to send you some pics.

F. T. VAN BEUREN
Mexico City, Mexico.

* * *

Hot Rod Magazine:

Why not have an Index to Advertisers in each issue? It would save everybody a lot of thumbing and hunting.

A. W. ALEXANDER
Crankshaft Co.
Los Angeles, Calif.

Starting with this issue, HRM carries an advertiser index in the back of the magazine. Thanx to Mr. Alexander for the suggestion.—ED.

* * *

Gentlemen:

. . . I'm very interested in your mag and own a ¾ race Merc in a '39 Ford convertible chassis. Also a member of the "Blow-By's," a Kansas City "rod" club.

PAUL D. WILSON, JR.
Kansas City, Mo.

Sirs:

After having looked through your March edition, I was interested enough to pay $5.00 for the copy from a person passing through my home town . . . Never saw a magazine of its kind before. I am building a cut-down '32 V-8 Roadster and your magazine has many helpful suggestions.

DICK ROADS
Marion, Ohio

* * *

Dear Sirs:

. . . I had no idea such a swell magazine existed until I purchased a copy of your March issue from Grancors in Chicago. We really don't get much Hot Rod info here in the Middle West and your mag is certainly doing a good job.

BUD ARMSTRONG
Kankakee, Ill.

* * *

Dear Sirs:

We saw your January issue and we are enclosing a subscription taken from that issue. Your magazine really hits the spot up here north of Frisco. Roadster racing has the crowd going in Oakland and we hope to have it here soon. Congratulations of your swell publication.

IVER HANSEN
DAVID CONDON
BILL FERGUSON
of Roadsters, Inc.
Marin County, Calif.

AFTER A RECENT RACE
P-F-T-T-T!

—Drawing by Ferguson

Dear Friends:

I was very glad to learn of your new magazine and I wish you lots of luck with it.

I teach Auto Shop at Montebello Sr. High School, and since I came into the field through hot rod activity, I am still very, very interested in the stuff. Also, I find it one of the best ways to get student interest in the shop program.

Therefore, will you please enter my name on your subscription list and start back with the first issue because I want to keep a full file of the magazine in my office for the students to use.

JOE COFFIN
Whittier, Calif.

* * *

Hot Rod Magazine:

. . . Your magazine certainly hits the spot! The sport is greatly benefitted by its work, both from good public relations it helps create and from the spreading of factual information to its fans and participants over a very large area.

BOB MCGEE
Gear Grinders, S.C.T.A.
Huntington Park, Calif.

* * *

Gentlemen:

Your March issue has arrived to give me quite a thrill. Having been present for Don's (Blair, Hot Rod of the Month, March.) original tinkering with a "hop up" (now "hot rod") and subsequently having watched its growth into a hobby and later a vocation, I was more than interested in your fine, though short, article entitled "Hot Rod of the Month." It is accurate and well written. I was also very pleased to see Don's picture on your cover. It has been two years since I saw my brother and I certainly had no idea he had come so far in this business of building and racing cars.

Thank you for a fine article and photograph to bring me up to date.

CECELIA BLAIR PALM
Trieste, Italy

Editor's Column

Hot Rod of the Month of June is Ed Iskenderian's custom-built T-V8. Most of the work, body and engine alike, on this smooth job was done by Ed himself.

For mechanical interest, HRM offers the readers Bob Tattersfield's PISTONS AND DESIGNS. The story, with illustrations, starts on page 8. Also, along a technical line, is W. I. 'Bill' Gieseke's article on CARBURETION AND SUPERCHARGERS. This feature, also fully illustrated, begins on page 18.

On pages 10 and 11, Wally Parks, Executive Secretary of S.C.T.A., Inc., does a complete write-up of S.C.T.A.'s first 1948 time trials. Parks, very active in the Association, has done much to further smooth operation of S.C.T.A.'s lakes meets.

Russetta Timing's first meet of the year also receives full coverage in this issue. Some of RTA's coupes are knocking off excellent times this year.

ORIGIN OF A SPEED SHOP gives readers an idea of the growth of hot rod building, racing, and timing. This feature is written by Lee Chapel, who still operates his own shop.

NCRRA, which presents some of the nation's finest hot rod racing, is well represented in HRM's June edition. Pictures of their races appear on page 9.

Interested in custom cams? Interested in redheads? In either case, don't overlook this month's PARTS WITH APPEAL. (Page 23, fellows!)

HOT ROD DRIVERS AT INDIANAPOLIS is another spot feature of HRM's June issue.

Remember, whenever you patronize our advertisers (and we hope it is often) be sure to mention that you saw their ads in HOT ROD MAGAZINE.

Beginning with our July issue we will carry a page of close-up news of the nation's leading hot rod builders and drivers. Will your Association be represented? If not, speak to your Association officers and ask them to contact HRM.

A REMINDER — that our new address is 7164 Melrose Avenue, Los Angeles 46, California. Please send all correspondence to this address.

You can't send us too many snapshots and stories. Just try!

—ED.

HOT ROD Magazine
WORLD'S MOST COMPLETE HOT ROD COVERAGE

TABLE OF CONTENTS

HOT ROD MAGAZINE, U.S. Copyright 1948 by the Hot Rod Publishing Company, 7164 Melrose Avenue, Los Angeles 46, California.

SUBSCRIPTION PRICE: $3.00 per year throughout the world.

VOL. I   **HRM—Published Monthly**   No. 6

Associate Editors .... Robert R. Lindsay
                                                                     Robert E. Petersen
Advertising Manager .... Richard Sabotka
Photography .... Lee Blaisdell, Dyson Smith
                                                             Alan Dean, Paul Schaeffer
Cartoons and Humor .... Tom Medley
Reporters .... Robert Williams, Glenn Glendening
                                                       Dick Robinson, Richard K. Martin
                                          Arthur Elliot, William H. Sippel, Bob Machin

QUESTIONS AND ANSWERS

Q. Can you get Johnnie Lucas' address for me?

FRANK HEATON,
Tucson, Arizona

A. Johnnie Lucas (President, California Hot Rods, Inc.) lives at 6525 Sunset Blvd., Hollywood, Calif.

Q. I have a coupe which I would like to clock. Since S.C.T.A. does not time them, I was wondering if you could tell me what timing assn. does and when.

Is there an age limit to run through and what are the safety rules?

HAROLD HADLEY
Santa Barbara, Calif.

A. Coupes run in several classes in the Russetta Timing Assn. The rules and schedule for R.T.A. were printed in the May issue of HRM. Drivers in Russetta meets must be 21 years old, or, if younger, have an affidavit signed by their parents and notarized—giving them permission to drive at the lakes meets.

Russetta Timing may be contacted by writing Nellie Taylor (Assn. president) at 2667 W. Whittier Blvd., Whittier, Calif.

Gentlemen:

I have a '36 Ford 3-window coupe with a '36 block bored .030 over. It has stock heads and cam. I am running an Edelbrock regular manifold with two Stromberg 97's. I have a 4.11 rear end and Zephyr gears in the transmission. My questions are, what you do for a cam, what type of heads should I use, or how much is advised for milling my own heads. I don't intend to port and relieve the block. With a cam, would I be better off by tipping the valves or putting in adjustable tappets? With the Zephyr, what gears would you put in the rear end for gear ratio? I want the most jump that I can get. . . . I thank you very much, and I think you have a wonderful thing. Keep it going. I will be looking forward to every issue of HRM to come.

—A Faithful HRM Subscriber
Glendale, Calif.

A. A semi-race cam is recommended for all-round performance in your particular case. There are several makes of heads that you could use. (Eddie Meyer and Cyclone). If you mill your own heads, it is advisable not to take off more than .100 or you may run into trouble. By all means, use adjustable tappets as you will find that they are actually cheaper in the long run. As for jump, a low gear in the rear end (preferably 4.11) should prove satisfactory.

Q. Could you inform me as to the top speed (clocked time) of 1947 or 1948 American sedan cars?

R. J. PHILLIPS
Vallejo, Calif.

A. No official clocked times have been given out on these models.

Q. Several weeks ago a new asphalt track opened here in Salinas, and a boy named Pat Flaherty from down Los Angeles way walked off with every race he entered. Flaherty drove car No. 88—a '27 T with a Wayne equipped Chevy engine. I have never seen a car handle so well; it never skidded appreciably on the turns and its control on them was unbelievable.

I think these characteristics may have resulted at least in part from the car's unorthodox front wheel setup. The thing I noticed was that the camber angle of the right front wheel was such that the top slanted toward the inside; that is, the whole wheel slanted so that the top was closer to the inside than the bottom was. Now, what I would like to know is exactly what the builders of the car did to the front wheels and steering mechanism, upon what theories they based their arrangement, what results may be expected, if other car builders have used such a setup, and any other information there may be pertaining to the subject.

CLAY ALSHERGE
Salinas, Calif.

A. At the time mentioned above, No. 88 was running with about a 5° angle on the right front. Recently the angle was changed to 3°. The steering mechanism didn't need alteration with such a small degree of slant. The builders believe this arrangement affords a better "grip" for the right front which carries a good deal of strain on the tracks.

This setup is not uncommon in hot rod track jobs. However, its use—and especially the degree itself—are up to the builders and drivers. (There is considerable difference of opinion on this point.)

Q. Could you tell me where I get adjustable tappets for a '29 Ford "A"?

ERIC W. MAURER
New Haven, Conn.

A. Tappets from a 4-cylinder Essex will fit a '29 Ford A. These, however, are very hard to find. Some builders recommend tappets from Plymouths, late 4's and early 6s. (These need some grinding to fit. At the same time the heads need reaming.)

Buck Taylor of Hollywood is using tappets from late Oldsmobiles. These are ground about 1/32" and fit very well.

Readers and Advertisers

We wish to take this opportunity to thank our many readers and advertisers for their complete support during the early months of our publication. Through their help and cooperation this magazine has been a complete "sell-out" since it was first put on sale.

*In the last six months the magazine has expanded to a present press run of 15,000. Eight pages have been added. Advertising has tripled since the first issue.

Our aim is to please the readers and advertisers. Whenever they have suggested changes or additions, these suggestions have been thoroughly considered, and, wherever practicable, enforced.

The magazine which boasts the "World's Most Complete Hot Rod Coverage" gratefully looks back on its first six months in existence and anxiously turns toward the future.

Sincerely yours,

ROBERT R. LINDSAY, ROBERT E. PETERSEN
Associate Editors and Publishers

*The certified statement of press run, 15,000 monthly, of Hot Rod Magazine is hereby acknowledged.

VER HALEN PRESS

Thos. A. Wood

by THOMAS A. WOOD,
General Manager

Hot Rod of the Month

Ed Iskenderian's T-V8 is an excellent example of craftsmanship on the part of hot rod builders. Ed not only did much of the custom work on the car's body but on the engine as well.

Iskenderian, a native Californian, was born in Tulare, moving to Los Angeles at the ripe age of one year. There he went through school, graduating from Dorsey High.

Long before leaving school, Ed began to work with cars. At 14 he did his first experimental engine work, tinkering with model T's, at that time considerably less expensive than they are today. When he was 16 he built his first hot rod, a Fronty T. After that he put together an 8 spark Multi-Flathead. (Riley equipped.)

The following year Ed decided to turn his attentions to V8's. It seemed that T cranks broke too often and too easily for the young mechanic. His first V8, however, was in a T body. In 1939 Iskenderian ran his V8 roadster at an S.C.T.A. meet on Harper Dry Lake, clocking 97 mph.

Ed built the cover car in 1940. Probably the most outstanding feature of the car is the Maxi Overheads, which Ed rebuilt to his own specifications. He made his own head covers, also filled the combustion chambers to suit the new setup. The block is '32 Ford. The roadster is running a Navarro dual manifold. Cylinders are bored to Merc. Engine is ported and relieved. Body work was done by Jimmy Summers. (Ed put on the finishing touches with a change here and there.) Also of his own design are the copper head gaskets which take

Top view of the engine shows overhead valve covers and scrolled firewall.

him two days apiece to build. The distributor is a Zephyr. (Ed did the converting.) The cam, of course, is Iskenderian. For the upholstery work, he finally had to get outside help. Laddie Jerbeck did the interior.

This car turned 120 mph at a Western Timing Association meet at El Mirage. Ed hopes to better that time in dry lakes competition in the near future. For the lakes he runs 600x16's on all four wheels. The car has a 3.78 rear end. Hydraulic brakes are a safety feature. The

attractive grill is made from the grills of two 1934 Pontiacs. (The top halves were cut off and fused together.) Steering is by Franklin. The car has Essex frame rails. Ed uses streamlined airplane struts for light brackets. The rear end suspension is '32 Ford with housing reversed (placing spring ahead of axle, lowering car a few inches).

Just one year ago Ed was married. He and his wife, Alice, are now the proud parents of a son, Roland. Right now Ed is biding his time 'til he can check Roland out in his hot rod. Mrs. Iskenderian thinks that the car is definitely not meant to be used by women with long hair. "I just finish getting all dressed up for a party, with my hair done up just so and . . . half a block's ride in the car finds my hair right back down in my face."

The car is nicknamed "La Cucaracha," a title jokingly given it in 1940 by a Mexican sheriff. The name has stuck with it ever since the Mexican trip.

Ed, a one-time cycle fan, drives his own car at dry lakes time trials. Years ago his hobby was radio building. However, he gave it up to devote all of his spare time to car building. Today Ed Iskenderian spends all of his time in automotive work. He manufactures Iskenderian custom cams in Los Angeles.

The June Hot Rod of the Month rates admiring comment wherever it goes. But, believe it or not, Ed bought the whole '24 T from which the body was made for only $4.00. That was in 1939. Just try to buy it now.

Interior has well-equipped dash with tachometer mounted in steering wheel bracket.

Pistons and Designs *By Robert Tattersfield*

Pistons, to the average individual, are just another moving part in a motor. This part, unlike most of the others in the motor, has been experimented with by engineers comparatively less than any of the other component working parts. It is generally understood that the purpose of a piston is to transfer the combustible power to the connecting rod, from there to the crankshaft, then to the transmission and to the rear end, then finally transferred to the drive wheels. With this in mind, a piston is the starting point for power in any combustible motor.

Through time, a few different types of pistons have been tried, some successfully while others not so successfully. Possibly the first piston ever used was of a cast iron nature, later steel pistons were introduced; then came the high speed era and the engineers decided that magnesium and aluminum were more suitable for hi-speed pistons.

However, there is a definite advantage to each metal used in piston design, taking first the use of cast iron in pistons. Primarily, the advantage for this is the long life and quiet operation derived in its use; its disadvantage is the excessive weight resulting in short bearing life at higher R.P.M.'s. The steel piston has the same advantages as iron while steel is slightly lighter and carries a much higher tensile strength. Metallurgists have been working on aluminum alloys for many years with a final outcome of some very close structure metal with an increasingly high tensile strength.

The aluminum alloys now largely used in pistons proves that lightness and strength is essential where higher speeds are concerned. With their use it has been found that this light metal has proven best for heat dissipation while other tests show that uniform heat, prevalent in this metal, has a definite advantage as far as wearing ability is concerned. So, from this point on, the conversation will be that of aluminum alloy in the manufacturing of pistons.

There are three specific designs on the market today that are most widely known and used. First we will take the tee slotted or trans-slotted types which are used extensively by the present-day car manufacturers. This is a piston that is slotted either diagonally or horizontally in the skirt of the piston to afford a closer fit. Naturally with a close fit and the expansion of the piston due to heat, the slots afford the expansion to take place with the least amount of wear, resulting in a quieter running motor. The second type used primarily in racing is the solid skirt design. These are usually made with all the stress afforded in a high compression racing piston. You will find this design being used where close tolerances are not being held. The last type is the so-called slipper type. This is similar to the second in construction with the exception of having the skirt extend down below the pin bosses while the skirt has been removed from the opposite sides. This idea being to make a piston as light as possible for the high-speed racing motors.

The next question in mind is that the average person has a fallacy that, because of all the cylinders being bored perfectly round, the pistons themselves should also be round. This is not true in most present-day pistons, so an operational procedure termed "CAM GROUND" is administered. The reason being to prevent a piston from sticking or galling the sides of the cylinder walls. Where a piston distorts through excessive wear and heat is at the pin bosses, consequently if the piston is turned slightly off center, it remedies the biggest cause of piston failures, and that being before-mentioned—no sticking or galling.

If the reader recalls, we have not mentioned the height variation of any of the present-styled pistons. It so happens that the present manufacturers have kept the doming height to a minimum, thus the piston moves up only slightly into the combustion chamber. This holds true in L-type motors only. Engineers have proven that the overhead-valve type motor is the best style of all for fuel flow. This being because of the way the valves are situated directly over the piston, consequently the cylinder is able to take a better charge of cumbustible gases at higher speeds than that of the L-type motor.

On overhead-valve type racing motors, engineers have proven that by piston design rather than combustion chamber design they are able to receive a better flow of fuel at all speed ranges so the high-domed piston was introduced on the market for overhead motors with remarkable results. The thought then came to mind about incorporating this same piston idea into the L-type motors, the result being a motor of high compression ratio as well as smoothness at every speed.

In the designing of high compression L-type motors, the combustion chamber has to be reduced to a point where the flow of gas into the piston chamber has been restricted, creating design problems.

When considering the advantages of the special high-domed piston over the conventional standard design, examine Figures 1 and 2.

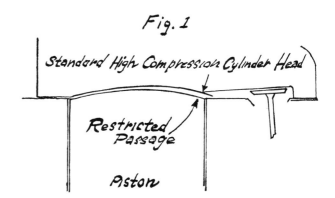

Fig. 1

Standard High Compression Cylinder Head

Restricted Passage

Piston

You will note, in Figure 1, the disadvantage of the standard design in a high-speed motor using high-compression heads and standard designed pistons. This naturally means at high speeds the motor is unable to receive a sufficient amount of fuel and the motor experiences a choking-off effect. In other words, the flow of fuel from the intake valves are restricted into the piston chamber. Thus the motor is unable to take full advantage of the high compressions needed for higher octane fuels.

Please note, in Fig. 2 (page 31) the advantage of the special high-domed piston protruding into the cylinder head. The results are that a motor running at higher speeds is able to receive a more nearly complete charge of combustible fuel at the time it is needed most and is able to take full advantage of higher compression fuels.

Referring to Figure 1, note the small passage into the piston chamber. Refer to Figure 2 and note how engineering design, utilizing the high-dome piston, enables us to an open passage into the piston chamber regardless of the compression ratio, whether it be 8 to 1 or 13 to 1.

(Continued on Page 31)

DANA PHOTOS by RI

NCRRA Drivers are off to a fast start of the featured main event. Double-decker stands are at Bayshore Stadium in San Francisco.

Al Neves (18) seems to be airborne as he trys to find an opening. Others shown are Al Berndt (38) and Larry Terra (far side). (Bayshore Stadium).

Northern California Roadster Racing Association

The Northern California Roadster Racing Association recently started its 1948 season. These pictures illustrate some of the fine action witnessed by Northern California fans. NCRRA, which was formed just two years ago, ranks with top racing associations in the United States.

NCRRA puts "safety first" ahead of everything else in staging its races.

Last year NCRRA raced before approximately 300,000 fans. In 1948 they expect to reach an even greater audience.

Listed here and on Page 30 are results from NCRAA pre-season and opening races.

HIGHWAY 99 STADIUM, Stockton, Calif—May 9—Fastest qualifying time, :16.82, set by Sam Hawks.

Trophy Dash (3 laps)—1, Lemoine Frey; 2, Sam Hawks. :50.40.

First Heat (5 laps)—1, Bob Earl; 2, Mel Alexander; 3, Chuck Harwood. 1:33.30.

Second Heat (5 laps)—1, Ernie Reyes; 2, Gene Smith; 3, Joe Huffaker. 1:33.10.

Third Heat (5 laps)—1, Al Germolis; 2, George Danburg; 3, George Mehalas. 1:28.30.

Fourth Heat (5 laps)—1, Wayne Selser; 2, Bill Sullivan; 3, Bob Machin. 1:26.80.

Fifth Heat (5 laps)—1, Lemoine Frey; 2, Sam Hawks; 3, Ed Elisian. 1:25.90.

Second Place Winner Final (6 laps)—1, Bill Sullivan; 2, Mel Alexander; 3, George Danburg. 1:59.20.

First Place Winner Final (6 laps)—1, Lemoine Frey; 2, Wayne Selser; 3, Al Germolis. 1:43.90.

Semi-Main (15 laps)—1, Al Germolis; 2, Larry Terra; 3, Ernie Reyes. 4:41.40.

Main (25 laps)—1, Sam Hawks; 2, Al Neves; 3, Joe Valente. 7:30.90.

BAYSHORE STADIUM, San Francisco—April 25—Fastest qualifying time, :18.05, was set by Sam Hawks.

Trophy Dash (3 laps)—1, Joe Valente; 2, Sam Hawks. :58.10.

First Heat (5 laps)—1, Carl West; George Danburg; 3, George Mehalas. 1:45.60..

Second Heat (5 laps)—1, Mel Alexander; 2, Al Berndt; 3, Bob McLean. 1:44.60.

Third Heat (5 laps)—1, Gene Tessian; 2, Lloyd Selacci; 3, George Pacheco. 1:40.80.

Fourth Heat (5 laps)—1, Lemoine Frey; 2, Bill Sullivan; 3, Al Neves. 1:40.60.

Fifth Heat (5 laps)—7, Wayne Selser; 2, Ed Elisian; 3, Sam Hawks. 1:43.20.

Second Place Winner Final (6 laps)—1, George Danburg; 2, Al Berndt; 3, Lloyd Sellacci. 2:01.10.

First Place Winner Final (6 laps)—1, Gene Tessian; 2, Wayne Selser; 3, Carl West. 1:59.10.

Semi-Main (15 laps)—1, George Mehalas; 2, Ed Huntington; 3, Gene Tessian. 4:58.50.

Main (25 laps)—1, George Pacheco; 2, Bob Machin; 3, Sam Hawks. 7:48.80.

During a race at Contra Costa Stadium (Pacheco, Calif.) Joe Valente (3) overtakes and almost overruns Al Germolis (15).

Lemoine Frey (9) Leads George Mehalas (2) and Al Germolis (15) into some three-lane traffic during a race in San Francisco. (Bayshore Stadium).

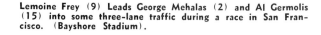

New three lane starting light system, allowing drivers to leave at 20 second intervals, proved a great success. Actress Sara Bianco (right) and Harvey Haller, first man through the course, officially open the 1948 S.C.T.A. season.

Owner Regg Schlemmer (above) congratulates driver Niel Davis on attaining an all time one-way roadster speed of 148.27 in the Merc. powered '27 T Ford. Powered by a Chevy 4 engine, the Spurgin-Giovanine roadster (below) captured the A class record with a two-way time of 113.95.

S.C.T.A. OPENS

On Saturday, April 24, the Southern California Timing Association opened its current season's Time Trials with the first of its two-day meets. Running at El Mirage Dry Lake, which is just 35 miles east of Palmdale in the Mojave Desert, the boys got off to a good start with several cars topping existing class records the first day.

Outstanding feature of Saturday's running was the setting of a new record for Class 'B' Streamliners by Stuart Hilborn's sleek black #11 which is powered with a '34 Ford V8 engine. Under the skillful piloting of Howard Wilson, Hilborn's car made the two-directional runs at an average speed of 145.640 mph.

Although the first day's trials were run under favorable conditions, a steadily increasing wind arose which boosted the times considerably as the day progressed, and blew so strongly on Sunday that visibility was impaired by the dust which arose from the lake. A new course was laid out for both Sat. and Sun. running, but the condition of the bed's surface made the trials difficult.

In keeping with its policy toward providing the utmost in safety precautions for these competition meets, S. C. T. A. had many new experimental features in evidence. A completely new set of course markers were in use and proved to be very successful in the face of the strong winds. They consisted of the new-type flexible rubber traffic cones painted red and white, and made an impressive appearance as they stretched in two lanes out across the lake bed's horizon.

A modern system of automatic starting was accomplished by use of an electrical traffic-light system which rotated cars out of three lanes on regular twenty-second intervals. This system was controlled by the Starter from high atop his starting line judges' stand where at a master panel he could control the interval between cars in order to prevent faster cars from overtaking their preceding cars on the course. A series of three observation stations were located alongside the course where their crews could watch from their lofty seats for any difficulties along the route and, through use of a new inter-communication system, keep the starters informed on the running and course conditions in their sectors. Each post was also equipped with a red signal light for warning approaching cars of any danger ahead.

Of the 230 cars entered in the meet, 191 completed timed runs through the course before the running was called off early Sunday due to hazardous wind and course conditions. Only 15 of these qualified under 100 miles per hour. Many of those waiting at the starting line when the meet was called off would undoubtedly have turned some very fast times had they been permitted to run.

That the Times and Speeds attained in S. C. T. A. competition are accurate beyond all doubt is assured through the fact that the personal services and equipment of Mr. J. O. Crocker were

B Class record holder at 129.356 is Doug Hartelt's Merc. bore '25 T roadster that has been consistently high in point standings. Powered by a '34 V-8 engine, Stuart Hilborn's B Class streamliner (left) set a new record of 145.64 with Howard Wilson at the wheel.

1948 SEASON

By WALLY PARKS

utilized. Mr. Crocker, who is also Chief Timer for the American Powerboat Assn., has handled the timing of these events over the past years and his equipment is of the most advanced and highly developed in use anywhere. Countless periodic checks and certified tests by outstanding chronological institutions have endorsed its accuracy to the most minute degree. The device is entirely electronic and uses tele-photo light-beam equipment that is effected by neither dust nor glare and can be used on courses of quarter-mile width or more if necessary. The timed distance is one-quarter mile in length with a one-and-one-half mile approach.

An amazing Roadster speed of 148.27 miles per hour was made on a one-way run by Regg Schlemmer's Mercury-powered '27 T Roadster. The car was driven by Neil Davis (this was his first ride in the car) and they established a new record for 'C' Class Roadsters at 138.975 mph average. This car at its initial appearance last season set a class record of 136.050 mph and presents a beautiful appearance.

In the 'B' Roadster class,' Doug Hartelt who held the record of 126.17 mph successfully raised it to 129.356 mph and made a one-way time of 134.93. Doug runs a Merc-bore engine, in the 183 to 250 cubic inch class, with a '25 T Roadster body and was the 1947 Season Champion in the Roadster competition for points.

In the small-engine 'A' class, which has been raised from 150 cu. in. to include engines up to 183 inches, the re-

juvenated Chevrolet 4 of the Spurgin & Giovanine team set a record for 'A' Roadsters at 113.950 mph average, and turned a qualifying speed of 120.32 mph on their one-way run. The car, a '25 Chevy Roadster has been lowered and streamlined into a neat appearing little machine which promises to add consistent interest in its class throughout the season. Bob Rufi, whose record of 140 mph set in 1940 has until this year remained unequalled in the Streamliner class, is an enthusiastic asset to the Spurgin-Giovanine team in keeping the car outstanding. The four-inch exhaust emerging from the center of the turtleback shows a definite Rufi touch, as does the performance attained.

A new all-time top speed for lakes cars was made by the Burke & Francisco rear-engine Mercury wing-tank Streamliner. This car, driven by Johnny Johnson, turned 149.75 on a one-way run and averaged 144.855 mph for a new 'C' Streamliner record. The chassis was constructed from a P-38 fuel tank by Bill Burke and started the present popular trend in streamliner construction. The engine is a product of the efforts of Don Francisco who has been developing its capabilities on exhaustive dynamometer tests to good advantage.

Many other interesting speeds were made among the various classes by cars which kept the competition very keen. Paul Schiefer, from San Diego, turned a speed of 141.95 with his '25 T Mercury Rdstr. on a record run but failed

(Continued on Page 27)

Driver Johnny Johnson waves to the timer as he passes the finish after piloting the Burke-Francisco C Streamliner record holder 149.97 one-way. High in the air timer J. O. Crocker (below) records a roadster's speed with unfailing accuracy.

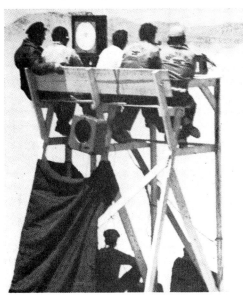

Burleigh Dolph of the Lancers in his rear-engine Class B roadster is pushed off from the starting line.

RUSSETTA TIMING ASSOCIATION

OPENING MEET OF '48 SEASON

The first Russetta meet under the new organizational setup was held at El Mirage Dry Lake in California on May 2, 1948, with many new records being set despite difficult weather conditions.

Fastest time of the meet was by Burleigh Dolph who turned 128.57 in his rear-engine Ford roadster. Ludwig Solberg in his '32 took the A Class roadster record with 126.97. Russetta vice-president, Bob Corbett, in his C Class '32 roadster clocked 122.78 to make another record.

Coupe times were very high with several coupes in the over 110 mph bracket. Bob Pierson drove his A Class '36 Ford through for the fastest coupe time recorded, a record 117.03. The B record went to Bill Young who turned 115.83 and the C record is 111.94 set by Carl Taylor.

Operation of the meet was well planned with members concentrating on strict technical inspections of fire extinguishers, safety belts, helmets, and running gear. Timing was done by Raymond Ingram, Russetta's official timer.

Russetta, a Greek name for the chariot drivers who drove red chariots pulled by white horses, is symbolic of winged speed. Brought up to date, the name is very appropriate for this rapidly expanding timing association.

Accelerating towards the traps is Ludwig Solberg in his '32 roadster. He holds Class A record at 126.97 mph.

Although very stock, the chow truck is quite popular with Russetta members and fans. A '40 Ford coupe (below) is piloted across the finish line by Ted Nielson at 106 mph.

At the timing truck Bob Pierson gets the good news that his '36 coupe turned a record time of 117.03. The engine is a full-Edelbrock '46 Merc. with a Harman cam.

MAY, 1948

ORIGIN OF A SPEED SHOP

By LEE CHAPEL

Some of our readers probably wonder how all this speed equipment and speed shops came about . .

The Speed Shop was located on San Fernando Road. (Note the "Hot Rods" parked outside.)
This building now houses the "Broken Drum Auto Supply."

It was quite by accident that I got started in this business early in 1930. Before that time there were no speed shops, as we know them now. There was considerable interest in Hot Rods and "Hopped-up Jobs," as we called them then, but anyone trying to build one was stymied as to where to get the necessary equipment. There were parts manufactured, to be sure, such as Morton & Brett, Rajo, Frontenac or Fronty, etc. The manufacturers were scattered all over the United States, and some of the equipment was pretty crude compared to what is available to-day at any large speed shop.

There had been hopped-up Model 'T' Fords running at the Dry Lakes as early as 1923.

In 1930 I worked at a wrecking yard at 3265 San Fernando Road in Los Angeles. At that time I had built a "Souped-up" Chevrolet into a one-man race car and was running at the old Legion Ascot Speedway. The car was stored at the wrecking yard where I worked. It was pushed out front each day, as it attracted quite a bit of attention.

One day the idea occurred to me to put a sign in the seat, listing a dozen or more assorted parts that I had accumulated and, for one reason or another, had not used. The sign was placed in the car. In a few days, the parts were sold. "Well," I thought, "those parts sold very easily. Why don't I gather all the odds and ends that other race car owners have around and sell them?"

So I proceeded to do so. Within three months, I obtained about half the building for a speed shop and was traveling California gathering up parts. They were mostly used ones, but readily sellable. My brother, Herman Chapel, took care of the shop. I remained in business at this location until 1933, then moved to larger quarters at 4557 Alhambra Ave., only a few blocks from the old Legion Ascot Speedway. I continued in business there until 1937, at which time the Speedway burned down.

When I finally closed up shop in Los Angeles, I toured the country with a Midget Race Car for about two years. I then settled in Oakland, California, where I re-opened and now operate a large shop.

Inside were thousands of parts hung from nails, rafters, whatever was handy.

TYPICAL TRACK ROADSTER
A NEW SPORT IS SWEEPING THE NATION

Gus Maanum

HOT ROD DRIVERS AT INDIANAPOLIS

Driver Rex May (left) and Mechanic Pete Clark, both former hot rod builders, ready their Indianapolis car for the big race.

Jack McGrath, CRA charter member and driver, will be among many hot rod representatives at the famed Memorial Day classic.

The Weidell entry (above) is powered by an Edelbrock equipped Mercury engine. Bob Estes, Inglewood, Calif., Lincoln-Mercury dealer, is sponsoring the car.

Manuel Ayulo of the CRA is scheduled to drive the Connie Weidell entry (left) in the big race. Ayulo is a veteran roadster pilot.

Connie Weidell poses in the car he built for the 1948 Indianapolis Race. He is noted for his Cadillac dry lakes entries.

Moving through the traps in his Merc. powered roadster is Lou Baney who clocked a time of 127.23 mph.
running Edelbrock equipment.

CHR drivers get the starting flag during a race at
Bonelli Stadium, Saugus, Calif.

To CHR victor, Jim Rathman, goes a kiss, but
Charlie the Clown seems just as happy to watch.

Jim Downie of Los Angeles in his '29 Roadster. Engine
is a '39 Merc. with Weiand heads and manifold. Cam
is by Smith.

Emile Leonardo (37) spins during NCRRA race at
Bayshore Stadium. George Danburg (5) passes him.

R.R.A.O. '27 T track pickup with a '41 stroked
Merc. 3/8 bore and Harman cam is property of Dick
Kamna of Oregon.

A '34 Ford roadster with a '37 La Salle engine
built by Bob Madrid of Santa Cruz, Calif.

D. G. Knezivich and his brother (left) with their
chopped '38 V8 sedan. The car has Lincoln V12
engine, Edelbrock manifold.

Chopped '32 Ford, 5 window, with Merc. bore Edelbrock engine is owned by Bill Pearson of Beverly Hills, Calif.

An unusual chain drive T roadster that made its appearance at a CHR meet, Bonelli Stadium, Calif.

At a Russetta meet is Bob Corbett in his '32 roadster with a 1/8 stroke Merc. engine using a Spalding ignition and Weber cam.

A "swell time" was had by participants in Russetta's first 1948 timing meet.

In the pits at Bonelli Stadium drivers get set for qualifying heats for a CHR race.

Midget driver Jimmy Reece of Oklahoma City runs this rod with Weiand, Spalding and Harmon equipment.

Jack Graden of Los Angeles built this '31 roadster with '46 Mercury engine.

This roadster is a '34 Ford with a Merc. stroker engine belonging to R.T.A. Timer Raymond Ingram.

CARBURETION & SUPERCHARGERS by W. I. "Bill" Gieseke

This column is written by W. I. "Bill" Gieseke of the Solv-X Chemical Company, manufacturing chemists for the jobbing trade. Mr. Gieseke is a member of the Society of Automotive Engineers of the American Chemical Society, with seven years as Automotive and Lubrication Engineer for a major oil company. For twelve years he was an instructor at Frank Wiggins Trade School in the Engine Test Laboratory and for two years served as an Air Corps Instructor.

RELATIVE HUMIDITY—Air contains not only its two chief ingredients, nitrogen and oxygen, but also a certain quantity of water. The capacity of air for holding water vapor varies with temperature, the capacity being greater as the temperature is raised. Air containing the maximum possible amount of moisture at a given temperature is said to be saturated; partial saturation is expressed as the relative humidity in percent. For example, a relative humidity of 50 percent indicates that the air contains only half as much moisture as it could contain if completely saturated. Temperature changes cause a variation in relative humidity, even though the total quantity of water vapor in the air remains the same.

AIR SATURATION — (DEW POINT).—To illustrate this point, air at 60°F. and 50 percent relative humidity is heated to 80°F. without the addition of moisture. At the increased temperature the percent of saturation is reduced. The relative humidity in this case will drop below 50 percent. On the other hand, a reduction in air temperature increases relative humidity, possibly to the point of saturation. If the cooling is continued after the saturation is obtained, precipitation must occur. The temperature at which moisture condenses from the atmosphere is known as the dew point. Relative humidity and dew point are somewhat related; in general, a high humidity will cause the dew point to be observed quite near the atmospheric temperature. A temperature of 70°F. and a dew point of 65°F. indicate a high humidity, since in this case a drop of only 5°F. will permit precipitation. Condensation of water vapor accounts for the water often observed on the outside of cold water pipes in damp weather. If conditions are such that precipitation occurs below 32°F., the moisture will be deposited in the form of frost and ice. Such formations are known to occur in some carburetion systems under certain conditions of operations.

LATENT HEAT OF VAPORIZATION.—During engine operation a decided drop in temperature will be noted in the carburetor barrels as a result of the rapid vaporization of fuel leaving the discharge nozzles. It is commonly known that a liquid absorbs heat as it enters the vapor state, this property being expressed as the latent heat of vaporization of a liquid. When large quantities of a liquid are vaporized the process often produces a temperature drop sufficient to freeze water; in fact, the principle involved is exactly the same as that employed in the operation of a mechanical refrigerator. Whenever the proper conditions of temperature and humidity are present, ice may form in carburetor passages in dangerous quantities.

FUEL AND AIR MIXTURES— Internal-combustion engines having carburetion systems are fairly sensitive to the proportioning of the fuel and air charge. In general, engines operating on gasoline will require approximately 15 pounds of air in order to burn 1 pound of gasoline completely. However, a theoretically perfect mixture ratio is not essential in all cases. Certain conditions may require the use of mixtures either richer or leaner than this average ratio. Gasoline and air mixtures can be ignited when the ratio is as rich as 7 to 1 and as lean as 20 to 1, but these values are most extreme and are therefore of little importance. In general, the useful mixture ratios are between 11 to 1 and 16 to 1, the exact setting being determined by consideration of power output, cylinder cooling, and other factors. It must be remembered in connection with fuel and air mixtures that proportions are expressed on the basis of weight, since a volumetric measurement of air would be subject to inaccuracies resulting from pressure and temperature variations. Fuel air ratios may be given either as a direct ratio, such as 12 to 1, or may be designated as a decimal fraction such as 0.083. The latter expression is best understood by converting it to a common fraction as follows: $0.083 = \dfrac{83}{1,000} = \dfrac{1}{12}$.

In either case the ratio is the same but the decimal fraction is probably more convenient, and so is quite often used in the calibration of instruments for indicating fuel air ratios.

In order to provide a continuous instrument indication of mixture ratio two methods are employed, direct measurement and exhaust gas analysis. Direct measurement involves the continuous indication of both fuel flow and mass air flow. Separate instruments may be used for those two readings, and the relative flow rates can be compared. Mixture ratio is determined by observing the comparative fuel and air consumptions. For example, a high air flow and a low fuel flow indicate a lean mixture, and conversely a low air flow and a high fuel flow are an indication of a rich mixture. Special scales can be provided in order to simplify the determination of the fuel air ratio. When properly corrected for variations in altitude and temperature, such instruments give very satisfactory results in laboratory work.

EXHAUST GAS ANALYSIS. — Exhaust analysis is based on the change in exhaust composition according to the mixture ratio of the charge being passed through an analyzing cell which explained, the mixture strength will alter the chemical nature of the exhaust gases, particularly the carbon dioxide and the carbon monoxide content. (This will be mentioned later in connection with the measurement of mixture ratios in a subsequent article). As the exhaust composition varies, the specific heat and thermal conductivity of the gases will be altered to such an extent that a sensitive electrical instrument will respond to such changes. Generally, a filtered sample of the exhaust gas is passed through an analyzing cell which contains resistance elements forming a part of an electrical circuit. In this way changes in exhaust analysis will cause the instrument to indicate such changes. The indicator proper is usually calibrated directly in fuel air ratios. Certain factors other than mixture strength, such as detonation and pre-ignition, will cause inaccurate readings, but such indications are generally not confusing if the basic principles of the instrument are understood.

MIXTURE VARIATIONS. — Improper mixtures will cause certain variations in engine performance and in many cases will seriously damage vital engine parts. Excessively rich mixtures are accompanied by a loss of power. Black smoke (free carbon) will appear in the exhaust when a rich mixture is burned, and carbon monoxide, a colorless but poisonous gas, will also be present. Very lean mixtures cause a loss of power and under certain conditions will result in serious overheating of the engine cylinders. Lean mixtures must be especially avoided when an engine is operating near its maximum output, and it is well to observe closely the cylinder head temperature whenever lean mixtures are used. If leaning is excessive, an engine may backfire through the induction system or stop completely. Backfiring is not to be confused with kickback, which is merely a tendency to reverse the direction of rotation when starting the engine and is caused by a highly advanced ignition timing or preignition. A backfire is caused by slow flame propagation resulting from a lean mixture, so that the charge is still burning when the cycle is completed (end of exhaust stroke). As the intake valve opens to admit the fresh charge to the cylinder, it is immediately ignited by the residual flame of the previous cycle. The flame travels back through the induction system burning all the combustible charge, and often will ignite any accumulation of gasoline near the carburetor.

VOLATILITY VS. STARTING CHARACTERISTICS.

When starting a cold engine, excessive quantities of liquid fuel are required in order that sufficient vapor may be present to form a combustible mixture. The non-volatile fractions of gasoline (heavy ends) do not assist in starting; in fact, such fractions are often harmful in that they tend to remove oil from the cylinder walls, thus lowering the compression in the cylinder. Since most gasolines possess only a moderate vapor pressure, some difficulty is generally experienced in starting engines at sub-zero temperatures. The use of highly volatile fuels for starting at low temperatures will reduce the difficulty providing the operator is familiar with the characteristics of such fuels. In all cases it is well to remember that gasoline and similar liquid fuels will not burn in their liquid state. They must be converted into a vapor or gas and mixed with the proper amount of oxygen before combustion can occur.

FUEL VAPORIZATION

Although internal-combustion engines may be operated on either gaseous (Butane, etc.) or liquid fuels, it is generally most convenient to utilize the latter type. Liquid fuels are available in large quantities and they represent a comparatively concentrated source of heat, since one volume of the liquid will form several hundred volumes of vapor. The rapid transition of a liquid into the vapor state is known as vaporization.

In carburetion systems, vaporization is accomplished as the fuel, discharged from the carburetor discharge nozzles, travels through the induction system. Because of the high air velocity through the carburetor venturi and the volatile nature of fuel, the vaporization process is quickly accomplished. As previously mentioned an absorption of heat is necessary whenever this change occurs, and this heat must ordinarily be extracted from the air flowing through the carburetor. In many cases, it is not at all unusual for the temperature in the mixture chamber to drop 40° to 60°F. (22° to 30°C.) below the temperature of the incoming air when a high rate of fuel flow is present. If the air contains a large amount of moisture, the cooling process may cause precipitation in the form of ice. The above conditions occur in aircraft engines to some extent under certain atmospheric conditions. To offset this in automotive equipment, the gases in the intake manifold are reheated by the well-known "hot spot", which promotes still further and more complete vaporization.

TYPES OF SUPERCHARGERS.

Although many types of superchargers have been designed, those illustrated in figure give best results on modern engines.

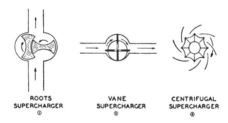

ROOTS SUPERCHARGER   VANE SUPERCHARGER   CENTRIFUGAL SUPERCHARGER

ROOTS SUPERCHARGER.

The Roots type supercharger (figure *a*) is generally mechanically driven from the engine at a moderate speed. It is fairly efficient but is usually somewhat heavier than other types of equal output and may offer some problems in lubrication. However, the Roots type may be used with good results on certain engines. The sliding vane type supercharger (figure *b*) is also satisfactory but appears to be less desirable in most cases than the centrifugal type (figure *c*).

CENTRIFUGAL SUPERCHARGER.

The centrifugal type supercharger is remarkably efficient for engines as it is simple, has few parts, and can be driven at rotative speeds far higher than would be permitted with other types. It is interesting to note that the centrifugal unit was first installed in radial type engines in order to overcome difficulties in charge distribution and not to increase the charge density. As better fuels developed, the natural procedure was to increase the gear ratios to obtain much higher manifold pressures. Centrifugal superchargers may be driven either through a gear train or by an exhaust gas turbine.

EXTERNAL AND INTERNAL SUPERCHARGERS. — In addiiton to their construction features, superchargers are also classified according to their location in the carburetion system. An impeller located in the induction system between the carburetor and engine cylinders is known as an internal supercharger, and when located on the air inlet side of the carburetor it is classified as an external supercharger.

SUPERCHARGER SYSTEMS

GENERAL.—The subject of supercharging is based on a study of mass, volume and density as applied to the properties of gases. Like liquids and solids, gases have weight, but unlike liquids and solids their weight is not of constant value under all conditions. For example, at sea-level pressure it requires approximately 13 cubic feet of air to weigh 1 pound, but at a higher pressure the same volume will be considerably heavier. For practical purposes, mass may be considered as identical with weight, that is, a measure of true quantity. Mass is not to be confused with volume, since volume merely designates the space occupied and does not consider pressure or density. The relation between these factors is explained in certain laws pertaining to the behavior of gases. At constant temperature, the relation between volume and pressure can be best shown by a study of a definite quantity of air in a closed cylinder fitted with a movable piston (fig. ABC).

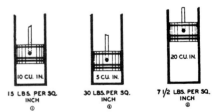

10 CU. IN.   5 CU. IN.   20 CU. IN.
15 LBS. PER SQ. INCH   30 LBS. PER SQ. INCH   7½ LBS. PER SQ. INCH

BOYLE'S LAW.—Assuming constant temperature and no leakage past the piston, it is apparent that volume and pressure are inversely related (Boyle's Law). The mass or quantity of air below the piston is the same in all cases, but as the volume is changed the pressure will be affected. Density, or the mass for a given unit of volume, is also explained by a consideration of these properties. In figure *a*, if the density of the air is taken as standard, the air in *b* will have a density of 2 and the air in *c* will have a density of only ½.

(Continued on Following Page)

(Continued from Page 19)

These facts have and important bearing on the performance of an internal-combustion engine, as the power developed depends principally upon the mass of induced charge. A nonsupercharged engine is able to induce only a definite volume according to its piston displacement and volumetric efficiency; therefore, in order to increase this mass of charge it is necessary to increase the pressure and density of the incoming charge by the use of a supercharger. Therefore, the function of a supercharger is to increase the quantity of air (or mixture) entering the engine cylinders.

EXPANSION FACTOR.—The elastic property of gases is also observed when temperature changes occur. If a given quantity of any gas is heated 1°C. the gas will, if not confined, expand 1/273 of its former volume (GayLussac's law). If heated 273°C. under the same condition, the gas will expand 273/273 or will simply double its former volume, and the density will be reduced to one-half of the original value. (figure).

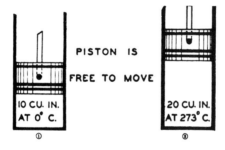

PISTON IS FREE TO MOVE

10 CU. IN. AT 0° C.

20 CU. IN. AT 273° C.

TEMPERATURE - PRESSURE DENSITY.—If a gas is confined so that free expansion cannot occur, an increase in temperature will result in an increased pressure (figure). The relation

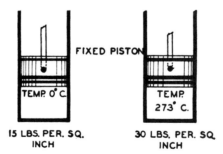

FIXED PISTON

TEMP. 0° C.

TEMP. 273° C.

15 LBS. PER. SQ. INCH

30 LBS. PER. SQ. INCH

between temperature and density must be considered in the operation of internal-combustion engines in order to insure the maximum power output.

ALTITUDE - PRESSURE. — The weight of the earth's atmosphere is sufficient to exert considerable pressure on objects at sea level. At altitudes above sea level the pressures will not only be lower but the density of the

air will also be reduced. At an altitude of 20,000 feet the pressure and density of the atmosphere are only one-half of the sea level value. Superchargers were originally developed to increase the density of the air taken into the cylinders at high altitudes so that full power output could be realized, and many superchargers are still employed for this purpose. However, with improved engines and better fuels, it is also very profitable to utilize a supercharger at low altitudes to increase the induction system pressure (and charge density) far above the normal atmospheric value. At one time, superchargers were considered merely an engine accessory but are now a vital part of every high output engine.

Manufacturer News

Phil Weiand announces his new line of Ford 60 equipment, including heads and manifold. The parts are designed similar to his Mercury line, constructed to give a more even distribution of fuel. Weiand's new Studebaker heads (shown below) offer increased mileage and power. Some drivers

report the heads give them the same power in overdrive as they had before in conventional drive. Others report up to 30 miles per gallon of gas with the new head.

* * *

Potvin Automotive of Anaheim, California, has a new aluminum flywheel on sale. The flywheel, proven by tests, is made of 356 T6 heat-treated aluminum alloy. The tensile strength is 40,000 # per square inch. Reinforced ribbing on the back side of the flywheel keeps spring out of the wheel. It will retail around $25.00, plus tax. Potvin also announces his line of leather-covered Cromwell de luxe helmets.

* * *

Electric & Carburetor Engineering Co. is in the experimental stages with a new supercharger. Tattersfield expects to run the blower in future S.C.T.A. time trials.

CHATTER . . .

Ohio Raceways, Inc., a NASCAR-sanctioned group (Akron, Ohio) announces the following schedule for the '48 season: May 30, Berea; May 31, Norwalk; June 6, Berea; June 13, Berea; June 20, Norwalk; June 27, Dover; July 4, Norwalk; July 5, Berea; July 11, Dover; July 18, Berea; July 25, Berea; August 1, Norwalk; August 8, Berea; August 15, Dover; August 22, Norwalk; August 29, Berea; September 5, open; September 6, Dover; September 12, Berea; September 19, Berea.

* * *

CRA will hold a 500-lap invitational race at Carrell Speedway, Gardena, Calif., on May 29. The event is expected to draw entries from many racing groups throughout the United States.

* * *

The S.C.T.A.'s newly acquired panel truck, sporting a red and white paint job courtesy of Bill's Auto Works, will be used for transporting equipment and carrying on promotion of the sport.

* * *

At a recent RTA meeting it was ruled that no motorcycles would be allowed to participate as guest entries. Also plans were formulated to acquire new course markers and to tighten safety regulations.

* * *

Officials of the S.C.T.A. and R.T.A. met with State Highway Patrol Officials to work out a more efficient system of controlling spectators at dry lakes timing events. This type of cooperation will do much to further safety campaigns of well organized roadster groups.

Parts With Appeal

Red haired Dean "Penny" Hales finds that a full race cam helps a great deal while practicing her daily calisthentics.

Perhaps, this is due to the fact that the cam is custom ground for the greatest high-speed performance. Maybe it can be attributed to the fact that the part is made of the most durable metal available. Or possibly it's because——Oh, well, who cares? The young lady likes the cam——and that's good enough for us.

Five foot-three inch Dean was born in Dallas, Texas. She graduated from high school there. After graduation she took a job, but remained only until she heard the call of the stage. At this time Miss Hales learned that a stock company was casting a road show to star Bert Wheeler. Dean applied for a part as a comedy-specialty dancer. She was chosen from over 100 applicants— and toured with the show for over a year. It was also a big hit in New York, the proving ground for theatrical productions.

Following this show, she turned to Hollywood where she was signed to a Paramount contract. Her next picture will be Warner Bros. "Silver Lining."

Surely this "super-race" Part With Appeal will meet with readers' approval.

Photo by Alan Dean

DEAN "PENNY" HALES WITH A FULL-RACE CAM

BELL AUTO PARTS

Featuring the FINEST IN RACING EQUIPMENT

For Roadsters-Boats & Race Cars

Send for our free
illustrated catalog

ROY RICHTER

BELL, CALIF   KImball 5728

3633 E. GAGE AVE.

Laughs...from here and there

By TOM MEDLEY

Joan: "My uncle is a safe driver yet he never slows down for crossings."

Jerry: "Impossible."

Joan: "Not at all; he drives a locomotive." —*Huntingtonian.*

* * *

A KISS IN A HAMMOCK MAY TAKE A MAN'S BREATH,

BUT A SMACK IN A FLIVVER IS FLIRTING WITH DEATH!

—*National Safety Council*

* * *

Stop and let the train go by,
It hardly takes a minute.
Your car starts off again intact,
And, better still, you are in it.

Woman's intuition isn't so impressive when she is deciding which way to turn in traffic.

* * *

Now I leap to cross the street,
I pray the Lord to help my feet.
Should I be hit before I cross,
I pray will be an easy loss.

Have you heard about the meanest man in Los Angeles?

Yea; he throws chewing gum on the streets for Crosleys to get stuck on.

* * *

Gone from this life
Is rush-along Bill.
He always would pass
other cars on a hill.

STROKER McGURK

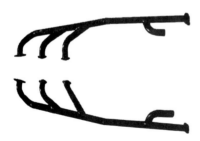 

S.C.T.A.

(*Continued from Page* 11)

to make the return run. Lloyd Kear of Upland qualified at 131.19 mph in his 'B' Class Rdstr. Randy Shinn, 1946 Champion, turned 136.98 in qualifying his Class 'C' Rdstr., and Don Blair turned 136.36 in the same class. Emil Dietrich's Mercury tail-job, with Schlemmer-built engine, made the one-way run at 147.54 driven by Neil Davis. Dietrich placed first in points in the Streamliner competition last season.

Chuck Daigh, in a front-engine wing tank, took first spot in qualifying times for the 'C' Streamliners at 148.76 miles per hour, beating Burke-Francisco's qualifying time by 25-hundredths of a mile an hour.

Phil Remington of Santa Monica, in his Mercury-powered Modified, turned 135.73 for second place in the 'B' Streamliner class while Dick Fugle with a new Ford-60 engine in '27 'T' Roadster placed second in Class 'A'

(*Continued on Page* 31)

S.C.T.A. Inc. — FASTEST QUALIFYING TIMES — APRIL 24-25

The car speeds listed here are the FASTEST QUALIFYING TIMES of each car entered in the El Mirage Dry Lake Time Trials conducted by the Southern California Timing Association, on April 24-25, 1948. The speeds shown below do not include times made in either direction runs and possibly faster speeds in record attempts. Our SCTA Competition Rules state that as a car breaks one of the existing class records, in qualifying, it is eligible to make its record attempt and return run in opposite direction within fifteen-minute elapsed time.

Asterisks (*) indicate cars which made record runs.

505—LeRoy Holmes	116.12
516—W. C. Gardner	115.83
519—Tom Nicklin	117.49
522—R. L. Reed	114.64
524—Don Waite	117.80
526—Jack Early	109.48
527—Richard Sagran	117.80
528—Gil Schmeister	102.97
529—George LaRue	118.11
537—Marvin Watson	111.94
538—Phil Weiand	123.45
540—Bob Bennett	121.13
541—T. Tompkins	115.83
543—C. R. Crawford	104.28
555—Xydias & Shaw	87.04
560—Bernard Couch	107.14
575—Reiff & Wells	113.49
576—Don Smith	110.97
578—Cook & Bashore	113.06
593—J. R. Badstubner	114.35
594—Calvin Peterson	117.95
600—Henrich & Seaton	112.07
611—Frank Sasnine	106.64
612—Lee Enfiajian	117.64
621—John B. Willis	113.92
624—G. W. Castera	122.11
625—Robert A. Camp	80.35
626—Oliver L. DePew	107.52
629—Harry Garlick	113.35
634—Ken Sills	123.11
637—E. B. Jochim	112.07
639—W. R. Murray	104.52
640—Loren E. Walker	116.88
650—Jim Plummer	106.25
655—Ted Peckels	108.04
656—Bob Griffin	117.34
666—T. A. Condon	118.57
667—Johnnie Adams	103.68
669—Phil Miller	97.40
672—Ted Colley	118.42
685—Ray Cawelti	98.14
688—Robert Hayes	110.42
699—Jim Bradford	101.46
701—Don Clark	113.63
702—Bill Roberts	108.69
703—Jim Bowman	112.92
707—Jimmy Khougaz	123.28
708—Ed Scott	106.13
710—Henry Simbro	107.65
711—Ed Harding	113.63
713—Thompson-Grsso	105.63
717—Harold Johansen	118.57
720—Stuart Harper	113.20
723—Bruce Brown	114.50
735—Johnson & Dahm	109.22
744—Bruce Boosey	108.56
766—Bob Maddocks	108.17
780—Howard Davis	110.15
790—Gordon Reed	105.50
798—Ralph Cagnacci	95.23
799—A. Youngblood	106.36

1-R—*Doug Hartelt	134.93
1-S—*Emil Dietrich	144.46
2—*Randy Shinn	136.98
4—*Burke-Francisco	148.51
5—Bob Riese	125.00
9—*Tom Beatty	129.68
11—*Stuart Hilborn	144.92
14—Phil Remington	135.73
15—*Spurgin & Giov	120.32
17—Ludvig Solberg	126.40
19—Burleigh Dolph	131.00
20—Harold Warnock	123.28
21—Ed Stewart	124.82
22—Bob Drew	123.45
23—*Regg Schlemmer	146.10
24—Dick Kraft	116.12
26—*Chuck Daigh	148.76
27—*Harvey Haller	128.57
29—Blackie Gold	124.48
30—*Don Blair	136.36
33—*Lloyd Kear	131.19
34—Akton Miller	120.16
35—Chuck Hossfeld	120.00
38—Bob Wenz	124.65
41—Byron Froelich	124.48
46—Bob Sykes	127.84
47—Frank Leonard	123.79
48—Bob Reemsnyder	124.48
52—Frank Beagle	128.20
53—Coshow Bros.	123.45
54—Wally O'Brien	125.87
55—Charles Scott	121.95
56—Shinn & Morgan	128.38
61—Jack Avakian	128.02
63—Roland Mays	123.79
65—Bub Marcia	122.44
66—Bud Swanson	120.32
67—Fred Bagula	123.28
69—Johnny Ryan	120.32
70—Mark Smith	121.62
101—Don Olson	125.52
102—Palm & Allen	123.45
103—Chuck Moore	109.48

104—George Barber	121.95
106—Alger & Starr	120.80
110—*Jim Guptill	129.12
111—Ernest Graham	118.73
113—Bob Beam	118.89
120—Meb Healey	82.87
123—E. Killingsworth	127.47
131—Breene & Haller	127.65
132—Dean Batchelor	115.68
143—Bill McBurney	114.64
144—Fred Riedman	117.80
145—Dave Cruz	112.35
147—Fred Renoe	110.29
157—Richard Fugle	104.16
166—D. A. Ratner	107.27
175—Ramon Marotta	119.52
177—Don Neary	98.14
180—Dave Glotch	115.08
191—Chuck Dunn	121.29
194—Leo Wise	77.12
197—Hershom Bros.	94.04
200—Kenny Parks	127.65
205—Davis & Pettigrew	84.11
214—Carl Caylor	120.96
220—Palma & Kukura	125.17
221—Bill Booth	115.68
222—Jim Lindsley	126.76
225—Bill Braun	122.95
234—Stanford Bros.	104.52
239—Ray Brummel	114.50
250—Richard Ohrbom	111.66
250—*Don Nicholson	128.38
263—Jim Kendall	120.64
268—Norman Way	117.80
273—Guy Wheatley	80.35
299—Lehman-Swrtrk	125.69
306—Ed Thrush	125.34
307—Ernest Dewey	121.62
313—Kenny Yenawine	119.36
315—*Paul Schiefer	136.77
317—John Bozoff	119.52
318—Norm Lean	121.45
319—Charles Rotter	117.64

320—Don Conroy	119.36
321—Dan Busby	123.96
322—Harison-Dorling	120.96
323—Dick Schilling	86.20
325—Harold Daigh	116.12
328—Donald Shutt	120.32
330—Robert Taylor	116.58
332—Ray Wymore	114.21
333—H. L. Whilldin	118.42
335—Coahran-Downey	114.64
336—W. H. Holden	94.14
337—John Collins	120.64
338—Taylor-Einhaus	125.00
340—Ted White	110.56
360—Dave McCartney	120.96
361—Eppard Bros.	111.66
366—Ray Morisette	111.94
368—Delbert Loomis	107.78
372—Wilmer McNatt	115.08
374—Keith Long	108.95
375—George Olafson	116.27
376—Jean L. Jones	111.38
380—Leonard Koch	105.38
399—Munroe-Merdith	109.22
415—Cannon-Darwin	111.80
417—Robert Fleischer	66.66
430—Art Hatfield	118.73
435—Charles Clark	121.78
442—Jim Rawding	122.61
443—Paterson-Dietz	117.95
444—Jack Morgan	117.18
445—L. Johnson	118.89
447—V. Schnackenburg	122.61
455—Arthur Tremaine	115.83
458—Hugh Romstedt	124.65
468—Lee Grey	97.40
465—Al Pahland	116.58
461—Harold Osborn	122.61
470—Fred Oatman	119.36
478—John Bayard	109.22
488—Jim Seabridge	96.46
494—G. Patterson	114.06
500—Jim Harber	116.42

Classified Advertisements

WILL MAKE a wooden semi-scale model of YOUR hot rod, convertible or hard top about 4" x 1 3/4". Complete with leather upholstering, your own license plates, numbers, etc. Please send photos, details and colors, etc. Also smaller ones suitable for hanging on rear view mirror. Prices: $2.50 up. HOT ROD—$5.00 (no fenders) Convertible—$8.00. Hard Top — $10.00 (seats inside). Boots, 1329 N. Kenmore Ave., Los Angeles 27

WANTED—'36 Ford front fenders. Call YO-1486.

RAELITE PISTONS for all engines. Special Pistons Made to Order. Alloy Casting and Machine work. PH. OS 6-8746, 14113 Ocean Gate Ave., Hawthorne, Calif.

'29 A PICKUP, channelled, full race '46 Merc., Zephyr transmission, hydraulic brakes. Extra parts included in price of $900. Call Jim Straub, NOrmandy 6011.

---

2 New S.C.T.A. Records
Established Using
EVANS SPEED EQUIPMENT

"B" Class Roadster
Doug Hartelt entry - 129.365 mph avg.

* * *

"C" Class Roadster
Regg Schlemmer entry.
138.975 mph average

EVANS Speed & Power Equipment
2667 Whittier Blvd., Whittier, Calif.
Phone: WHittier 422-387

Custom Motor Builders
BLAIR'S AUTO PARTS

Boring • Porting • Balancing
Large Valves Installed

SPEED and POWER EQUIPMENT

Send for Catalog

826 Arroyo Parkway
Pasadena, Calif.
SYcamore 2-4798

★ FOR SALE ★

V-8 60 midget - New engine - Meyer's equipment - Winfield 3-R Cam - Extra wheels, tires and spare parts - Good torsion bar trailer - $1400.

NORMAN HALL
8913 Sunset Blvd., Hollywood 46, Calif.
CRestview 5-0311

FOR SALE—'34 V8 engine, ported and relieved, Harmon-Collins 3/4 race cam, Meyer heads. '32 Ford chassis & running gear with '32 cabriolet channeled & dropped 8", perfect filled '32 shell and radiator cut 5". First $190 takes engine, first $300 takes body and gear, will trade for stock car. Malvern Gilmartin, Jr., 787 W. 7th St., Ontario, RR3, Calif.

ROADSTER—Edelbrock manifold, Meyer's heads, 2-spring front end, chrome axle, Winfield super cam, hydraulic brakes, ported, relieved, new tires, 3/8 stroke, 3 5/16 bore, chrome backing plates, 354 gears, black paint, split windshield, perfect condition, has clocked 123.28 S.C.T.A. Scotty's, 888-4th Street, San Bernardino, California.

STROKED MERC CRANKS. Pistons, Balancing. Crankshaft Co. 1422 So. Main St., Los Angeles 15, PRospect 6597.

CAR PARTS FOR SALE — Private party. Very reasonable. 1—'42 Merc. transmission, Zephyr gears, steering control type shift. NEW. 1—'42 Merc steering column with shifting mechanism and wheel. 1—'41 3.54 rear end and spring. '46 hydraulic brake set-up complete, master cyl., wheel cyl., backing plates, drums and shoes, emergency brake handle and cable. NEW. 5—'46 Ford wheels. NEW. 1—'41 front stabilizer. 1—'41 front axle with wishbone tie rod and spring, new bushings and spindles. 1—'41 Ford frame, good condition and straight. Phone George Mills, GL-0556.

LOWER THE FRONT OF YOUR CAR WITH A DROPPED AXLE
(Fits '28-'34 Ford A & V8)
Dealership Available — Wholesale and Retail
BRUCE BLAIR
826 ARROYO PARKWAY, PASADENA, CALIF.

CRA

CARRELL SPEEDWAY, Gardena, Calif.—May 8—½-mile, dirt. Fastest qualifying time, :22.65, was set by Jam. Oka.
Trophy Dash (3 laps)—1, Yam Oka; 2, Troy Ruttman. 1:07.62.
First Heat (6 laps)—1, Puffy Puffer; 2, Elmer Arndt; 3, Tim Timmerman. 2:28.44.
Second Heat (6 laps)—1, LeRoy Nooks; 2, Chuck Leighton; 3, Bob Ascot. 2:27.78.
Third Heat (6 laps)—1, Joe James; 2, Red Amic; 3, Don Freeland. 2:23.95.
Fourth Heat (6 laps)—1, Troy Ruttman; 2, Yam Oka; 3, Jay Frank. 2:21.84.
Semi-Main (15 laps)—1, LeRoy Nooks; 2, Puffy Puffer; 3, Chuck Leighton. 6:03.10.
Main (25 laps)—1, Troy Ruttman; 2, Lou Figaro; 3, Jim Davies. 10:15.02.

CULVER CITY SPEEDAY — May 14 — ¼-mile, paved, banked.d Fastest qualifying time, :12.40, set by Ed Barnett.
Trophy Dash (3 laps)—1, Roy Prosser; 2, Ed Barnett. :45.95.
First Heat (10 laps)—1, Bob Cross; 2, Red Amic; 3, Dwight Gunn. 2:20.00.
Second Heat (170 laps)—1, Puffy Puffer; 2, Ken Stansberry; 3, Lou Figaro. 2:20.15.
Third Heat (10 laps)—1, LeRoy Nooks; 2, Jay Frank; 3, Jim Davies. 2:19.20.
Semi-Main—Called at the 6th lap due to water on the track. Finishing order at that time: 1, Bob Cross; 2, Puffy Puffer; 3, Dick Hughes.
Main (30 laps)—1, Jim Davies; 2, Ed Barnett; 3, LeRoy Nooks. No time given.

CARRELL SPEEDWAY—May 15 — ½ mile, dirt. Fastest qualifying time, :22.41, set by Troy Ruttman.
Trophy Dash (3 laps)—1, Troy Ruttman; 2, Don Freeland. 1:08.25.
First Heat (6 laps)—1, Dempsey Wilson; 2, Ed Papac; 3, George Smith. 2:28.60.
Second Heat (6 laps)—1, Chuck Leighton; 2, Fred Pope; 3, Ken Stansberry. 2:30.05.
Third Heat 6 laps)—1, Jay Frank; 2, Bob Cross; 3, Dick Hughes. 2:23.72.
Fourth Heat (6 laps)—1, Don Freeland; 2, LeRoy Nooks; 3, Red Amic. 2:9.95—new record.
Semi-Main (15 laps)—1, Fred Pope; 2, Ed Papac; 3 Les Harvey. No time given.
Main (25 laps)—1, Don Freeland; 2, Jim Davies; 3, Jay Frank. 9:56.42.

NCRRA

PACHECO STADIUM, Pacheco, Calif.—April 18—Fastest qualifying time, :17.29, set by Ernie Reyes.
Trophy Dash (3 laps)—1, Gene Tessian; 2, Ernie Reyes. :53.30.
First Heat (5 laps)—1, George Pacheco; 2, Ed Huntington; 3, Jack Myers. 1:34.30.
Second Heat (5 laps)—1, Larry Terra; 2, George Danburg; 3, Bob Veith. 1:33.80.
Third Heat (5 laps)—1, Mel Senna; 2, Bob McLean; 3, Bob Machin. 1:34.60.
Fourth Heat (5 laps)—1, Joe Valente; 2, Al Neves; 3, Al Germolis. 1:30.30.
Fifth Heat (5 laps)—1, Sam Hawks; 2, Bill Sullivan; 3, Ernie Reyes. 1:31.90.
Second Place Winner Final (6 laps)—1, Ed Huntington; 2, George Danburg; 3, Bob McLean. 1:51.10.
First Place Winner Final (6 laps)—1, George Pacheco; 2, Joe Valente; 3, Mel Senna. 1:48.70.
Semi-Main (15 laps)—1, George Pacheco; 2, Ed Huntington; 3, Dan Kern. 4:43.60.
Main (25 laps)—1, Bob Machin; 2, Al Berndt; 3, Sam Hawks. 7:45.40.

CONTRA COSTA STADIUM, Pacheco, Calif.—March 21. ¼ mile. Fastest qualifying time, :15.69, set by Joe Valente.
Trophy Dash (3 laps)—1, Lemoine Frey; 2, Joe Valente. :49.50.
First Heat (5 laps)—1, Mel Senna; 2, Jack Barlow; 3, Chuck Harwood. 1:35.70.
Second Heat (5 laps)—1, Wayne Selser; 2, Bob Veith; 3, Ed Eliisian. 1:27.80.
Third Heat (5 laps)—1, Al Neves; 2, George Pacheco; 3, Mike Andrews. 1:26.80.
Fourth Heat (5 laps)—1, Gene Tessian; 2, Al Germolis; 3, Al Berndt. 1:28.40.
First Handicap (6 laps)—1, Bob Veith; 2, George Pacheco; 3, Al Germolis. 1:43.80.
Second Handicap (6 laps)—1, Sam Hawks; 2, Mel Senna; 3, Gene Tessian. 1:46.50. (3 laps under yellow flag.)
Semi-Main (15 laps)—1, Mel Senna; 2, Ed Elisian; 3, Bob Veith. 4:36.40.
Main (25 laps)—1, George Pacheco; 2, Al Berndt; 3, Gene Tessian. 7:21.60.

CHR

HUNTINGTON BEACH SPEEDWAY, Huntington Beach, Calif—May 7, 1948—1/5 mile. Fastest qualifying time, 15:87, set by Colby Scroggins.
Trophy Dash (3 laps)—1, Colby Scroggins; 2, Bob Lindsey. 46:62.
First Heat (10 laps)—1, Don Nicholson; 2, Ed Lockhart; 3, Dale Brooks. 3:42:26.
2nd Heat (10 laps)—1, Bill Steves; 2, Bud Gregory; 3, Stan Kross. 3:07:78.
3rd Heat (10 laps)—1, Dick Vineyard; 2, Bud Van Maanen; 3, Grant Lambert. 3:08:91.
4th Heat (10 laps)—1, Archie Tipton; 2, Jim Rathman; 3, Ed Ball. 3:07:82.
Consolation Race (8 laps)—1, Dan Tracey; 2, Tom Wiley; 3, Chuck Shaw. 2:46:14.
Semi-Main (25 laps)—1, Bud Gregory; 2, Bill

FOR SALE

'40 V-8 Custom Convert., '39 Hood and Grill, all molded. Overdrive, '46 mill bored .90 over Merc. Full cam, ported and relieved. Elect. doors, Carson top. DICK - YOrk 1486.
7164 Melrose Ave., Rm. 4, L. A.

Steves; 3, Stan Kross. 6:47;61.
Main Event (Race stopped on 25th lap—no time)—Stopping order—1, Dick Vineyard; 2, Mickey Davis; 3, Bob Lindsey.

BONELLI STADIUM, Saugus, Calif.—May 9, 1948—Fastest qualifying time, 19:37, set by Bud Van Maanen.
Trophy Dash (3 laps)—1, Bud Van Maanen; 2, Bud Gregory. 1:00:31.
1st Heat (10 laps)—1, Colby Scroggins; 2, Dick Benninger; 3, Bruce Emmons. 3:36:30.
2nd Heat (10 laps)—1, Stan Kross; 2, Mickey Davis; 3, Vern Slankhard. 3:25:12.
3rd Heat (10 laps)—1, Archie Tipton; 2, Bob Lindsey; 3, Dan Tracey. 3:20:88.
4th Heat (10 laps)—1, Bob Cross; 2, Stan Kross; 3, Dick Vineyard. 3:51:23.
Match Race (3 laps)—1, Stan Kross; 2, Colby Scroggins. 1:06:01.
Semi-Main (20 laps)—1, Colby Scroggins; 2, Dick Benninger; 3, Mickey Davis. 6:54:03.
Main Event (40 laps)—1, Bill Steves; 2, Bob Lindsey; 3, Stan Kross. 13:25:32.

HUNTINGTON BEACH SPEEDWAY, Huntington Beach, Calif.—May 14, 1948—Fastest qualifying time, 14:91, set by Archie Tipton.
Trophy Dash (3 laps)—1, Archie Tipton; 2, Jim Rathman. 46:45.
1st Heat (10 laps)—1, Mickey Davis; 2, Vern Slankhard; 3, Dale Brooks. 2:42:47.
2nd Heat (10 laps)—1, Bud Gregory; 2, Don Nicholson; 3, Stan Kross. 2:39:18.
3rd Heat (10 laps)—1, Dan Tracey; 2, Fred Ryness; 3, Dick Vineyard. 2:35:60.
4th Heat (10 laps)—1, Bill Steves; 2, Wayne Tipton; 3, Archie Tipton. 2:35:34.
Consolation Race (8 laps)—1, Curtis Hayes; 2, Ed Lockhart; 3, Gordon Cox. 2:12:83.
Semi-Main (20 laps)—1, Mickey Davis; 2, Bud Gregory; 3, Vern Slankhard. 3:28:08.
Main Event (40 laps)—1, Dan Tracey; 2, Dick Vineyard; 3, Wayne Tipton. 7:29:60.

BONELLI STADIUM, Saugus, Calif—May 15, 1948—Fastest qualifying time, 19:07, set by Jim Rathman.
Trophy Dash (3 laps)—1, Jim Rathman; 2, Pat Flaherty. 58:75.
1st Heat (10 laps)—1, Curtis Hayes; 2, Don Tripp; 3, Dick Benninger. 3:37:81.
2nd Heat (10 laps)—1, Jim Graham; 2, Colby Scroggins; 3, Grant Casper. 3:30:00.
3rd Heat (10 laps)—1, Archie Tipton; 2, Dick Vineyard; 3, Vern Slankhard. 3:23:58.
4th Heat (No contest due to accident).
Semi Main (15 laps)—1, Curtis Hayes; 2, Grant Casper; 3, Colby Scroggins. 5:17:53.
Main Event (30 laps)—1, Dick Vineyard; 2, Vern Slankhard; 3, Jim Rathman. 10:05:42.

ASC

VALLEY SPEEDWAY, Fresno, Calif. — April 25, 1948—5/8 mile. Fastest qualifying time, 22:90, set by Don Bailey.
Trophy Dash (3 laps)—1, George Seeger; 2, Don Bailey. 1:09:50.
3, Dan Maruffo. 2:34:60.
2nd Heat (5 laps)—1, Bruce McClaire; 2, Buck Knight; 3, Bud Hetzler. 2:33:72.
1st Heat (5 laps)—1, Bernie Miller; 2, Jack Jones; 3rd Heat (5 laps)—1, Pat Patrick; 2, Bob Ascot; 3, George Seeger. 2:32:10.
Match Race (3 laps)—1, Jack Jones; 2, Willie Perren. 1:11:34.
Semi Main (10 laps)—1, Jack Jones; 2, Bob Ascot; 3, Bernie Miller. 4:12:60.
Main Event (25 laps)—No time due to accident. 1, George Seeger; 2, Pat Patrick; 3, Bud Hetzler.

NASCAR

BEREA FAIRGROUNDS, Berea, Ohio—April 25, 1948—Main Event won by Bob James.
BEREA FAIRGROUNDS, Berea, Ohio, May 9, 1948—Main Event won by Bob James.

PISTONS & DESIGNS
(Continued from Page 8)

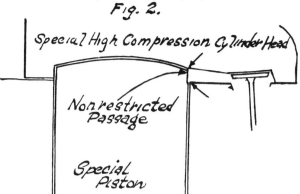

Fig. 2.
Special High Compression Cylinder Head

Nonrestricted Passage

Special Piston

Figure 2 has shown how the high-domed piston and special-designed heads have speeded the flow of fuel into the piston chamber or gives us "better motor breathing." Consequently the next step has to be taken in the design of a special intake manifold that will supply enough air and fuel to feed the pistons at high speeds. It has been found, through tests, that the most satisfactory unit would have to be designed to use four carburetors or eight venturis, so designed to give turbulence as well as velocity. A manifold to handle eight venturis with a minimum amount of pulsation occurring within the manifold, and yet having each venturi port connected by equalizing tubes in a manner as to not connect any three in a straight line. Tests have shown this to be very essential in decreasing pulsations in the tubes themselves.

With the three units run as a combination, PISTONS, HEADS, and MANIFOLD, you will find an L-type motor resembling the actions of an overhead valve and cam-type motor. The instant surge of power, the smooth acceleration, and the R.P.M.'s are but a derivative of this special-designed piston combination.

SCTA
(Continued from Page 27)

Rdstr. competition at 104.16 mph. This latter car featured a pointed nose fashioned from a fuel tank and created much comment on its 'ant eater' appearance.

Other cars utilizing a 'new look' front-end appearance were Ak Miller's Cadillac with its '23 Dodge Rdstr. body, engine in rear, and wing-tank front-end construction, and a new low-slung tank-nosed '27 'T' Roadster with full belly pan and form-fitting tarp cover. These new diversions from the conventional roadster will no doubt start an all-out phase of streamlining among the classes of competition and should further the growing trend toward creation of strictly 'lakes' cars, which are towed or transported to the Time Trials meets and are not suited to running on the streets.

With five more two-day meets on their 1948 schedule, officials and members of the S.C.T.A. are hopeful of presenting the most interesting and successful season of Time Trials in the history of Dry Lakes Racing. By establishing a strict 20 mph speed limit on the lake bed for all non-competing cars and with assurance of full support and co-operation from the California Highway Patrol in helping to control the thousands of spectators that are in attendance at every meet, they hope to continue their activity in providing a SAFE means of testing cars developed under the natural energies of youthful American ingenuity. While speed is the goal, the primary aim of S.C.T.A. is to preserve its present record of "Ten Years In Automotive Timing Without One Casualty In Competition." By exercising its governing control over the activities of the members of their 37 Southern California clubs, S.C.T.A. is undoubtedly the country's most extraordinary and effective Safety organization.

TATTERSFIELD-Baron

Racing

Equipment

● **NEW** ●

→ 4 Carburetor Manifold
→ Special High Compression Cylinder Heads
→ Special Pistons
→ Venturi Type Stacks
→ Large Cast Gas Lines

2 ADVANTAGES

MULTIPLE VENTURI SYSTEM

A Tattersfield-Baron four carburetor manifold has eight venturi tubes. On a Ford V8 and Mercury installation, for example, this means one venturi tube for each cylinder insuring the absolute packing of every cylinder with a power-loaded charge of combustible gas. This multiple venturi construction, by reducing the demand on each tube, produces even mixture with plenty of air and thus gives greater power and speed.

ISOLATION OF GASES

With ordinary manifolds there is often a tendency for one cylinder to "rob" another. This cannot happen with a TATTERSFIELD-BARON manifold. Provision has been made for individual distribution of gases to each cylinder, with complete partitioning to prevent any possibility of "theft" or over-lap. The net result is the packing of each cylinder with a uniform and complete charge of fuel.

For thrilling new economy or speed install a

TATTERSFIELD-BARON FOUR CARBURETOR manifold on your Ford or Mercury

A COMBINATION DESIGNED FOR EVERY SPEED RANGE

IF IT'S A RECORD YOU WANT, INSTALL A TATTERSFIELD-BARON SPEED UNIT TODAY

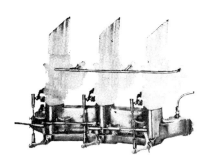

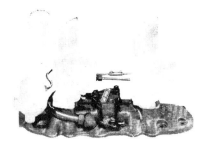

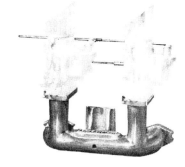

—FORD 6—

This manifold is designed to use 2 or 3 carburetors more efficiently than with only 1 carburetor.

—FORD 60—

Illustrated is the new Ford 60 manifold with many new added features—Adds more dynamic power to your 60 midget.

—FORD "A"—

This manifold can be purchased in either single or dual carburetion.

→ **Many other types of Manifolds are available for your truck or passenger car.**

→ **Write today for information regarding dual Carburetion on your own car.**

Manifold Division

ELECTRIC & CARBURETOR ENG. CO.

2321-23 E. 8th St.,   TR. 4863   Los Angeles 21, California

HOT ROD
Magazine

udy Ramos in his Track Roadster JULY, 1948 **25¢**

It's in the Bag . . .

Editor:

. . . That magazine of yours is out of this world, and what results on your classified advertising (May issue) . . . we're well satisfied. . . .

ROBERT DOKE
JOHN ACKERMAN
Dearborn Speed Shop
Dearborn, Mich.

Dear Sirs:

. . . I am in the market for a good '39 Ford Coupe De Luxe or '40 Ford Convertible De Luxe. Any information on same as to where I might get a good one would be highly appreciated. It may be fixed up or I'll fix it up.

KEITH E. KENNEDY
Oceanside, Calif.

All of our readers will find it to their advantage to try HRM's classified advertising. Compare our rates with other publications.—ED.

Dear Sir:

. . . Being on the East Coast has its bad points. Here we have what you would call "Cold Rods"; just bright paints, fur (fox) tails, and some chrome, with nothing under the hood.

THOMAS FLEMING
Philadelphia, Pa.

Do all of our Eastern readers agree?—ED.

Gentlemen:

. . . Certainly is a wonderful publication. Have shown it to many friends and you will probably have more subscribers from here. Am a member of the Hawaiian Motor Racing Association . . . in the process of having a track built. . . .

W. L. RANKIN
Honolulu
Territory of Hawaii

Dear Sirs:

. . . One of our members . . . happened to find a copy of the book (HRM) at Indianapolis. He brought it to our meeting . . . I only had a chance to glance through it, but in the short time I had to look at it, I knew it was what I wanted. I am president of a newly formed organization known as the "Volunteer Stock Car Racing Association," VSCRA. We plan on running stock, modified, hot rods, etc. I think this magazine will be of great help to the boys in the club . . . I lived in San Diego . . . a short few years ago, and I know you boys (Southern California) are "on the ball" when it comes to any kind of racing. Stay that way, by all means. . .

W. C. 'Wild Bill' FERGERSON
Nashville, Tenn.

Dear H.R.M.

Until recently I was a resident of No. Hollywood. When you brought out your publication I believed it was one of the greatest mags that I had ever run across. Since I have moved to this part of the country, I have been cut off from all the finer things in life. To see another lakes trial or a track race I would gladly pay plenty. I'm telling you fellows, I'm the most homesick guy there is for the sound of a roadster screaming through the traps. Included is a poem I wrote while in one of my dark moments of despair.

Vince Ketzler
Bellville, Texas

THAT DUSTY RUN

A quarter over Merc,
    And a three-eighths stroke,
Ten to one heads,
    Not a trace of a choke.
Four chrome jugs
    That were pretty slick,
A Kong ignition,
    And a full ground stick.
A Zephyr transmission
    With a column shift,
A chopped flywheel
    That a baby could lift.
Out of Shelby tubing
    He had made his frame,
With a channeled "T" body
    to fit the same.
Twenty-five coats
    Of lacquer paint,
The cost of the chrome
    Would make you faint.
With Carson upholstery
    And all the fine gear,
Of a more beautiful rod
    You seldom hear.
He'd built her all winter
    For the run in the spring,
He'd sweated blood
    And was skinny as a string.
Then came the word
    Of the first lakes trial,
When the boys'd run
    That Long, short mile.
He was there that morn
    With the rise of the sun,
First on the list
    Of that dusty run.
The final check
    Was stamped O.K.
He was ready to go,
    Get outta the way.
Fire gutted headers
    That gleamed in the sun,
The nineteens screamed
    As he giv 'er the gun.
Sixty in low
    And then the next cog,
Eighty in second
    Was just a jog.
Four pots screaming
    As he gave it high,
Lake dust boiling
    Into the sky.
The drive-in boys
    Will tell you the rest
At least they'll say,
    "He did his best."
He'll try next year,
    As you all know,
To beat his time,
    Of ninety-nine point O.

(Continued on Page 20)

Editor's Column

July's HOT ROD OF THE MONTH is Rudy Ramos' combination track and dry lakes roadster. Two-page coverage of our feature car is designed to please our many readers who have asked for more photos.

Questions have been pouring in . . . some pretty tough. This month's QUESTIONS AND ANSWERS are on page 8.

ENGINE STROKING is explained on page 9 by Don Blair, popular Pasadena, California, hot rod builder.

Pages 10 and 11 feature Wally Park's story on S.C.T.A.'s second 1948 speed trials. The article is supplemented with many pictures.

California Roadster Association's 500-lap race at Gardena, California, drew a record crowd of spectators. Those who missed the big race will enjoy Dorothy Sloan's review of the evening's events. Those who were at the race will be interested in the close-up of the race's winner, Dempsey Wilson. Story and photos on page 12.

Superstitious? Russetta Timing members aren't. They held their June timing meet on the thirteenth of the month. In accord with this, the story of that meet is on page 13.

The 1949 Ford has caused considerable interest in an automotive-minded country. HRM's readers will appreciate the excellent photographic studies of both of the new Ford engines—the Six and V-8. (Pages 14 and 15.)

Our thanks to William G. Briegleb of the El Mirage Soaring School for the use of his plane to take aerial photographs of S.C.T.A.'s timing meet. Further thanks goes to Joe Green for his excellent pilotage.

Due to the many fine stories and photos available for the July issue, our promised club news section will have to be omitted this month.

For the benefit of the many readers who have written in asking that we print the popular poem, "His Car Was Hot," we will mention that it was printed in our February issue (Vol. 1, No. 2.)

Continue to tell our advertisers that you read their ads in HRM. They appreciate it—and so do we.

Next month's Hot Rod Magazine will feature an unusual cover car. Don't miss it! SUBSCRIBE TODAY!!

—Ed.

HOT ROD Magazine

WORLD'S MOST COMPLETE HOT ROD COVERAGE

TABLE OF CONTENTS

HOT ROD MAGAZINE, U.S. Copyright 1948 by the Hot Rod Publishing Company, 7164 Melrose Avenue, Los Angeles 46, California. Second Class mailing permit pending.
SUBSCRIPTION PRICE: $3.00 per year throughout the world.

Vol. I   *HRM—Published Monthly*   No. 7

Associate Editors .... Robert E. Petersen
Robert R. Lindsay
Technical Advisers .... W. I. "Bill" Gieseke
Wally Parks
Advertising .... George Peterson
Art Director .... Alice Van Norman
Photography .... Dyson Smith, Alan Dean,
Paul Schaeffer, Kirk Harris
Cartoons and Humor .... Tom Medley
Reporters .... Robert Williams, Glenn Glendening
Dick Robinson, Richard K. Martin
Arthur Elliot, William H. Sippel, Bob Machin
Subscription Department .... Marilyn Lord
Distribution .... Gordon Bain

HOT ROD MAGAZINE $3.00 Per Year

Subscription Dept.
7164 Melrose Avenue
Los Angeles 46, California

Please send me HRM for one year beginning with the .... issue.

Name ....

Street Address ....

City ...., Zone ...., State ....

(Check one)   Cash ☐   Check ☐   Money Order ☐

Capacity crowd looks on as Roy Prosser (left), Chuck Leighton (center) and Don Freeland line up for a gruelling 500-lap speedfast. Eighteen of the 33 starters finished the race.

Hot Rod of the Month

A Veteran of Roadster Racing Since 1946, Car No. 5 Still Ranks High in California Track Competition with Roy Prosser at the Wheel.

Cover Car owner Rudy Ramos is one of those rare California exceptions, a native son. Born in Los Angeles, 20-year-old Rudy has great expectations for his combination lakes-track roadster. The car is likely to justify his beliefs. Number 5 won four C.R.A. trophy dashes out of the first five starts in 1948. These events were taken with Roy Prosser at the wheel. Number 5 has known other top-ranking hot rod drivers—Pat Flaherty, Don Freeland, Wally Pancratz and the idol of feminine hot rod followers, Troy Ruttman.

Rudy's roadster clocked an S.C.T.A. C Roadster time of 118 mph in 1945. At that time the car was running Meyers heads and Weiand manifold.

He runs his car at the S.C.T.A. time trials as a member of the Albatas.

Number 5's present engine is: '46 Merc. block, Sharp heads, Sharp triplet manifold, Spalding ignition, 5/16″ bore, 1/8″ stroke, ported and relieved, 3/4 cam. The engine is dynamically balanced throughout. No. 5 uses Stromberg 97 carburetors. The car's '27 T body sits on a '32 frame. Rudy uses a Stelling gear box, Knudsen full-floating (4.11-1) rear end, Franklin steering. For safety's

Roy Prosser is pushed off from the pits during the 500 Lap C.R.A. Invitational Meet at Carroll Speedway in Gardena, California.

Photo by Ted Tanner

Side view of car displays clean low-slung lines that provide for better maneuverability on the track.

sake, and association regulations, No. 5 has the aircraft-type bucket seat with safety belt. Also featured are the fuel shut-off valve and hydraulic brake setup.

Rudy runs the car with 700-16 rears and 550-16's on the front. Every builder has at least one automotive idea he likes to experiment with. With Rudy Ramos, it's the engine's cooling system. "With two water pumps," he says, "the water is thrown out of the overflow. Soon the engine overheats." His solution: one '34 water pump, with the other side blocked off. "This is just right to agitate the water and keep cooling at a maximum." Rudy is a charter member of the California Roadster Association, having raced with the group since its inception in 1946. He builds his own engines. He is a graduate of Washington High School in Los Angeles. Rudy claims his primary interests (sports, hobbies, past-times) are in hot rods. Secondary interest: "Women."

At the recent 500 lap hot rod race at Carrell Speedway, Gardena, California, the car took the lead for the first 25 laps, alternating between first and second position for the next 22 laps at which time it was forced to withdraw due to a damaged oil tank.

Following the C.R.A. "500," Rudy took his roadster north to Oakland, California, where he raced with Racing Roadsters, Inc. On Friday night, June 11, his car was top qualifier at Oakland, finishing third in the Main Event.

Ramos will return to Southern California in time to enter C.R.A.'s 4th of July 100 lapper at Gardena, Calif.

If past performances are any indication, racing fans may look for Rudy Ramos' No. 5 to come out on top on the Fourth and in future races.

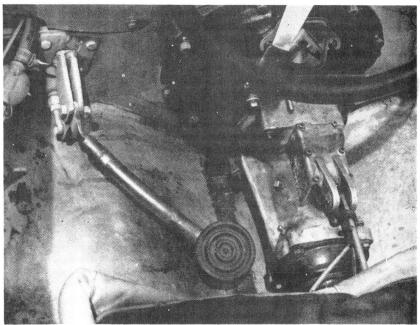

A driver's eye view of the cockpit. Gear box is a Stelling in and out type. On far left the gasoline shut-off valve

Below is the engine, a '46 Mercury with Spalding Ignition, Sharp Heads and Manifold.

QUESTIONS AND ANSWERS

Q. Would it be possible for you to give me some information as to times, dates and places of the time trials held by the Southern California Timing Association?

I am planning a trip to Los Angeles this summer and would like to have the trip coincide with one of the meets.

A. S.C.T.A., Inc. has set up the following schedule for 1948 meets:

July 17 and 18
August 28 and 29
September 25 and 26
October 23 and 24

In case any of the above meets are called off, due to rain or other causes, an alternate date has been set for November 20 and 21.

All of the dates given here are Saturdays and Sundays. Timing begins as early as possible after sunup.

Q. I have a '29 Chevy and I would like to know if a late model manifold ('34-'39) would fit on the old block and if a late model head would fit.
JACK LITTLE
Reno, Nevada

A. Chevy heads and manifolds of 1937 or later will fit with slight adjustments. The Hi-torque '42 or later models are preferable in that they have the large (7/16") bolts in the crankshaft flange. However, it is suggested that Mr. Little get ahold of a complete late model engine. They sell at a very reasonable price, because of the low trade-in value set on them.

Q. I have one question . . . as an avid fan and constant track attender I don't know what the ——— is meant by "stroking, stroked Merc., stroked pistons, etc."
O. G. JOHNSON
Major. USAF
Dayton, Ohio

A. Stroking means lengthening the stroke of the crankshaft; therefore a stroked Merc. is a Mercury (engine) in which the crankshaft stroke has been lengthened.

Stroked pistons are pistons on which the pins have been moved to compensate for the difference in crankshaft stroke.

Q. Would you please send me some information on the Mojave Timing Association because our club . . . would like to join. Also could you send me the name and address of the person I should see?
M. L. PHENIX
El Monte, California

A. For information regarding the Mojave Timing Association, contact Mr. Arnold Birner (Association President) at 2639 Palm Grove, Los Angeles 16, Calif.

Q. While at the Hot Rod Show in Los Angeles I saw some engines painted with a metalic base paint. Light blue was the color I remember seeing . . . I thought you might tell me where I could purchase that paint.

MARIO BAFFICO
San Francisco, Calif.

A. The paint mentioned is Polychromatic Synthetic and can be purchased from any Ditzler Store or DuPont Store. Lacquers will not withstand the heat.

Q. I would like to know who makes the dropped axle and the price of it. The axle is the one in your May issue (Parts With Appeal) which Ellen Koller is using as a swing.
EDWARD SANDERS
Pomona, California

A. The dropped axle featured in our May Parts With Appeal is sold by the So-Cal Speed Shop for $20.00.

Q. Are there any timing associations out here on the East Coast?
DONALD HURTER
Norwood, Massachusetts

A. As far as we can find out, there are none. If any of our readers know of any, please drop a line to HRM.

Q. I have a chance to buy . . . a 10-inch McCullough Blower. I have been told that low compression heads are better than high while using a blower. What grind cam would you suggest?
DEL THOMAS
Oakland Roadster Club
Oakland, California

A. You were rightly informed about the heads. As for a cam, a super race model would best fit your needs.

Q. I would like to know . . . the addresses of the Winfield and Crager racing parts companies.
JEFF HASTE
Glendale, California

A. The Winfield Company is located at 4515 Alger Street in Los Angeles. The original Crager company is out of business. However, Bell Auto Parts might be able to supply you with the necessary information and possibly Crager equipment.

NASCAR
1948
RULES AND ROADSTER SPECIFICATIONS

ENGINE
1. Any engine can be used as long as it is a stock American block.
2. No overhead valves can be used on an L head engine.
3. Any special head can be used as long as it is the original design.
4. Carburetors, pistons, rods, oil system, cams, intake manifolds, fuel mixtured and radiators may be altered in any way.
5. Ignition system may be altered in any way.
6. Magnetos will be permitted.
7. Position of engine may be changed.

TRANSMISSIONS AND REAR ENDS
1. No limitations.
2. Gear boxes and dog clutches are optional.
3. Driver must be able to disengage rear wheels.
4. Rear end should be locked.

SHOCK ABSORBERS
1. Every car must have shocks on all four wheels. They may be of any type providing they work efficiently.

WHEEL BASE
1. 90 inches minimum and a maximum of 120 inches recommended.

FRAME
1. Any stock frame can be used.
2. Frame can be shortened providing it isn't cut between cross members.
3. Cross members may be moved and new members inserted.
4. Width of frame may only be altered beyond outer limits of cross members.

BODIES
1. Bodies are required to cover whole frame and top half of hood.
2. Body must be 30 inches wide at seat.
3. Home made bodies and factory made speedster bodies will be permitted.
4. Home made bodies will be subject to inspection by Safety Committee.
5. Hoops are optional but not recommended.
6. Body must have doors or space closed and they may be welded shut and cut down.
7. Doors must be welded, bolted or strapped shut.
8. All cars must have fire wall between motor and driver.
9. Windshield optional. Must be of non-shatterable construction if installed.

STEERING
1. Any type steering may be used providing it is in good working order.
2. Welded pitman arms, draglinks, tie rod ends, and steering arms are not permitted.
3. Radius rods may be mounted at the side of frame.
4. Knurfing bars are required and should

be rounded and must be in front of rear wheels.

BRAKES
1. At least two-wheel brakes, in good working order, are required.
2. Brakes may be operated by hand or by foot.
3. Brakes may be mechanical or hydraulic.

WHEELS
1. Any metal wheel may be used.
2. Any stock size may be used.

AXLES
1. Any type front and rear axles may be used.
2. Tread must be standard.

BUMPER
1. Bumper is optional but should not extend beyond width of car.
2. Bumper must meet frame on both sides.

APPEARANCE
1. All cars must be neatly painted with permanent number at least 16 inches high.
2. Duplicate numbers will be altered with white wash.
3. Any color paint may be used. Don't spare this item.

GENERAL
1. Superchargers may be used if it is a rule of local group or association but will not be allowed in the proposed N A S C A R National

(Continued on Page 31)

Engine Stroking

By DON BLAIR

Stroking an engine raises the compression ratio by increasing cubic inch displacement. There are advantages as well as disadvantages to stroking an engine. Particularly important is the added low speed power of a stroked engine. At the same time, stroking gives lower RPM and, therefore, higher ratio gears are needed. Engines may be stroked anywhere from 1/8″ up to as high as 1/2″. The 1/8″ stroke is the most popular.

In breaking down a stroked engine, it should be explained that the actual stroking process is performed primarily on the crankshaft throws (journals). In the case of an 1/8″ stroke, for instance, the cylindrical throw is milled 1/8″ on the side towards the center of the crankshaft cycle. This milling is gradually decreased from 1/8″ to "no mill" on the outside (180 degrees from the 1/8″ spot). When this is done on a Mercury crank, Ford rods and bearings will fit the altered engine. (The operation has brought the Merc. crank throws down to normal Ford size.)

The above-mentioned procedure has increased the travel distance of the piston 1/8″; that is, 1/16″ closer to the head at top center and 1/16″ further away from the head at bottom position.

In line with crank stroking are

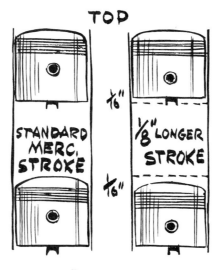

TOP

STANDARD MERC. STROKE

1/8″ LONGER STROKE

BOTTOM
(With Standard Piston)

stroked pistons. These are special-made pistons in which the pin holes have been moved to compensate for the greater length of stroke. Stroked pistons also have shortened skirts to prevent them from traveling too low in the cylinders. While the pin hole is moved but half of the added stroke length, the skirt is trimmed the full length of the stroke. This is necessary in that the changed position of the pin hole puts the skirt one-half the stroke length lower than its normal position. Add to this the fact that the stroked crank throw pulls the piston half of the stroke length further down in the cylinder. Therefore, the skirt must be

trimmed an amount equal to the added stroke.

A few figures may help to make this article more useful to readers:

INCREASE IN DISPLACEMENT
(Mercury engine)

Added Stroke	Normal Disp.	New Disp.	Cu. in. added per cyl.	Cu. in. added to engine
1/8″	239.312 cu. in.	247.288 cu. in.	.997	7.976
1/4″	239.312 cu. in.	255.272 cu. in.	1.995	15.960
3/8″	239.312 cu. in.	263.240 cu. in.	2.991	23.928

COMBINATIONS FOR:

1/8″ stroke: Mercury crankshaft, Ford rods (21A-6200), Ford bearings (81A6211-basic no.).

1/4″ or 3/8″ strokes: Mercury crankshaft, Mercury rods, Mercury bearings.

For a stroke of more than 1/8″, the ground throws must be metal-sprayed. The spray is applied hot to the roughened throws, fusing itself into a circle about them.

AMOUNT OF SPRAY NECESSARY:

Stroked	Amt. milled off	Amt. spray needed
1/4″	.250″	approx. 113″
3/8″	.375″	approx. 236″

The thickness of the spray added is one-half of that of the amount stroked.

At this point, a mention of "destroking" is in order. The process of destroking an engine is just the opposite of stroking. A destroked engine will, therefore, have a lower cubic inch displacement and will possibly fall into a lower classification for timing and racing purposes.

EVOLUTION OF A FORD

1928

JOE'S JUNK YARD

1938

1948

ABOVE—The starting line early Sunday morning before the crowd has gathered. LEFT—A roadster leaves the start in a cloud of dust as other drivers await turn. Note the signal-type starting lights that dispatch the cars at 20 second intervals.

Shinn Sets New

S.C.T.A.—JUNE 5-6

As a result of careful planning and much hard work on the part of alert Timing Committees, the S.C.T.A. produced its most successfully run meet in the history of dry lakes racing. Running on July 5 and 6, under favorable weather conditions, and a very rough course, they set three new class records and turned in some enviable qualifying times.

Due to the streamlined methods now in use, they have entirely eliminated the long waiting in line that has always posed such a problem. The new electrical starting light system allows cars to be run off on regular twenty-second intervals, or oftener if conditions permit. No longer do members have to push their way along a seemingly endless line of cars to the starting line. Instead, the Starters Eber Bailey and George Prussell, were often calling for more cars.

A new simplified phone communication system now gives a complete report of all the conditions, activities, and instructions along the running course. Through this media operators on signal posts along the course are able to receive the times on cars as

they are made, thereby relieving the monotony of a long and lonely watch.

That the expert timing facilities of Chief Timer J. O. Crocker have been continuously improved upon was demonstrated in the fact that not one car's time was missed during the running of Saturday's meet and only one on Sunday, which was caused by an error of timing personnel. Newly installed equipment affords absolutely accurate timing regardless of temperature, dust or humidity. This is a factor rarely heard of in timing devices and is the result of years of research by Mr. Crocker.

Through the co-operative efforts of two crews who manned the new time station, cars were able to return to the station and find their correct time ready for them. This station, located at the starting line end of the lake, eliminated the dust and confusion formerly encountered under the old system of picking up times at the finish

stand. Car times and speeds are now relayed by direct line from the recorder's stand to the time station.

One of the biggest assets toward the success of the meet was attributed to the new colorful windshield stickers supplied by the association. These were applied to all cars coming onto the lake at check stations at the entrances. They contained information on the 20 m.p.h. enforced speed limit, as well as reminders for Careful Driving and No Firearms. Through this method of giving advance notice to drivers, the entire problem of crowd control was eliminated.

Under supervision of Gordon Kenward and John Cannon, the job of patrolling the meet was carried out with commendable success. Frequent announcing of times at the starting line

LEFT — Kenny Parks' unique '27 T with a fuel tank nose attracted a great deal of attention. Car clocked 123.96 mph. RIGHT — Officials watch Doug Hartelt's roadster as it speeds through the finish beam.

ABOVE—Finish stand and SCTA truck can be seen at extreme right of the well-patrolled crowd of spectators. RIGHT—Randy Shinn in the Edelbrock powered '27 T that carried him to a new roadster record.

Roadster Record

By Wally Parks

area and continuous announcement of times at the finish line kept the large crowds of spectators under amazingly co-operative control.

First of the new records was set by Randy Shinn in the C roadster class. This 27T turned an average 139.760, a remarkable time for any roadster, let alone a car that is also driven on the highways.

Paul Schiefer was handicapped by engine trouble, but did manage to do 135.13 one way.

In his V-8 60 powered aircraft fuel tank Alex Xydias set the first A class streamliner record. Alex's time for two runs averaged 127.120.

The third record to be broken was in the A roadster class by Spurgin and Giovanine with their four-cylinder

Chevrolet. The two-way time was 117.515.

With the meets running smoothly under the new system, car builders are looking forward to the next event for faster times.

NEW RECORDS MADE JUNE 5-6

"A" Roadster—117.515 mph. aver.
.... Spurgin & Giovanine

"A" Streamliner—127.120 mph. aver.
.... Alex Xydias

"C" Roadster—139.760 mph. aver.
.... Randy Shinn

CLUB POINTS STANDINGS JUNE, 1948

Pos.	Club	June	Total
1	Road Runners	1,340	2,650
2	Low Flyers	830	1,630
3	Lancers	500	1,610
4	Strokers	550	940
5	Dolphins	600	860
6	Gaters	600	760
7	Albata	300	720
8	Gear Grinders	230	690
9	San Diego Road Club	460	640
10	Gophers	410	620
11	Southern California Road Club	220	490
12	Sidewinders	350	390
13	Mobilers	190	380
14	Glendale Stokers	30	360
15	Pasadena Road Club	20	250
16	Clutchers	180	220
17	Hornets	130	130
18	Road Masters	50	50

OTHER EXISTING SCTA RECORDS

"B" Roadster—129.365 mph. aver.
.... Doug Hartelt

"B" Streamliner—145.640 mph. aver.
.... Stuart Hilborn

"C" Streamliner—144.855 mph. aver.
.... Burke & Francisco

"D" Roadster—130.76 mph. aver.
.... Randy Shinn

"D" Streamliner—As yet, no record set: 130 mph. min. req.)

LEFT — An association member pastes a safety reminder on the windshield of a spectator's car. RIGHT — This beautiful gold & white V-8 '60' streamliner was driven by owner Alex Xydias for a class A-S record.

CRA Holds Hot Rod '500'

By Dorothy Sloan

Winner Dempsey Wilson is surrounded by fans. His T roadster has a big bore Mercury engine with Weiand heads and manifold.

History was made and another forward step taken for the Roaring Roadsters when the California Roadster Association presented its 500-lap "Little Indianapolis" race for the Memorial Day week-end at Carrell Speedway in Gardena, California. A record crowd of over 17,000 turned out for the race.

The race was patterned after the big Indianapolis yearly classic. On the half-mile dirt track, the total was 250 miles instead of 500, but it was still the longest race in the history of roadsters.

The same number of cars—33 in all —were started and paced around the track by 'Pop' Ruttman, father of the famous Troy and a renowned driver in his own right, having been dirt-track champion in the Middlewest.

It was a beautiful sight; witnessed by a sell-out crowd, plus standees, that were deafened by the roar of motors as Babe Ouse gave them the green flag and they were away for the gruelling contest.

Very generous donations from local business houses, to be given as lap money, made first spot a desirable position to hold, and Don Freeland, sitting on the pole with fastest qualifying time, pulled into the lead in the first turn with an eye to getting his share. Bad luck rode with him in the second turn, however, and he spun out in the center of the turn with 32 cars hard on his heels.

It was nothing less than a small miracle that they all got past him safely and Roy Prosser gathered a few laps to his credit before Andy Linden took it away from him.

Andy was going good in the Chevy '6' he was driving for Nick Brajevich, until he pulled into the infield for a pit stop and hit a pole marker wiping out his whole undercarriage and putting him out of the running. The same thing happened to Jimmie Davies in Vince Duarte's famous No. 4.

Ed Korgan led the race for his share

of laps, giving way to Ed Barnett, Troy Ruttman, and Jim Rigsby, in that order, but by the 208th lap Dempsey Wilson had worked his way up from 17th spot in the line-up to take the lead and hold it uncontested all the way to the checkered flag. Dempsey had no car trouble with his big-bored Merc, No. 37, and only made two pit stops for refueling. He drove the whole 500 himself.

A good many of the boys spurned the aid of relief drivers, including Ed Barnett who took second place, and Puffy Puffer who finished third.

Lou Figaro and Jim Rigsby also fought it out unaided, and both of them worked under handicaps. Lou suffered badly blistered feet when his water hose broke early in the race, and Jim ran the last 100 laps driving with one hand while he held his car together with the other. The constant beating had jarred one of his welded doors open and broken the gas tank loose, so they wired the door and he held the gas tank in the seat beside him.

A great deal of respect was earned by the much-criticized "hot rods" when eighteen of them—a higher percentage than Indianapolis itself had — crossed the finish line, and a big step was made in getting the fact across to the public that the racing roadsters are no longer street jobs but highly specialized racing cars.

J. C. Agajanian, promoter of Carrell Speedway, was very happy about the whole thing when he arrived in Indianapolis the next morning to find that news of the California race had beaten him there.

Next year's "Little Indianapolis" is already a definite plan. In the meantime the C.R.A. will present a special Fourth of July holiday race of 100 laps with a line-up of 16 cars instead of the usual 12. Qualifying will take the place of the heat races and places will be determined by that alone. The show will also have a semi-main and a trophy dash.

Smiling Ed Barnett just pulled into the pits after finishing second.

BELOW—Coming into the stretch are Jim Rigsby (15), Chuck Leighton (59) and Bob Rozzano (41).

Vince Duarte's driver Jim Davies gets last minute instructions before leaving the pits.

In 37 is Dempsey Wilson getting pus off at the start of the race. Dick Hug in 35 is waiting for his push truck.

The Hartman, Wayne & Spalding trio with the full torsion bar Chevy 6 roadster which turned 134.52.

Gopher Club member Roland Mays' V-8 roadster had a time of 121.29 with Evans equipment and Weber cam.

Chevy 6 Turns 134.52 At Russetta Meet

A speed of 122.28 was reached by this A class roadster owned by Gene Jackson and Bob Holbert.

Bob Rufi's old Chevy 4 now belongs to driver Howard Markham. Present engine is a Ford 4 with 4 port Cook head and Dulen cam.

RUSSETTA—JUNE 13, 1948

Car No.	Name	Fastest Time	Av. Time
"A" ROADSTERS			
33A	John Ryan	121.78	118.97
44A	Roland Mays	121.29	
55A	J. E. Collins	117.80	
57A	Roy Burton	104.04	
78A	Don Olson	119.99	116.10
156A	Fred Norton	106.63	
166A	Frank Cox	110.02	
171A	Holbert-Jackson	122.28	113.02
199A	Kenneth Arnold	111.11	
210A	James Lambert	111.94	
218A	LeRoy Titus	110.56	
220A	David Whitmyer	105.88	
248A	Douglas Barlow	118.73	
332A	Edwin Perry	98.25	
"B" ROADSTERS			
64B	Roy C. Padgett	99.22	
181B	Joe Daleo	122.61	115.76
209B	Howard Helvik	88.34	
B	Doug Hartelt	133.13	128.53
213B	Charles Quesnel	112.07	
217B	Robert Thomas	111.52	
225B	Husting Freeman	111.52	
252B	Richard Jones	112.78	
253B	Joseph Warner	110.70	
306B	Robert Bentz	95.94	
305B	Ken Black	109.48	
258B	Phil Weiand	124.82	
"A" COUPES			
14A	Robert Cautley	121.29	
17A	John Perdue	97.08	
22A	Manuel Butkie	113.20	107.80
29A	James Henry	99.33	
30A	William King	97.72	
50A	David Dudley	94.73	
59A	Marion Thompson	102.85	
106A	Thomas Cobbs	86.76	
145A	Robert Pierson	115.28	111.13
219A	Clinton Dexter	109.75	
307A	Earl Smith	94.53	
336A	Charles Townsen	99.44	
300A	John Ford	87.46	
"B" COUPES			
91B	Donald Ness	102.85	
121B	Don Towle	109.62	106.19
198B	Bill Young	111.24	106.54
206B	Bob Brannigan	110.82	
335B	Herbert Ast	112.35	106.46
324B	Willy Werder	103.68	
"C" ROADSTERS			
8C	Nat Good	98.90	
106C	Thomas Cobbs	119.84	
245C	Edwin Davis	100.89	
13C	Dean Cottle	111.11	
"C" COUPES			
5C	Carl Taylor	106.76	102.99
10C	R. C. Kietzman	92.21	
12C	Ray Ingram	101.46	
STREAMLINERS			
65B	Howard Markham	123.96	
86	Hunter & Barnes	122.78	
GUEST ENTRIES			
501	Bill Spalding	134.52	
502B	Paul Wheeler	95.61	
503B	Vince Duarte	118.42	
504A	Tommy Tompkins	119.04	
505A	Milton Vogel	118.11	
506B	Fred Steinbroner	110.83	
219A	Clinton Dexter	109.75	
509B	Navarro	124.82	
507C	Beatty	123.62	

LEFT — From left to right, Russetta officials Technical Committeeman Dean Cottle, Treasurer C. E. Camp, Vice President Bob Corbett and Starter LeRoy Burton pose beside new starting stand.

Johnny Ryan's record A class '32 roadster runs Evans heads and manifold. Time 121.78.

171

Photos by Arch Heatherwick

Presenting

The new Ford has made its debut with radical changes in almost every respect.

Clean functional body lines with a minimum of ridges and chrome are in accord with the California custom trend, which professes removal of moldings and hood strips. Dash panel design also stresses simplicity. The dash is now rid of the usual clutter of plastic trimmings.

Chassis improvement is highlighted by the use of box section side rails. Coil springs in front and two semi-elliptical leaf springs in the rear provide for easy riding and roadability. Another comfort feature is the Hotchkiss drive.

Of primary concern to Hot Rod enthusiasts are the design changes in the engines. A choice of either '6' or V-8 is offered.

The famed V-8, holder of almost all track and dry lake Hot Rod competition records, is basically the same. The greatest single change is removal of the distributor from low on the front of the block to a higher position on the right side. It is angle-driven from the front of the camshaft. Crankshaft runs on three wide bearings with $\frac{7}{16}$ journal overlap. Aluminum pistons are used with three rings above and one below. Timing gear is also aluminum constructed.

SIX ENGINE

Type	L-head
No. cylinders	6
Bore x stroke, in.	3.3 x 4.4
Piston displacement, cu. in.	225.9
Taxable (S.A.E.-A.M.A.) horsepower	26.1
Max. brake horsepower at rpm	95 @ 3600
Compression ratio	6.8 to 1

The 1949 Ford

Oil filler pipe has been moved from rear of the manifold to the left side of the engine, permitting easier accessibility when changing oil. Cylinder head water connections are in the front of the head instead of in the center as in older models. Cylinder heads have been changed, making a new market for speed equipment to fit this engine.

Inline enthusiasts will note changes in the Ford Six which may help to get those essential extra miles per hour.

As with the Eight, the distributor is mounted on the side with the coil close to assure a hot spark.

Self-locking screw-type adjustable tappets are accessible through a removable cover on the right side of the engine.

With a longer crankshaft, the Six runs on four main bearings. They are all of the steel-back replaceable type.

Piston ring arrangement has the four rings above the pin with none below.

Spark is regulated by using difference between vacuum at the carburetor throat and at manifold as the controlling factor.

These new engines may be expected to make their appearance at the dry lakes and on the tracks in the near future.

V-8 ENGINE

Type	L-head, 90° "V"
No. cylinders	8
Bore x stroke, in.	3 3/16 x 3¾
Piston displacement, cu. in.	239.4
Taxable (S.A.E.-A.M.A.) horsepower	32.5
Max. brake horsepower at rpm	100 @ 3600
Compression ratio	6.8 to 1

This unusual accident took place during a hot rod race at Soldier's Field in Chicago. Luckily, Drivers Nick Karelas (2) and Wally Edwards (1) escaped serious injury.

Warren Thatcher, vice-prexy of the Pan Draggers Club of San Mateo, in "Little Joe." The car runs Edmunds heads, Edelbrock manifold, Winfield cam, stroked crank, bored, ported and relieved.

At the Farmington, Minnesota, track Tom Adelman wheels his fast roadster. The '46 Merc. mill has overbore, dual manifold and full race cam.

Milo Berg of Sacramento, California, runs this sleek job. The body is '36 Ford coach on '32 rails. Engine is '40 Merc. with Edelbrock heads and manifold.

From Visalia, California, comes this snap of Arnold Bremler's track roadster's engine. The power plant is Ford B Fargo. Car has been timed at 115 mph.

Sue Christensen of Racine, Wisconsin, with Bob Hansen's roadster. Bob hopes to enter it soon in local hot rod racing. (Word has it the engine is all chrome.)

This custom '33 V-8 belongs to A. A. Davis of Beverly Hills, Calif. Car has new Merc. engine, Thickstun manifold, special heads.

Nick Brajevich's C.R.A. track job runs '41 Chevy block, 3¾" stroke, 3⅝" bore, Wayne head and manifold, Riley carbs., Spalding ignition and cam.

Robert Dokes and Johnny Ackerman of the "motor city," Detroit, drive this sharp V-8 powered roadster. Body work is almost complete. Next step will be interior, then further engine improvements.

At the Porterville Speed Bowl Jerry Cherest (21) and Gene Perdu (1) speed past the grandstand. Cherest runs a T V-8 with Weiand manifold, Cyclone heads, Winfield cam and Spalding ignition.

Eugene Le Blanc of San Jose, California, built this custom '34 Ford coupe. Car runs Edelbrock heads and manifold, custom cam, is stroked and bored.

Bob Lindsey leaves this trail of steam during an invitational race at Riverside, California. Lindsey is a popular driver in California Hot Rods, Inc.

This track roadster, shown here at the 4/10 mile track at Farmington, Minn., is owned by Mike Siakooles. Engine runs Thickstun manifold, Winfield cam.

An excellent view of El Mirage Dry Lake sent in by Norman Grose of Los Angeles. In foreground, pretty 17-year-old Anita Smith, regular dry lakes attender.

Larry Lunetta's track job pictured on display in a Southern California Ford dealer's showroom window. Many of the Ford dealers sponsor track jobs.

Sunday is roadster day in San Mateo, California. Here drivers meet in a drive-in to begin a weekly road trip. This shot shows cars just before "takeoff."

LUBRICANTS *by W. I. "Bill" Gieseke*

This column is written by W. I. "Bill" Gieseke of the Solv-X Chemical Company, manufacturing chemists for the jobbing trade. Mr. Gieseke is a member of the Society of Automotive Engineers of the American Chemical Society, with seven years as Automotive and Lubrication Engineer for a major oil company. For twelve years he was an instructor at Frank Wiggins Trade School in the Engine Test Laboratory and for two years served as an Air Corps Instructor.

GENERAL. A lubricant may be defined as a substance having greasy properties and used almost exclusively for reducing friction between bearing surfaces; however, it may also be used as a rust preventive on metallic parts subject to corrosion.

Common lubricants may be classified as animal, vegetable, and mineral, according to the source from which they are derived.

Animal lubricants, such as tallow, sperm oil, lard oil, etc., are excellent lubricants provided they are not subject to high temperatures. They are not suitable for lubricating internal-combustion engines, since above certain temperatures they form fatty acids. Porpoise-jaw oil, used for lubricating expensive watches, is an excellent high-quality animal oil.

Certain vegetable lubricants, such as castor oil, olive oil, and cottonseed oil, have satisfactory lubricating qualities but are chemically unstable under conditions prevailing in internal-combustion engines. Straight mineral oils of high quality have almost completely replaced the blends of castor oil formerly used in high-output engines.

Mineral lubricants have many desirable properties for use in the lubrication of internal-combustion engines and are, therefore, described in detail in subsequent paragraphs.

DESCRIPTION AND CLASSIFICATION OF MINERAL LUBRICANTS. Lubricants may be readily classified according to their physical properties as solids, semisolids, and fluids. Solid lubricants, such as mica, soapstone, and graphite in finely powdered form, serve to fill the low spots in a bearing surface to form a perfectly smooth surface and at the same time to provide a slippery film to reduce friction. A finely divided solid lubricant also acts as a mild abrasive, smoothing the surface previously roughened by machining or excessive wear. Solids are fairly satisfactory on slow speed machines but lack the ability to dissipate heat, which is often an essential requirement. Certain solid lubricants have the ability to carry heavy loads and for this reason are often added to fluids to reduce wear between surfaces subjected to high unit pressures.

Semisolid lubricants include such substances as extremely heavy oils and greases. Modern industrial operations require a great number of such lubricants for special applications. Greases give good service when applied periodically, but because of their consistency they are not suitable for continuous or circulating lubrication systems. Fluid lubrication will be emphasized, especially the requirements of internal combustion engines.

Fluids (oils) are universally used in internal combustion engines for many reasons. They may be readily pumped or sprayed, they provide a good cushioning effect, and are effective in absorbing and distributing heat. In theory, fluid lubrication is based on the actual separation of surfaces so that no metallic contact occurs. (Fig. 1.)

In this way, as long as the oil film is unbroken, metallic friction is replaced by the internal friction (fluid friction) of the lubricant itself, and obviously under such an ideal condition no wear can occur. Many vital engine parts are given adequate protection by supplying oil under direct pressure, but where this method is impractical a mist or spray will generally be satisfactory. Parts carrying heavy loads at high rubbing velocities are, where possible, lubricated by direct pressure. In the process of circulating through the engine, oil absorbs heat from different parts and will later dissipate most of the heat through suitable coolers or heat exchangers. In this way engine parts are protected from both wear and excessive temperatures.

An ideal fluid lubricant would be capable of providing a strong oil film to prevent metallic friction, and at the same time create a minimum amount of oil drag or viscous friction. Unfortunately, however, the body or viscosity of oils is affected by temperature changes to such an extent that ideal conditions are difficult to attain. Variations in climatic temperatures alone will often create an astounding change in oil viscosity. It is not at all uncommon for some grades of oil to become completely solid in cold weather with consequent high oil drag and impaired circulation. Conversely, at high operating temperatures oil may thin out to such extent that the oil film is broken, which permits rapid wear of the moving parts. The major problem in lubrication is to obtain a satisfactory compromise between the above conditions.

ENGINE LUBRICATING OILS. Crude petroleum, which furnishes the fuel for internal-combustion engines, also supplies the most satisfactory oils for its lubrication. The numerous individual compounds contained in crude oil are arranged in groups, such as the paraffin series (Fig. 2) [saturated hydrocarbons], naphthalene series (Fig. 3), olefin series, aromatic series (Fig. 4), and others of lesser importance. A single crude sample may contain all of the above groups of the hydrocarbons in varying proportions. As a group the paraffins are most satisfactory for engine lubricants since they are very stable, have good lubricating qualities, and are affected least by temperature variations. Almost any crude contains a certain percentage of paraffin compounds, but the crudes taken from eastern United States oil fields contain a higher proportion than midcontinent or western crudes.

Since the paraffin hydrocarbons are most desirable in a finished oil, the refining process should endeavor to

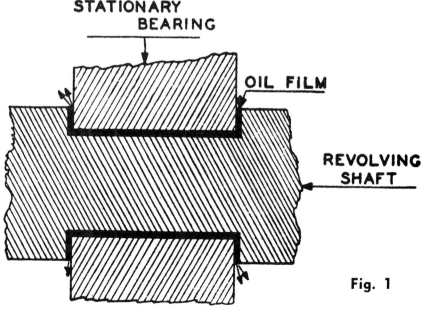

STATIONARY BEARING

OIL FILM

REVOLVING SHAFT

Fig. 1

eliminate all of the undesirable constituents without damage to the paraffin compounds. Two principal methods of refining are in common use: acid extraction and solvent extraction, the latter being of more recent development.

The acid extraction process involves the treatment of the lubricating stock with sulphuric acid which reacts chemically with many of the undesirable compounds, thus removing them from the mixture. The acid concentration and the duration of the treatment must be carefully controlled, since insufficient exposure will fail to remove the undesired compounds, and an overtreatment will destroy a part of the valuable constituents. In most cases, the type of crude has a direct bearing on the quality of the finished product when acid extraction is employed. Thus it would be very difficult, if not impossible, to produce a superior lubricating oil by this process, except from crudes containing a high

(Continued on page 31)

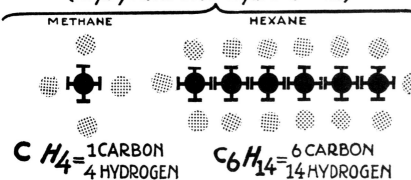

PARAFFIN SERIES
(Highly Saturated Hydrocarbons)

METHANE

HEXANE

$CH_4 = \begin{array}{l}1\ \text{CARBON}\\4\ \text{HYDROGEN}\end{array}$

$C_6H_{14} = \begin{array}{l}6\ \text{CARBON}\\14\ \text{HYDROGEN}\end{array}$

Fig. 2

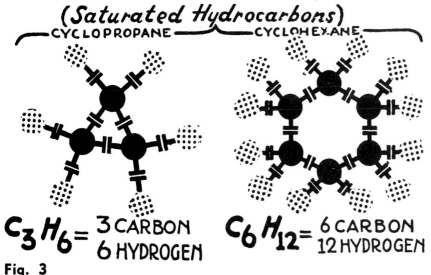

NAPHTHENE SERIES
(Saturated Hydrocarbons)

CYCLOPROPANE

CYCLOHEXANE

$C_3H_6 = \begin{array}{l}3\ \text{CARBON}\\6\ \text{HYDROGEN}\end{array}$

$C_6H_{12} = \begin{array}{l}6\ \text{CARBON}\\12\ \text{HYDROGEN}\end{array}$

Fig. 3

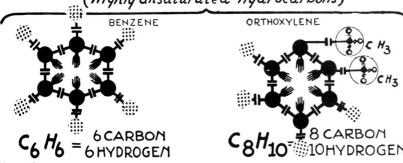

AROMATIC SERIES
(Highly Unsaturated Hydrocarbons)

BENZENE

ORTHOXYLENE

CH_3

CH_3

$C_6H_6 = \begin{array}{l}6\ \text{CARBON}\\6\ \text{HYDROGEN}\end{array}$

$C_8H_{10} = \begin{array}{l}8\ \text{CARBON}\\10\ \text{HYDROGEN}\end{array}$

Fig. 4

HOT ROD

(Continued from page 4)

Dear Sirs:

... I am from Washington and have been interested in roadsters for some time. I have owned one myself and intend driving one when I'm discharged from the service. What appealed to me most (in HRM) was your advertising. In Washington it is hard to find equipment ... Your magazine seems to leave nothing out as to what you may buy and where. ...

PFC GORDON F. HILL
USMC
Oceanside, Calif.

———

Dear Sirs:

A couple of months ago a friend of mine told me about your wonderful magazine and showed me a copy. I was so interested in it that I showed it to the PX officer in charge of sales and asked if he would be able to carry your magazine in the PX. Last week I noticed a few HOT ROD MAGAZINES on sale in the PX... the salesgirl said that they sell very well and that everyone is interested in them. So, now I feel right proud of myself for having introduced your HOT ROD MAG into the Service!

E. H. BERESFORD
Sgt. USMC
Santa Ana, Calif.

MUTUAL RACING ASSN.

By MELVIN DUDLEY

**Roadster Racing Is Gaining Popularity in the East
With Fans Eager to See the New Type Cars
Entering in Competition**

●

Indiana's Mutual Racing Association is fast becoming one of the country's most popular racing groups. Shown here are some of the association's top drivers and cars.

Also pictured on this page is "Dutch" Hurst, famed track anouncer and manager. "Dutch" races as a sideline, having many years of experience and much love for the racing game. When he was a kid, Hurst began racing out-board motorboats. He organized a racing club called The Hoosier Kids. The group made a great name for themselves in the outboard field. In later years "Dutch" turned to promoting boat, midget and stock car racing in the Midwest. He started the Velodrome in Indiana, which was the first midget track in that part of the country. Recently Hurst sold his interest in the Velodrome and has turned all his efforts to stock cars.

MRA scheduled an open roadster race for June 6 to be held at Winchester, Indiana. The race, however, was rained out and has been postponed until June 20. (This will be reviewed in a future

issue). The results should prove particularly interesting, as the track was recently resurfaced and is said to be very fast. The old track record of :23.68, set by Red Renner in a Ford 6, is expected to fall during the time trials for the race.

Mutual Racing is now using reverse starts for all of its events including the feature races. A new handicap system is being introduced into the association at present.

All of the drivers are looking forward to the opening of the Sun Valley Track at Anderson, Indiana. The oval is expected to present some record times, as it is being set up for 15 foot banks and the best racing surface. Owner Joe Helping is going all-out to make this an excellent short track.

Fans feel that Mutual's best shows are on the shorter tracks, most of the tracks, in use being ¼, ⅓ and ½ mile. So far this year, Mutual races are averaging $1,000 payoffs. Incidentally, hot rods in the Midwest are often referred to as stock cars.

Keep your eye on Mutual for greater racing in the future.

TOP TO BOTTOM:
At Mt. Lawn, Indiana, Dick Frazier (32) and John Arnold (62) tool around spinning Sam Skinner (58, facing camera) and all three cars reached the finish line. ● Mutual Officials are (left to right): Ralph Broadwater, Sec.-Treas.; Harry Modlin, Flagman; and Walter Straber, President. ● Ford 6 owned by Art Rhonemous was driven by Red Renner for the Winchester half-mile track record of :23.68 sec., Labor Day, 1947. ● Track manager and announcer Harold "Dutch" Hurst presents a trophy to Red Renner. ● Mutual's 1946 Champion, Ralph "Smokie" Stover, is seated in Joe Wall's (standing, left) Hudson 6 with Bob Lindsey, Luke Bratten, Leo Mills and Bob De Bord looking on.

Laughs...from here and there

By TOM MEDLEY

A woman driver had been hailed into court, and, when her name was called, the judge asked what the charges were against the prisoner.

"Suspicious actions, your Honor," answered the officer who had made the arrest.

"Suspicious actions?" queried his Honor. "What was she doing that seemed suspicious?"

"Well," replied the officer, "she was running within the speed limit, sounding her horn properly, and trying to keep on the right side of the street, so I arrested her."

"Just happened to run into an old friend down town."

"Was he glad to see you?"

"Heck no; I smashed his whole right fender."

Lawyer: "Then you say this man was drunk?"

Witness: "I do not; I simply said that he sat in his car for three hours in front of an excavation waiting for the light to turn green."

"LOOKS LIKE WE'LL HAVE TO RUN ON GASOLINE TODAY!"

"The doctor said he would have me on my feet in a fortnite."

"And did he?"

"Sure; I had to sell my roadster to pay his bill."

The best way to quit smoking is to carry an automatic lighter.

"I thought you owned a roadster!"

"I did, but I taught my wife to drive it and now I'm back to the street cars."

"Did anybody comment on the way you handled your new car?"

"One man made a brief remark: 'Fifty dollars and costs'."

STROKER McGURK

Photo by Alan Dean

VIRGINIA LEITH WITH A RACING PISTON AND ROD

Parts With Appeal

◀◀◀

Here's Virginia Leith with a racing piston-and-rod combination.

The unit is designed to withstand the high pressures of a speeding engine as well as the high temperatures developed. The piston has been cast to specifications required for a stroked engine. In all, this "part with appeal" is in four sections: piston, pin, rod and bearing. Basically, however, it's a two-piece outfit — which brings us to further specifications.

Twenty-one year old Virginia was born in Cleveland, Ohio. She attended Cleveland Heights High School in that city. Following graduation, she trekked to New York City for a try at modeling. It proved successful, and Miss Leith did modeling stints for some of the nation's largest agencies including John Powers. After two years modeling in New York she turned to Hollywood where she has continued her career under the supervision of the Mary Webb Davis Agency.

Virginia is now being groomed for screen work and can be assured of a very bright future.

Other specifications: 5'7", brown hair, green eyes.

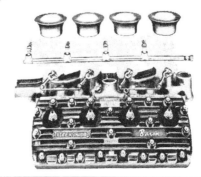

MANUFACTURERS' NEWS

Roy Richter at Bell Auto Parts has announced that a new addition to his shop is being built. This addition will house his mail order offices.

* * *

Electronic Balancing Company has installed a new Clayton dynamometer that will register up to 500 horsepower. Owner Bill Fisher stated that it is one of the largest in the country. This fine machine will be at the disposal of engine builders on a rental basis to determine power ratings and acceleration curves.

* * *

John T. Jenkins of Sherman Oaks, California, announces the new Jenkins distributor.

* * *

A new Super H cam has been developed by Harman & Collins, Inc., for use in straightaway racing. This is the same grind used in the 99.114 mph world's record 225 cubic-inch Hydroplane, *The California Kid*.

CHATTER

Understand that a Midwest roadster driver was unofficially clocked at :21.62 for ½ mile at the paved Winchester, Indiana, track. This time is reported faster than any midget record set there and only .51 seconds slower than the track record set by a big car Offy. (270 cu. in.). This is, without a doubt, a great accomplishment for a hot rod.

* * *

Frank Crowley has announced completion of the Lakeland Stadium at 1800 South Durfee in El Monte, California. The ¼-mile dirt track, with a 5,000 seating capacity, will run daylight roadster and midget races.

* * *

Latest ASC Standings

CAR	DRIVER	POINTS
1	George Seeger	134
5	Bruce Emmons	109
2	Bill Steves	92
2	Lewie Shell	83
3	Grant Lambert	83
4	Chuck Burness	77
5	Pat Patrick	72
75	Len Shreenan	69
6	Len Shreenan	68
33	Pat Patrick	66
7	Bill LeRoy	62
8	Mickey Davis	60
22	Bob Goux	60
9	Dan Maruffo	58
20A	John Kelley	55
10	Bruce McClaire	54
9	Roy Tremaine	54
58	Bruce McClaire	54
70	Perry Logan	53
44	Larry Mueller	48

GRANT'S RACING COMBINATION
For Speed Records

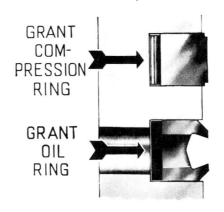

GRANT COMPRESSION RING

GRANT OIL RING

1. Keeps film of oil on cyl. walls.
2. Allows much freer running engine. Quick break-in.
3. Prevents blowby and power loss.
4. Gives upper ring lubrication.

1. Carries off only Excess oil.
2. No spring used in back of oil ring in racing set-ups.

They Never Dry Your Cylinder Walls

Make it run even better
—Use Grant Inserts and Mains for Fords and Mercurys — Use Grant Piston Pins

Aurora Stadium Speedway in Seattle, Washington, has invited the "boys" to "come up anytime. Would make a nice vacation trip . . . Bring your hot rods."

* * *

S.C.T.A. has a new red-and-white panel truck. This attractive and practical truck has been long needed to carry on Association activities. Incidentally, S.C.T.A. has completed plans for a new office. The address will be announced in the near future.

* * *

As this issue goes to press, the hot rods will make their initial appearance at the popular Gilmore Stadium in Los Angeles. The show will feature the top drivers of California Hot Rods, Inc.

* * *

Johnny Lucas has retired as President of the CHR. His new occupation will be as press agent to newspapers and radio stations in the Imperial Valley district. New business manager of the association is Ad Man Bill Hunter.

* * *

Hot rods will go to San Bernardino track on June 29.

The car speeds listed are FASTEST QUALIFYING TIMES of each car entered in the El Mirage Dry Lake Speed Trials conducted by the Southern California Timing Association, on June 5-6, 1948. These speeds shown do not include times made in either direction on record attempts. S.C.T.A. Competition Rules state that as a car breaks one of the existing Class Records, in qualifying, it is eligible to make its record attempt with return run in the opposite direction within a 15-minute elapsed time.

CLASS "B" ROADSTERS

1-R—Doug Hartelt	127.84
6—Jim Palm	116.12
22—Bob Drew	114.35
27—Harvey Haller	120.96
38—Robert Wenz	122.11
41—Myron Froelich	116.27
50—Jay Andrews	109.63
61—Jack Avakian	124.48
63—Roland Mays	117.49
101—Don Olson	117.34
106—Alger & Sterr.	119.04
110—Jim Guptill	120.48
121—Fred Hadley	116.42
124—Stanley Betz	105.14
132—Dean Batchelor	110.42
143—Bill McBurney	110.29
144—Fred Riedman	110.62
148—Don Baker	118.89
149—Dick Finkle	108.30
154—James Woods	108.17
155—Lee Enfiajian	113.20
156—Dick Megugorac	105.50
214—Carl Kaylor	119.20
220—Palma & Kukura	116.27
225—Bill Braun	119.68
238—Booth & Dugan	112.92
250—Richard Ohrbom	116.73
259—Don Nicholson	116.73
260—Spalding Bros.	125.35
262—Frank Morimoto	106.13
292—Porazzo Bros.	109.22
299—Lehmnn-Swatrk	113.20
156—Dick Megugorac	105.50
214—Carl Keylor	119.20
220—Palma & Kukura	116.27
225—Bill Braun	119.68
307—Ernest Dewey	117.34
318—Norm Lean	118.26
319—Chuck Rotter	111.66
320—Don Conroy	115.38
321—Dan Busby	121.45
323—Dick Schilling	111.52
330—Bob Taylor	113.78

333—Harold Whilldin	117.95
335—Downey & Cohrn	116.42
337—John Collins	115.68
342—John Cramer	102.04
350—Bob Holden	113.63
362—Eckloff & Hutton	99.33
366—Ray Morisette	108.56
360—Dave McCartney	117.03
361—Eppard Bros.	90.27
367—Ernest Laby	93.45
371—Glenn McNatt	100.11
376—J. J. Jones	101.58
380—Leonard Koch	97.19
416—Robert Riggs	88.92
435—Charles Clark	119.68
442—Jim Rawding	118.11
455—Arthur Tremaine	118.57
458—Hugh Romstedt	113.57
465—Albert Pahland	116.58
468—Lee Grey	97.19
470—Fred Oatman	120.00
494—Gordon Patterson	107.01
505—LeRoy Holmes	110.29
506—J. E. Tucker	93.55
516—Wesley Gardner	109.35
519—Tom Nicklin	110.29
524—Don Waite	111.11
528—Gil Scirmeister	106.76
535—Roy Siegner	107.78
536—Buz Buswell	110.15
575—Reiff & Wells	88.23
629—Harry Garlick	108.56
639—W. R. Murray	95.23
640—Loren Walker	113.06
701—Clark & Roberts	115.83
710—Henry Simlo	102.38
712—Teddy Miller	113.47
717—Harold Johansen	117.08
742—Harry Tham	92.59
750—Charles Mohr	94.24
751—Neil Berrong	104.28
790—Gordon Reed	101.80
799—A. Youngblood	96.56
866—Beckham-Clews	104.89

868—Donald Cox	96.35
875—M. J. Collins	102.04
881—Ralph Weston	100.78
882—B.T. Cantarini	116.12

GUESTS
(CLASS "B" ROADSTERS)

901—J. B. Morris	91.64
908—Marvin Phillips	96.98
909—Nelson Morris	105.63
910—Ray Ingalls	98.90
911—W. Gotchall	102.85

CLASS "C" ROADSTERS

2—Randy Shinn	140.62
17—Ludvig Solberg	120.80
20—Harold Warnock	117.49
21—Ed Stewart	122.11
30—Don Blair	114.50
35—Chuck Hossfeld	112.64
47—Frank Leonard	121.29
48—Bob Reemsnyder	123.11
52—Frank Beagle	118.57
53—Coshow Bros.	118.11
54—Wally O'Brien	114.79
55—C. W. Scott	121.62
59—Don Arnett	116.58
65—Bub Marcia	118.26
67—Fred Bagula	123.45
69—John Ryan	120.00
104—Don Olson	117.34
135—Peterman-Carillo	114.20
160—Jim Nairn	120.16
165—L. McCormick	119.52
170—Vern Ellyson	113.73
173—Don Lenk	115.83
191—Chuck Dunn	112.21
200—Kenny Parks	123.96
255—John Goldman	115.97
273—Guy Wheatley	95.44
313—K. Yenawine	112.21
315—Paul Schiefer	135.13
322—Dorling-Lyons	114.21
325—Harold Daigh	125.17
331—Doug Harrison	116.73
338—Taylor-Einhaus	117.64

340—Ted White	121.13
341—Jack Trousdale	103.92
372—Wilmer McNatt	109.22
461—Harold Osborn	119.36
473—James Hawley	113.20
500—Harber Bros.	117.34
520—Major Gilbert	115.23
540—Bob Bennett	119.20
541—Tommy Tomkins	117.49
544—Arthur Crane	107.01
593—Calvin Peterson	113.35
624—Geo. Castera	117.80
634—Ken Sills	113.49
636—Dale Simpson	108.04
637—Bruce Jochim	112.50
650—Jim Plummer	109.89
707—Nick Khougaz	108.30
821—Nick Christos	98.90
882—B. T. Cantarini	116.12

CLASS "A" ROADSTERS

15—Spurgin-Giov.	116.27
157—Richard Fugle	100.89
422—Jack Kempster	63.69

CLASS "A" STREAMLINERS

555—Alex Xydias	124.48

CLASS "B" STREAMLINERS

11—Stuart Hilborn	142.63
131—Breene & Haller	128.93
14—Phil Remington	128.75
16—Lee & G. Wise	118.73
147—Fred Renoe	106.64
197—Hershom Bros.	93.94
222—Jim Lindsley	119.68
490—Kay Kimes	84.90
493—G. L. Patterson	107.01

CLASS "C" SREAMLINERS

4—Burke-Francisco	144.69
205—Davis-Pettigrew	102.04
459—Dean Moon	114.21
600—Henrich-Bishop	115.53
720—Stuart Harper	117.18
800—Dowell-Anderson	136.57

CLASS "D" ROADSTERS

34—Akton Miller	120.48
384—F. Livingston	110.15
452—J. K. Triplett	103.92

DEFINITION OF CLASSES

The Car Classes shall be divided into Roadsters and Streamliners, with four classes in each body type as follows:

"A" Class—0 to 183 cubic inches engine displacement.

"B" Class—183 to 250 cubic inches engine displacement.

"C" Class—250 to 350 cubic inches engine displacement.

"D" Classs—350 and over cubic inches engine displacement.

Classified Advertisements

RACE RESULTS

CRA

CULVER CITY SPEEDWAY—May 21—¼-mile, paved, banked. Road race. Fastest qualifying time, 1:36.25, set by Roy Prosser.
Trophy Dash (3 laps)—1, Roy Prosser; 2, LeRoy Nooks 1:36.25.
First Heat (10 laps)—1, Red Amic; 2, Walt James; 3, Johnny Palmer. 3:24.55.
Second Heat (10 laps)—1, Don Freeland; 2, Puffy Puffer; 3, Elmer Arndt. 3:17.99.
Third Heat (10 laps)—1, Chuck Leighton; 2, Red Amic; 3, Dick Hughes. 3:11.98.
Fourth Heat (10 laps)—1, Don Freeland; 2, Roy Prosser; 3, Bob Cross. 3:20.96.
Semi-Main (15 laps)—1, Red Amic; 2, Lou Figaro; 3, Chuck Leighton. 13:45.87.
Main (25 laps)—1, Don Freeland; 2, Roy Prosser; 3, Ken Stansberry. No time given.

CARRELL SPEEDWAY, Gardena, Calif—May 22—½-mile, dirt. Fastest qualifying time, :24.09, set by Troy Ruttman.
Trophy Dash (3 laps)—1, Jimmy Davies; 2, Troy Ruttman. 1:12.13.
First Heat (6 laps)—1, Edb Papac; 2, Bob Scott; 3, Les Hervey. 2:35.05.
Second Heat (6 laps)—1, Don Freeland; 2, Chuck Leighton; 3, Dempsey Wilson. 2:33.71.
Third Heat (6 laps)—1, Puffy Puffer; 2, Walt James; 3, Bruce Blair. 2:33.9.
Fourth Heat (6 laps)—1, Troy Ruttman; 2, Red Amic; 3, Jimmy Davies. 2:26.95.
Semi-Main (15 laps)—1, Chuck Leighton; 2, Don Freeland; 3, Ed Papac. 6:30.80.
Main (25 laps)—1, Jimmy Davies; 2, Troy Ruttman; 3, Jay Frank. 10:21.36.

CARRELL SPEEDWAY—May 29—½-mile, dirt.
(500 laps)—1, Dempsey Wilson; 2, Ed Barnett; 3, Puffy Puffer.

CARRELL SPEEDWAY—June 5—½-mile, dirt. Fastest qualifying time, :23.06, set by Bob Cross.
Trophy Dash (3 laps)—1, Ed Kassold; 2, Bob Cross. 1:11.06.
First Heat (6 laps)—1, Ed Papac; 2, Bob Scott; 3, John Bray. 2:38.72.
Second Heat (6 laps)—1, Walt James; 2, Jay Frank; 3, Ed Barnett. 2:31.48.
Third Heat (6 laps)—1, Puffy Puffer; 2, Ken Stansberry; 3, Dick McClung. 2:30.87.
Fourth Heat (6 laps)—1, Don Freeland; 2, Lou Figaro; 3, Bob Cross. 2:25.74.
Semi-Main (15 laps)—1, Walt James; 2, Bob Garrett; 3, Jay Frank. 6:64.19.
Main (25 laps)—1, Bob Cross; 2, Lou Figaro; 3, Red Amic. 13:90.86.

CARRELL SPEEDWAY—June 12—½-mile, dirt. Fastest qualifying time, :23.49, set by Don Freeland.
Trophy Dash (3 laps)—1, Ed Kassold; 2, Don Freeland. 1:12.19.
First Heat (6 laps)—1, Bob Ascot; 2, Les Hervey; 3, Jim Bray. 2:34.02.
Second Heat (6 laps)—1, Ed Korgan; 2, Walt James; 3, Elmer Arndt. 2:39.00.
Third Heat (6 laps)—1, Roy Prosser; 2, Bob Rozzano; 3, Jimmy Davies. 2:27.77.
Fourth Heat (6 laps)—1, Lou Figaro; 2, Don Freeland; 3, Bob Cross. 2:26.55.

Semi-Main (15 laps)—1, Ken Stansberry; 2, Walt James; 3, Elmer Arndt. 6:11.95.
Main (25 laps)—1, Jimmy Davies; 2, Roy Prosser; 3, Bob Cross. 10:29.41.

CARRELL SPEEDWAY—June 19—½-mile, dirt. Fastest qualifying time, :23.85, set by Bob Cross.
Trophy Dash (2 laps)—1, Ken Stansberry; 2, Bob Cross. :53.02.
First Heat (6 laps)—1, Bob Rozzano; 2, Frank Danielson; 3, Bob Ascot. 2:39.49.
Second Heat (6 laps)—1, Lou Figaro; 2, Ed Papac; 3, Puffy Puffer. 2:36.52.
Third Heat (6 laps)—1, Roy Prosser; 2, Chuck Leighton; 3, Jimmy Davies. 2:29.44.
Fourth Heat (6 laps)—1, Don Freeland; 2, Ed Kassold; 3, Bob Cross. 2:27.28.
Semi-Main (15 laps)—1, Bob Rozzano; 2, Lou Figaro; 3, Frank Danielson. 6:26.72.
Main (25 laps)—1, Chuck Leighton; 2, Ed Kassold; 3, Roy Prosser. 10:39.71.

OSA (Ohio Speedway Association)
BEREA, OHIO—May 30—Main Event won by Mike Lesick (Akron Speed Shop Special).
NORWALK, OHIO—May 31—Main event won by Mike Lesick.

ASC
OCEANSIDE RECREATION PARK, Oceanside, California—May 29.
Trophy Dash (3 laps)—1. George Seeger, 2. Bud Hetzler. :55.23.
1st Heat (6 laps)—1. Gene Reed, 2. Ray Sharp, 3. Paul Hoak. 2:01.77.
2nd Heat (6 laps)—1. Ray Sharp, 2. Don Trippe, 3. Bill Donivan. 1:57.85.
3rd Heat (6 laps)—1. Chet Stafford, 2. Dan Maruffo, 3. Bill Lewis. 1:52.66.
4th Heat (6 laps)—1. George Seeger, 2. Len Shreenan, 3. Bud Hetzler. 1:50.89.
Semi Main (12 laps)—1. Paul Hoak, 2. Gene Reed, 3. Ray Sharp. 3:50.81.
Main (25 laps)—1. George Seeger, 2. Ray Sharp, 3. Dan Maruffo. 8:01.36.
OCEANSIDE—May 22.
Trophy Dash (3 laps)—1. George Seeger, 2. Grant Lambert. :53.15.
1st Heat (5 laps)—1. Curtis Hayes, 2. Bill Donivan, 3. Willie Perren. 1:55.94.
2nd Heat (5 laps)—1. Len Shreenan, 2. Pat Patrick, 3. Bud Hetzler. 1:51.71.
3rd Heat (5 laps)—1. Pat Patrick, 2. Mickey Davis, 3. Bud Hetzler. 1:49.64.
4th Heat (5 laps)—1. Grant Lambert, 2. Dan Maruffo, 3. Chet Stafford. 1:49.51.
Semi Main (12 laps)—1. Curtis Hayes, 2. Len Shreenan, 3. Bill Donivan. 3:49.24.
Main Event (25 laps)—1. Len Shreenan, 2. Dan Maruffo, 3. Grant Lambert. (no time, due to accident).
OCEANSIDE—May 15.
Trophy Dash (3 laps)—1. Bill Steves, 2. Bud Hetzler. 1:06.00.
1st Heat (5 laps)—1. Scott Caine, 2. Dan Maruffo, 3. Len Shreenan. 1:38.55.
2nd Heat (5 laps)—1. Grant Lambert, 2. Bill Steves, 3. Chet Stafford. 1:33.22.
Special (3 laps)—1. Bill Steves, 2. Grant Lambert.
Main Event (30 laps)—1. Bill Steves, 2. Len Shreenan, 3. Grant Lambert. 10:09.00.

NASCAR 1948 Rules and Roadster Specifications

(Continued from page 8)

Roadster Championship at Daytona Beach. Due to the expense involved, it is recommended that superchargers be barred from all roadster competition in 1949.

2. All welding and construction methods used throughout the car must measure up to strict N A S - C A R standards.

3. Exhaust pipes should extend past driver's seat.

Local or association rules will apply in all races excepting National Championship events when N A S C A R rules will apply.

LUBRICATION

(Continued from page 19)

percentage of paraffin hydrocarbons.

Solvent extraction, on the other hand, does not require a chemical reaction but, as the name implies, separates the various compounds by dissolving them with certain selected solvents. Advantage is taken of the fact that the desirable compounds are soluble in particular fluids such as propane, whereas the undesirable ingredients are soluble in other liquids. By the use of one or more solvents the lubricating stock may be accurately divided into the desired fractions. By this process a good lubricating oil may be produced from practically any crude.

Oils extracted by either of the above methods require many treatments other than the basic extraction process. In order to remove heavy wax which will cause cold weather difficulties, the oil is chilled as low as -30° F., and the solid wax is removed by special filters or centrifugal separators. Filtration through fuller's earth or other decolorizing earth is an essential and valuable part of must refining methods. After being properly purified, the various "cuts" taken by low pressure distillation are accurately blended to give the various grades of oil required by modern industrial operations.

Additional copies may be obtained by sending 25c per copy to SOLV-X CHEMICAL COMPANY, "Manufacturing Chemists for the Jobbing Trade", 3608 Roselawn Ave., CHurchill 9-3533, Glendale 8, California.—Copyright 1946 (Permission to reprint reserved).

HOT ROD
Magazine

25¢

F 145A

Photo by Floyd Wheeler

ob Pierson's '36 Competition Coupe AUGUST, 1948 **25¢**

SHARP SPEED EQUIPMENT

6225 Wilmington Avenue   **LOgan 5-1329**   **Los Angeles, Calif.**

Dept. B

* ★ DUAL AND TRIPLET MANIFOLDS
* ★ HIGH COMPRESSION HEADS
* ★ CAMS—ROAD, TRACK and LAKES
* ★ SAFETY HUBS
* ★ FOOT PEDALS
* ★ CENTER MOUNT IDLER BRACKETS

●

CAMS

A SHARP EQUIPPED ENGINE   *Ground to Your Engine Specifications*

See Your Dealer Or Write For Information

It's in the Bag . . .

Dear Sirs:

. . . We have had a hard time getting useful information on Hot Rod construction, but your magazine really fills the bill.

. . . Please enter my name on the subscription list starting me out with the first issue or, if you are sold out, please begin with the earliest possible issue.

MARTIN BRAUNS
Chicago, Ill.

Literally hundreds of readers have requested back issues of HRM. There are still a limited number of copies of HRM for January, March, April, and June available.—ED.

———

Dear Sirs:

In your last issue I saw a comment in "It's in the Bag." It states that on the east coast all we have are cold rods. I disagree. Within a ten-mile area, there are three A-V8's and two '32's with Mercury engine, cam, heads and setup.

I belong to the Eastern Roadster Racing Club. . . . We race mostly on half-mile tracks in Virginia. Enclosed is a picture of my track roadster. It's a full Winfield. . . .

BILL WINTERBOTTOM
Wallingford, Pa.

———

Dear Sir:

. . . I saw Thomas Fleming's letter on Cold Rods in the July issue and I beg to differ with him. . . . There aren't any large number (of hot rods), but I wouldn't say there isn't anything under the hoods. He must be talking about the boys who try to make people think they have something under the hood. . . .

C. R. KURKA
Pocomoke, Md.

Thanks to readers Winterbottom and Kurka, as well as others, who have let us know that there are HOT RODS on the east coast. We had a hunch that there were.—ED.

Hot Rod Magazine:

Please send me HRM for one year beginning with the July issue.

RON E. KNITT,
Toronto Racing Drivers' Club,
Toronto, Canada

Hot Rod Magazine:

. . . I live in central Nebraska where Hot Rods are few and far between. We have no club around here but are trying to get one started.

JIM GESSFORD
Holdrege, Neb.

Hot Rod enthusiasts interested in joining this proposed club may obtain Mr. Gessford's address by dropping a card or letter to HRM asking for same. —ED.

———

Dear Sir:

After reading your Questions and Answers (HRM, July, 1948), we thought it might be advisable to inform your magazine that Arnold Birner vacated his office as President of Mojave Timing Association, Inc. . . . Our new President is Robert F. Baldwin.

M.T.A., Inc. is limited to not more than one hundred members nor more than five clubs at any one time. At this time we have the five clubs—the BH Club, Rumblers, 4 Barrel Club, Lobers, and the Roadsters. There are, on the average, five memberships open in the above-named clubs. . . .

M. J. BUTLER,
Secretary, M.T.A.
Los Angeles, Cal.

Editor's Column

Without a doubt, the biggest news of the month is Dick Frazier's amazing world's record half mile time—:21.37—set in a HOT ROD. Complete coverage, including photos, will be in the September HRM.

Many clubs and individuals have written us regarding public opinion on hot rods. One club offers its practical solution in this issue. A HELPFUL HAND, appears on page 31.

Members of California Hot Rods, Inc. recently bowed in at Gilmore Stadium in Los Angeles. Action photos of the opening races are on pages 8 and 9.

Most current news in this issue is coverage of SCTA's July 17 and 18 timing meet. This pictorial feature is on pages 10 and 11.

Indiana roadster racing is featured on pages 12 and 13.

Don't say we didn't tell you! Parts with Appeal (page 22) is a "must" in this issue.

Turn to page 26 for news of your favorite club or association. Our thanks to those who are contributing to this new feature. If your hot rod organization is not represented, ask your club secretary to contact HRM.

The August Hot Rod of the Month is Bob Pierson's beautiful white coupe. This custom-built car represents an important phase in hot rodding. Story and graphic breakdown of this car are on pages 6 and 7.

In answer to many requests—we do have some back issues available. Those issues still in stock are January, March, April and June.

Many of our readers have requested figures on gear ratios, engine displacements, dry lakes time computations, etc. Through the helpful cooperation of the Southern California Timing Association, Inc., HRM's technical page for August gives a complete breakdown of: cubic inch change on bored and stroked engines, cubic inch displacement on American automotive engines, tachometer-gear ratio-tire size relationship and quarter-mile speed computations in seconds. All of this information has been printed on a single page for the convenient use of hot rod enthusiasts everywhere.

Your letters and photos are still welcome.—ED.

HOT ROD Magazine

"World's Most Complete Hot Rod Coverage"

TABLE OF CONTENTS

Vol. 1   HRM—Published Monthly   No. 8

Associate Editors .... Robert E. Petersen, Robert R. Lindsay

Technical Advisers .... W. I. 'Bill' Gieseke, Wally Parks

Advertising .... George Peterson

Art Director .... Alice Van Norman

Photography .... Dyson Smith, Paul Schaeffer, Floyd Wheeler, Paul Panghorn, Rick, Pete, Vic Drake, Al Moss

Cartoons and Humor .... Tom Medley

Reporters .... Robert Williams, Glenn Glendening, Dick Robinson, Richard K. Martin, Arthur Elliot, William H. Sippel, Bob Machin, Pauline Bayer and Robert Seth

Subscription Department .... Marilyn Lord

Distribution .... Gordon Behn

ON THE COVER: Caught in action at a recent Russetta Timing meet, Bob Pierson drives his record coupe through the course.

This Fast Coupe is a Typical Russetta Timing Entry

Bob Pierson's '36 Ford is an outstanding example of a clean appearing, high performance competition coupe.

Plans for the car were formulated in 1943 when Bob, who was attending Inglewood High, started to build his first '36 Ford. The car was only partly completed when Pierson entered the Air Corps as an aviation cadet. He sold his car and began planning a new one.

While still in the service, he found a car near Denver, bringing it home after his discharge. Then followed the task of finding the necessary parts and a suitable '46 Mercury engine. Work was done in Bobbie Meek's garage with Bobbie adding his skill to the building and designing.

After two years the car made its first appearance at the dry lakes. At the first Russetta Timing Meet of the 1948 season, the car clocked 106, with the speed being raised at each of the two succeeding meets. Fastest speed to date was turned at the last meet when Bob did 117.03, running alcohol fuel, to take the A class record.

Active in club activities, Bob is Vice-President of the Coupes Club and Secretary of Russetta Timing Association. He is employed by a used car dealer who has found Pierson's automotive know-how a worth-while asset.

In the future a new car will be built embodying the best points of this car with certain improvements. The car will be a chopped and channeled full-belly-pan '36 Ford, designed strictly for dry lakes competition.

Until then he'll continue development of his present car with an eye toward higher speed and performance.

Interior displays chrome dash, steering shift, tan and brown Runyan upholstery.

Side view shows car with full equipment as it is driven on the highway.

Engine is a '46 Mercury, most popular engine at time trials today.

Bob Pierson beside his coupe. Car is stripped of accessories for lakes competition.

Photos by Pete

Construction Cutaway

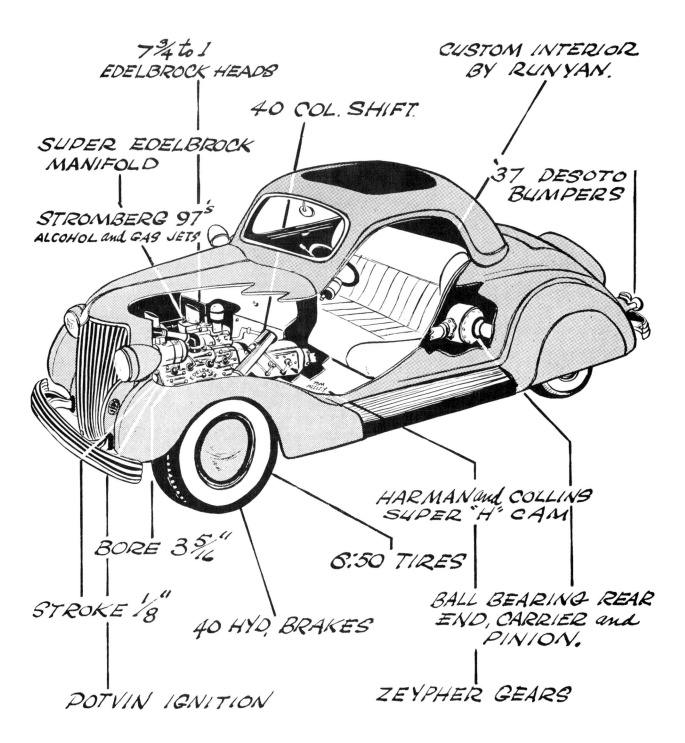

7¾ to 1
EDELBROCK HEADS

CUSTOM INTERIOR
BY RUNYAN.

40 COL. SHIFT.

SUPER EDELBROCK
MANIFOLD

'37 DESOTO
BUMPERS

STROMBERG 97's
ALCOHOL and GAS JETS

HARMAN and COLLINS
SUPER "H" CAM

BORE 3⁵⁄₁₆"

6:50 TIRES

STROKE ¹⁄₈"

40 HYD. BRAKES

BALL BEARING REAR
END, CARRIER and
PINION.

POTVIN IGNITION

ZEYPHER GEARS

C.H.R. Opens At Gilmore Stadium

Photo by Paul Panghorn

Photo by Pete

ROADSTERS GET GREEN FLAG IN MIDGET TERRITORY

A total of more than 15,000 spectators watched drivers of the California Hot Rods, Inc. during their first three races at Gilmore Stadium in Los Angeles.

It was Gilmore Manager Gene Doyle's foresight that led to the start of roadster racing at the stadium.

The CHR bowed in at Gilmore on June 21, followed up on June 28, skipped the Fourth of July week-end, returned July 12 to thrill the crowds with their excellent roadster events. Main event winners of these races were (pictures on page 28), in order of race date: Stan Kross, Dick Vineyard, and Mickey Davis.

Especially interesting is Vineyard's No. 53. The track job is chain driven. Also unusual is number 53's motor, a G.M.C. truck engine. (This is similar to a Chevy.) Dick claims the arrangement performs without fault.

Long an ambition of hot rod race drivers, Gilmore is a clay-surfaced ¼ mile oval. Most important to the purses is the stadium's convenient location, close not only to Los Angeles but Hollywood and other suburban communities.

Roadster racing fans are in for exciting shows each Monday night when the CHR takes over Gilmore Stadium.

(Upper left) After Len Shreenan (76) spun out on the north turn, Bud Gregory (55) ran into trouble trying to avoid him. Veteran hot-rod driver Andy Linden (5) passed safely by going high.

(Lower left) Pat Flaherty (6) succeeds in passing Dick McClung (57) during a main event. Flaherty wound up third in this feature race.

(Right) Freddie Hayes' (27) spin resulted in this unusual shot. Bob Lindsey (28) climbs out of his roadster as Hayes ponders the geyser-like effect of a broken radiator connection.

Photo by Paul Panghorn

LD FAITHFUL?

A long line of spectators watch Eugene Perello leave the start.

Hilborn Clocks 150.50 MPH at S.C.T.A. Meet

By WALLY PARKS

Stuart Hilborn, in his Class B Streamliner (HRM, April, 1948) reached just beyond the coveted 150-mile-an-hour mark to time 150.50 one way at El Mirage on July 17. Running a '34 V8 block, Stu set this amazing record. On the following day of the meet, he set a new B Streamliner record of 146.47 mph.

Close competition between former record holder Randy Shinn, Harold Daigh and Paul Schiefer ended with Daigh setting a new C Roadster record.

Alex Xydias, Doug Hartelt and the Spurgin-Giovinni team raised their previous record times.

Records attained at the meet include:

Class	Car	Record	Old Record
A Streamliner	Alex Xydias	129.05	127.120
A Roadster	Spurgin-Giovinni	118.48	117.515
B Roadster	Doug Hartelt	131.005	129.365
C Roadster	Harold Daigh	140.955	139.760

Many unusual cars turned out for the meet, including Charles Dimmit's elongated Caddie V16, shown below.

S.C.T.A., Inc. has announced that the driver who holds the Class B Roadser record at the end of this season will receive a new television set. This set will be donated by Tommy Lee.

With safety and achievement as their foremost goals, S.C.T.A. can be proud of its July 17-18 timing meet. Five out of eight classes had new records established.

Photos by Pete

Don Waite brought this Ford 4 rear engine "T" to the Lakes. With a Miller head, Bertrand cam and Wico ignition the car turned 121.25.

New C Roadster record holder Harold Daigh leaves the traps. His 268 cu. in. '46 Merc. engine has a Smith cam, Kurten ignition, Navarro heads and manifold.

This unusual 16 cyl. Cadillac rear engine Zephyr built by Charles Dimmitt made its first lakes appearance.

Arnold Birner tunes his 141.06 m.p.h. Four Port Riley. The '32 Ford block has 205 cu. in. displacement.

The fuel injection system that Stuart Hilborn used on his '34 Ford engine to break the 150 m.p.h. mark. Howard Wilson drove.

Starting officials check safety belts, goggles, extinguishers, and give last minute course information to drivers awaiting the green light.

INDIANA ROADSTER RACING

With ever-increasing popularity, Indiana's Mutual Racing Association continues to entertain thousands of midwest roadster racing fans.

No small news item is the new world's record for the half-mile set by Dick Frazier of Mutual. Dick set the new mark of :21.37 in his roadster at Winchester, Indiana. Since that time was clocked, much has been done in the Chicago area to regain the title. It was Chicago's Duke Nalon who formerly held the record. His time, :21.42, was set in 1941 in a big car Offy.

On behalf of the roadster racing fraternity, Frazier has taken a big step up the ladder of success. His story (which will appear in the September issue of HRM) is one that is causing a great deal of furor in the midwest, and it is likely to lead to interesting racing achievements in the near future.

There is talk in the Indiana area of a possible match race between Dick and one of the long-established drivers like Spider Webb. Such a race would undoubtedly carry a considerable side bet.

Shown on the right-hand page is Tom Cherry, one-time president of the Mutual Racing Association. He is now a star midget driver in the Midwest Association. Tom served in the U.S. Navy during the war as Chief Warrant Officer. When he was with Mutual, the group had only seven cars. Now it is one of the largest and certainly most popular racing groups running.

Photo by Paul Hemberger

Start of a race at Mt. Lawn. Crowded grandstand vouches for attendance at Indiana roadster races.

At Funk's Dayton Speedway, Dayton, Ohio, drivers pull into line for start of a feature race. This shot was taken during an open race last year.

Photo by John Weiser

Photo by Burnside

An air view of the famed Mount Lawn Speedway (Note irregular course of track). Situated six miles west of New Castle, Indiana, the track is known as the "Home of Mutual." This speedway is owned by Dr. "Doc" George Swiegart.

Tom Cherry, now a midget racing star, was president of Mutual in 1942. His efforts aided in getting the association started on its way.

Two members of Indiana's roadster racing fraternity "match wheels" during night show at Mt. Lawn.

Photo by Way Side Studio

CHECK YOUR TACHOMETER AND GEAR RATIO WITH TIRE SIZE

NOTE: — The following table of Tachometer readings and speeds cannot be absolute for every car as different brands of tire treads will vary in design and change the circumference or "roll of the tire." Also, tire wear, unless compensated for, is an unknown quantity. Unless you measure the driving wheel distance travel and allow for some slippage, depending on the day's course conditions, we can only repeat again, that the best Tachometer reading is never the final check for accurate speed at the Dry Lakes' Meets. We print the following Table of Gear Ratios to enable the car owner to check "roughly" the engine speeds relative to miles per hour. It is also very likely that there will be many tire changes due to swapping of the bigger "skins" for the smaller wheel setups, each driver figuring the outcome will better his speed by several miles per hour.

R.P.M. of Motor	3.27 — 1 28"	3.27 — 1 29"	3.27 — 1 30"	3.54 — 1 28"	3.54 — 1 29"	3.54 — 1 30"	3.78 — 1 28"	3.78 — 1 29"	3.78 — 1 30"
	28 inch is 600x16 or 650x15			29 inch is 650x16 or 700x15			30 inch is 700x16 or 750x16		
	MILES PER HOUR			MILES PER HOUR			MILES PER HOUR		
3500	88.7	92.0	95.5	82.0	85.1	88.1	77.0	79.7	82.7
3600	91.2	95.1	97.9	84.7	87.6	90.7	81.5	82.3	85.0
3700	83.8	97.8	100.8	87.0	90.2	93.2	82.1	84.4	87.2
3800	96.3	100.0	103.6	89.3	92.6	95.8	83.8	86.8	90.3
3900	98.9	103.0	106.0	91.8	95.0	98.3	86.0	89.0	92.4
4000	101.4	105.5	108.9	94.2	97.5	100.9	88.2	91.4	94.5
4100	103.9	108.0	111.7	96.5	99.9	103.3	90.4	93.6	96.3
4200	106.5	110.8	114.4	98.9	102.0	105.9	92.6	95.9	99.1
4300	109.0	113.6	117.0	101.2	104.8	108.2	94.8	98.2	101.5
4400	111.6	116.0	119.8	103.5	107.2	110.9	97.0	100.4	103.9
4500	114.1	118.9	122.6	105.8	108.6	113.3	99.2	102.7	106.2
4600	116.6	121.6	125.0	108.2	111.9	115.8	101.3	104.9	108.6
4700	119.2	124.2	127.9	110.5	114.2	118.3	103.5	107.2	110.9
4800	121.7	126.9	130.6	112.8	116.8	120.9	105.7	109.5	113.2
4900	124.3	129.8	133.5	115.3	119.3	123.4	107.9	111.6	115.7
5000	126.8	132.2	136.2	117.9	121.7	125.8	110.1	114.0	117.9
5100	129.3	134.8	139.4	120.0	124.3	128.8	112.9	116.2	120.0
5200	131.9	137.3	142.0	122.2	126.8	131.1	115.0	118.2	122.8
5300	134.4	140.0	144.8	125.7	129.1	133.8	117.4	121.1	125.0
5400	139.0	142.7	147.5	127.0	131.6	136.2	119.5	123.2	127.5
5500	141.5	145.3	150.2	129.3	134.0	138.8	121.8	125.4	130.0
5600	144.0	148.0	153.0	131.5	136.4	141.2	124.0	127.8	132.2
5700	146.6	150.8	155.8	134.0	138.9	143.8	126.2	130.0	134.5
5800	148.0	153.2	158.5	136.4	141.3	146.2	128.5	132.4	136.0
5900	150.7	156.0	161.0	138.8	143.8	148.8	130.5	134.5	139.2
6000	153.2	158.7	164.0	141.0	145.1	151.3	133.0	136.8	141.6
6100	155.7	161.0	165.6	143.4	148.6	154.0	135.0	139.0	144.0
6200	158.3	163.8	169.4	145.8	151.0	156.4	137.2	141.4	146.2
6300	160.8	165.5	172.0	148.0	153.5	159.0	139.4	143.8	148.7
6400	163.4	169.0	174.9	150.4	156.0	161.5	141.7	146.0	151.0
6500	165.9	171.7	177.5	152.8	158.3	164.0	144.0	148.3	153.4

When You Bored and/or Stroked Your Mercury

ENGINE	BORE	STROKE	INCREASE	TOTAL CUBIC INCHES
Ford V-8	3.0625	3.750	Stock	220.935
Ford V-8	3.1225	3.750	.060 bore	229.70
Ford V-8	3.1875	3.750	.125 bore	239.39
Merc. V-8	3.1875	3.750	Stock	239.39
Merc. V-8	3.2475	3.750	.060 bore	248.49
Merc. V-8	3.2575	3.750	.070 bore	250.10
Merc. V-8	3.2675	3.750	.080 bore	251.56
Merc. V-8	3.2775	3.750	.090 bore	253.10
Merc. V-8	3.3125	3.750	.125 bore	258.53
Merc. V-8	3.3750	3.750	.187 bore	268.39
Merc. V-8	3.4375	3.750	.250 bore	278.42
Merc. V-8	3.1875	3.875	.125 stroke	247.50
Merc. V-8	3.1875	3.927	.187 stroke	250.80
Merc. V-8	3.1875	4.000	.250 stroke	255.50
Merc. V-8	3.2425	3.875	.125 S and .06 B	256.77
Merc. V-8	3.3125	3.875	.125 S and .125 B	267.15
Merc. V-8	3.3750	3.875	.125 S and .187 B	277.33
Merc. V-8	3.4375	3.875	.125 S and .250 B	287.70
Merc. V-8	3.4375	4.00	.250 S and .250 B	296.98
Ford A-B	3.875	4.25	Stock	200.49
Ford A-B	4.00	4.25	.125 bore	213.63
Ford A-B	4.062	4.25	.187 bore	220.36
Ford A-B	4.125	4.25	.250 bore	227.19
Ford B	3.875	4.625	.375 stroke	218.18
Ford B	4.00	4.625	.375 S and .125 B	232.48
Ford B	4.125	4.625	.375 S and .250 B	247.24
Ford V-8 (60)	2.60	3.20	Stock	135.92
Ford V-8 (60)	2.69	3.30	.10 S and .09 B	150.04

QUARTER-MILE SPEED CHART IN SECONDS

SECS.	MPH	SECS.	MPH	SECS.	MPH
9.00	100.00	7.75	116.12	6.76	133.13
8.91	101.01	7.69	117.03	6.71	134.12
8.82	102.04	7.62	118.11	6.66	135.13
8.73	103.09	7.55	119.09	6.61	136.15
8.65	104.04	7.50	120.00	6.56	137.19
8.57	105.01	7.43	121.13	6.52	138.03
8.49	106.00	7.37	122.11	6.47	139.10
8.41	107.01	7.31	123.11	6.42	140.18
8.33	108.04	7.25	124.13	6.38	141.06
8.25	109.09	7.20	125.00	6.33	142.18
8.18	110.02	7.14	126.04	6.29	143.08
8.10	111.11	7.08	127.11	6.25	144.00
8.03	112.07	7.03	128.02	6.20	145.16
8.00	112.50	6.97	129.12	6.16	146.10
7.96	114.06	6.92	130.05	6.12	147.05
7.89	113.06	6.81	131.00	6.08	148.02
7.82	115.08	6.81	132.15	6.04	149.00
				6.00	150.00

Stock American Automotive Engines

ENGINE	CU. INS.
Ford Ferguson	119.5
Willys 4	134.2
Ford V-8 (60)	136.0
Stude. Champ	169.6
Graham 6	169.6
Hudson Std. 6	175.0
Chevy 4	170.9
Ford Model T	176.7
Graham 6	199.1
Fords A, B	200.5
Plymouth 6	201.3
Hudson 6	212.1
Terraplane 6	212.1
Oldsmobile 6	216.0
Chevrolet 6	216.5
Dodge 6	217.8
Plymouth (42)	217.8
Ford V-8	221.0
Pontiac 6	222.7
Ford 6	226.0
Stude Comdr. 6	226.2
De Soto 6	228.1
Oldsmobile 6	229.7
Nash 6	234.8
Oldsmobile 8	238.1
Mercury V-8	239.3
Chrysler 6	241.5
Packard 6	245.0
Hupmobile 6	245.3
Buick Spec. 8	248.6
Pontiac 8	248.9
Stude Pres. 8	250.4
Hudson 8	254.5
Oldsmobile 8	257.1
Nash 8	260.8
Zephyr 35-39	267.0
Packard Std. 8	282.0
Cord V-8	288.6
Zephyr 40-41	292.0
Hupmobile 8	303.2
Zephyr 42-47	305.0
Buick Cent. 8	320.0
LaSalle V-8	322.0
Chrysler 8	323.5
Cadillac V-8	346.0
Packard Super 8	356.0
Cadillac V-12	368.0
Pierce-Arrow 8	385.0
Lincoln V-12	414.0
Cad V-16, 38-40	431.0
Cad V-16, 35-37	452.0
Pierce-Arrow V-12	462.0
Packard V-12	473.0
Marmon V-16	490.8

S.C.T.A. Times Scout Motorless Midget Races

By HOWARD REDDING

The Motorless Midget Races were started in 1946. It was planned as a summer program for the cub scouts of Pack 508-C in Highland Park, California. Since that time the race has gained national fame. The 1946 meet had 24 cars entered and, for the first meet, they put on a wonderful show.

The 1946, 1947 and 1948 winner was Wayne Bates in Car #13. The fathers of the boys help build the cars, as the age of the drivers runs from 9 to 11. The 1946 and '47 meets were run on an elimination basis, running two cars at a time.

The winner of the 1947 meet was Douglas Redding, driving car #9, with a field of 30 cars entered. Many prizes and trophies were given the winners by local merchants. Louie Meyer came early and stayed late to wave the flags and award the cups and trophies.

The racing committee turned in such a good job on the 1946 and '47 meets that all the scouts in the town were talking about the Motorless Midget Races; so the committee thought if it was good for one group, why not invite all the units in the Foothill District to enter. It was given the green flag at the Los Angeles Area Scout Headquarters, and the 1948 meet was held open to the entire Foothill District.

The rules for the 1948 meet were changed around as far as the running of the meet goes. Instead of running on an elimination basis, it was decided to run on a time basis; so the S.C.T.A. was called upon to time the meet. George Prussell and Tommy Silvernail officiated as starters. J. Otto Crocker had his timing equipment on hand to clock the boys.

Thanks are in order for the fine job the S.C.T.A. turned in on the meet. Akton Miller and Wally Parks worked for months planning the meet. The U.R.A., headed by Roscoe Turner, had Sam Hanks, Rodd Simms and Louie Meyer on hand both days of the meet to act as track officials.

The 1948 winner was Jim Foley, driving Car #2, which turned in a time of 21.80 over a 880-ft. course.

Plans are under way now to hold three meets a year for the boys in order that they may have a better way of testing their cars under competition. Past successes indicate that we shall soon see these races on a national scale with the entire cub scout organization taking part.

HOT ROD MAGAZINE

Photo by Pete

Lou Meyer gives Willard Yates the checkered flag as he streaks past the finish. Roscoe Turner, Akton Miller, Fred Woodard, Jim Lindsay and Timer J. O. Crocker are in the Judges' stand.

Photo by Paramount

S.C.T.A. official Wally Parks explains to James Creighton (Hope Car) and Robert Green (Crosby Car) how the intricate timing mechanism will clock their cars.

Photo by George Axt

Winner of last year's meet, Cub Scout Douglas Redding with the trophy awarded him.

Photo by Pete

Fastest Boy Scout of the day, John Quackenbush receives his trophy from S.C.T.A. President Ackton Miller.

205

Casey Boghosian's Chevy roadster passes the grandstand at the Porterville, Calif. Speed Bowl during
qualifying heats.

Charles Ryan of Tustin, Calif., runs a Cyclone triple
manifold, Harman & Collins cam on his '32 V-8.

Sacramento's Ed Ohanesian owns this sleek custom
hot rod. Offenhauser manifold, Edelbrock heads and
Harman cam add power to the '46 Mercury block.

On the pole, at start of main event at Oshkosh,
Wisconsin, is Tom Friedman's roadster. Car was built
by Hank Gieser of Milwaukee.

At Farmington, Minn., Howie Hoffman (left) and Mel Hansen (background) throttle onto the straight-away. Hoffman runs Navarro manifold, Meyers heads.

This '42 Merc. has Meyer manifold, Harman and Collins cam. At the wheel is owner Doreen Gatehouse of San Bruno, Calif.

Dana Photo by Rick

Chuck Ford (12) flips at Belmont Speedway while trying to avoid collision with Bob Kelleher (99).

Ralph Potter drove from Los Angeles to Indianapolis towing this oversized trailer. The roadster averaged 18.7 miles per gallon on the trip.

Lubricating Oils

By
W. I. "BILL" GIESEKE

Mr. Gieseke is a member of the Society of Automotive Engineers of the American Chemical Society, with seven years as Automotive and Lubrication Engineer for a major oil company.

DETERMINING PROPERTIES OF LUBRICATING OILS. Since mineral oils are produced in many grades it is highly important to examine particular specifications when selecting oils for use in internal combustion engines. Of special significance are the factors of viscosity, flash point, and pour point, each of which will be discussed in detail.

Viscosity is generally considered as the resistance the oil offers to flow. Thus, if an oil flows readily it is known to possess a low viscosity. As previously stated, the body or viscosity of an oil determines the amount of fluid friction. In general, it is desirable to select an oil of the lowest viscosity which will provide an unbroken film, so that friction may be held to a minimum. However, when consideration is given to the fact that the oil must often lubricate through a temperature range of 0 degrees F. to 300 degrees F., the problem becomes a very complex one and worthy of extensive study .

In order to measure oil viscosity, the Saybolt viscosimeter is employed. By a suitable arrangement, a certain amount of oil is heated to a standard testing temperature, generally 130 degrees F. or 210 degrees F. The oil tube is provided with with an outlet orifice through which oil is permitted to flow into a 60 cubic centimeter flask. The time (in seconds) required for the delivery of 60 cubic centimeters of oil gives the Saybolt universal viscosity at that temperature. For example, if the time required for a particular sample is 120 seconds at 210 degrees F., the oil is said to have a Saybolt viscosity of 120.

If actual Saybolt numbers were used to designate the viscosities of various oils on the market, there would probably be several hundreds of grades listed and the purchaser would be faced with a complex problem. In order to simplify the selection of oils, they are often classified under an SAE rating system which divides all oils into seven groups (SAE 10 to 70, incl.) according to viscosities at either 130 degrees F. or 210 degrees F. These SAE ratings are purely arbitrary and bear no direct relationship to the Saybolt or other ratings. They

are defined, however, in terms of the Saybolt universal viscosity. By reference to the chart (fig. 1), the relation

SAE VISCOSITY NUMBER	VISCOSITY RANGE SAYBOLT UNIVERSAL SECONDS			
	AT 130° F.		AT 210° F.	
	MINIMUM	MAXIMUM	MINIMUM	MAXIMUM
10	90	LESS THAN 120		
20	120	LESS THAN 185		
30	185	LESS THAN 255		
40	255			LESS THAN 75
50			75	LESS THAN 105
60			105	LESS THAN 125
70			125	LESS THAN 150

Figure 1

between Saybolt seconds and SAE ratings can readily be determined. It will be noted that grades 10 to 40 are tested at 130 degrees F. and the heavier grades at 210 degrees F., a procedure which is quite normal since the heavier oils are intended for use at higher engine temperatures. To determine the SAE rating of an oil sample, it is first tested at the correct temperature in the Saybolt viscosimeter. The reading thus obtained is compared with the ranges listed on the chart. For example, if an oil tests 82 Saybolt seconds at 210 degrees F. it is evidently an SAE 50 oil, because the 50 classification covers all oils between 75 and 105 seconds. By the same method, an oil testing 130 seconds at 130 degrees F. is found to be an SAE 20 grade. Occasionally the letter "W" will be included in the SAE number giving a designation such as SAE 20W. This letter indicates that in addition to meet-

ing the viscosity requirements at the testing temperature the oil also meets additional low temperature specifications, showing that it is a satisfactory oil for winter use.

Although the SAE number indicates grade it does not indicate quality or any other essential characteristics. It is well known that there are good oils and inferior oils having the same viscosities at a certain temperature and are therefore subject to classification in the same grade. The SAE letters on an oil container are not an endorsement or recommendation of the oil by the Society of Automotive Engineers.

In order to appreciate the difference between apparently similar oils, viscosity must be known at more than one temperature. Fig. 2 shows two oils of

SAYBOLT VISCOSITY VS TEMPERATURE						
OIL	TEMPERATURE	300° F.	210° F.	130° F.	100° F.	32° F.
SAE 50 SAMPLE A	SAYBOLT VISCOSITY	44	80	350	840	20000
SAE 50 SAMPLE B	SAYBOLT VISCOSITY	42	80	480	1480	65000

Figure 2

the same SAE rating but having widely different characteristics, as their temperatures are changed through the range required by engine operation.

This chart clearly indicates a need for a *more complete study of the viscosity temperature characteristics of lubricating oils.* Sample A is obviously superior to sample B in its ability to withstand temperature changes with less change in body or viscosity. Sample B congeals readily at low temperatures thus causing excessive drag and cold starting difficulty, and at 300 degrees

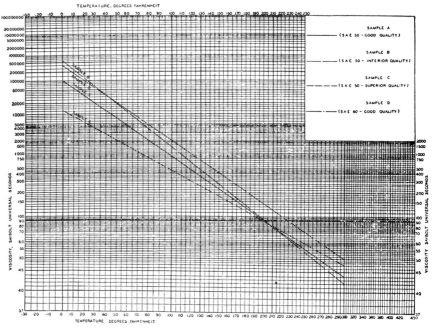

Figure 3

F. is actually lower in viscosity than sample A.

A convenient method of recording viscosity temperature curves is by the use of a special graph prepared by the American Society for Testing Materials (A.S.T.M.), a copy of which is shown in fig. 3. By intricate spacing of the temperature and viscosity readings on the graph, resultant curves will appear as straight lines. To examine an oil it is tested in a Saybolt viscosimeter at two temperatures, such as 130 degrees F. and 210 degrees F., and the viscosities are properly located as points on the chart. A straight line is then drawn through the two points so as to include all temperature readings. It is then a simple matter to determine the viscosity at any temperature between 30 degrees F. and 450 degrees F., although the temperature values below 0 degrees F. and those above 300 degrees F. are of little significance, because most oils reach their chill points near zero temperatures and are seldom subjected to engine temperatures above 300 degrees F.

Upon examination of the oils plotted on the graph in fig. 3 certain significant points are observed. Sample A is a good grade of SAE 50 oil; sample B is an inferior grade of SAE 50 oil; sample C is a superior grade of SAE 50 oil, and sample D is a good grade of SAE 60 oil. Sample B line on the chart indicates that at low temperatures this oil is actually more viscous than the SAE 60 oil represented by the sample D line on the chart. Sample C line shows less tendency to congeal at low temperatures and to thin out at high temperatures than other samples tested, thus indicating its superior characteristics. Many other comparisons may be readily made by use of the A.S.T.M. graph. It is generally agreed that an oil of 60 to 100 Saybolt seconds at all temperatures represents an ideal lubricant for internal-combustion engines, but it is highly improbable that such a lubricant will ever be available.

For somewhat greater convenience in indicating the viscosity temperature characteristics of oils, a viscosity index chart (fig. 4) may be used. This is an arbitrary chart on which superior oils of any grade will give a reading at the higher end of the scale, and inferior oils will show much lower readings. Indexes are determined by performing two Saybolt tests at different temperatures and locating the readings thus obtained on the proper lines on the left side of the chart. A straight line is then drawn through these two points and projected so as to cross the index scale at the right. The point of intersection of the viscosity line and

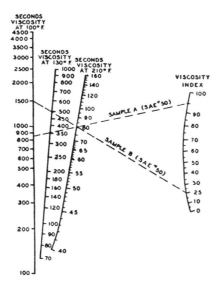

Figure 4

index curve gives the index rating of the particular oil. The two oils listed in figure 2 furnish an excellent sample of oils having similar SAE ratings but widely different index values. When compared on the index chart, sample A oil is found to have a viscosity index of 95, and sample B (also an SAE oil) has a rating of only 26. This further emphasizes the fact that an SAE rating alone can be interpreted as an indication of quality in lubricating oils. *In general high index ratings are very desirable in all grades of oil, a quality which is found particularly in compounds of the paraffin series. Some oils containing high percentage of paraffin hydrocarbons have indexes well above the 100 figure.*

The lubrication of cylinder walls and pistons of internal-combustion engines requires consideration of factors other than oil viscosity. Because of the large amount of heat generated in cylinders during the power stroke, the flash test of an oil assumes considerable importance. The test is performed by heating an oil sample in an open cup (fig. 5), and as the temperature rises a flame is periodically passed slowly over the surface of the oil. The first test which momentarily ignites the oil vapor above the cup is recorded as the flash point. Other factors being equal, an oil of high flash test is preferred because of the greater degree of protection afforded cylinders and pistons and the probable lower oil consumption during continuous engine operation. A fire point test, which indicates the temperature of continuous burning, is often performed along with the flash test.

In addition to the above properties, a good oil must show a high degree of chemical stability in order to resist the action of high temperature, moisture, and acids, all of which are often

(Continued on Page 20)

LUBRICATING OILS
(*Continued*)

present in engine crankcases. *Here again, the paraffin hydrocarbons (saturated series) (fig. 6) show a marked superi-*

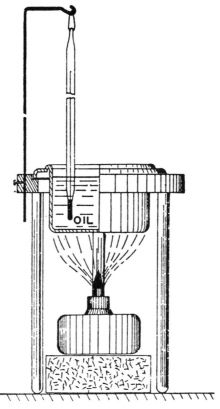

Figure 5

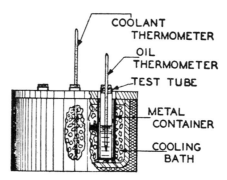

Figure 6

ority over the other groups of petroleum products.

Cold weather starting and operation also require special consideration. It is not at all uncommon for internal combustion engines to be started cold at temperatures of 0 degrees F. or below. A study of the A.S.T.M. chart (fig. 3) reveals that at these low temperatures oil viscosities reach surprisingly high figures, which, of course, necessitates a very high cranking torque in order to rotate the crankshaft. Furthermore, at certain low temperatures oil will congeal or chill completely so that circulation is impossible even if starting is accomplished by special means.

In regard to the question of whether a *low pour point or a good viscosity curve (high viscosity index) is best* for low temperature starting of internal combustion engines, experience indicates clearly that both are essential. *The viscosity curve must be good (viscosity index about 95 or above is desired), and the pour point should be within 5 degrees F. of the average starting temperature.* The pour point of an oil is the lowest temperature at which it will pour or flow when it is chilled without disturbances. The oil to be tested is placed in a glass test jar and cooled in a cooling bath and held in a horizontal position for exactly 5 seconds.

In response to readers' requests, we reprint the following poem.

HIS CAR WAS HOT
By HOWARD BITTNER

(Reprinted from "Throttle" Magazine)

All kinds of stuff, and a winfield "pot";

No doubt about it, his car was hot!

He could peel in high, when others could not

No doubt about it, his car was hot!

Solid panel, fastened by lock,

When asked what he had; he'd say "strictly-stock."

But we all knew that that was rot,

'Cause we all knew, that his car was hot!
He even got tickets, as tickets go;

But not for speeding; for flying so low!

He'd "gow out" in low, cause his car was hot,

And still be "peeling," eighty feet from the spot,

Winding his motor, pipes that "blubber,"

Crackling mufflers, and the scream of rubber!

Tight in second, the same in low,

No doubt about it, his car would go,

Meshing of gears, to him, was an art,

In a race with him, you were "chopped" from the start.

He'd "speed shift" to second, and "snap" it in high,

His car was hot, and that's no lie!

But all things must start, and all things must end,

Iron will give, and steel will bend.

He got his on a Saturday night.

He was feeling good, and his motor was tight.

He really shouldn't have tried to pass,

But he "dropped" in second, and gave it the gas.

Head-lights were shining in his face,

For once he was going to lose a race!

Even then, he could have turned back,

But his car was hot, so he wouldn't slack.

A deafening crash, that was heard for miles,

And two fast cars were worthless piles.

A wisp of smoke from his motor came,

And soon his car was a sheet of flame,

It had turned over twice, and burnt on the spot,

No doubt about it, his car was hot!

Second in a series of Harman and Collins record-holders.

117.03 m.p.h.

Fastest A class coupe time ever recorded at a Russetta Timing event was by Bob Pierson's Mercury-powered '36 Ford coupe using a HARMAN and COLLINS cam.

HARMAN & COLLINS, INC.

5552 ALHAMBRA AVENUE   LOS ANGELES 32, CALIF.

CApitol 4610

Parts With Appeal

LORELEI VITEK DISPLAYS A GENERATOR BRACKET

Most dual racing manifolds are made without a generator mount on the front, so this part is bolted to the top studs on the left head to provide a side bracket.

The highly polished, durable aluminum part holds a generator very nicely; Miss Lorelei Vitek holds the bracket very nicely.

The 5' 3" lovely was born in Chicago in 1926, leaving there at an early age to live in Texas. She received her schooling in Dallas, where she danced her way to top honors in the 1936 and 37 Pan American Exhibition Personality Contests. From there Lorelei embarked on a USO tour ending up in Hollywood.

Her blond hair, green eyes and other attributes were soon brought to the attention of studio casting offices. Lorelei has appeared in numerous pictures, her most recent was an R.K.O. picture, "Interference."

As to favorite recreations, dancing comes first, with eating and just soaking up a good tan following in order. Sophisticated clothes appeal to her most, but we're sure that our readers will agree that she also does wonders with a bathing suit and a generator bracket.

QUESTIONS AND ANSWERS

Q. I have a '38 V-8 roadster and am interested in lowering the body and rounding it out some.

ALLEN E. GREB
Cedar Rapids, Iowa

A. Lowering the body can be accomplished by using lowering blocks or long shackles in the rear. The front may be lowered with a dropped axle. Another method is channelling which is done by cutting away the floor boards and lowering the body over the frame. After channelling the fenders may be removed or raised. Also, solid side panels and fender skirts would help with, perhaps, excess exterior chrome and handles removed. Additional ideas may be obtained by keeping tab on other builders' cars pictured in HRM.

Q. I do a great deal of driving and my greatest operating expense is fuel. I want to obtain the best possible mileage per gallon of fuel and still maintain normal power operation. That is, sufficient pull on hills, steady pickup and smooth power at highway speeds. The only record I am out to break in my '46 Ford V-8 is distance between gas stations.

RICHARD C. DE LA MATER
International Correspondence Schools
San Bernardino, Calif.

A. Equipment built to give an engine greater speed efficiency will also increase performance. A high type manifold and increased compression should bring your mileage up.

Q. What kind of a manifold can I get for my '32 Lincoln V-12?

RICHARD BLACKMAN
Los Angeles, Calif.

A. Demands for manifolds for this type engine have been so small that there are none in production at present. Your solution is to either have a manifold custom made or alter your stock one.

Q. I am 14 years old and plan to build a hot rod next year. Could you tell me if I can get full race parts for engines earlier than a '36? Also, just what does a full race engine consist of?

CLINT ANDERSON
Glendale, Calif.

A. Race parts are available for engines as far back as Ford T. (At the last S. C. T. A. Meet, a T clocked 121, a 4-cylinder Ford timed 142, and a '34 Ford did 150.50.)

A full race engine is one that has a special cam, heads, manifold, ignition, is ported and relieved, etc. The more race parts, the fuller the engine.

Q. I would like to know what gear ratio should be used on the transmission and rear end of a full house V-8 running 600x16 tires. I am using a conventional three-speed shift and my car doesn't seem to have much jump in second.

DAVE McGUIRE
Wilmington, Calif.

A. Try Zephyr gears in the transmission and 3.11's in the differential.

Q. We have a '40 Ford and are rebuilding a Mercury engine with genuine Ford steel sleeves and steel pistons. Would like to know types and brands of heads you would advise and what compression ratio. We don't want the speed too severe as we are using the car for every-day driving in the city. Also, what dual intake manifold can be used successfully without changing generator bracket?

KENNETH W. LOHMEYER
St. Louis, Missouri

A. For street driving an 8¼/1 compression ratio is suitable. Brand is a matter of personal preference. You can confidently make your choice from HRM's advertisers. Most manufacturers have high type manifolds with generator mount on the front for street use.

Q. I am building a roadster for track racing and would like to know what your advice would be as to setting up the front camber and caster. I have a '33 Plymouth front axle and brakes. Also, can you recommend a steering column other than Franklin and in the same price range?

(Name Withheld)
Maywood, Calif.

A. Amount of caster and camber will differ with various length tracks. A 6° caster with no camber or toe in is proving satisfactory on many local track roadsters.

The Norden steering column may fill your needs.

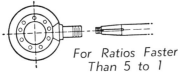
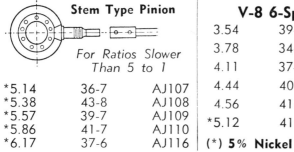

L.A.P.D. Traffic Educ Unit

YOU CAN'T GET ANOTHER! Drive it safely, Brother! If you smash up THIS car, where are you going to get another? You may have PILES of money, but you can't afford to drive recklessly if you want to keep on driving. Remember, SAFETY SAVES YOUR CAR!

Yam Oka ranks high in California hot rod racing. Shown on Gilmore ¼ mile track.

South Pasadenan Dick Durkee's former Indianapolis car is rigged for street use.

Bob Ingram in Lloyd Griswell's '32 V-8 at Porterville, California, Speed Bowl.

Dan Tracey, active in California Hot Rods, Inc., shown in qualifying laps.

CLUB NEWS

Albuquerque Road Pilots
(New Mexico)
By J. Robert Seth

Several members made a week-end trip to Santa Fe over June 19-20. Everything went fine with the exception of the weather. It rained during the entire trip. Upon arriving in Santa Fe the drivers felt right in place. The town was a sea of mud due to a sudden cloudburst. The Rodneys looked as though they had been swimming in a river of mud.

Mrs. May Vanderslice, the mascot of the Road Pilots, returned to Albuquerque after her recent operation. Nearly all of the club members were on hand to meet her train. She wasn't on the train they expected her on, however. Hereafter, people who sneak into town are apt to be shot on sight.

Periodical Fox Hunts are regular activities of the club. A whitewash trail is left by the fox and followed by the rest. The June 24 hunt was a rather surprising event. Ray Pilon and Clyde Vanderslice broke the regular procedure and took off for Belen, New Mexico, a small town south of Albuquerque. Local residents were in for a shock recently. Imagine driving down the street and suddenly spotting a PURPLE T roadster with GREEN wheels pull alongside. Local drivers have. It is the new Mercury T roadster of Vernon Leweke.

Bill Hall of the Road Pilots is piling up points in Albuquerque midget racing competition. He is, at present, second in point standings. It is expected that Bill will garner the top position before long.

Roadster Racing Association of Oregon
By Dick Martin

Readers may have seen in the papers (*Who hasn't?*) that we've had some floods up here. Our Portland track is . . . as per latest reports . . . some THIRTY feet under water. Also, there are some college buildings floating around over it. Maybe we can take up speed-boating until the waters subside.

The weather has caused us to run all of our races out of town. We have run several in conjunction with the Washington Roadster Racing Association. (The WRRA has most of its members located around Seattle & Everett, Wn.)

NEWS FROM TEXAS
By Pauline Bayer

On May 25 of this year the Texas Roadster Racing Association was formed. The group elected Marvin Brandt as its President and Treasurer, Charley Farrell of the same city as Vice-President and your reporter as Recording Secretary.

The initial forming of this group listed thirty-one members, eighteen hot rods. On June 22 eight new members and five more cars joined the association. The new members include R. L. Billy, J. R. Roland, Johnny Dunn, R. G. Lungstrom and B. H. Roland, all of Corpus Christi; J. B. Meyer of San Antonio; and V. W. McGee of Mathis, Texas.

TRRA's present record standings are as follows: Harry Elbel (Ford V-8) holds the record for the one-quarter mile Pan American Speedway in San Antonio. The time: :17.10. The surface: clay. Freddie Elbel and Eddie Callahan are all tied up for the record at the Corpus Christi Speedway in that Texas city. The one-quarter clay surfaced track has a record of :19.70. At Jacksonville, Texas, it's Harry Elbel again holding the record time. The track is a one-half mile oval, sand top. The time: :28.41. Freddie Elbel has the record for the Arrowhead Speedway at Houston. The track is one-half mile sand. The record time: :33.31.

The Elbel clan carries many of the top honors in the Texas Roadster Racing Association. It is fitting that we give a little biographical data on one of these lads.

Freddie Elbel (pictured here) was

born in Kendalia, Texas. He is 26 years old, is married and the father of one child. Freddie was reared in and around his dad's garage. In 1940 he drove his first hot rod race on the Devil Bowl Speedway in San Antonio. The following year he wound up as high-point man at that track, receiving his first gold trophy.

(Continued on Page 29)

Laughs...*from here and there*

By TOM MEDLEY

If all the autos in the world were laid end to end, it would be Southern California on a Sunday afternoon.

Mechanic: "*Would you have the price if I said you needed a new engine?*"

Car owner: "*Would you say I needed a new engine if you thought I didn't have the price?*"

I envy you, little lightning bug,
You worry not a bit,
For when you see a traffic cop
You know your tail light's lit.

An easy way to find the horsepower of a car is to lift up the hood and count the plugs.

He: "How much gas do we have?"

She: "It points to one-half, but whether it means half full or half empty, I don't know."

TREES

I think that I shall never see
Along the road an unscraped tree
With bark intact and painted white
That no car ever hit at night;
For every tree that is near the road
Has caused some auto to be towed;
Side-swiping trees is done a lot
By drivers who are not so hot.
God gave them eyes so they could see
Yet any fool can hit a tree.

"SORRY, OFFICER, BUT WE ROADSTER BOYS AREN'T ALLOWED TO DIVULGE OUR SPEED SECRETS"

Salesman: "Yes, sir, of all our cars, this is the one we feel confident and justified in pushing."

Customer: "That's no good to me. I want one to ride in."

"Well, your car surely does run smoothly," gushed the high school girl on her first date.

"Wait a minute—I haven't started the engine yet," said her escort.

"What kind of oil do you use in your new car?" said the hotel clerk to the traveling salesman.

"What?"

"What kind of oil do you use?"

"Oh, I usually start off by telling them how lonesome I am and then ..."

It takes thousands of nuts and bolts to hold a car together, and only one nut to scatter it all over the country!

STROKER McGURK

WINNERS AT GILMORE *(Continued)*

Stan Kross puts No. 4 through qualifying paces at Gilmore Stadium.
Car is Weiand equipped.

Dick Vineyard's chain-driven roadster houses a G.M.C. truck engine.
'53' is a car to watch at any CHR roadster race.

Photos by Al Moss.

Mickey Davis gets set to drive the "Double Question Mark," No. 99.
Davis piloted the car to main event first place at Gilmore on July 12.

Classified Advertisements

CLUB NEWS
(Continued)

At this point in his racing career, Freddie parked his hot rod for a matter of three and one-half years while he donned the uniform of the United States Navy. He served as a motor machinist mate, first class.

After receiving his discharge, Freddie wasted little time before resuming his role as an able hot rod pilot. In August of 1947, he walked off with another gold trophy, this time awarded for being high-point man at the Spillway Speedway in San Antonio. The following year he received the same high honor.

Freddie owns his own roadster — a 1932 V-8—as well as holding down driver and mechanic duties for the track car.

Freddie Elbel seems to be the driver to beat in the Texas Roadster Racing Association. A record such as his will prove a tough one to top.

Mutual Racing Association
By Melvin Dudley

Biggest news in this section of the nation is a new world's record for the half mile track set by Dick Frazier in his Mercury-powered hot rod at Winchester, Indiana. This important event took place June 20. The new record time, :21.37. The old record was :21.42, set by Duke Nalon in 1941. Nalon set this time in a big car. (HRM will give readers complete coverage of this occasion.)

Here are the point standings for the association as of June 29:

		Points	Car
1—Dick Frazier (Muncie)		634	Merc.
2—Jim Morrison (Muncie)		561	Ford 6
3—John Arnold (Muncie)		418	Ford 6
4—Sam Skinner (Muncie)		348	Ford 6
5—Ralph Stover (Muncie)		345	Hudson
6—Bob Beeson (Shirley)		328	Chevrolet
7—Red Renner (Woodburn)		310	Ford 6
8—Gene Pyle (Redkey)		202	Champion
9—Jr. Fort (Anderson)		188	Dodge
10—Curly Burton (Lewisville)		151	Merc.

During the association's recent Winchester showing, Ralph Stover took his Hudson to the open races at South Bend, Indiana, returning with First Place honons. We have had many interesting races with the use of the inverted starts.

This year there have been several midget drivers turning to stock cars for the summer season. This is reversing the trend of the past few years.

The word around Mutual and Hurricane (Chicago) now is "Beat Frazier." Dick and his car are a tough combination to top.

Dry Lakes and Race Results

MOJAVE TIMING ASSOC., INC.
JULY 11, 1948

Car No.	Name	Time in M/H	Engine	Club	Pts.	Class
31	IVAR HOWMANN	109.09	Riley 2 pt.	4 Barrel	6	A, Roadster
42	ED. DONAVAN	108.56	Winfield	4 Barrel	5	A, Roadster
100	TOM HYNES	93.17	SO Miller	Roadusters		A, Roadster
5	BUD HAND	128.21	Riley 4 pt.	4 Barrel	6	A, Modified
10	CLEVELAND—LARSON	113.78	Winfield	Bungholers	5	A, Modified
3	BILL BARTLETT	118.58	V-8	Bungholers	5	B, Roadster
17	DAVE BOURKE	121.79	V-8	Bungholers	6	B, Roadster
19	LEHMANN—SCHWARTZROCK	115.68	V-8	Bungholers	3	B, Roadster
47	JIM McALLISTER	100.78	V-8	Rumblers		B, Roadster
61	ANDREWS—GOSHAY	113.78	V-8	Lobers	2	B, Roadster
63	BILL KIMBALL	117.80	V-8	Lobers	4	B, Roadster
70	DON SEDGELEY	110.02	V-8	Lobers		B, Roadster
84	DICK LAZO	104.05	V-8	Roadusters		B, Roadster
85	GEORGE RUBIO	96.98	V-8	Roadusters		B, Roadster
91	SHAW—MELCHERT	100.33	V-8	Roadusters		B, Roadster
95	ELMER CHIODO	104.77	V-8	Roadusters		B, Roadster
99	BILL JOHNSON	103.93	V-8	Roadusters		B, Roadster
1	BOB DE SHIELDS	138.04	V-8	Bungholers	6	B, Modified
25	PATH—MOORE	122.12	V-8	4 Barrel	5	B, Modified

RECORDS:
1—Bob De Shields: Cl B. Modified.
 Time up: 138.04, Time down: 134.33, Average time 136.19 (6 points.)
5—Bud Hand: Cl. A Modified.
 Time up: 127.30, Time down: 128.21, Average time 127.76 (6 points.)

GUESTS:
110—Rod Parker	106.38	Cl. B Roadster
113—Stu Harper	115.09	Cl. B Modified
117—R. S. Oster	110.29	Cl. B Roadster
118—Joe Milliorn	95.64	Cl. B Roadster

There was a steady crosswind throughout the Time Trials which averaged out, according to our new Wind Recorder, to be 7.08 M/H.

RECORDS TO DATE
Class A Roadster
1947—Eugene von Arx ....114.50 M/H
 Riley V-8
Class A Modified:
1948—Bud Hand ....127.76 M/H
 Riley 4 Port
(Previously held by Cleveland-Larson at 114.06 M/H)
Class A Streamliner: open.
Class B Roadster:
1948—Bill Bartlett ....121.95 M/H
 V-8
(Previously held by Bob DeShields at 120.81 M/H)
Class B Modified:
1948—Bob DeShields ....136.19 M/H
 V-8
Class B Streamliner: open.
Class C Roadster: open.
Class C Modified:
1947—John Chambard ....119.55 M/H
 Dusenberg
Class C Streamliner: open.

POINT STANDINGS BY CLUBS
BUNGHOLERS	85
4 BARREL CLUB	46
RUMBLERS	4
LOBERS	13
ROADUSTERS	6

TEN HIGHEST MEMBERS IN PT. STANDING
1. Bob De Shields 24
2. Bill Bartlett 23
3. Ivar Howman 18
3. Bud Hand 18
4. Cleveland-Larson 16
5. Lehmann-Schwartzrock 13
6. Dave Bourke 9
7. Ed Donavan 5
7. Path-Moore 5
8. Bob Baldwin 4
8. George Rubie 4
9. Bill Kimball 4
9. Don Sedgeley 3
10. Andrews-Goshay 2

RRAO
YAKIMA SPEEDWAY, May 16, 1/8 mile, dirt.
Andy Wilson set a new track record of :45.31.
 Trophy Dash: 1. Andy Wilson, 2; Don Moore, 3. G. Livingston
 Main Event: (Reverse start) 1. Andy Wilson, 2. Bob Gregg, 3. Don Moore.

AURORA SPEEDWAY, Seattle. 1/4 mile asphalt. May 21.
A new qualifying record of :16.23, set by Len Sutton.
 Trophy Dash: 1. Len Sutton, 2. Frank McGowan, 3. Don Moore.
 Main Event: 1. Len Sutton, 2. Bob Gregg, 3. Andy Wilson.
 Semi Main: Won by George Amick.

PORTLAND SPEEDWAY, May 23, 5/8 mile asphalt.
 Trophy Dash: 1. Bob Gregg, 2. Don Moore, 3. Len Sutton.
 Semi Main: 1. G. Livingston, 2. Darmond Moore.
 Main Event: 1. Bob Gregg, 2. Andy Wilson, 3. Gordy Youngstrom.

SALEM FAIR GROUNDS, Salem, Oregon. May 30. 5/8 mile, dirt.
 New track record of :27.83 set by Bob Gregg.
 Trophy Dash: 1. Bob Gregg, 2. G. Livingston, 3. Len Sutton.
 Semi Main: Won by Don Crocket.
 Main Event: 1. Don Moore, 2. Bob Gregg, 3. Dick Boubel.

AURORA SPEEDWAY, Seattle. June 18.
 Trophy Dash: Won by Len Sutton.
 Main Event: 1. Len Sutton, 2. Frank McGowan, 3. Augie Scoville.

AURORA SPEEDWAY, Seattle. June 25.
 A new track record set by Max Humm. Time: :16.22.
 Trophy Dash: 1. Max Humm, 2. Len Sutton.
 Semi Main: Won by Don McPherson.
 Main Event: Won by Max Humm.

CHR
GILMORE STADIUM—July 19—1/4 mile, dirt.
Fastest qualifying time, 15.17, set by Mickey Davis.
 Trophy Dash (3 laps)—1, Yam Oka; 2, Ed Mall. 46.52.
 First Heat (8 laps)—1, Jimmy Graham; 2, George Seeger; 3, Colbey Scroggins. 2:12.23.
 Second Heat (8 laps)—1, Grant Casper; 2, Wayne Tipton; 3, Bob Lindsay. 2:10.12.
 Third Heat (8 laps)—1, Dick Vineyard; 2, Yam Oka; 3, Archie Tipton. 2:18.13.
 Fourth Heat (8 laps)—1, Bud Van Maanen; 2, Vern Slankard; 3, Bud Gregory. 2:09.95.
 Semi-Main (25 laps)—1, Yam Oka; 2, George Seeger; 3, Dick Vineyard. 6:52.02.
 Main (25 laps)—1, Vern Slankard; 2, Ed Ball; 3, Bob Lindsay. 6:56.90.
 Runoff (10 laps)—1, Yam Oka; 2, Ed Ball; 3, Vern Slankard. 2:41.83.

GILMORE STADIUM, July 12.
Fastest qualifying time, :15.13, set by Yam Oka.
 Trophy Dash (3 laps)—1. Pat Flaherty, 2. Dick McClung, :46.81.
 1st Heat (8 laps)—1. Freddie Hayes, (Tie for 2nd spot between Don Tripp and A. A. Knight, 2:02.91.
 2nd Heat (8 laps)—1. Bud Van Maanen, 2. Bob Lindsey, 3. Dick Benninger. 2:12.38.
 3rd Heat (8 laps)—1. Ed Ball, 2. Vern Slankhard, 3. Dan Tracey. 2:09.09.
 4th Heat (8 laps)—1. Mickey Davis, 2. Yam Oka, 3. Bud Gregory. 2:09.04.
 Semi Main (15 laps)—1. Bob Lindsey, 2. Bud Van Maanen, 3. Archie Tipton.
 Main Event (30 laps)—1. Mickey Davis, 2. Yam Oka, 3. Pat Flaherty. 8:21.09.

GILMORE STADIUM, Los Angeles. 1/4 mile, dirt. June 28. Fastest qualifying time, :15.26, set by Yam Oka.
 Trophy Dash (3 laps)—1. Stan Kross, 2.Yam Oka. :47.87.
 1st Heat (8 laps)—1. Dick Benninger, 2. Mickey Davis, 2:15.22.
 2nd Heat (8 laps)—1. George Seegar, 2. Ed Lockhart, 3. Corvie Tullio. 2:12.10.
 3rd Heat (8 laps)—1. ob Lindsey, 2. Ed all. 2:17.97.
 4th Heat (8 laps)—1. Wayne Tipton, 2. Dempsey Wilson, 2. Stan Kross. 2:08.97.
 Semi Main (15 laps)—1. George Seegar, 2. Archie Tipton, 3. Ed Lockhart. 4:12.45.
 Main Event (30 laps)—1. Dick Vineyard, 2. Bud Van Maanen, 3. Wayne Tipton. 8:32.92.

A Helpful Hand

By J. Robert Seth

So-called "street jobs" have been branded as a nuisance in many spots throughout the nation. Partly, the blame has been due. In other cases (these, the majority) the rod drivers have been blameless. On record are hundreds of instances wherein newspaper reporters and editors . . . eager to 'make' a story . . . have looked over an accident involving a FENDERLESS auto (of any year, make, engine, and construction) and labeled the story "HOT ROD ACCIDENT." The weight of such stories must, in turn, be borne by the law-minded Rodney as well as the Pest. Hot Rod owners and enthusiasts can help to remedy this situation. Mr. Seth of New Mexico offers the solution, picked by the Albuquerque Road Pilots. It is a sound remedy. There are others equally as good. If you or your club have found one, please let us know. We'll be only too glad to pass the word along to the thousands of Rodneys in need of such a plan.

* * *

Several months ago the Albuquerque Road Pilots formed their club. To prove that unity would be an advantage, they began their co-operative program.

Embarking on such a program proved a greater task than expected. Citizens of the city had been told by newspapers, motion pictures, and . . . in some cases . . . radio, that all Hot Rods were death traps driven by irresponsible nincampoops, bent on leaving a destructive path wherever they went. Such adverse publicity caused people to shy away from Hot-Rodders much as they would from lepers.

Bucking odds that seemed hopeless, the Road Pilots began their work. They decided to give aid to any motorist in need of the type of help the skilled Rodney could give. It wasn't long before people were commenting to the local Chamber of Commerce about the

aid they had received from members of the Road Pilots. On the lonely stretches of highway in New Mexico, often up to 50 miles between stations, many stalled motorists have breathed a sigh of relief when they've seen a low-slung, fenderless car stopping next to them. The policy of the club forbids accepting pay for anything other than parts.

Second phase of the program includes scenic tours to New Mexico's many spots of interest. It has become a common sight to see a caravan of hot rods traveling and safely spaced, at even speeds, rolling along the highways.

People of Albuquerque no longer refer to "Those Hot Rods" with the bitterness so common in the past. It is not unusual to hear a statement like: "I was towed in by a Rodney last night when my gas line broke," or, "I went with the Rodneys to Hyde Park for the snow display last week." Albuquerque is proud of its Rodneys.

Many club activities and recreations are planned to keep the membership entertained. Drag races are unknown on the streets of Albuquerque. Club-sponsored acceleration tests are held periodically to afford an outlet for the interests of the speed-minded members. The tests are held with the aid of local and state police.

Club members aid other community activities by doing odd jobs. At a recent turkey shoot held by the Chamber of Commerce, target pits were manned by members of the Road Pilots. By aiding in such activities, the club has placed itself in a community standing to be envied by many of the Hot Rod Clubs throughout the nation.

Helpful unity in New Mexico has proven that the Rodneys can make themselves welcome. By lending a helping hand, they have become established as a bigger aid than hindrance. Let's all be Rodneys!

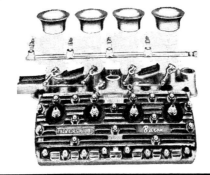

New Custom Mercury Engines

C O M P L E T E

1/8 STROKED $725.00

1/4 OR 3/8 STROKED $750.00

ALL TYPES OF ENGINE REBUILDING

LOOK TO SOUTHERN CALIFORNIA FOR THE
BEST IN RACING EQUIPMENT

Send for Catalog

BLAIR'S AUTO PARTS

PHONE SYcamore 2-4798

826 ARROYO PARKWAY   **PASADENA, CALIF.**

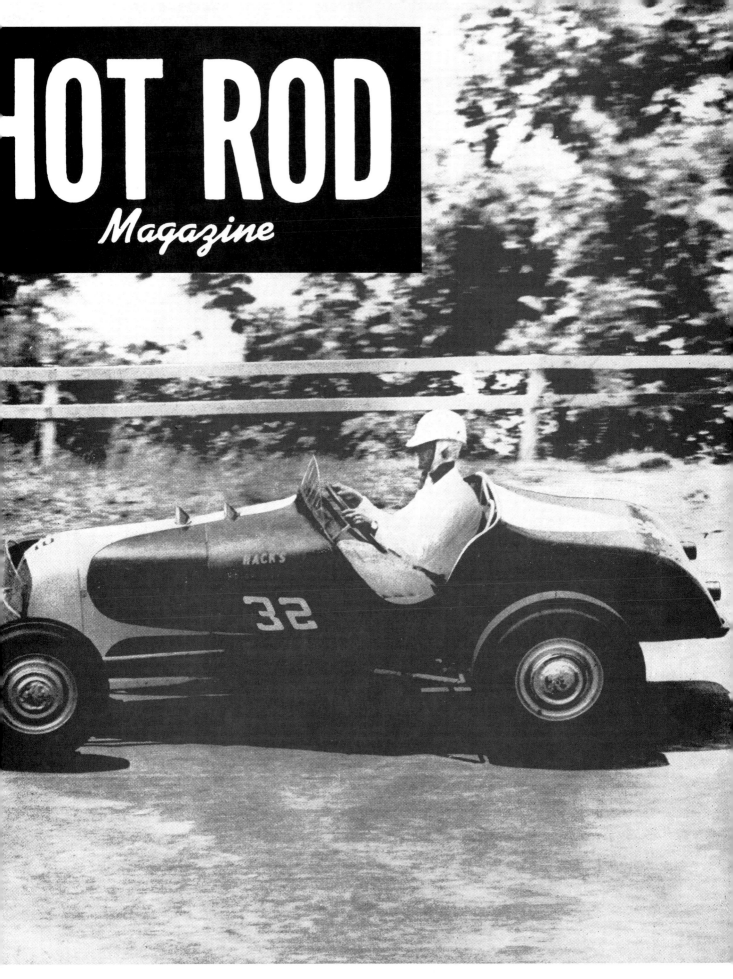

HOT ROD
Magazine

32

Record Holder Dick Frazier SEPTEMBER, 1948 **25c**

It's in the Bag . . .

Dear HRM:

I bought my first copy of your magazine . . . in January of this year. Right then and there I knew that this new magazine had in it everything that I wanted in a magazine of this kind.

. . . Since then I have met with a slight accident and have been confined to the U.S. Naval Hospital . . . I have been eagerly awaiting every issue of your magazine. Everyone in the ward wants to read it and now they sell it in the Ship's Store here at the hospital.

I . . . talked my doctor into letting me go to a lakes meet last month. It was really great up there, getting to see all my buddies again. Nothing can keep me from a lakes meet.

DON HAMMER
U.S. Naval Hospital
Long Beach, Calif.

P.S.—Have been trying to figure out how to mount a Merc. stroker in a wheel chair. Have any suggestions?

D. H.

---

*We turned your order over to our cartoonist, Tom Medley, who replied with the accompanying drawing.—*ED.

Dear Editor:

While looking through the July issue of Hot Rod Magazine I came across the photo of very pretty Virginia Leith. On showing the photo to the rest of the men at the Diesel Mechanic School, she was elected the pin-up girl of the 013 School (Diesel Mechanic).

The men hope you can fulfill our request for an autographed photo of Miss Leith.

PFC ROBERT MELUH
Fort Warren, Wyo.
463rd A.F.B.U.

*Miss Leith sends her thanks to the fellows of the 013 School at Fort Warren. The autographed photo is on the way.—*ED.

Hot Rod Magazine:

. . . As far as we know, we are the only speed shop in the state of Florida that caters exclusively to Hot Rods . . . We have attempted to form a hot rod club here, but failed miserably many times since all we could get were enthusiasts . . . no car owners or prospective owners. We intend to try again in the near future.

WILLIAM OTTO
Titusville, Florida.

To the Editor:

It's about time that, in the interest of better racing, a "Commissioner" or "Public Relations Officer" be appointed to represent all concerned with hot rod and/or midget racing.

Certain large publications take a great deal of interest in featuring the slightest infraction (where so-called hot rods are involved) which leads to accidents on the road, whether or not hot-rodders are to blame. It makes good reading and something to "talk about."

Such a Commissioner should enforce regulations about professional drivers' equipment, inspection of safety belts, helmets, goggles, automobile frames, etc. He should inspect track conditions and penalize any management permitting unusual holes and bumps to go unrepaired. Smart drivers learn how to drive under all kinds of conditions, but sometimes even cleverness cannot prevent accidents. It should be the duty of the Commissioner of Racing, or Public Relations Officer, to get to the public first with the truth to prevent distortion. Big industry does this today.

Race driving has become such an industry it can no longer afford haphazard situations to exist which can give rise to public "indignation." Careful supervision should be taken now to prevent unreasonable criticism to develop. A good Public Relations Officer or Commissioner-at-large could do much to hold together in a favorable light this infant, but large, sport.

JOHN C. BARTLETT
Los Angeles, Calif.

(Continued on Page 22)

Editor's Column

Dick Frazier, featured in HRM's HOT ROD OF THE MONTH, is one of the nation's leading hot rod record holders. The story of Dick and his car, which appears on pages 6 & 7 of this issue, illustrates the fact that Indiana plays a big role in the world of hot rod racing.

INSIDE THE DAVIS gives readers a chance to see and understand the functions of the new tri-wheel Davis automobile. The car, manufactured in Southern California, reportedly will appear on western markets within the next 90 days.

Photographer Rick Mann outdid himself with the exceptional action sequence shown on pages 8 & 9. The pictures were taken with a motion picture-type camera. The accident took place at Oakland Stadium during a Racing Roadsters, Inc., race. Five cars were involved, only one minor injury sustained.

Builders will be interestetd in FRONT DRIVE ROADSTER, story of the Sosic Brothers' track job, to be found on page 12 & 13 of this issue.

Bill Gieseke's September article is concerned with BREAK IN OIL. This feature is supplemented by a group of questions and answers on the subject. Turn to page 16.

A little strip entitled EL MIRAGE BEFORE DAWN shows a humorous side of dry lakes attendance. Some of our readers may find that HRM's early morn photographer caught them napping recently. This strip is on page 19.

PARTS WITH APPEAL proves that piston rings can have more than one use. Don't guess! Turn to page 20!

At last some pictures from Chicago, thanks to Burdette Martin. Hurricane Hot Rod followers will find their favorites on page 23.

John Bartlett's letter, which appears in this month's IT'S IN THE BAG column (opposite), tells of his proposed solution to unfavorable publicity given to hot rods. This problem is becoming more pronounced. Before long some steps will have to be taken in defense of hot rod activities. Possibly Mr. Bartlett's idea is the solution. HRM would appreciate hearing from readers with helpful suggestions regarding hot rod functions.

Those news items and photographs are still welcome.

Don't forget! Our advertisers appreciate your mention of their ads in HOT ROD MAGAZINE. Thanks!—ED.

"World's Most Complete Hot Rod Coverage"

TABLE OF CONTENTS

Vol. 1   HRM—Published Monthly   No. 9

Associate Editors	R. E. Petersen, Robert R. Lindsay
Technical Advisers	W. I. 'Bill' Gieseke, Wally Parks
Art Director	Alice Van Norman
Photography	Dyson Smith, Paul Schaeffer, Rick, Pete, Vic Drake, Paul Panghorn
Cartoons and Humor	Tom Medley
Reporters	Robert Williams, Glenn Glendening, Dick Robinson, Richard K. Martin, Arthur Elliot, William H. Sippel, Bob Machin, Pauline Bayer, J. Robert Seth
Subscription Department	Marilyn Lord
Distribution	Gordon Behn

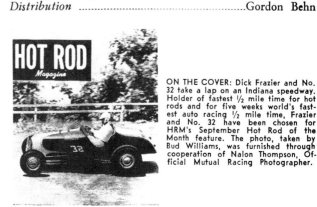

ON THE COVER: Dick Frazier and No. 32 take a lap on an Indiana speedway. Holder of fastest ½ mile time for hot rods and for five weeks world's fastest auto racing ½ mile time, Frazier and No. 32 have been chosen for HRM's September Hot Rod of the Month feature. The photo, taken by Bud Williams, was furnished through cooperation of Nalon Thompson, Official Mutual Racing Photographer.

Photo by George Hornbeck

Photo by Bud Williams

WINCHESTER, INDIANA
JUNE 20, 1948

DRIVING A HOT ROD RACING CAR
DICK FRAZIER OF MUNCIE SET A
NEW WORLD'S RECORD OF :21.37 FOR
½-MILE AT WINCHESTER SPEEDWAY
TODAY.

This news certainly qualifies Dick Frazier and his #32 as the Hot Rod and Hot Rod Driver of the Month.

Dick "Rapid Richard" Frazier was born April 18, 1918, on a farm northeast of Newcastle, Indiana. His early sporting career consisted of membership in the Moreland Bob-Cats basketball team. In later years, however, Dick took an avid interest in automobile racing. He drove his first race at Jungle Park Track, Rockville, Ind., in 1938. From then on Dick stayed in the racing game, driving midgets, hot rods, stock cars, three-quarter and big cars.

Frazier is one of the original members of the Mutual Racing Association. He is a topnotch mechanic, but his real love lies in racing. When he takes #32 around the track he becomes a part of the car. His perfect sense of balance with the car seems to be the secret of his success.

"Cup Cake," as Dick's closest friends affectionately call him, hopes to one day drive the "500." His qualifications for the big race include:

1940—Placed second in Mutual championship; 1941—Won the Mutual championship; 1941—Drove Art Hartley's stock car for the 1941 championship title; 1942—Won the mutual championship; 1945—Won the Mutual championship; 1946—Placed third in the Mutual championship; May, 1948—Was running second to Spider Webb when race was halted. (This was his first ride in big cars. A.A.A.); 1948—Placed first in 21 out of 30 feature starts in No. 32. Placed second 6 times, third, fifth, and eighth once each.

#32 is owned by Frazier and Hack Winninger, Muncie automobile mechanic.

Dick's record stood until July 25 when top-ranking driver Ted Horn was clocked in :20.863. This doesn't dismay Frazier, as he feels he can make the circuit in :20.80.

Dick is married and has one son.

HRM tips its masthead to Driver Dick Frazier.

TOP—Dick takes a "winner's lap" with the starter's checkered flag. ABOVE—Frazier passes John Arnold on the same day he set his world's record lap. RIGHT—The engine is well back against the firewall. FAR RIGHT—From the driver's eye view. Note exhaust covers, which save the driver from possible burns.

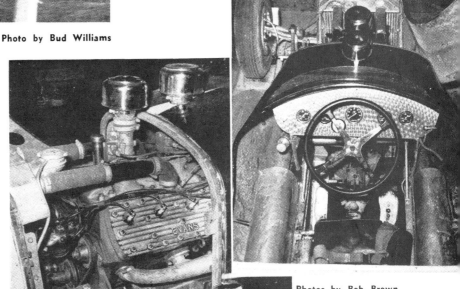

Photos by Bob Brown

Construction Cutaway

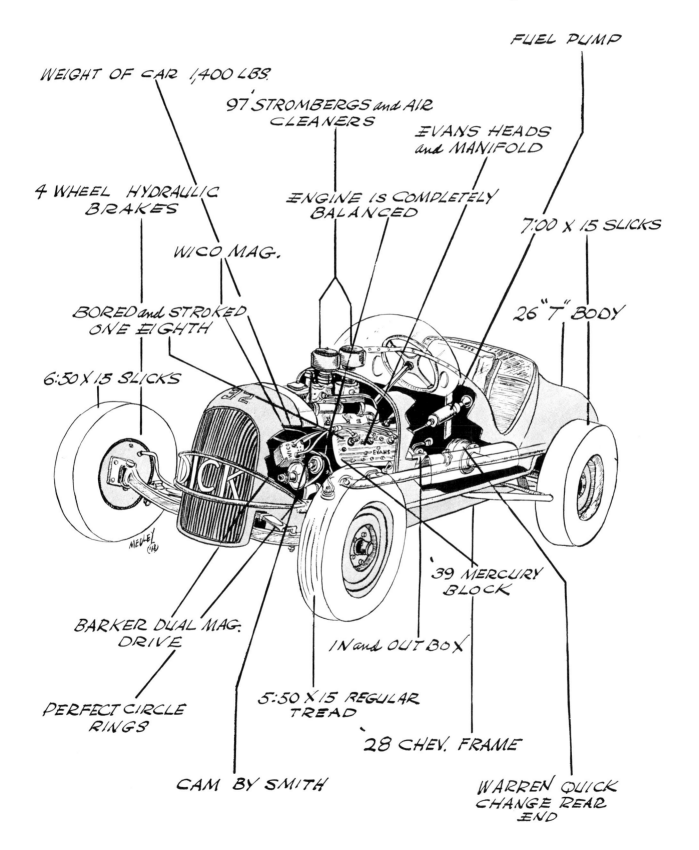

FUEL PUMP

WEIGHT OF CAR 1,400 LBS.

97 STROMBERGS and AIR CLEANERS

EVANS HEADS and MANIFOLD

4 WHEEL HYDRAULIC BRAKES

ENGINE IS COMPLETELY BALANCED

7:00 X 15 SLICKS

WICO MAG.

26" "T" BODY

BORED and STROKED ONE EIGHTH

6:50 X 15 SLICKS

'39 MERCURY BLOCK

BARKER DUAL MAG. DRIVE

IN and OUT BOX

PERFECT CIRCLE RINGS

5:50 X 15 REGULAR TREAD

'28 CHEV. FRAME

CAM BY SMITH

WARREN QUICK CHANGE REAR END

ACTION AT OAKLAND STADIUM

Walt Davis (4) of Los Angeles breaks a drag link in the 35th lap. Bob Kelleher (2) is too close behind to avoid collision.

Frank Santos (16) piles into the wreck, knocking Kelleher to the ground. A

moment later Bill Ryan (73) joins the wreck. Kelleher tries to

avoid the moving wreckage as Ryan begins his roll.

Three-quarters of the way over and still rolling, Ryan's

safety belt holds him in his seat. Davis, after several jolts

from the rear, looks back and decides it's all clear, leaves car.

Ryan, out of his collapsed racer, helps a pitman out of path of Troy Ruttman (19). No one was injured.

Davis body design is characterized by extreme frontal streamlining.

With many hot rod builders looking toward three-wheel construction for wind resistance reduction, HRM has endeavored to give to its readers an inside view of the construction features of the most widely discussed car of this type.

A product of California race car builders, the Davis incorporates speedway and aircraft ideas into a unique streamlined automobile.

The big question that has arisen regarding this car is, "Will three wheels work?" The answer seems to be "Yes."

Company head, Gary Davis, answers this with a test routine that emphasizes the outstanding characteristics of the car.

This routine includes demonstration of the action that throws the driver back instead of forward when the disc-type brakes are applied. Maneuverability is displayed by making high-speed turns inside the factory and putting the car into a tight turn and leaving the driver's seat, the car continuing to circle without a driver. Another test has the auto jumping large bumps with no hands on the wheel to prove roadability.

It's difficult to scoff at this streamlined tricycle after a demonstration such as this.

Power is supplied by a four-cylinder 60-horsepower Hercules engine. This small 133 cubic inch power plant has a 3 1/4 bore and a 4-inch stroke. Ignition is an Auto-lite and carburetor is a special-built Zenith; cam is of the high-lift type.

Although the engine is small, the acceleration qualities are good. This can be attributed to the lightness of the 1385-pound, all-aluminum body and the low gear ratios.

Conventional rear end runs 4.10 gears with the transmission a direct drive in high gear.

Coil sprung, the body rides 18 inches from the ground with hydraulic oleo shock absorbers to smooth out the bumps.

Secured by four toggle bolts, the top is easily removable, changing the car from coupe to roadster in a few moments.

Interior fittings are simple; seat is 64 inches wide, providing ample room for four passengers.

Upholstery is similar to that used in

Cutaway diagram gives a closer insight to the construction details.

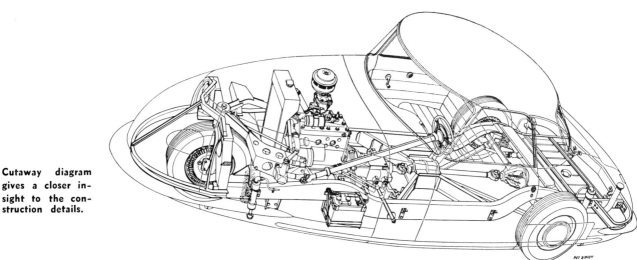

THE DAVIS

Front wheel components are amazingly simple and sturdy.

race cars, being easily installed or removed by snap fasteners.

In case of damage to the body, panels held by lock nuts may be quickly replaced.

Extras will include a four-point jack arrangement operating off of the engine that lifts all three wheels from the ground for tire repairs. Gary Davis also plans to manufacture his own speed equipment and special accessories.

At the present time the four-seat model described is being readied for production. A seven-passenger car, a station wagon, a panel pickup, and other designs are being readied for the future.

ABOVE — The 60 horsepower Hercules engine is mounted between the channel steel frame rails.

LEFT—Coil springs and tubular shock absorbers are combined in the rear for easy riding.

FRONT DRIVE ROADSTER

By

WALTER A. WORON

•

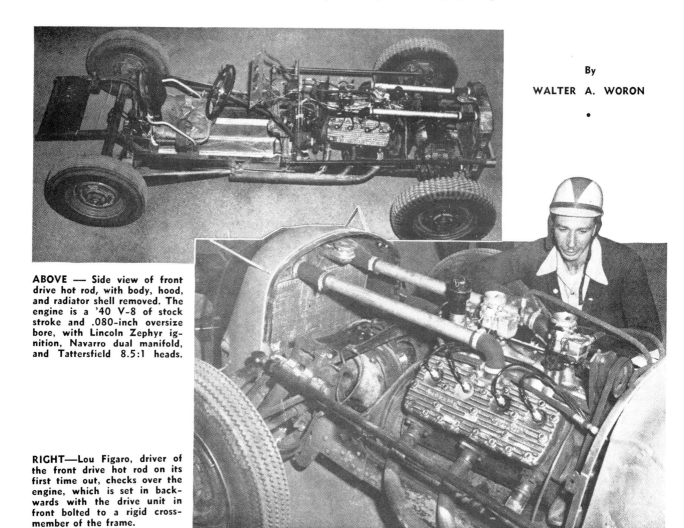

ABOVE — Side view of front drive hot rod, with body, hood, and radiator shell removed. The engine is a '40 V-8 of stock stroke and .080-inch oversize bore, with Lincoln Zephyr ignition, Navarro dual manifold, and Tattersfield 8.5:1 heads.

RIGHT—Lou Figaro, driver of the front drive hot rod on its first time out, checks over the engine, which is set in backwards with the drive unit in front bolted to a rigid cross-member of the frame.

Again proving that the pioneer spirit is still alive in America, the Sosic brothers of Los Angeles have come up with a creation new to the racing fraternity —a hot rod with front drive. Not that hot rods, or front drives, in themselves, are new, but when combined, that is something again.

The idea was born when the first hot rod race was conducted on Labor Day, 1946, at Carrell Speedway, then known as Gardena Bowl. George and Dave Sosic had always been front drive enthusiasts, and having watched front drive big cars at Indianapolis compete with the best of them, they were certain that a hot rod of the same type would prove to be the master of anything else in the hot rod class.

At first being ridiculed and scoffed at, they nevertheless continued undiscouraged, assembling detail data and listening to helpful advice given by such racing stalwarts as the late Ralph Hepburn, Lou Moore, Bud Winfield, Emil Dietz, and Leo Goossen. In a few months, they began to gather parts for

use in the car, taking almost six months for this project.

Truck drivers George (an A&E mechanic in the AAF during the war) and Dave (a Motor Sergeant in his divisional headquarters) devoted all their spare time to the assembly of the car: cutting and welding the frame, mounting the engine, designing a front end for the drive unit, installing the body, and the countless other details involved in building up a car.

And then, on July 21, 1948, the car was ready for its initial race date, and as it should be, the place was where the idea was born, Carrell Speedway.

The car was driven by Lou Figaro, well-known driver of the California Roadster Association, who had never before driven the car, nor any other front drive car. Nonetheless, Figaro qualified the car in the fairly fast time of :25.43 seconds for one lap around the half-mile dirt track.

The car was entered in the first six-lap heat race, and starting on the outside front line, held off the challenge of the other five cars to wind up in first

place. Starting on the pole for the 15-lap semi-main event, Figaro finished in second place. The Sosic brothers feel that it was a good beginning for a new car, and that when the right gear ratio with the proper size tires is found, they will have a well-nigh unbeatable combination.

POWER PLANT AND DRIVE UNIT

The power plant used in the hot rod is a 1940 Ford V-8 of stock stroke and .080-inch oversize bore, developing around 135 horsepower. It uses Lincoln Zephyr ignition, which was built up by Regg Schlemmer. A Harmon and Collins full-race cam is used.

For its first race the Sosic brothers used Tattersfield 8.5:1 heads and a Navarro dual intake manifold.

The engine is set in the chassis with the front end at the firewall and the rear end forward, with the clutch housing attached to the front drive unit. Diamond (four-point) solid-type suspension is used; one point at the rear to a cross-member of the frame, two points at the side toward the front, attaching to the two longitudinal members of the frame, and the fourth point where the front drive unit bolts to a frame cross-member (the drive unit being bolted to the clutch housing, which is, in turn, bolted to the engine.)

The drive unit is a Pat Warren quick-change rear end (using possible gear ratios of from 2.24:1 to 6.95:1) with the necessary modifications to make it adaptable to the Sosic car. In effect, it is a transmission with the gear box end cut off, and a differential added in its place. The primary shaft is hooked to the Ford drive shaft, which has been made special to fit the crankshaft, making a straight-through drive shaft.

Spicer universal joints are used to transmit power from the drive unit to the wheel drive shafts, while Spicer constant-velocity universal joints are used at the wheels.

Between the drive unit and the engine is a conventional Ford clutch, with a heat-treated, aluminum alloy flywheel that weighs but three pounds instead of the usual 21 pounds.

SUSPENSION

The car features rigid-frame, torsional suspension, using longitudinal torsion bars fore and aft, with dampers consisting of Gabriel shocks in the front and Houdaille shocks in the rear. In a rigid design of this type, the unsprung weight (that part of the car that takes the road shock) is kept to a minimum.

At the front end, the upper control arm (a "wishbone") is connected flexibly to the frame and to the wheel spindle, while the lower control arm is connected flexibly to the torsion bar and the wheel spindle, making the wheels independently sprung. The Gabriel shock absorber attaches to the lower control arm at the lower end and to the frame at the upper end.

The forward torsion bars run longitudinally, inboard of the box frame, attaching to the lower control arm with rubber bushings fore and aft, and are welded to the cross-member of the frame that is just aft of the engine.

Each of the rear wheels uses a short vertical link from the wheel to a two-foot horizontal steel plate linkage that transmits vertical loads to the longitudinal torsion bar. The two torsion bars are but seven inches apart, side motion being prevented by the fact that they are both bolted to the same "T" fitting that, in turn, bolts to the rear cross-member of the frame. At this point, two rubber bushings are bonded to each shaft and are also bonded to an outer shell. This gives the bar not only the effect of a torsion bar, but also the effect of a torsilastic spring, since the first linear loads are taken up by the rubber (the torsilastic effect) and then by the bar (the torsional effect).

FRAME AND BODY

The frame, or chassis, is the box-type, consisting of two longitudinal box sections, with six cross-members. The cross-members include the following: a crome-moly tubular bumper in front of the radiator, the front axle channel section, a steel plate to which the forward end of the engine attaches, a channel at the rear of the engine, and two additional channels, one forward and one aft of the bucket seat location.

The rear wheel tread is five inches less than the front wheel tread, being 54 inches, as compared to 59 inches. All tires are size 6.00x16, those on the front having winter-cleat tread, the rear tires having rib tread.

The body is a combination of a '25 Model A cab and a specially built hood made for the Sosic brothers by Emil Dietz. The body can be quickly removed, being held in place by a few bolts.

Instead of the conventional Plexiglas windshield, a fine-mesh screen is used. The advantage in having a windshield of this type is that on a dirt track, when dirt on the windshield begins to impair the vision, a flick of the finger will remove the dirt.

STEERING GEAR

The steering gear is the conventional race gear type; the gears were made by the Advance Gear Company, while the rest of the mechanism was made by the Conze Brothers. Pitman arms connect the gear mechanism (outside of both sides of the cab) to a longitudinal steering rod that runs forward to adjustable steering links above the upper control arm on each front wheel. The most important point in this adjustment, the Sosic brothers feel, is that a straight line drawn from the same point thru any turn to the center of each front wheel, must be exactly perpendicular to the fore-and-aft axis of each wheel. In this manner, maximum control is assured through any and all turns.

HANDLING OF CAR

The Sosic brothers believe that the biggest advantage of a front drive car

(Continued on page 29)

RIGHT — Top view of stripped Sosic brothers' front drive hot rod. Note individual suspension of front wheels, box-type frame, and Pitman arm-longitudinal rod type of steering.

BELOW—Troy Ruttman tooling the Sosic brothers' front drive hot rod through a turn during a trial spin at Carrell Speedway.

WHAT'S NEW

TWENTY-ONE STUD HEADS

Twenty-one stud heads are now in production by Evans. Designed for V-8's from 1932 to 1937, the heads have the waterpump mount in the front. Compression ratios, finish and chamber design are the same as in the later model V-8 heads.

FORD "60" RACE PARTS

Ford V-8 "60" racing heads and manifolds may now be obtained in the Weiand design. Manifold differs from the "85" in that the fuel pump mount is part of the casting. Heads have an external water manifold connecting with each of the four cylinders.

BALL-BEARING REAR END

Ball-bearing rear ends for roadsters are being turned out by the Drake Brothers Machine Shop with the bearings being used in the wheel hub, ring and pinion gears. Special axles have $1\frac{3}{8}$" spline. Big-car type safety hubs complete the assembly to prevent loss of wheels.

FLAT SURFACE TRACK SLICKS

Rusty Accornero has developed a new surface design for asphalt slick tires. The surface is absolutely flat across, having no raise in the center with a $\frac{3}{8}$-inch raise on the high side. No burning in is needed with this type of tread.

TWO TYPES V-8 IGNITIONS

Kurten Aero-Motive is now making two types of V-8 distributors. One, made from a Lincoln Zephyr, mounts the double coils on the case. The other, made from a late Ford case, has the double coils mounted separately. Both units have Scintilla points.

DUAL CARBS FOR CHEVS

A new two-carburetor heated Chevrolet manifold complete with linkage is being manufactured by the Sharp Speed Equipment Co. Designed for use on 1937 to 1949 models, the finned set-up will come in sand blast or black crackle finish.

RACING V-8 BOAT HEADS

Special heads for V-8 racing boat engines are now available from Navarro Racing Equipment Co. Water outlet is on top of the front instead of in the middle. The outlet hole is $\frac{1}{2}$ inch in diameter with head ratios 9.75 and 10.1.

HORSEPOWER TESTING

High-speed chassis dynamometer service is being offered by C & B Motortest. Horsepower and torque charts may be made on roadsters and motorcycles without removing the engine from the chassis.

HEADS FOR '49 V-8'S

Heads for the 1949 Fords and Mercurys have been announced by Vic Edelbrock. A wide range of compression ratios are being offered for both cars.

RUSSETTA TIMING RESULTS

EXISTING RECORDS
as of Aug. 23

A Coupe	114.80	Anderson	Coupes
B Coupe	117.11	Towle	Coupes
C Coupe	120.40	Brown	Coupes
A Roadster	124.56	Guptill	Lancers
B Roadster	129.59	Hartelt	Lancers
C Roadster	123.11	Miller	Drifters
A Streamliner	122.12	Hunter	Moles
B Streamliner	123.88	Markham	Blo Bys

POINT STANDINGS

Place	Club	Points
1	Coupes	277
2	ARC	144
3	Gophers	137
4	Drifters	125
5	Velociteers	84
6	Blo Bys	79
7	Rhodents	75
8	Lancers	73
9	Vultures	71
10	Moles	52
11	Screwdrivers	42
12	Gophers	39
13	Rotors	36
14	Gazelles	30
15	Screechers	19
15	Cam Twirlers	19
17	Stockholders	13
18	Hutters	11
19	Roadhogs	8

MEET OF AUG. 15, 1948

"A" COUPES
RECORD: Harold Anderson (Coupes)—114.80 Avg.

Place	Name	Average	Club
1	Bob Pierson	115.38	Coupes
2	Harold Anderson	115.23	Coupes
3	R. Lock	110.02	Rhodents
4	R. Brannigan	108.56	Gophers
5	P. Andrews	108.43	Rhodents
6	C. Goodin	106.88	Coupes
7	Ed Rice	106.63	Drifters
8	J. Walker	106.13	Cam Twirlers
9	C. Townsen	103.9	Coupes
10	D. Moon	102.85	Hutters

"B" COUPES
RECORD: Don Towle (Coupes)—117.11 Avg.

1	Don Towle	117.80	Coupes
2	D. Gaudreau	111.52	Drifters
3	D. Ness	108.30	ARC
4	B. Pierson	106.50	Coupes
5	J. Spencer	105.38	Rhodents
5	J. Thomassin	105.38	Coupes
7	B. Smith	105.13	Gazelles
8	D. Rock	103.92	Screechers
9	R. Bowen	103.12	Gazelles
10	L. Walker	102.50	Drifters

"C" COUPES

Place	Name	Average	Club
1	Bob Meeks	116.58	Coupes
2	Bob Cantley	107.14	Coupes
3	Carl Taylor	106.50	ARC
4	E. Husting	99.66	Stockholders
5	D. Blanchard	99.00	Rhodents
6	J. Eccman	98.25	Coupes
7	D. Corwin	95.23	Coupes
8	Richardson	90.36	Coupes

"A" STREAMLINERS
RECORD: Dave Hunter (Moles)—123.12

1	Dave Hunter	122.28	Moles
2	S. C. Davidson	117.95	ARC

"B" STREAMLINERS

1	H. Haller	139.96	Drifters
2	H. Haller	120.10	Drifters

ABOVE—Don Brown's 120.40 mph record coupe is pushed to the starting line with the help of a pretty crew member.

BELOW—Driver Fernandes goes past in a hard top '32 Ford coupe.

BELOW LEFT—A roadster leaves the start in a cloud of dust.

BELOW RIGHT—Don Towle's chopped '34 clocking over 115 mph.

Break In Oil

By

W. I. "BILL"

GIESEKE

Mr. Gieseke is a member of the Society of Automotive Engineers of the American Chemical Society, with seven years as Automotive and Lubrication Engineer for a major oil company.

Introduction

The phrase "Break in Oil" has been with us in the automotive and mechanical field a lot longer than the average mechanic can remember. It no doubt originated back in the early days of the internal combustion engine. It was then decided that lubricants made from mineral oil were more readily available and to a large degree were more generally suitable, especially insofar as their physical and chemical stability was concerned. However, when engines were first started they would freeze or tighten up. It was soon discovered that vegetable or animal oil when added to regular oil would help to get them by this critical period— thus the phrase "break in oil."

Mineral or petroleum oils (providing they are properly manufactured from the better lube stocks) can be used to accomplish the following:

1. It can be pumped and circulated.
2. When supplied to rotating or reciprocal bearings or parts, it changes friction from solid to fluid friction; thus reducing wear and drag.
3. It has the ability to further seal piston rings, etc.
4. It functions as a coolant to carry away heat.
5. To some extent it carries away impurities.
6. It resists shock load, heat, dilution, etc.

The six foregoing advantages are what made the early-day engineers decide to use an oil derived from petroleum.

This does not mean that mineral oil possesses all of the qualities desired for a perfect lubricant.

Listed below are some of the disadvantages or shortcomings inherent in a mineral lubricant.

1. It usually has a very low affinity for metal; very high surface tension, poor penetrating value, low oiliness value (does not adhere like vegetable, animal oils or other chemicals) (the vegetable oils are classed as fixed oils).
2. Low film strength.
3. Thickens or congeals when cold.
4. Thins out or loses body when hot.
5. Becomes oxidized when exposed to the elements present in the average crankcase, especially when air and oil temperatures become excessive; thus resulting in varnish-like formation or generally classed as high temperature or oxidation sludge.
6. Becomes highly acid when drain periods are over-extended, causing corrosion and thus erosion. *The greatest cause of engine wear.*
7. Lacks high enough solvent power to clean up a dirty engine.
8. Immiscible in water. This fact alone is in the writer's opinion the cause of sludge formation in most engines, especially when average crankcase temperatures are below 180°F. When water, oil, gums, waxes, soot, dust, acids and metallic particles are constantly agitated within the engine, it is no wonder that we produce a lot of what the mechanic calls "African Mayonnaise," "goop," "gunk," "sludge," etc. This type of sludge is more technically known as low temperature and/or emulsion sludge.

Mineral or petroleum oil as it comes from the earth has in many respects better actual lubricating ability because of the oxygen and/or sulphur, etc., it contains. However, when it is refined it loses its natural solvent, wetting ability, oiliness or lubricity and film strength. Many valuable components of mineral oil are removed by refining for the sake of greater chemical and physical stability.

In recent years some oils have been over-refined for the sake of increasing their chemical stability or improving some physical property such as viscosity or pour points, etc.

In the United States and throughout the world, mother earth yields three main types of oils. They are in the order of their importance:

1. The Paraffin series (highly saturated hydrocarbon — chain group) considered quite stable chemically.
2. The Napthene series (saturated hydrocarbons — ring group) considered fairly stable.
3. The aromatic series (highly unsaturated — ring group) considered very unstable.

Above three series are also known as eastern, mid-continent and western oil.

All three types of crude when properly refined produce lubricating oil of varying quality.

In spite of the fact that acid and/or solvent refining has in many cases removed the oiliness "germ" or the so-called "missing link" in lubricating oils it is now possible, thanks to synthetic chemistry, to impart the good characteristics of vegetable or animal oil (fixed oils) to any well refined mineral oil regardless of type.

ENGINE DEPOSITS FROM FUELS AND LUBRICANTS

Deposits such as carbon sludge, etc., forming within the engine, regardless of type or fuel used, have been a serious problem ever since the internal combustion engine turned its first revolution.

Hydro-carbon fuels and oils, that all internal combustion engines must have for producing power and lubrication, are subject to chemical and physical changes, such as oxidation, acidity, dilution and many others. As an example, when iron or steel is exposed to the elements too long, oxidation (rusting or corrosion) sets in.

There are many variables connected with the operation of an internal combustion engine that greatly affect the service period of the oil in the crankcase. We change oil, not because it wears out, but because it becomes contaminated with impurities; or because certain chemical changes take place that make it unfit for further use.

Many Variables

Following are a few of the many variables we have to contend with in the operation of all types of engines:

1. Air fuel mixture ratio, ranging from rich to lean;
2. Ring and valve efficiency, ranging from good seal to poor seal;
3. A wide range of ignition and timing characteristics;
4. Engines operating from too cold to too hot;
5. Engines operating from load to overload;
6. Low speed to high speed;
7. Dry air to moist air;
8. Clean air to dirty air.

There are other variables too numerous to mention, including driving habits, to say little about the many types and grades of fuels and oils consumed. This should serve to remind us that we can hardly ever expect to be entirely free from engine deposits.

A great many men in the industry can remember when it was necessary to change the oil almost daily, or at least every Sunday, before they took the old gas buggy out for a spin. In those days the average owner was more interested in how good a lubricating job he was doing than in how far he could run without adding to or draining the crankcase oil. In this respect we have gone perhaps from one extreme to the other. As a matter of fact, there have been several attempts to prepare a no-change motor oil Other devices have been developed to keep oil clean, which permit greatly extended drain intervals, and some have done a remarkable job.

Improved Motor Oil

The oil industry has given the motoring public a greatly improved motor oil, especially since the advent of solvent refining which has generally increased the chemical stability and permitted more miles between drains.

If the engine builders were to hold still long enough and not continually strive for higher and higher output from a given displacement, the oil companies would no doubt make it possible to safely run the oil, let us say an average of 10,000 miles. Of course that is not possible or progressive. It would be like asking a 12-year-old boy to stop growing. Instead, the motor car industry has made some wonderful strides in the past ten years, resulting in our present-day units that are highly efficient.

There has been close collaboration between the automotive and petroleum industries, in so far as furnishing fuels and lubricants to meet many changes, such as greatly increased pressure, temperatures, speed, leaner mixtures, closer clearances and tolerances.

But in spite of this close cooperation, the tighter fit of engine parts and higher temperatures have brought on a new problem, the "varnish problem." This varnish is partly caused by the baking down of "gum" that comes from using the new and improved cracked or polymerized fuels that have been on the market for the past 10 years. However, the writer has noticed that the varnish has been traced to the oil in a great majority of the cases.

It has been found in the laboratory that these gum and varnish deposits that form on valves, rings, cylinder walls, piston assemblies and bearings throughout the engine vary greatly in their density and solubility characteristics. Many solvents or chemicals that will dissolve such deposits when an engine is disassembled are extremely harmful to internal parts of the engine during the process of combustion as they combine with the water vapors to form corrosive gases and acids.

It has been very definitely proven by many that the formation of gum from gasoline is the cause of rings sticking, resulting in a loss of power due to blow-by and the blow-by gases plug oil slots, which suddenly increases oil consumption, as well as helps to contaminate the lubricating oil with products of combustion, and at the

(Continued on next page)

BELL AUTO PARTS
Featuring the FINEST IN RACING EQUIPMENT
for Roadsters-Boats & Race Cars

DASH MOUNT HAND AIR PRESSURE PUMP
FOR ROADSTER AND BOAT USE
POLISHED AND COMPLETE, READY TO INSTALL — $9.00
Plus 5% Mfg. Tax

This pump is principally the same as the race car side mount pump, with a flange mounting, for fitting in the instrument panel. Is equipped with the same highly efficient check valve featured in the race car pump. Made of 24 ST Dural with heat treated cast alloy ends.

Send for our free illustrated catalog
ROY RICHTER

BELL, CALIF.   **3633 E. GAGE AVE.**   **KImball 5728**

EDELBROCK
POWER and SPEED EQUIPMENT

COMPRESSION RATIOS:

FORD—
7½-8-8½-9

MERCURY—
8-8½-9-9½

Edelbrock Announces New Heads for '49 Fords and Mercurys
SEND FOR FREE CATALOG
VIC EDELBROCK

1200 N. Highland Ave.   Dept. H   Hollywood 38, Calif.   HE. 2223

PAT WARREN
Quick Change Rear Ends
- **Indianapolis**
  - **Dirt Tracks**
    - **Midgets**
      - **Roadsters**
COMPLETE REAR-ENDS
Write for Literature and Gear Ratio Charts
Center Section to Fit Ford Rear Ends

DOWNEY MACHINE COMPANY
8313 E. FIRESTONE BLVD.   •   **LOgan 2656**
DOWNEY, CALIFORNIA

same time the greatest damage of all is excessive cylinder wall wear from corrosion and erosion. Moreover it is also observed that more compression is lost from stuck rings than from bad valves. Carbon formation is faster and in greater quantities when using a fuel with a high gum content.

Symptoms of Increased Friction

"Gum" or "varnish" together, when allowed to accumulate, due to their high frictional properties, in the average case, will cause an increased frictional drag in the engine. These symptoms as noted by the operator are:

1. Blow-by fumes up through the floor boards;

2. Surging flow of power at a given speed with a fixed throttle, many times with a variation of three to five miles per hour. Oftimes the tune-up specialist confuses the symptom with fuel pump or carburetor vapor lock, flat spot, etc.;

3. A gradual falling off in power, as well as many other performance factors;

4. Hard for the starter to turn engine after coming to a fast stop; also dies easily when hot; and in acute cases, varnish deposits cause complete seizure, resulting in costly repair.

It has been proven by the trade (especially those operating the modern chassis dynamometer) that this gradual loss of power can suddenly be restored, amounting to an average of 15 per cent, by the use of the proper "chemical tune-up."

As one very well-known authority puts it, "The use of chemicals must always precede the mechanical tune-up."

While the formation of "gum" and "varnish" cannot be entirely eliminated, it can be materially retarded in the modern engine by:

1. Selecting a fuel with low gum content;

2. Using an oil that forms the least varnish;

3. Draining the oil at proper intervals, which may be anywhere from 500 to 5,000 miles, depending on how pure the oil is kept;

4. Using a good oil filter (keep it clean);

5. Using a good "add" oil in the crankcase continuously to retard formation of "gums," "varnish" and sludge;

6. And last, but not least, a complete mechanical and chemical tune-up every 5,000 miles.

PART III
QUESTIONS & ANSWERS
On the Important Subject
How Often Should I Change My Oil?

Q. *What are these "conditions" that affect oil change mileage requirements?*

A. Physical conditons—the human element — and the mechanical condition of the engine in question.

Q. *What do you mean by "physical conditions"?*

A. Percent of dirt in air, dust storms, winds; rain, fog, snow; freezing temperatures, ice; heat in varying degrees; city traffic, country traffic, level ground, hills; cement, oiled, macadam, or dirt roads.

Q. *Why do these "conditions" have such an effect on the oil change period?*

A. Example: One motorist m a y have come only 75 miles through a dust storm and should change his oil immediately, regardless of the low mileage; another may have the ideal conditions of fine weather, level cement highways, no traffic tie-ups—and be a good driver . . . his car may be allowed many more miles before a change is absolutely necessary.

Q. *What do you mean by the "human element"?*

A. Motorists themselves. There are all kinds—good, bad, hard, fast, slow and indifferent drivers—each one can be reflected in the condition of his car by the way he operates it.

Q. *What do you mean by "mechanical condition"?*

A. The engine itself, and the state of wear in rings, pistons, bearings, valves; efficiency of cooling system; use and care of oil filters; crankcase oil level and the rate of oil consumption.

Q. *Are these factors so important if I use a good oil?*

A. Yes, because to give proper performance in today's compact, high-speed, high-compression motors, oil must carry out successfully four major duties — it must lubricate, cool, seal and clean better than ever before.

Q. *Why is "lubrication" so hard?*

A. Higher compressions, closer fits, greater speeds, and more power per weight of engine mean much greater heat—a tougher lubrication job all around. In 10,000 miles each piston travels 3,700 miles up and down within its cylinder—6,000 times each mile over a 4-inch distance. The crankshaft revolves 30,000,000 times, each valve opens and shuts 15,000,000 times!

Q. *Doesn't water do all the "cooling" that is necessary?*

A. No! Higher compressions, closer fits, higher piston ring pressures, heavier bearing shock loads that now reach 3,000 lbs. per square inch, explosion temperatures that hit 3000°F. at the firing point, and greater speed mean

(Continued on page 29)

EL MIRAGE BEFORE DAWN

Photos by Dyson Smith

Here are a few studies in sleep, taken

at a recent S.C.T.A. dry lakes meet just

before sun-up. Impromptu sleeping quar-

ters include sleeping bags, car seats, hot dog stands and good old terra firma.

Parts With Appeal

◀◀◀

VIRGINIA BATES

When it comes to piston rings, pretty Virginia Bates has found them decorative as well as useful. Here she demonstrates how piston rings can fill the bill in the way of costume jewelry.

The rings are, of course, built specifically for racing service. Hot rod enthusiasts will be interested to note that the manufacturer boasts, "They Never Dry Your Cylinder Walls." Our readers will find further interest in some facts about trim Miss Bates.

Virginia, blue eyed brunette, was born in Phoenix, Arizona, some twenty years ago. It was in that city that she received her early schooling. Later she enrolled at the University of Southern California. While appearing in a school dance recital, Miss Bates was spotted by a Metro-Goldwyn-Mayer talent scout. Within twenty-four hours she was interviewed, tested and signed to a contract.

Virginia Bates will soon appear with Esther Williams and Red Skelton in "Neptune's Daughter."

M-G-M Photo by Clarence Bull

Third in a series of Harman & Collins record-holders

90.114 m.p.h.

The world record for 225 cubic inch hydroplane in Division 2 of the American Power Boat Association was set at the Salton Sea by Tommy Hill in George Mattucci's CALIFORNIA KID using a HARMAN & COLLINS cam.

HARMAN & COLLINS, INC.

5552 ALHAMBRA AVENUE   LOS ANGELES 32, CALIF.

CApitol 4610

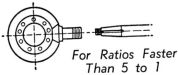
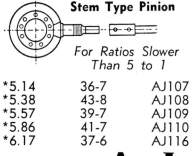
It's in the Bag
(Continued from page 4)

Dear Sirs:

Having just left Los Angeles for the T.T.O. (Texas Theater of Operations) I'm cut off, but definitely, from the roadsters . . . I gave up home and a roadster for Aviation Cadets . . . You don't know a Texan with a '32 roadster, do you?

A/C ELLIOT TOURS
Sherman, Texas

Dear Sirs:

Please allow me to point out a couple of mistakes in an otherwise perfect magazine. In your "Dry Lakes and Race Results" (August, 1948) you stated that the Yakima Speedway was an eighth-of-a-mile track and in the R.R.A.O. The track is a MILE-and-an-eighth and in the Washington Racing Association.

I also want to thank your magazine for all the information it has given me in building my own "rod."

CURTIS MILLER
Bremerton, Wash.

HRM erred in listing Yakima Speedway as a one-eighth-mile track. Although the mile-and-an-eighth track is unusually long for hot rod racing, a one-eighth-mile track might prove ridiculously cramped quarters for a group of racing roadsters. Yakima Speedway surely falls within the realm of the Washington Roadster Racing Association. However, as stated in the club news section of the same issue of HRM, RRAO — ". . . Portland track is . . . some thirty feet under water . . . The weather has caused us to run all of our races out of town. We have run several in conjunction with the Washington Roadster Racing Association . . ."
—ED.

Dear Sir:

Having just arrived in Los Angeles from Miami, Florida, I found . . . a July issue of your magazine. On the Questions and Answers Page, Don Hurter of Norwood, Mass., asked if you knew of any timing associations on the East Coast. The only one I know of is the Greater Miami Timing Association. If Don would like to get in touch with the president, Al Powell, here is his address: 3714 Royal Palm Ave., Miami Beach, Florida.

TOMMY GOSCH
Hollywood, Calif.

Soldiers Field Favorites

Photos Courtesy Burdette Martin

"Wild" Willie Stirnquist of Evanston, Ill., was 1947 champ of Hurricane Association.

Former C.H.R. pilot Jim Rathman has been doing well in the Midwest circuits.

Local boy Vince Granatelli of Chicago runs Grancor equipment in a Blair chassis.

QUESTIONS AND ANSWERS

Q. Is Winfield still putting out equipment for Ford 6 engines? If so, I would like his address.

JERRY MARTIN
Claremont, Calif.

A. There has been quite a bit of misunderstanding on this point. Winfield never did commercially manufacture Ford 6 equipment. He did design a manifold and head for Wilbur Houghton, who later manufactured the parts under the designers name. Further information may be obtained by writing Wilbur Houghton, 1245 W. Glen Oaks, Glendale, Calif.

Q. I would like to know who makes, if anyone, a dual spark plug high compresion head for a '47 Mercury engine. Also, I have '32 spindles on my rod, and I am very desirous of putting Milan disc type brakes on. I have the brakes, but I find they will not fit '32 spindles and will fit the later model Ford spindles. This will necessitate a complete change in my steering geometry. Is there any other way I can mount these brakes without changing my steering, which is the original steering on the model?

PRESTON TUCKER, JR.
Ypsilanti Machine & Tool Co.
Ypsilanti, Michigan

A. Bert Letner, 912 W. Center St., Hynes, Calif., is manufacturing a limited number of dual-spark plug heads (HRM May), and they are now being used on car 19 in the CRA. Installation of the Milan brake on '32 spindles is quite difficult. They may be mounted easily on late spindles with no change in steering arrangement. Bolt an L shaped bracket on the left backing plate with the four bolts that hold the brake unit together. The steering rod is bolted to the top of the L bracket. If you don't have the facilities to make a bracket, they may be purchased from most speed shops.

Q. I am trying to build up a Midget V-8 "60" roadster and wondered if you could tell me what kind of a frame is best suited for this.

MORTON HICKS
Altadena, Calif.

A. Ford "T," "A" or '37 Willys frame rails should be satisfactory, the lighter the better to compensate for the lower horsepower of the "60." Many builders are using tubular frames made of surplus pipe.

Q. I am in the process of building a chopped-channeled-'32 V-8 sedan, and was wondering whether or not I might be permitted to run it through the lakes.

I am running a suicide-dual spring front end. Is it permitted with the association? Any information you can give me would be greatly appreciated.

BILL D. BEVANS
San Diego 9, Calif.

A. Russetta Timing Association has facilities for timing coupes and sedans. You may either join their association or pay a six dollar guest entry fee. The suicide-dual front end is permitted, provided that it is constructed sturdy enough to pass the technical committee.

Q. I have put a pair of Denver or High Altitude Ford heads on my '46 V-8. Could you tell me the compression ratio of these heads. I have been running my car without a fan and it gets very hot. How do other guys keep their hopped up cars cool, or do they? What harm can I do by running without a fan. Would the use of Zephyr gears in my transmission increase my performance in low and second to any great extent?

BILL EADIE
San Bernardino, Calif.

A. Denver heads have a compression ratio of 7.5. It is difficult to keep a V-8 engine cool without a fan. When running minus a fan, the driver can best keep the engine cool by avoiding idling and striving to maintain a constant flow of air through the radiator. Increased radiator area and large water capacity heads will also help. Excessive overheating of the engine may result in cracked heads, stretched bearings or any number of difficulties. Zephyr gears will enable you to wind longer in low and second.

Q. I have a '29 Ford roadster now running dual 97's and .090 pistons. Would like to run a 3/4 cam. What must I alter in the valve assembly? How much can I mill off my heads for better compression without being too hard on the motor. Where and for how much can I get a hot ignition?

RICHARD DURBIN
El Segundo, Calif.

A. When a cam is installed in a V-8 engine, Zephyr valve springs should be substituted to assure complete closing of the valves at high engine speeds. The valves must be lengthened or adjustable tappets used to compensate for the shorter cam lobes. By milling your stock heads .070 you will obtain a compression of about 7.5. This should suffice for your requirements. As to an improved ignition, you may check with our advertisers for types and prices.

Laughs...from here and there

By TOM MEDLEY

A speed cop raised his hand. The woman motorist stopped with a jerk.

"As soon as I saw you, miss," the cop declared, "I said to myself, 'Forty-five, at least.'"

"Oh, no!" said the woman, "it's this hat that makes me look so old."

"My wife has just run away with a man in my car."

"Great Scott! Not your new car?"

Back in 1942 a warning picked up by a U.S. freighter in the Mediterranean indicated that Germans were using observation balloons to spot Allied ships and to direct U-boats to them. Late one afternoon the eager lieutenant in charge of the ship's Navy crew noted a faint, round speck in the sky and excitedly ordered General Quarters sounded. The crew was rushing to its guns when the ship's skipper approached the youngster.

"What's the target?" he asked.

The lieutenant passed his glasses and pointed to the speck. "We're going to shoot it down, sir."

The older officer looked, and then lowered the glasses.

"I wish you wouldn't do that, son," he said. "We've got to have something to navigate by—that's Venus."

The automobile has proven a great moral force. It has stopped a lot of horse stealing.

A station wagon is something a city person buys when he moves to the country so the country people will know he's from the city.

He could neither read nor write. When a distant relative died and left him a small fortune, he arranged with the bank to sign his checks with two crosses. One day he handed the cashier a check which was signed with three crosses.

"What's this?" asked the clerk. "You've got three crosses here."

"I know,' was the reply; "my wife's got social ambitions. She says I have to have a middle name."

A guard from the lunatic asylum rushed up to a farmer who was standing on the road. The guard said, "I'm looking for an escaped lunatic. Has he passed this way?"

The farmer puffed thoughtfully on his corncob pipe. Finally, he asked, "What does he look like?"

"He's short," said the guard, "and very thin, and weighs some 350 lbs."

"How can a man be short and thin and still weigh 350 pounds?"

"Don't be so surprised," replied the guard, angrily, "I told you he's crazy."

"Does she know much about cars?"

"No. She thinks you cool the motor by stripping the gears."

STROKER McGURK

Proof of hot rods in Florida is this photo of Tom Gosch's '32 roadster which runs a '37 engine. Clocked 107.63.

Barney Navarro, popular speed merchant of Glendale, California, makes an engine adjustment after clocking his blower job at El Mirage.

After breaking the track record at Corpus Christi Speedway, Texas, Harry Elbel relaxes in his roadster. The combination has set numerous records in Texas

Excellent body workmanship is displayed on Bruce Brown's '36 Ford at San Mateo, California. The '41 Ford mill has a H&C cam. Clocked: 106.12 S.C.T.A.

CLUB NEWS

Acceleration Tests Held By The Albuquerqe Road Pilots

By J. ROBERT SETH

Recently the Albuquerque Road Pilots held their first acceleration tests. The tests were held on the mesa west of the city of Albuquerque where a paved stretch was acquired for the event. The course was semi-hazard, with two 90° turns, one to the left and the other to the right. Each test was run according to the following procedure:

1) Inspection of car.
2) Standing start.
3) Acceleration at the starter's signal, finishing the stretch at the highest possible speed.
4) Time averaged from start to finish. (Official time for each car taken from average of three runs.)

Most Road Pilot members completed their tests. Several stock cars were allowed to run for comparative data.

Official places were as follows:

First—Leo Pilon — Mercury engine; custom roadster.

Second—Vernon Leweke — Mercury engine; T roadster.

Third—Byron Ward—'38 Ford engine; '34 roadster.

Fourth—Bud Stagner—'32 Ford engine; '32 custom sedan.

Fifth—Elroy Vanderslice—'36 Ford engine; '35 custom coupe.

Sixth—J. Robert Seth—Ford 4 engine; '26 Dodge roadster pickup.

Seventh—Don Roof—'41 Ford engine; '34 Ford coupe.

The top seven places averaged official times from 43 mph to 49.76 mph.

Texas Roadster Racing Ass'n

By PAULINE BAYER

The T.R.R.A. has been adding a few cars in the last few weeks now that racing fans have really found out that the Association is here to stay. The crowds have increased at every meet and the Association boasts a record of only one serious spill: Wade Bedell flipping a car upside-down and receiving a skinned nose which healed without medical care. There is better than $1200 in the hospital fund at present.

The C.C. Speedway at Corpus Christi, Texas, is a new $30,000 racing plant which opened May 9 of this year for Sunday afternoon racing. With the Texas sun beating down so hard, the Promoters J. R. Lungstrum and C. F. Roscher, got together and added a few more dollars to the stadium and installed a lighting system for night racing in July. They also signed up the T.R.R.A. With ever-increasing popularity of roadster racing, the grandstands now are being enlarged for this Saturday night weekly of hot rod races.

Geo. Carroll set a new record for the C.C. Speedway of :19.05, only to have it broken by Harry Elbel, August 7, with :19.02.

Charles Ferrell and Roy McCall towed the McCall Special Ford V8 #300 to the Midwest Circuit for a week of racing July 16 to 25. They stopped by Carl Johnson's CeJay Stadium in Wichita, Kansas, leaving after racing there. They joined the Hurricane Association in Chicago to race at Soldiers' Field. Here they were joined by their hometown buddies, Harry Elbel and his flying V-8 #20 and B. C. Ryan in his V-8 #77. Racing at Indianapolis 16th Street Speedway, Ryan was very unfortunate, spinning in the south turn, he was hit by his close competitor and eliminated for the rest of the evening. Loading up the following morning they headed back to Texas with plenty of ideas, as all the cars are now coming on the tracks with lighter bodies and faster motors.

Freddie Elbel (8) crowds Charles Ferrell at Corpus Christi Speedway.

Wade Bedell in Cecil Littlefield's T-V8.

Congratulations to Andy Granatelli for such wonderful cooperation in the Hurricane Association; and the best of luck to our friend, Dick Frazier, for setting the new world's record.

(Continued on Page 30)

Race Results

LAKES
MOJAVE TIMING RESULTS
Aug. 8, 1948—Rosamond Dry Lake

Name	Time	Eng. Wnfld.	Club	Pts.	Class
J. Rogers	104.53	Winfield	Rumblers	0	A Rdstr.
I. Howman	102.04	Riley 2-Pt.	Bungholers	6	B Rdstr.
J. McAlister	93.75	V-8	4 Barrel	0	A Rdstr.
M. Melchert	93.65	V-8	Rumblers	0	A Rdstr.
S. Joseph	84.67	Cyclone	Rdusters.	0	A Rdstr.
Bud Hand	129.87	Riley 4 Pt.	Lobers	0	A Rdstr.
R. Grow	107.27	Winfield	4 Barrel	6	A Mdfd.
B. Bartlett	127.50	V-8	4 Barrel	0	A Mdfd.
J. Nelson	124.65	V-8	Rumblers	0	A Rdstr.
Lehmann-Schwartzrock	124.31	V-8	Bungholers	5	B Rdstr.
B. Kimball	121.29	V-8	Bungholers	4	B Rdstr.
Andrews-Goshay	118.42	V-8	Lobers	5	B Rdstr.
McCausland	117.65	V-8	Lobers	2	B Rdstr.
Shaw-Melchert	116.13	V-8	Bungholers	1	B Rdstr.
D. Bourke	115.53	V-8	Rddusters.	0	B Rdstr.
J. Turton	110.70	V-8	Bungholers	0	B Rdstr.
E. Chiodo	105.02	V-8	Rumblers	0	B Rdstr.
Rath-Moore	137.40	V-8	Rddusters.	0	B Rdstr.
			4 Barrel	6	B Mdfd.

RECORDS
Name	Time up	Time down	Ave.	Pts.
Bill Bartlett	125.00	119.21	122.11	6
Bill Bartlett	127.30	118.58	122.94	6

GUESTS
Name	Time	Eng.	Class
Bill Dunning	115.24		B Roadster
Al Hruska	92.88		A Roadster
Jim Rigsby	104.05	Riley 2 pt.	A Roadster

DEFINITION OF CLASSES
Class A; Displacement up to 230 cu. inches
Class B; Displacement from 230 to 290 cu. inches.
Class C; Displacement from 290 cu. inches and up.
D.O. and supercharged engines are in the next higher class than their cubic inch displacement.

S.C.T.A. RESULTS
July 17-18—El Mirage Dry Lake
CLASS "B" ROADSTERS

ENTRANT	CLUB	Speed	Points
Doug Hartelt, Lancers		135.33	300
Tom Beatty, Glendale Stokers		135.13	190
Alger & Starr, Lancers		132.74	180
Conkle & Palm, Lancers		131.19	170
Lloyd Kear, Mobilers		128.57	160
Jack Avakian, Road Runners		128.38	150
Bob Wenz, Low Flyers		128.22	140
Dan Bushy, Dolphins		127.65	130
Bill Spalding, Mobilers		127.65	130
Fred Oatman, Strokers		127.65	130
Don Olson, Lancers		125.87	120
Ernest Dewey, SoCalRdstrClub		125.52	110
Bill Braun, Gear Grinders		125.34	100
John Collins, San Diego Rdstr Club		125.17	90
Guptill & Howard, Lancers		125.00	80
Lehmann & Swartzrock, Albata		125.00	80
Coahran & Downey, SD Rdstr Club		125.00	80
Dave McCartney, Pasadena Rdstr Cl		124.82	70
Jim Rawding, Clutchers		124.82	70
Arthur Tremaine, Strokers		124.82	70
Dean Batchelor, Road Runners		124.48	60
Kukura & Palma, Gear Grinders		124.30	50
Harold Whilldin, SD RdstrClub		123.96	40
Carl Taylor, Gear Grinders		123.28	30
Paul Swanson, Glendale Strokers		122.95	20
Bob Drew, Low Flyers		122.78	10
Donald Baker, Road Runners		122.78	10

CLASS "C" ROADSTERS
Paul Schiefer, SoCalRdstrClub		148.02	200
Randy Shinn, Road Runners		142.18	190
Harold Daigh, Dolphins		140.84	*280
Bob Reemsnyder, Strokers		134.93	170
Coshow Brothers, Lancers		133.33	160
Frank Beagle, Strokers		130.05	150
Don McLean, SoCalRdstrClub		130.05	150
Ed Stewart, SanDiegoRdstrClub		128.93	140
Don Blair, Pasadena Rdstr Club		128.75	130
Brown-Carl-Pete, Road Runners		128.75	130
Chuck Daigh, Dolphins		128.02	120
Bob Sykes, Lancers		127.84	110
Dowell & Sullivan, Dolphins		127.29	100
Geo. Castera, Almega		126.58	90
Charles Scott, Hornets		126.40	80
Richard Sagran, Sidewinders		125.34	70
Ted White, SanDiegoRdstrClub		125.00	60
Marty Sullivan, Strokers		124.65	50
Leland McCormick, Gophers		124.65	50
Major Gilbert, Sidewinders		124.48	40
Harold Osborne, Strokers		124.65	40
Walt Noble, Sidewinders		123.96	30
Jim Nairn, Low Flyers		123.79	20
John Ryan, Gophers		123.79	20
Wally - O'Brien, Strokers		123.79	20
Harold Warnock, Lancers		123.62	10

*Includes 100 points for fastest avg. speed: 140.955

CLASS "A" ROADSTERS
Spurgin & Giovanine, Albata	123.79	300
Richard Fugle, Low Flyers	120.16	190
Ray Brown, Road Runners	117.64	180
Jack Ratledge, Road Runners	115.23	170
Don Parkinson, Low Flyers	100.44	160

CLASS "A" STREAMLINERS
Alex Xydias, Sidewinders	131.19	300
Stanford & Lynn, Gear Grinders	110.02	190

CLASS "B" STREAMLINERS
Stuart Hilborn, Low Flyers	150.50	300
Arnold Birner, Throttlers	141.06	190
Phil Remington, Low Flyers	136.77	180
Breene & Haller, Road Runners	136.57	170
Rath & Moore, Lancers	134.12	160

CLASS "C" STREAMLINERS
Burke & Francisco, Road Runners	148.02	200
Henrich & Bishop, Quarter Milers	131.96	190
Chuck Rotter, Dolphins	131.57	180

CLASS "D" ROADSTERS
Fred Woodward, Strokers	127.29	200

TRACK
CHR
GILMORE STADIUM—Aug. 2—1/4-mile, dirt. Fastest qualifying time: :15.12, set by Yam Oka.
Trophy Dash ((3 laps) — 1, Colby Scroggins; 2, Yam Oka. 47.52.
First Heat (8 laps) — 1, Grant Casper; 2, Chuck Burness; 3, Bob Lindsey. 2:07.60.
Second Heat (8 laps) — 1, Vern Slankard; 2, Grant Lambert; 3, Bob Chaplin. 2:10.31.
Third Heat (8 laps) — 1, Bud Gregory; 2, Mickey Davis; 3, Dan Tracey. 2:09.67.
Fourth Heat (8 laps) — 1, Dick McClung; 2, Dick Vineyard; 3, Colby Scroggins. 2:08.63.
Semi-Main (25 laps) — 1, Grant Casper; 2, Bud Van Maanen; 3, Chuck Burness. 7:43.23.
Main (25 laps) — 1, Dick McClung; 2, Yam Oka; 3, Vern Slankard. 6:43.50.
Lap Runoff ((10 laps) — 1, Grant Casper; 2, Chuck Burness; 3, Bud Van Maanen. 2:43.95.

CULVER CITY SPEEDWAY — August 6 — 1/4-mile, paved, banked. Fastest qualifying time, :13.43, set by George Seegar.
Trophy Dash (3 laps) — 1, —George Seegar; 2, Bud Van Maanan. :41.55.
2, Grant Lambert; 3, Ed Lockhart. 1:54.26.
First Heat (8 laps) — 1, Bruce McClaire; 2, Grant Lambert; 3, Ed Lockhart. 1:54.26.
Second Heat (8 laps) — 1, Mickey Davis; 2, Dan Tracey; 3, Chuck Burness. 1:52.20.
Third Heat (8 laps) — 1, Bud Gregory; 2, Dick Benninger; 3, Colby Scroggins. 1:53.62.
Fourth Heat (8 laps) — 1, Dick McClung; 2, Archie Tipton; 3, Dick Vineyard. 1:51.75.
Main (30 laps) — 1, Bud Van Maanan; 2, Archie Tipton; 3, Dick Vineyard. 7:08.71.

GILMORE STADIUM—August 9—1/4-mile, dirt. Fastest qualifying time, 15.30, set by Yam Oka.
Trophy Dash (3 laps) — 1, Yam Oka; 2, Dick Vineyard. 47.71.
First Heat (8 laps) — 1, Jimmy Graham; 2, Wayne Tipton; 3, Stan Kross. 2:11.76.
Second Heat (8 laps) — 1, Chuck Burness; 2, Grant Lambert; 3, Bob Chaplin. 2:09.85.
Third Heat (8 laps) — 1, George Seegar; 2, Mickey Davis; 3, Bud Gregory.
Fourth Heat (8 laps) — 1, Yam Oka; 2, Dick Benninger; 3, Colby Scroggins. 2:08.63.
Semi-Main (25 laps) — 1, Dick Vineyard; 2, Mickey Davis; 3, Bud Gregory.
Main (25 laps) — 1, Chuck Burness; 2, Dick McClung; 3, Archie Tipton. 6:45.22.
Lap Runoff (10 laps) — 1, Dick McClung; 2, Archie Tipton; 3, Dick Vineyard. 2:46.83.

GILMORE STADIUM — August 16 — 1/4-mile, dirt. Fastest qualifying time, :15.05, set by Yam Oka.
Trophy Dash (3 laps) — 1, Wayne Tipton; 2, Yam Oka. :47.87.
First Heat (8 laps)—1, George Seegar; 2, A.A. Knight; 3, Grant Casper. 2:12.28.
Second Heat (8 laps) — 1, Bob Lindsey; 2, Don Tripp; 3, Freddie Hayes. 2:11.70.
Third Heat (8 laps)—1, Dick McClung, 2, Mickey Davis; 3, Colby Scroggins. 2:09.27.
Fourth Heat (8 laps)—1, Yam Oka; 2, Jimmy Graham; 3, Wayne Tipton. 2:06.71.
Semi-Main (25 laps)—1, Dick McClung; 2, George Seegar; 3, Bud Gregory. 6:45.84.
Main (25 laps) —1, Chuck Burness; 2, Archie Tipton; 3, Wayne Tipton. 6:54.30.

GILMORE STADIUM—August 23—1/4-mile dirt. Fastest qualifying time :15.14, set by Wayne Tipton.
Trophy Dash (3 laps)—1, Archie Tipton; 2, Colby Scroggins. :47.12.
First Heat (8 laps)—1, Jack McGrath; 2, Bob Lindsey; 3, Chuck Burness. 2:10.58.
Second Heat (8 laps)—1, Grant Lambert; 2, Bud Gregory; 3, Wayne Tipton. 2:08.22.
Third Heat (8 laps)—1, Bob Lindsey; 2, Bud Gregory; 3, Joe DeHart. 2:09.50.
Fourth Heat (8 laps)—1, Dick McClung; 2, Colby Scroggins; 3, Archie Tipton. 2:04.03.
Semi-Main (15 laps)—1, Chuck Burness; 2, Jack McGrath; 3, George Seegar. 4:04.02.
Main (30 laps)—1, Dick McClung; 2, Colby Scroggins; 3, Wayne Tipton. 8:10.43.

still greater heat—a need for tremendous cooling powers to carry off these higher temperatures that water alone cannot do. True, 1940 cars have larger water jacket capacities—one, and even two powerful pumps—yet heat is still so great that modern high pressure oil systems must pump up to 6½ gallons of oil per minute, at from 30 to 45 lbs. pressure, for oil to do its cooling job right.

Q. *What do you mean by "sealing"?*

A. Clearances between pistons, rings and cylinder walls must be sealed by oil alone against wasteful blow-by that could result from the higher compression pressures of the modern engine. These pressures have increased some 200% in the past 25 years.

Q. *How does oil "clean" the motor?*

A. Because of ever increasing speed, heat and load duties, oil must flush away all dirt—and still combat oxidation and the formation of sludge.

Q. *Won't my oil and air filters do this for me?*

A. Oil filters seldom provide complete protection against wear from dirt, and can't catch the oxidized products of fuel and oil which may deposit on the pistons and working parts. Motorists often forget entirely that oil filters need regular attention, which varies in its frequency according to operating conditions.

Carburetor air cleaners, to cope with the dust that must enter the engine even under ordinary operating conditions, would have to be built larger than the motor itself to be 100% efficient. In one large city, Public Health Department records show an average dust fall of 2,580 lbs. per cubic mile per day—a high of 11,760 lbs.

The average car breathes in about 6,000 cubic feet of air per hour—and oil must overcome the abrasive powers of the dirt that gets into the motor in that time.

Then there is crankcase ventilation, too. Ordinarily, from 3 to 27 cubic ft. of air per minute is forced through engine crankcases to ventilate them—and most crankcase ventilators do not have real good air-cleaning equipment. HAVE YOUR OIL AND AIR FILTERS CHECKED AND SERVICED FREQUENTLY!

Q. *Well, how often should I change my oil?*

A. No one can say, to the mile, when you should change your oil without an expensive laboratory test for your particular car at a given time. However, we may say in a general way — that beyond 1,000 mile point there may be risk—a real risk to the expensive investment you have in your car—in increased wear, possible bear-

ing failures, or stuck rings.

Q. *But won't 1,000 mile oil changes cost me a lot of money?*

A. No matter at what mileage you may change your oil, today, sticking to the safe 1,000 mile oil change period will only cost you a few cents more per year. This is amazingly cheap insurance against the risk of expensive engine repairs that may result from not doing so.

Q. *Why do you recommend 1,000 miles as the safe oil change period?*

A. Because constant agitation of oil in the crankcase together with water condensation, unburnt fuel dilution, carbon particles, dirt—plus heat—combine to make oil less efficient. According to most lubrication engineers, safe oil conditions can be assured for about 1,000 miles of normal summer driving, the exact interval depends on when, where and how you drive your car. Beyond 1,000 miles each mile traveled may add to the burden of the oil—decrease the operating efficiency of your motor—invite serious damage to your engine—jeopardize the expensive investment your car represents—reduce its trade-in value.

FRONT DRIVE
(Continued from page 13)

is in the wheel adhesion, which is at its maximum in a car of this type. In other words, the horsepower is being put into the point where the differential between the sliding of the wheels and the track is the least. Therefore, less engine horsepower output is required to obtain the same power of a conventional drive.

Driving a front drive hot rod is quite different from a conventional drive, the Sosic brothers assert, the most noticeable being these:

Unlike the conventional drive in which the rear wheels are shoving and therefore trying to join the front wheels, the front end is pulling. For this reason, the wheels should always be headed in the general direction of travel.

It is important not to spin under full power, for under this condition, control over the car is lost. Additional power is the only thing that will then pull the car out of a spin.

If the car is in a slight slide, and the wheels begin to slip slightly, backing off on the throttle will cause the wheels to spin slower. Traction is regained in this manner and additional throttle will then pull the car ahead.

With front drive, it is also possible to pass another car in a turn without moving the steering wheel. Sudden full throttle will cause the front wheels to spin, resulting in the rear end sliding. As the car moves to the side, easing up on the throttle will cause the wheels to spin slower and traction is regained, making possible the application of additional throttle.

Although the Sosic brothers do not believe that their front drive hot rod will set a pattern as far as front drives are concerned, they do think that more hot rods will begin to feature independent wheel suspension. But even if the car does not set a pattern, it is a certainty that other hot rod owners and drivers will be hearing and seeing more of the Sosic brothers and their radical new venture.

Classified Advertisements

CLUB NEWS
(Continued)

MUTUAL RACING NEWS

(INDIANA)

By MEL DUDLEY

We understand that Jim Rathman,
Ed Ball, and Pat Flaherty will be with
us for some time. They are welcome,
as they have good cars and are hard,
clean drivers. Flaherty has done the best
here, but Ball seems to have captured
the fancy of the fans.

Funny thing about Flaherty. In a
recent race here, he placed second to
Dick Frazier. He didn't ask or seem
to care how much money he had won.
All he wanted to know was how much more
Frazier had made than he did.

Mutual's racing schedule is relatively
slow now. MRA races at Sun Valley
Speedway Friday nights; Dayton, Ohio,
Saturday nights and at Mount Lawn
on Sunday nights.

Hurricane of Chicago is also running
a three-way schedule: Monday nights
at Milwaukee, Wednesdays at Soldiers'

Field and Thursdays at Indianapolis.

On September 19 there will be an
open roadster race at Winchester, Indiana. The race will have a 25-lap
feature event. At the same track, on
October 24, there will be a 100-lap
championship event. There have been
no other 100-lap dates set here.

Before we can realize all of the
drawing power of auto racing, we will
have to have better tracks. Race cars,
fast as they are today, cannot run on
the rough tracks of the past.

TIMING SCHEDULE FOR EL MIRAGE DRY LAKE

R.T.A.	S.C.T.A.
Sept. 12	Sept. 25-26
Oct. 10	Oct. 23-24
Nov. 7	Nov. 20-21

RUSSETTA TIMING RESULTS
(Continued)

"A" ROADSTERS

1	Jim Daleo	121.62	Vultures
2	Holbert Jackson	120.96	Velociteers
3	H. Hukurkin	119.36	Vultures
3	R. Mays	119.36	Gophers
5	H. Petersen	118.42	Drifters
6	R. Paite	117.80	Gophers
7	D. Piersall	115.83	Screechers
8	B. Robinson	114.06	Gophers
9	C. DeWitt	113.35	Drifters
10	F. Norton	112.07	Velociteers

"B" ROADSTERS

1	Jim Daleo	121.95	Vultures
2	H. Haller	121.62	Drifters
3	P. Prinsel	113.20	Lopers
4	D. Jones	111.95	Blo Bys
5	F. Williams	107.14	Rhodents
6	J. Brendell	104.89	Screechers
7	Larsen	94.53	Screwdrivers

"C" ROADSTERS

RECORD: A. Miller (Drifters)—123.11 Avg.

1	A. Miller	126.58	Drifters
2	Ken Smith	111.94	Coupes
3	Joe Warner	104.65	Blo Bys
4	Tom Cobbs	101.35	Rotors

Channelled...A Pair

These twin '39 Ford coupes were built by Arthur Lellis and Jerry Moffatt.

Art's car, painted metallic green, is completed except for planned engine modifications. The engine is a '41 Mercury 3/8 stroker.

The topless coupe, Jerry's, has a 1/8 stroke '42 Mercury engine. Body is painted a metallic gold.

The builders, who have their own body shop, constructed the cars in their spare time at a cost of over 2,000 dollars each.

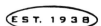

TOP—Rear of Art's car is smooth down to DeSoto bumpers.

ABOVE—Art Lellis and Jerry Moffatt standing beside their cars.

LEFT—Low lines of Jerry's car are clearly illustrated.

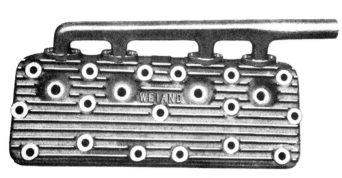

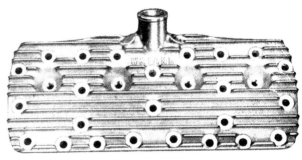

HOT ROD
Magazine

Bob McGee on the S.C. Campus OCTOBER, 1948 **25c**

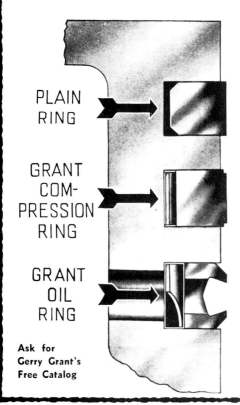

It's in the Bag . . .

TWIN COUPES

Dear Sir:

I am writing to you in reference to an article which appeared in the August issue . . . Bob Pierson's 1936 Ford coupe, which was featured as the Hot Rod of the Month. . . .

I would like very much to contact Mr. Pierson, and thought you might help me by forwarding his address if you have it on hand.

My interest in Bob Pierson's Ford lies in the fact that I built one that greatly resembles it. . .

GENE SCHLIESKE
Philadelphia, Penn.

Bob Pierson's car (above) and Gene's (below).

Bob Pierson's address is: 537 W. Olive Inglewood, California.—ED.

RODS GET A GOOD NAME

Gentlemen:

. . . In my estimate your magazine has done much to give hot rod racing a better name . . . You have . . . shown that, by proper leadership, in the form of hot rod associations, this sport can and has been made a safe . . . and constructive enterprise. . . . May the green flag be flown on your course at all times.

PERRY COHEN
Chicago, Illinois

Thanks to Reader Cohen and many many others for their praises. We believe that hot rod timing and racing are worthwhile and constructive activities. Some publications have suggested that the worthiness of such activities no longer contributed to the progress of the automobile and its component parts. In sharp contrast to this is the evidence of PAID subscriptions to HRM, ordered by some of the nation's biggest automotive manufacturers. Obviously,

these people think the amateur and semi-professional auto building group is one not to be overlooked when styling their future models. So, who's to judge the hot rods. . . the progress-minded or headline-happy? We think the final word will be accepted from the progressive group.—ED.

SOUTH AMERICA READS HRM

Hot Rod Magazine:

. . . I remember seeing your magazine in Brazil . . . The magazine was read by most of my friends who are interested in hot rods and probably they are going to write to you.

We already have some hot rods (in Brazil).

RENATO PAULO ROMERO
San Paulo, Brazil

NEW EAST COAST CLUB

Dear Sirs:

. . . Nothing better could happen to hot rods than to have this magazine published. It will clean up a lot of false impressions given the boys and their rods by certain news reporters. . .

I am trying to get a club started here in Jersey. I think the winter will see it actually started. Hope to bring the rods to as much popularity here as in California.

The Rodneys (Albuquerque Road Pilots, HRM, August, 1948) have built up a good name for themselves, and I had in mind doing the same here. . .

RALPH SCHANTZ
Eatontown, New Jersey

Editor's Column

Bob McGee and his beautiful roadster appear in the HOT ROD OF THE MONTH feature in this issue. With increased interest in "pleasure" jobs, it is befitting that Bob's roadster should take the spotlight in HRM. His car, rigged with every safety feature, has plenty of "eye-appeal." The story, photos and cutaway diagram are on pages 6 & 7.

In mentioning the cutaway diagram, we'd like to welcome Artist Rex Burnette to our staff. Rex has done a fine job on this month's Hot Rod of the Month.

John Vinther gives readers a complete accounting of the PACIFIC COAST INVITATIONAL CHAMPIONSHIP RACES held recently at Stockton, California. The story begins on pages 8 & 9, with accompanying pictures. This race attracted drivers and cars from five different California roadster racing associations. Qualifying races had as many as twenty cars in a single line-up.

When the Southern California Timing Association recently entered the National Safety Council en masse, HRM's reporter was on hand to get the story and pictures shown on page 10.

Theory and operation of a magneto are explained in A. L. Brownlee's illustrated story on page 11 of this issue.

A new personalty feature by Tom Medley appears on page 18. This month's featured driver is the CHR's Yam Oka, popular Japanese-American.

Ted Tanner deserves credit for the excellent photos he supplied for the September feature, FRONT DRIVE ROADSTER. His photographic efforts can be associated with all CRA events.

Next month's featured car will be a track roadster, one familiar to racing fans. The car, unusual in every respect, stands at the head of its association.

Other November features will include action and notes from Mutual Racing Association, more photos of the Texas rods (recently converted to "strictly" track jobs), news and pictures of the northwest's Oregon Roadster Racing Assocation as well as many other stories and photos.

You can't help but notice that our chest is way out to here this month. The reason? Well, it so happens that there are over 40,000 copies of this issue of HRM in circulation, a new record for us. That's an increase of eight hundred per cent since our first issue, some ten months ago.

Thanks to our readers for the hundreds of letters. We appreciate them.—ED.

HOT ROD Magazine

"World's Most Complete Hot Rod Coverage"

TABLE OF CONTENTS

HOT ROD MAGAZINE, U.S. Copyright 1948 by the Hot Rod Publishing Company, 7164 Melrose Avenue, Los Angeles 46, California. Second Class Mailing Permit Pending. SUBSCRIPTION PRICE: $3.00 per year throughout the world. Circulation: 40,000 monthly. On sale on newsstands, tracks and speed shops across the country. Phone: WEbster 3-4433.

Vol. 1	HRM—Published Monthly	No. 10

Associate Editors	R. E. Petersen, Robert R. Lindsay
Technical Advisors	Wally Parks, W. I. "Bill" Gieseke
Art Director	Alice Van Norman
Diagramatic Art	Rex Burnette
Photography	Paul Schaeffer, Vic Drake, Rick, Pete
Cartoons and Humor	Tom Medley
Reporters	Dick Robinson, Richard K. Martin, Pauline Bayer, J. Robert Seth, Melvin Dudley
Subscription Department	Marilyn Lord
Distribution	Gordon Behn

ON THE COVER: Bob McGee cruises along a campus street at University of Southern California. His sleek red roadster is an excellent example of hot rod craftsmanship. Bob is a student at S. C., where he is an active member of the college's famed football squad.

HOT ROD O

WITH THE GROWING DEMAND FOR SMART STREET ROADSTERS, BOB McGEE'S CAR SHOULD SERVE AS A MODEL TO HOT ROD BUILDERS

Bob McGee of Huntington Park, California, drives a roadster which is undoubtedly one of the most beautiful examples of hot rod efforts to be seen.

The bright red car shows the maximum body and upholstery work, result of much planning and many days labor.

Bob, a student at the University of Southern California, was born in California, which qualifies him as one of those rarities of the western state . . . a native son.

He began work on his first hot rod, also a roadster, back in 1940. When he completed that car, he joined the Gear Grinders, one of the associated clubs of the S.C.T.A. It was in 1941 that Bob made his initial dry lake runs, setting some admirable roadster times.

Later McGee entered the U.S. Army, serving three years during the recent war. He wound up his military term as an M.P. in the Philippine Islands. Bob began work on his present roadster in May of 1947, had it on the road in August of the same year.

At present he is busying himself by building up a new engine for his car. When this mill is in, Bob hopes to turn in some good times at S.C.T.A. dry lake meets.

Bob McGee wants everyone to know that he doesn't expect his roadster to become a top record holder, as it is designed primarily as a pleasure car.

Model roadster that it is, Bob's car was chosen to represent the S.C.T.A. when the group recently joined the National Safety Council in Los Angeles. Readers should take a good look at the cover picture on this issue as it is rumored to be one of the few photos ever taken of the modest roadster owner, Bob McGee.

Above—Dropped axle brings the front end close to the ground.

Below—Inside door hinges give a cleaner external view.

Bottom (center)—Note absence of water pumps due to Thermo Flow cooling.

Bottom (right)—Inside features padded leather upholstery and dash molded into steering wheel.

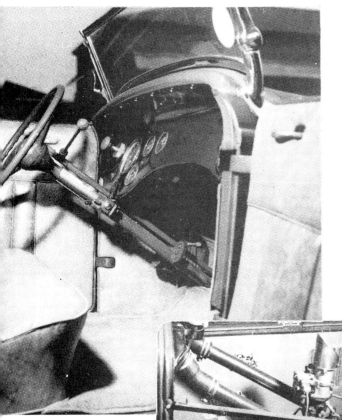

Photos by Pete

Construction Cutaway

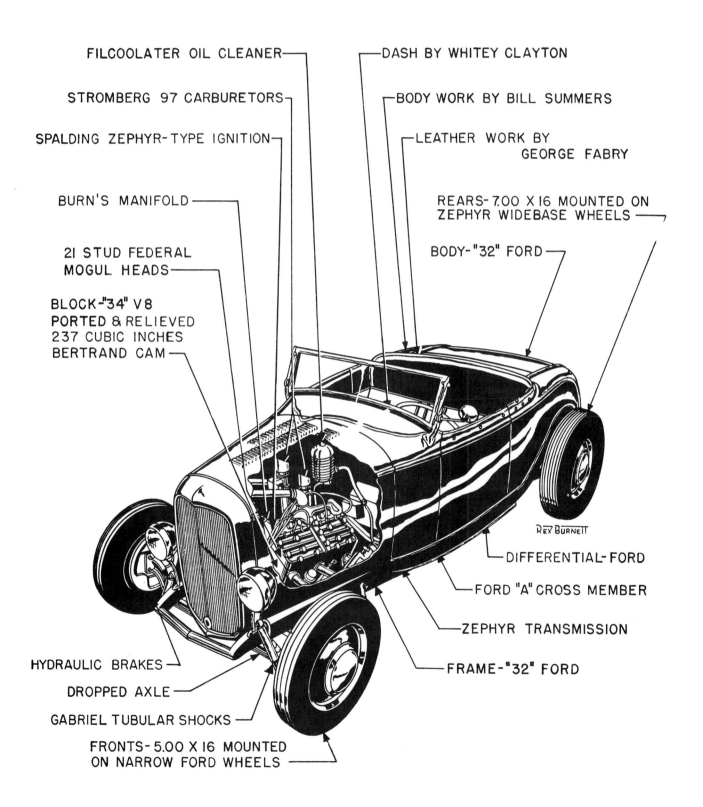

FILCOOLATER OIL CLEANER

STROMBERG 97 CARBURETORS

SPALDING ZEPHYR-TYPE IGNITION

BURN'S MANIFOLD

21 STUD FEDERAL
MOGUL HEADS

BLOCK-"34" V8
PORTED & RELIEVED
237 CUBIC INCHES
BERTRAND CAM

DASH BY WHITEY CLAYTON

BODY WORK BY BILL SUMMERS

LEATHER WORK BY
GEORGE FABRY

REARS-7.00 X 16 MOUNTED ON
ZEPHYR WIDEBASE WHEELS

BODY-"32" FORD

REX BURNETT

DIFFERENTIAL-FORD

FORD "A" CROSS MEMBER

ZEPHYR TRANSMISSION

FRAME-"32" FORD

HYDRAULIC BRAKES

DROPPED AXLE

GABRIEL TUBULAR SHOCKS

FRONTS-5.00 X 16 MOUNTED
ON NARROW FORD WHEELS

A large field of 18 top California hot rod drivers line up for the second 50-lap event.

Photo by Pete

Pacific Coast Hot Rod

West Coast Rods Gather for Big Race at Stockton, California

After many weeks of preparations the date was finally set for the big race of the 1948 season . . . with the hot bed of Roadster racing, Stockton's "99" Stadium, being picked as the site of the Labor Day Championships. Cars and drivers representing five different Roadster Associations in California were on hand for the afternoon's events. Point standing leaders from four of these organizations were around to place their combined reputations on the block while fans from all over the state witnessed the largest qualifying field ever to assemble for one racing meet.

The championship race was held under the sanction of the Northern California Roadster Racing Ass'n with their very capable business manager, Nils Liljedahl, directing the huge program. The five Roadster Associations were California Hot Rods Inc. headed by their point standing leader, Dick Vineyard of Los Angeles, driving Ed Walker's chain-driven G.M.C. sponsored by Blue Crown Spark Plugs of Indianapolis fame . . . the California Roadster Ass'n, represented by Ken Stansberry and Walt James. Stansberry of Hollywood drove the Green Brothers entry, the same car that finished third in the Roadster "500" at Carrell Speedway in Gardena, California, earlier this season. The Central California Roadster Ass'n was headed by Paul Kamm of Hollister, their point standing leader, driving his own

Mobile Service Special. The Racing Roadsters, Inc, were led by top point men Johnny Key of Salinas and Don Kilb of Castro Valley, while the Northern Californio Ass'n point standing leader from Berkeley, "Jumpin' Joe" Valente, was there with "Cash" Slayton's Mercury-powered job from Manteca. Responsibility of coordinating such a huge field of cars from all over the state of California was handled very smoothly as the packed stands at "99" Stadium watched one of the fastest moving programs of the '48 season.

The time trails began at 10 A.M. and the sixty car field was topped by Bill Steves of Stockton, who drove #100 to a new one lap record on the ten-foot banked asphalt oval. Steves' time of :16.13 gave him the fastest mark and placed him at the rear of the four-car field in the trophy dash. Steves was matched with Gene Tessien of Oakland in the Hubbard entry #4, with Wayne "Bromo" Selser of Sacramento in the Capitol City entry #130,

Photo by Pete

Above—Joe Valente (57), N.C.R.R.A.'s high-point man, overtakes Carl West (66) on a turn.

Right—Bob Machin (9) sets the pace for the start of the 10-lap feature race.

Photo by Rick

vitational hampionship

By JOHN VINTHER

and Ed Hungington in Johnny Dickman's #6 from Manteca. Selser moved into the lead on the first turn and held the top spot for two laps until Huntington jumped into the lead in car #6. The Northern California Ass'n driver went ahead to win the Dash in the new record time of 1:22.35 with Tessien second, Steves third and Selser fourth. The "proper" Trophy presentation was made by Miss Barbara Rain of Stockton. Huntington's record time for the five lap distance broke the mark which was set during the Fourth of July races at "99" Stadium by Lemoine Frey of Lodi, California.

The ten lap Consolation race, open to the drivers failing to make the time requirements for the main events, was won by Joe James of the C.R.A. in a new car fielded by Gino Rosso of L. A. Second place honors went to Wade Halstead of the N.C.R.R.A., third to Johnny Key of the R.R.I. and fourth to Don Kilb, also of the Racing Roadsters Inc. The time by

James was a very fast 2:58.50 . . . and paved the way for the two 50 lap main events to come. Each of the 50 lap features found a field of eighteen starters competing for the top three positions which would place them in the ten lap Championship Race to climax the Labor Day program at "99" Stadium.

The first of the two 50 lap events was won by Lemoine Frey of Lodi in a Los Angeles car owned by Phil Weiand. Frey, holder of two track records at Stockton, went into the lead on the tenth lap and held off some stiff competition afforded by a fellow N.C.R.-R.A. driver, Sam Hawks of Stockton.

Hawks was driving a Chrysler

6, owned by "Herk" Viglienazone, and was riding in the lead for the first ten laps when he lost the cap off his right rear tire and was forced to the pits for change. Returning to the race a few moments later, Hawks fought the terrific handicap of being down three laps and had to be content with eighth position. Meanwhile Walt James in Nick Valenta's car was challenging for third place on the 47th lap when he too was forced to leave the race because of engine trouble. Following the Lodi Speedster across the finish line was George Pacheco, N.C.R.R.A.'s defending Champion from Oakland in the Errecalde-Dal

(Continued on Page 19)

Photo by Pete

Photo by Pete

Above—Winner of 2nd 50-lap event Bob Machin. His time of 14:25.10 was 9 seconds faster than other 50-lapper.

Left—It's 8 barrels against 4 as Ed Elisian (56) goes into south turn with Bill Steves (100) close at his heels.

S.C.T.A. members raise their hands while taking the National Safety Council oath. They were sworn into membership by Municipal Judge Roger Pfaff (on speakers' stand, far right).

S.C.T.A. Joins National Safety Council

On September 19 members of the Southern California Timing Association met at the Lincoln-Mercury Plant in Maywood, California. This meeting was held as a formal acceptance of the S.C.T.A. into membership in the National Safety Council.

The occasion marked the first time any such large group has joined the Council en masse. S.C.T.A. members, representing some thirty-seven clubs,

pledged to assist the Council in a drive to reduce accidents on the highways as well as in the home. The oath of the Safety Council was administered to the hot rod group by Municipal Judge Roger Pfaff. "The program of education in safety carried out by the National Safety Council is not only to prevent injuries and deaths but also to keep people out of the courts by educating them in respect to traffic," he said.

Others who spoke to the S.C.T.A. membership were Police Captain R. E. Murdock, State Highway Patrol Captain Otto Bauer and James Bishop of the Safety Council, as well as officials of the timing group.

As the police officials stated at the meeting, S.C.T.A. is noted for their low traffic violation record. The by-laws of the association are such that members convicted of traffic violations are suspended from association activities and, upon repeated offenses, dismissed from membership in the group.

BELOW—Judge Pfaff tells S.C.T.A. members of their responsibility in joining the Safety Council. On Judge Pfaff's left are S.C.T.A. officials George Prussell, Safety Director; Thatcher Darwin, Recording Sec. Business Manager Wally Parks and Leonard Mikules of Lincoln-Mercury Public Relations Department.

Photos By Pete

ABOVE—Akton Miller, S.C.T.A. President (standing in car) places the first sticker on Bob McGee's roadster. Officials participating in the program were (left to right) State Highway Patrol Captain Otto Bauer, Police Captain R. E. Murdock, Safety Council Representative James Bishop, Miller and Municipal Judge Roger Pfaff.

MAGNETOS

by
A. L. Brownlee

In accord with HRM's technical stories, we print this article concerning magneto principles and useage. In a future article we will review the special ignitions which are also in popular use with hot rod builders.—ED.

Much has been said about the relative merits of magneto ignition and battery ignition. It is usually agreed that battery ignition must be satisfactory for general automotive use, else it would not be standard equipment on millions of automobiles. Many racing drivers feel that magneto ignition is best if top performance is to be expected from the high speed, high compression engines employed in racing cars today. Some of them possibly may not realize the reasons for this; and it might be of great help, therefore, to discuss just what is happening under the conditions imposed upon an ignition system at high speeds.

How is a spark generated by a conventional battery ignition system? It is created by passing battery current through the primary winding of the coil and thereby building up magnetism in an iron core inside it. When the magnetism suddenly dies down as a result of opening the points and shutting off the battery current that created it, a high voltage is generated in the many thousands of turns of fine wire in the secondary winding. This voltage is high enough to produce a spark at the plug. A weakness of battery ignition that makes it inadequate for high speed engines is the fact that it takes *time* to build up the magnetic field with current from the battery. When the breaker points close, the battery circuit is completed through the primary winding but the current does not build up to its normal at once. Actually, it takes an appreciable length of time, even though it is only a fraction of a second, for the current to flow sufficently to create the necessary magnetism in the coil core. Now when it is considered that at 3000 r.p.m. of a six-cylinder engine a set of breaker points must close and open 150 times a second, it can be understood that not much time is available for current to build up. On most automobile engines peak ignition current starts to fall off at 3000 r.p.m.; and in many cases, at 4000 r.p.m. only one-half the desired value of current is reached at the time points must be opened and spark obtained.

Of course, several things can be done to improve performance of a battery system at high speed, such as increasing the battery voltage, increasing the relative length of time the points are on, decreasing the spark gap, etc.

In direct contrast to the above, a magneto operates best at high speeds. This is because a magneto does not depend on a battery to build up magnetism in the coil core but does it directly with a rotating, permanent magnet which builds up and reverses magnetism as fast as the magneto shaft can be driven. It is true that a primary winding in a magneto coil is necessary, but only to give accurate timing and to improve the low speed performance. The current that flows in this primary through the breaker points is the result, not the cause, of magnetism changing in the coil.

A magneto consists basically of a magnetic circuit and two electrical circuits, together with the mechanical structure necessary to maintain them in their proper relation to one another. These requirements are shown in their simplest form in Figure 1. This funda-

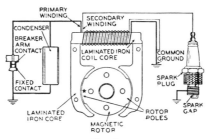

PRIMARY WINDING
SECONDARY WINDING
CONDENSER
BREAKER ARM CONTACT
LAMINATED IRON COIL CORE
COMMON GROUND
FIXED CONTACT
SPARK PLUG
LAMINATED IRON CORE
MAGNETIC ROTOR
ROTOR POLES
SPARK GAP

Fig. 1

mental magneto consists of:

1. A source of flux . . . the magnets which are contained in the rotor.
2. A set of laminated iron cores to carry the magnetic flux around.
3. A primary coil which is in series with . . .
4. A set of breaker contacts shunted by . . .
5. A condenser.
6. A secondary coil containing many turns of fine wire wound around the primary, and in series with . . .
7. The spark plug.

The position of the rotor at the beginning of the spark producing cycle is shown in Figure 2. The rotor poles are

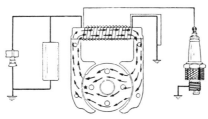

Fig. 2

fully covered by the core laminations, creating a strong magnetic flux through the coil core. Since the rotor is stationary, however, there is no change of flux and, consequently, there is no current flowing in the primary.

Turning the rotor diminishes the area of the rotor poles covered by the core, resulting in a constantly decreasing strength of the magnetic field. This change in flux throughout the iron core causes electrical energy to flow in the closed primary circuit, as shown in Figure 3.

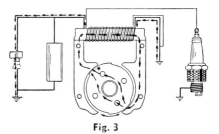

Fig. 3

Throughout the interval prior to the opening of the contacts, the changing of the flux value is held back or choked by the current in the primary circuit. When the contacts open, the choke effect of the coil is removed and there is an extremely rapid change in flux.

At the interval shown in Figure 4,

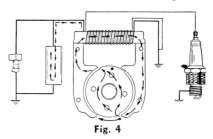

Fig. 4

the primary current has reached its highest value and the primary circuit is opened by the mechanical action of a cam (not shown in these diagrams) against the breaker arm. When this occurs, the resistance of the primary circuit increases rapidly until it is infinite. As the resistance increases and the current drops to zero, the voltage momentarily rises very rapidly. This increase in voltage and the breaking of the current, tend to make an arc at the contacts. To prevent this arcing, which is very detrimental to the contacts and which would continue the choke action on the flux, a condenser is connected across the contacts. The energy that would normally be discharged across the opening gap at the contacts rushes into the condenser.

When the contact opening is sufficiently large to insure an open circuit, the energy which surged into the condenser is discharged back through the primary coil to ground. This discharge back through the primary aids the rapid change and reversal of flux. This flux

(Continued on page 28)

MORE S.C.T.A.

Burke-Francisco Entry Reaches 153.32 m.p.h. at August 28-29 Meet

Three new Class records were shattered at the August meet of S.C.T.A., and a few near-misses were scored. First off was the new 'A' Class Roadster record made by Spurgin and Giovanine with their 'Hi-point' Chevy Four. This car, #15, has successfully established a new record in its class at every meet so far, this season. Their newest record average is 119.855 mph.

Ray Brown, running his #36 rear-engine Ford-60, in this same class, made an attempt on the record which resulted in an average of 119.760. Later, after a qualifying run at 124.30 mph, Ray made the two opposite-directional runs in an average of 122.080 mph, but this record was not held as official, due to technicalities.

In the 'C' Streamliner Class, the Burke-Francisco #4, rear-engine Mercury powered wing-tank, raised its own record of 144.855 to 149.400 mph, after qualifying at 150 mph flat. On the following day, Sunday, the same car turned a top speed of 153.32 mph, which is an all-time record for Dry Lakes time trials one-way runs. The car was driven by Wally Parks.

TOP TO BOTTOM—

Jim Badstubner in his modified T. The car features unique blisters on the hood.

This streamliner Chevy 6, built by Marvin Lee, made its first appearance at the lakes causing a great deal of comment amongst onlookers.

Driver Jay Andrews and his friends pull into Bill Albright's Lazy K Ranch for a cooling swim.

Studebaker Champion, owned by Jack McAfee, took 2nd place in A Streamliner class on its first trip to the lakes. Engine is Cannon equipped.
Photos by Pete

RECORDS FALL

By WALLY PARKS

Third car to better its own Class record was the So-Cal Speed Shop Special, #555, Ford-60 wing-tank, driven by owner Alex Xydias, who raised his average from 129.050 to 130.155 mph. This was a new record in the 'A' Streamliner Class (engines up to 183 cubic inches, unblown).

Harold Daigh, whose #325 '27-T Mercury Roadster made the day's top qualifying time in the 'C' Roadster Class, tried unsuccessfully to raise his Class record of 140.955 but slowed down on his return run, which resulted in a 138.331 average.

A fitting finale to the week-end's events was Stuart Hilborn's 150 mph Fuel-Injection Ford V-8 Streamliner which ran the quarter mile, from a standing start, in 14.60 sec. The car, driven by Howard Wilson, was traveling well over 123 mph when it crossed the finish of the quarter-mile distance.

With this interesting exhibition, made on a loose and dusty course, S.C.T.A. members are looking forward to the future presentation of some official short distance acceleration trials, plans for which are now in progress.

TOP TO BOTTOM—

Addition of a streamlined tail gives Phil Remington's sleek V-8 modified the "new look".

In the foreground Driver Frank Leonard watches the starting stand . . . and the girl recording times is well worth looking at.

Entrants line up at the registration tent to sign in with S.C.T.A. Official Thatcher Darwin for their positions on the starting line.

Guest entrant Stanley Wilson traveled all the way from Oregon to time his well-constructed pickup.
Photos by Pete

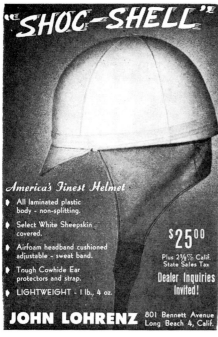

CLUB NEWS

Mutual Racing Ass'n
BY MEL DUDLEY

Ed Gimbel announced the sale of the #23 Ford Six to the Heuer Bros. of Muncie and he is returning to California soon. We were all very happy to hear that Ed Ball is planning to stay a while at least. This outfit is very popular both in the stands and pits. They have been in there trying every minute with a good car and driver and their quiet, efficient manner has won them a host of friends.

Jimmy Morrison announced the birth of his son, James Robert and Jim is the proudest father you ever saw. The boys chipped in and presented him with a baby carriage one night at Mt. Lawn. Dutch took Jim for a ride in it down the track and everyone had a good time.

The man of the hour is Bobby Beeson and the car is Tuck Mutersbaugh's #7-11 Chev. six. This car was new in '46 and always ran well up in front but Tuck put a new motor in it and we don't know as yet just what it will do. There is no doubt it is almost as fast as Frazier's #32 Merc. and Flaherty's #20.

Walt Straber is putting a new Merc. in his #39, replacing the Ford Six which he had run since '45. Walt was the first to use a Ford Six around here and started a trend which seems to have reached its peak. The sixes perform well but seem to fly apart after a few races and when they let go they usually wreck everything, block, cam and all.

The Bulldog Auto Club Of Southern California
By H. M. FOULDS

This Club is for and by drivers of cars, trucks or motorcycles who are interested in maintaining the Sport of Racing, Race Drivers and their Families, to the extent of starting and maintaining a permanent Benefit Fund for Race Drivers, their Wives and Children that will in a small way to help to offset hardship brought about by Accident, Disability or Death to any Racing Car Driver that occurs during the performance of his profession. This fund will be maintained by proceeds derived from Hot Rod Shows, Dances, Picnics, etc., and various other types of entertainment acceptable to the general public and from donations of persons interested in this particular sport.

This is strictly a non-profit organization. Limited membership, 200.

Oregon Roadster Racing Association
BY RICHARD MARTIN

Because of the floods, roadster racing up in the Northwest has been largely confined to Northern Washington, with the R.R.A.O. and the W.R.R.A. racing together at Seattle (¼ mile), Vancouver (80 ft. short of ¼ mile), and Yakima (1⅛ mile) and Centralia (½ mile, dirt).

Len Sutton of the O.R.R.A. holds the records on all of these tracks with the exception of the Yakima Speedway, which is held by Andy Wilson. Len holds the record at Seattle at :15.80, at Vancouver of :15.37, and at Centralia of :29.05. This last record at Centralia was established at the last race there, and was just barely made, as Don Moore in the Clevinger Special, #19, was only .01 of a second slower, and Don McPherson in the Brownie U Drive #1 car was only .01 second behind Moore, which made for a very nice dash.

Sutton not only holds his share of the records, but is also high point man by over 150 points. He has won almost every dash of the season, and has made close to a dozen clean sweeps. His #27 is owned by Rolla Vollstedt, who bought it last year and replaced its Lincoln Zephyr engine with a stroked and bored Mercury with Offy manifold, Meyers heads and a Smith cam. The car is built on an "A" frame, has a '27 "T" roadster body, '41 front and rear ends, and is equipped with a Stelling gear box.

It has a belly pan, a bright yellow paint job, and a novel oil cooling system. The pan on the engine has been enlarged a great deal, and tubes have been run through the pan for air to pass through to cool the oil while the car is running.

The Yakima track record of :45.31 was set by Andy Wilson in Don Waters' '21 "T" roadster. Wilson has gone back East now, and Max Humm, one of last year's high point men, has been driving the car. He has been fighting it out with Sutton quite regularly for firsts, and has taken the Seattle record away from Sutton several times. Waters' car is a 3/8 by 3/8 Mercury with Offy heads and manifold, Harman cam and Spalding ignition.

(Continued on Page 27)

COUPE CLOCKS 121.13 AT LAKES

RUSSETTA TIMING ASSOCIATION MEET OF SEPTEMBER 12, 1948

The September meet was held at El Mirage Dry Lake on a course chewed up by much useage this year. Many high speeds were turned although drivers complained of slippage in the soft spots.

Fastest A Class Roadster time of 127.84 was set by Jim Guptill of the Lancers. Doug Hartelt's B Class Roadster turned 137.19, 8 mph faster than the closest competitor. C Roadsters were headed by Frank Leonard with a time of 130.24.

Coupe competition has advanced well into the 120-mile-an-hour realm. Fran Hernandez of Offenhauser Engineering timed his fenderless '32 coupe at 121.13 mph, a new high. Close at his heels was Don Brown in his heavier '36 with a time of 120.24.

Running his sedan chassis with a chopped '34 coupe body, Don Toole raised his speed from 115 to 117.64 for the fastest B Coupe time. A Class top speed of 119.84 was made by Bob Pierson in his '36 Ford. Close behind was Bob Wittington of the Drifters with a time of 117.95.

The Hallman-Garrould entry topped the A Streamliner class with 128.93 mph. There was only one entry in the B Class Streamliners, Frank Williamson of the Prowlers who timed 105.26.

The next event for Russetta Timing Association is to be held on October 10, also at El Mirage. Association members expect to turn in some new records at the coming meet.

ABOVE—A "comfortable" 105.26 mph was clocked by Frank Williamson in his V-8 modified.

BELOW—Friends kibitz as Doug Harrison works on his 123 mile an hour roadster in the shade.

BOTTOM-RIGHT—Inside the Association truck Timer Raymond Ingram clocks the contestants.

BOTTOM-LEFT—A full bellie pan extends back from a '39 Buick grill on Paul Wheeler's '32 Coupe.

—Photos by Pete

ENGINE OPERATION AND TROUBLE SHOOTING

By
W. I. "BILL"
GIESEKE

Mr. Gieseke is a member of the Society of Automotive Engineers of the American Chemical Society, with seven years as Automotive and Lubrication Engineer for a major oil company.

In Operating the Average Car 10,000 Miles

1. Contact points open and close 90,000,000 times.
2. Each spark plug fires 15,000,000 times.
3. Coil delivers 90,000,000 charges of 15,000 volts.
4. Spark plug cables deliver a total of 1,350,000,000 volts.
5. Carburetor mixes 2,810,000 cu. ft. air with 825 gal. gas.
6. Distributor shaft and rotor revolve 15,000,000 times.
7. Fuel pump pulsates 15,000,000 times.
8. Speedometer cable revolves 10,000,000 times.
9. Each valve opens and closes 15,000,000 times.
10. The 1915 car was in its day good for about 40,000 miles. Its motor turned over at about 1,800 revolutions per minute at full speed. Repairs were frequent and expensive. Today's automobile has doubled that life expectancy—but its motor turns over a lot faster — 3,600 revolutions per minute is not too high for motor speed today.
11. Each piston travels up and down, over a 4″ distance inside the cylinder, 6,000 times each mile — or 3,700 miles during those 10,000 miles.
12. The crankshaft revolves 30,000,000 times.
13. Piston and bearing clearances have been reduced from about the thickness of heavy wrapping paper in 1915 to one-half the thickness of cigarette paper today.
14. Modern high pressure oil systems must pump about 6½ gallons of oil per minute throughout the engine, at from 30 to 45 lbs. pressure, for oil to do its *cooling* job right.
15. Compression ratios have gone from about four to one in 1915 to almost seven to one in 1940. This means more than 200% increase in compression pressures on the pistons, and therefore the crankshaft bearings, producing corresponding high pressures on the oil film protecting the bearing surfaces.

16. Oil is exposed to explosion temperatures that reach as high as 3,000 degrees F. at the firing point. With ever increasing speed, heat and load duties, oil must also clean—flush away all dirt, carbon, water condensation—and still stay tough . . . avoid sludge. There is an *average* of 2,580 lbs. of dust per cubic mile of air in one large city—a high of 11,760 lbs.! An engine normally breathes in about 6,000 cubic feet of air per hour . . . and oil must overcome the scratching powers of the dirt that gets into the motor in that time. Today these four jobs are vitally important because greater speeds, higher compressions, closer clearances, bearing shock loads of 3,000 lbs. per square inch, induce greater heat in cylinders, around rings, on bearings, in crankcases. All that heat promotes rapid formation of carbon and oxidation.
17. More than one gallon of water vapor is formed in the burning of every gallon of fuel. This water vapor must escape somewhere . . . and while most of it does escape through the exhaust, some of it is bound to enter the crankcase as piston blow-by, carrying soot and smoke from the combustion chamber down with it. There, the contact of the oil and this mist with air, heat and dirt induces the formation of sludge and "goo" . . . causing screen blockage, line clogging, faulty oil circulation and destructive wear.
18. Oil was changed in the old 1915 jalloppy every 500 miles and freshened with 3 to 4 quarts of make-up oil between times. Yet today, some people brag that they never change their oil.
19. Science today has made oil better than it ever was, and its performance is further perfected with the help of oil and air filters. But all the oil does not pass through the oil filters often enough to really clean the oil, and give complete protection against wear from dirt. And filters don't catch dissolved, oxidized products of fuel and oil which may deposit on the pistons and working parts. Most motorists forget that their oil filters need attention frequently—and as a result most filters don't work right half the time.

20. Carburetor air cleaners, to be 100% efficient, would have to be bigger than the motor itself, because the average car ordinarily breathes in about 100 cubic feet of air per minute! So lots of dust must get into the engine. Here again, motorists should be reminded to check and clean filters.
21. There is crankcase ventilation, too. Ordinarily, from 3 to 27 cubic feet of air per minute is forced through engine crankcases to ventilate them — and most crankcase ventilators don't have real good air-cleaning equipment.
22. According to most lubrication engineers, *safe* oil conditions can be assured for about 1,000 miles of regular summer driving.

Trouble-Shooting Guide—

The following is a list of reasons for (1) Hard Starting; (2) Slow Warm Up; (3) Poor Pick Up; (4) Loss of Power and Speed; (5) Poor Idling; and (6) Low Mileage.

1. Hard Starting
a. Low battery voltage
b. Excess starter drag
c. Low cranking speed
d. Stiff engine
e. Oil too heavy (Pour point too high)
f. Voltage to coil too low
g. Points burned or pitted
h. Condenser capacity off
i. Coil weak and wiring bad
j. Spark plug gaps too wide
k. Fuel (Distillation range)
l. Fuel (Vapor lock)
m. Fuel dirty
n. Choke not closing or releasing properly
o. Throttle open too wide
p. Air leaks in intake system
q. Mixture too lean
r. Mixture too rich
s. Valves and ring condition
t. Starter gear to fly wheel ratio incorrect for racing equipment, where compression ratio has been increased beyond stock car ratio.
u. Over extended battery to starter lead wire, ground wire too long, battery of too low ampere hour capacity, starter leads of too small gauge. All of the above would permit too much voltage drop.

2. Slow Warm Up
a. Insufficient heat on hot spot
b. Oil too heavy

c. Spark late (Sluggish governor action)
d. High engine friction
e. Valves and rings sticking
f. Plug gaps too wide
g. Water and oil temperatures too low
h. Mixture too lean
i. Grade of fuel (Does it measure up to standard?)

3. Poor Pick Up
a. Insufficient gas on acceleration
b. Insufficient heat on intake manifold
c. Mixture too lean
d. Mixture too rich
e. Spark plug gap too wide
f. Ignition system in bad order including points, condenser, coil, wiring, timing
g. Compression low from some mechanical fault; valves adjusted too close

4. Loss of Power and Speed
a. Engine in poor mechanical condition. Low compression and/or high friction
b. Clutch slippage
c. Dragging brakes
d. Fuel supply limited
e. Mixture too rich or lean
f. Wrong gear ratio and/or tire size
g. Improper or insufficient lubrication
h. Rolling resistance high due to misalignment or unduly high running gear resistance. Tires under-inflated
i. Vapor lock
j. Varnish on pistons and walls
k. Over heated air and fuel
l. Air cleaner restricted
m. Throttle fly not opening wide
n. Manifold restriction
o. Too high compression ratio or too low compression ratio
p. Not enough carburetor venturi area. Double carburetors do not always give adequate air volume for high speed. Always use Ford '48 carburetors instead of '97 carburetors, as the former is $\frac{1}{16}$" larger in size
q. Valve area and seating angle should be changed when bore and stroke are increased, or speed is increased. Use 30 degree seating angle
r. Insufficient valve port area. Insufficient block relief or cylinder head relief (surface volume ratio too great)
s. Cam grind too radical
t. Plugs too hot, causing pre-ignition
u. Carburetors not of the balanced type
v. Needle seat too small, should be about .115" diameter
w. Incorrect spark advance; distributor should have some manual advance

(Continued on Page 22)

PERSONALITIES By TOM MEDLEY

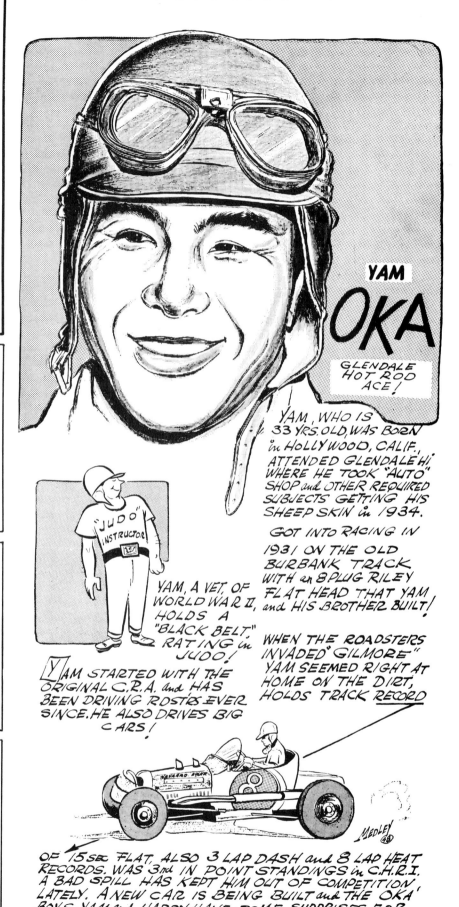

YAM OKA

GLENDALE HOT ROD ACE!

YAM, WHO IS 33 YRS. OLD, WAS BORN in HOLLYWOOD, CALIF., ATTENDED GLENDALE HI, WHERE HE TOOK "AUTO" SHOP and OTHER REQUIRED SUBJECTS GETTING HIS SHEEP SKIN in 1934.

GOT INTO RACING IN 1931 ON THE OLD BURBANK TRACK WITH an 8 PLUG RILEY FLAT HEAD THAT YAM and HIS BROTHER BUILT!

WHEN THE ROADSTERS INVADED "GILMORE" YAM SEEMED RIGHT AT HOME ON THE DIRT, HOLDS TRACK RECORD

YAM, A VET. OF WORLD WAR II, HOLDS A "BLACK BELT" RATING in JUDO!

YAM STARTED WITH THE ORIGINAL C.R.A. and HAS BEEN DRIVING ROSTIES EVER SINCE. HE ALSO DRIVES BIG CARS!

OF 15sec FLAT. ALSO 3 LAP DASH and 8 LAP HEAT RECORDS. WAS 3rd IN POINT STANDINGS in C.H.R.I. A BAD SPILL HAS KEPT HIM OUT OF COMPETITION LATELY. A NEW CAR IS BEING BUILT and THE OKA BOYS, YAM and HARRY, HAVE SOME SURPRISES FOR THEIR COMING OUT PARTY!

P. C. CHAMPIONSHIPS

(Continued from page 9)

Porto entry from Stockton. Third position was taken by Rex McCapes of Petaluma in his own #99. Bob Veith of Modesto placed fourth. Lloyd Selacci, another Petaluma driver from the N.C. R.R.A., placed fifth. The time for the 50 laps by Lemoine Frey was 14:33.90.

The second 50 lapper found another eighteen car field fighting it out for those three top positions. The green "Go" flag dropped and Bob Machin of Alameda went out in front in Al Dickman's #9 from Manteca. He set a very fast pace for the first 32 laps at which time the event was slowed down as the yellow caution flag went into effect. The Thomas Special from Lodi, driven by Butler Rugaard of the R.R.I. went into a spin directly in front of the main grandstand. Rugaard escaped uninjured. Ed Huntington, who was riding in second spot, failed to see the yellow flag and moved into the lead at this point.

At the forty lap mark, Huntington was still leading with Machin second, Bill Steves third, Joe Valente fourth and Dick Vineyard fifth. Steves left the race on the 48th lap with engine trouble leaving third spot wide open to Valente. Huntington was the first to take the checkered flag from starter Les Pine, followed by Bob Machin, Joe Valente, Dick Vineyard of the C.H.R. and Stan Dean of the R.R.I. The event was awarded to Machin's #9 as Huntington passed illegally under the yellow caution flag on the 32 lap. . . with the trophy dash winner taking the runner-up position. The time for the distance was 14:25.10 . . . almost a full nine seconds faster than the opening 50 lap feature. Next came the big race.

The green flag dropped and the big race of the afternoon was on!! Ten laps for the Pacific Coast Invitational Hot Rod Championship between the six top cars of the Labor Day program.

Rex McCapes went into the lead on the first turn and held that position for three laps while Huntington, Valente and Veith were moving into contention. Huntington took over the lead on the fourth lap as he passed McCapes on the outside with the Petaluma driver hanging on to second position. Huntington's #6 was out in front and going away . . . leading by a full six car lengths when the unexpected happened! The drive shaft broke. Huntington was out of the race with only a half lap left to go. Rex McCapes hit the final turn in the lead with Pacheco, Valente and Veith right on his heels. The traffic came out of the last turn and it was a dash to the finish line where the check-

ered flag . . . the prize money . . . the Trophies and the Pacific Coast Hot Rod Championship awaited.

Wheel to wheel down the straightaway came Rex McCapes and George Pacheco . . . fighting it out to the final yard with the checkered flag falling on car No. 99 . . . and Rex McCapes of Petaluma!

McCapes, one of the best liked Northern California Association's drivers, received the top honors of the afternoon's program. The trophy, donated for the occasion by Stockton's track manager Billy Hunefeld, was presented by Miss Mona Bradberry of Los Angeles . . . and a very fitting ceremony it was, as the photographs will attest.

It was a great day for McCapes . . . but one couldn't forget the thrilling moments turned in by the other drivers . . . like Sam Hawks and his battle to regain the lead in the first 50 lapper after leaving the race for that tire change . . . like Walt James and how he must have felt when his engine failed just as he was about to move into third place . . . like Bill Steves when he was riding in third spot and when he, too, developed engine trouble in the car that had previously set the new one-lap record. How Ed Huntington must have felt when he broke that driveshaft while he was so far out in front and all set to take the checkered flag in the Championship race. All these facts go into making Roadster racing the most popular and fast-rising Speed Sport in the Nation. The Labor Day program at Stockton's "99" Stadium did much to further Hot Rod racing in the Golden State.

TIMING SCHEDULE FOR EL MIRAGE DRY LAKE	
R.T.A.	S.C.T.A.
Oct. 10	Oct. 23-34
Nov. 7	Nov. 20-21

Parts With Appeal

◀◀◀

The Ford V-8 header really shines when displayed by pretty Lee Stacy. That's either because the header is chrome-plated or because Miss Stacy has taken an interest in it.

The header is an efficient means of removing exhaust gas without back pressure. It also aids in eliminating excess heat, as well as adding general beauty to the car.

Lee, a blue-eyed brownette, was born in New Jersey some 18 years ago. She began her dramatic education at the tender age of seven.

From dramatic school she graduated to little theatre work, receiving billing in both dramatic and dancing roles.

Miss Stacy has been doing modeling jobs since she was 15 years old. She stands 5 ft., 4½ in., loves to eat and to work in show business. Also among her interests she lists bicycling and snow sports. Her dislikes include hypocrites and bananas.

Recently she was chosen for a starring role in "Lend an Ear," a show that has won critics' acclaim as a smash hit. Following her Hollywood appearance with the popular show, Lee will trek to Broadway for the eastern opening, realizing a long-standing ambition to appear on the New York stage.

Photo by Pete

Photo by Bob Magill

Fourth in a series of Harman & Collins Record Holders

Karl Orr's K. O. Special driven by Bud Sennett has made an impressive record in big car competition using a HARMAN & COLLINS CAM.

Set new Record at Sacramento 1⅛ flat dirt July 4th, 1948—:42.10 (fastest qual.). Won trophy dash, fastest heat and 45-lap Main event.

Oakland Stadium ⅝ asphalt banked July 11th, 1948—broke 25-35 and set a new 40-lap track record—16:30.80.

Oakland Stadium Sept. 5th, 1948, New 1-lap track record—:23.52. Won trophy dash.

HARMAN & COLLINS, INC.

5552 ALHAMBRA AVENUE   LOS ANGELES 32, CALIF.

CApitol 4610

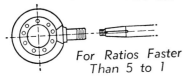
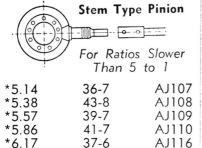
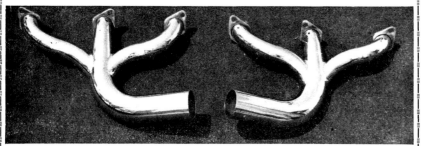
TROUBLE SHOOTING
(Continued from page 17)

    x. Fuel not designed for racing. Flame travel should be slightly in excess of piston speed at extreme top speed

5. Poor Idling (Assuming even and maximum compression)

a. Plugs spaced too close
b. Leak in valve guides
c. Leak in manifold or vacuum operated units
d. Spark too fast or slow
e. Ignition cutting out due to condenser, points, coil, spacing, shorted cap or rotor, and wiring
f. Valves or rings sticking
g. Valve spacing and timing
h. Carburetion and ignition not properly synchronized
i. Mixture too rich or lean

6. Low Mileage

a. Mixture too rich or lean
b. Float level too high
c. Fuel pump pressure too high
d. Fuel pump leaking externally
e. Fuel pump leaking into crankcase
f. Leak in gas tank and lines
g. Leak in carburetor while running as well as idling or standing
h. Manual or automatic choke not releasing properly
i. Air cleaner restricted by being dirty or too small
j. Insufficient heat on manifold at hot spot junction
k. Too much heat on manifold and carburetor system (watch for stuck hot spot valve)
l. Vapor lock in fuel system
m. Gas boiling in carburetor bowl
n. Ignition system in bad order
o. Spark set late
p. Improper governor advance
q. Muffler back pressure
r. Valves not seating or adjusted too close; valve timing off
s. Rings stuck and blowing by
t. Engine friction high due to improper clearance or varnish deposits; improper lubrication
u. Power step-up jet stuck open in cruising range or set to come in at too high vacuum
v. Chassis drag; including brakes
w. Wasteful driving habits
x. Wrong gear ratio
y. Head winds

Eddie Meyers, veteran speed merchant of Southern California, is recuperating from a recent traffic accident. The wreck occurred when another car smashed into the rear of Eddie's new Mercury as he was stopped at a signal. He received back and arm injuries, has been in and out of the hospital several times since the accident. Everyone hopes Eddie will soon be well again.

Laughs...from here and there   By TOM MEDLEY

"THAT'S THE GUEST ENTRY FROM CHICAGO."

STROKER McGURK

NCRRA'S 1947 president, Bob Machin, in his track job at Oakland Stadium. According to current rumors, Bob has $5500 in the car, a tidy sum.

To conform with laws in effect in some eastern states, James Flynn has designed fenders from '36 Ford spare tire covers for his A Ford pickup.

Don Frew of Salt Lake City got 26 miles per gallon in this coupe on a trip to west coast. Engine runs Edmunds heads, is bored and stroked.

Dry Lakes Results

"A" ROADSTERS

Place	Car	Entrant	Club	Speed	Points
1	15	Spurgin-Giovanine	Albata	119.68	300*
2	36	Ray Brown	Road Runner	119.20	190
3	157	Richard Fugle	Low Flyers	116.27	180
4	156	Don Parkinson	Low Flyers	113.78	170

"B" ROADSTERS

Place	Car	Entrant	Club	Speed	Points
1	1-R	Doug Hartelt	Lancers	131.57	200
2	6	Palm & Conkle	Lancers	131.19	190
3	106	Starr & Alger	Lancers	130.81	180
4	321	Dan Busby	Dolphins	129.68	170
4	363	Vogel Bros.	Pasadena Roadster	129.68	170
5	9	Tom Beatty	Strokers	129.49	160
6	117	Guptill & Howard	Lancers	128.75	140
7	101	Don Olson	Lancers	127.84	130
8	33	Lloyd Kear	Mobilers	12.84	130
9	38	Robert Wenz	Low Flyers	127.65	120
10	27	Harvey Haller	Road Runners	125.69	110
11	61	Jack Avakian	Road Runners	125.52	100
11	393	Blinn & McCartney	Pasadena Roadster	125.52	100
12	470	Fred Oatman	Strokers	123.96	90
13	227	Bailey & Bingham	Gear Grinders	123.45	80
13	299	Lehmann & Schwartzrock	Albata	123.45	80
14	307	Ernest Dewey	So. Cal. Rd. Club	122.44	70
15	275	Jerry Ashton	Mobilers	120.80	60
16	455	Arthur Tremaine	Strokers	120.48	50
17	220	Palma & Kukura	Gear Grinders	120.32	40
18	22	Bob Drew	Low Flyers	120.16	30
19	442	Jim Rawding	Clutchers	119.68	20
20	13	James Culbert	So. Cal Road. Club	119.52	10
20	50	Jay Andrews	Strokers	119.52	10
20	337	John Collins	San Diego Road Club	119.52	10
20	113	Beam & Noble	Lancers	119.52	10

"C" ROADSTERS

Place	Car	Entrant	Club	Speed	Points
1	325	Harold Daigh	Dolphins	141.73	200
2	315	Paul Schiefer	So. Cal. Rd. Club	139.75	190
3	104	Barber & Dolph	Lancers	132.93	180
3	259	Don Nicholson	Stokers	132.93	180
4	47	Frank Leonard	Gophers	131.19	170
5	200	Kenny Parks	Gaters	129.49	160
6	160	Jim Nairn	Low Flyers	128.93	150
7	46	Bob Sykes	Lancers	127.84	140
7	48	Bob Reemsnyder	Strokers	127.84	140
8	21	Ed Stewart	San Diego Rd. Club	127.29	130
9	527	Richard Sagran	Sidewinders	125.00	120
9	624	George Castera	Almega	125.00	120
10	59	Don Arnett	Clutchers	124.65	110
11	55	C. W. Scott	Hornets	124.48	100
11	135	Peterman & Carrillo	Road Runners	124.48	100
11	305	Don McLean	So. Cal. Rd. Club	124.48	100
12	69	John Ryan	Gophers	124.13	90
13	331	Doug Harrison	Dolphins	123.75	80
14	52	Frank Beagle	Strokers	123.11	70
14	164	Dave Glotch	Gophers	123.11	70
15	53	Coshow Bros.	Lancers	122.44	60
15	173	Don Lenk	Gophers	122.44	60
16	54	Wally O'Brien	Strokers	121.62	50
17	108	Bill Potts	Lancers	121.45	40
18	541	Tommy Tompkins	Sidewinders	121.13	30
19	324	Dowell & Slawson	Dolphins	120.80	20
20	115	Guy A. Hyde	Lancers	120.48	10

"D" ROADSTERS

Place	Car	Entrant	Club	Speed	Points
1	216	Stan Jones	Gear Grinders	132.54	200
2	34	Akton Miller	Road Runners	128.20	190
3	19	Burleigh Dolph	Lancers	124.65	180
4	463	Fred Woodward	Strokers	123.45	170
5	632	Albert Sterkin	Almega	120.00	160

"A" STREAMLINERS

Place	Car	Entrant	Club	Speed	Points
1	555	Alex Xydias	Sidewinders	129.31	300*
2	403	McAfee, Seely & Cannon Bros.	Throttlers	109.91	190
3	557	King & Hansen	Sidewinders	100.67	180

"B" STREAMLINERS

Place	Car	Entrant	Club	Speed	Points
1	11	Stuart Hilborn	Low Flyers	146.10	200
2	131	Breene & Haller	Road Runners	141.73	190
3	365	Marvin Lee	Pasadena Rd. Club	138.24	180
4	31	Arnold Birner	Throttlers	137.19	170
5	103	Path & Moore	Lancers	133.13	160
6	14	Phil Remington	Low Flyers	131.38	150
7	222	Jim Lindsley	Gear Grinders	121.29	140

"C" STREAMLINERS

Place	Car	Entrant	Club	Speed	Points
1	4	Burke & Francisco	Road Runners	153.32	300*
2	180	Hallman & Garrould	Gophers	128.93	190
3	319	Chuck Rotter	Dolphins	128.75	180

NOTE: Points marked with an * carry 100 points for new class record.

CLUB POINTS

Pl.	Club	Total Pts.		Pl.	Club	Total Pts.
1	Road Runners	5090		12	Gaters	930
2	Lancers	4530		13	Glendale Stokers	910
3	Low Flyers	3630		14	Pasadena Rd. Club	900
4	Strokers	2330		15	Mobilers	860
5	Dolphins	2320		16	Throttlers	550
6	Gear Grinders	1510		17	Clutchers	420
7	Albata	1480		18	Almega	400
8	Sidewinders	1460		19	Hornets	310
9	So. Calif. Rd. Club	1320		20	Quarter Milers	190
10	Gophers	1270		21	Road Masters	50
11	San Diego Rd. Club	1190				

NEW RECORDS, AUGUST 28, 29, 1948

Car	Class	Entrant	Club	No. 1 Run	No. 2 Run	Average
15	A-R	Spurgin-Giovanine	Albata	118.42	121.29	119.855
555	A-S	Alex Xydias	Sidewinders	128.93	131.38	130.155
4	C-S	Burke-Francisco	Road Runners	147.29	151.51	149.400

"A" ROADSTERS

Pts.	Name	Speed	Club
10	Jim Guptill	127.84	Lancers
9	Doug Harrison	123.79	Drifters
8	Norm Lean	121.45	Drifters
7	Bruce Robinsn	119.99	Lopers
6	James V. Daleo	118.26	Vultures
5	Holbert & Jackson	117.80	Velociters
4	Bob Wilcox	115.53	Nt. Hawks
3	Val Clenard	114.35	Lopers
2	Ed Perry	109.09	Screwdrivers
1	Meyer Rabin	106.45	Lopers

"B" ROADSTERS

Pts.	Name	Speed	Club
10	Doug Hartelt	137.19	Lancers
9	Milton Vogel	129.31	Coupes
8	Dean Moon	125.00	Hutters
7	Rod Starers	124.82	Lopers
6	Harvey Haller	123.45	Drifters
5	Joe Daleo	120.96	Vultures
4	Dick Jones	120.48	Blo Bys
3	Robert Maben	119.20	Blo Bys
2	Rulan McGregor	118.57	Stockholders
1	Phil Weiand	116.58	Lopers

"C" ROADSTERS

Pts.	Name	Speed	Club
10	Frank Leonard	130.24	Gophers
9	Akton Miller	127.24	Drifters
8	Don Olson	126.58	Lancers
7	Pat O'Brien	112.21	Gazzelles
6	Gerald Butler	110.15	Velociters
5	Jim Hurley	108.82	Velociters
4	Mike Daleo	102.85	Vultures
3	Ken Black	100.33	Vultures
2	Joe Warner	89.46	Blo Bys

"A" COUPES

Pts.	Name	Speed	Club
10	Robert Pierson	119.84	Coupes
9	Robert Whittington	117.95	Drifters
8	Robert Douns	109.89	Gophers
7	Dean Moon	109.75	Hutters
6	Dick Barlett	106.88	Prowlers
5	Ray Beck	106.50	Coupes
4	Barry Bollman	102.62	Gophers
3	Wally Randstrom	101.12	Coupes
2	Frank Breene	100.55	Drifters
1	Robert Thomas	100.22	Screwdrivers

"B" COUPES

Pts.	Name	Speed	Club
10	Don Towle	117.64	Coupes
9	Marla Christenson	111.66	Drifters
8	Joe Thomassin	110.02	Coupes
7	Bob Branninan	108.82	Gophers
6	Paul Wheeler	107.39	Screwdrivers
5	Bradt & Yarbrough	103.44	Road Hogs
4	Vic Roberts	100.89	Road Hogs
3	Charles DeWitt	97.72	Drifters
2	D. Whitmyer	97.19	Screwdrivers

"C" COUPES

Pts.	Name	Speed	Club
10	F. A. Hernandez	121.13	Coupes
9	Don Brown	120.48	Coupes
8	Bob Cantley	112.92	Coupes
7	Paul Andrews	109.48	Roadents
6	Glenn Ludvickson	105.24	Roadents
5	John Spencer	100.78	Roadents
4	John Eckman	100.55	Coupes
3	Don Corwin	99.55	Coupes
2	Walt Richardson	94.76	Coupes
1	Ray Britton	93.94	Coupes

"A" STREAMLINERS

Pts.	Name	Speed	Club
10	Hallman-Garrould	128.93	Gophers
9	Dave Hunter	122.95	Moles
8	S. C. Davidson	119.84	A.R.C.
7	Richard Lauder	96.98	Throttle Merchants

"B" STREAMLINERS

Pts.	Name	Speed	Club
10	Frank Williamson	105.26	Prowlers

CLUB NEWS
(Continued from page 14)
NEW MEXICO
By J. Robert Seth
GALLUP, N. M., AUG. 29

There was an exceptionally large field with cars from three states. Several of the Albuquerque Road Pilots attended. There were cars from Durango, Colo.; Prescott, Ariz.; Holbrook, Ariz.; Roswell, N. M., and several local cars.

As there are very few true hot rods in this locality, the races are mostly dirt track. Most cars have racing-type bodies, etc. The Albuquerque group was the only group which had true rods. Their bodies were reworked stock production bodies as well as their engines.

The results were as follows:

Fastest time trial:
Malcolm Dean, Roswell. Stroked Merc. :32.70.

Trophy Dash:
TWO LAPS—TIME: 1:76.60
First—Malcolm Dean, Roswell. Merc.
Second—E. J. Theron, Williams. Buick.

First Elimination:
FOUR LAPS—TIME: 2:15.00
First—L. Adderton, Prescott. Crager A.
Second—C. Montgomery, Holbrook. Plymouth.

Second Elimination:
FOUR LAPS. TIME—2:25.20
First—D. Turk, Gallup. Hudson.
Second—Jay Gunn, Gallup. Chevrolet.

Third Elimination:
FOUR LAPS—TIME: 2:29.30
First—Eddy Savoy, Gallup. GMC.
Second—A. Ray, Gallup. Ford 4.

Fourth Elimination:
FOUR LAPS—TIME: 2:51.50
First—Leo Pilon, Albuquerque. Merc.
Second—J. R. Seth, Albuquerque. Ford 4.

Main Event:
TWENTY LAPS
First—C. Montgomery, Holbrook. Plymouth.
Second—Stan Owens, Holbrook. GMC.
Third—D. Turk, Gallup. Hudson.

The new "Shoc-Shell" helmets are now available. This racing-timing headpiece is manufactured by John Lohrenz of Long Beach, California.

They weigh 1 lb. 4 ozs., come in sizes: small, medium, medium large and large.

The helmet itself is formed of low temperature, low pressure tough laminated plastic. This is covered with white sheepskin. Headbands are lined with thick foam rubber cushion.

One of the "mechanics-type" magazines recently ran an article on Frank Kurits's new sports car. The story said the car cruised "for hours at 120 mph" across the prairie. Such an exceptional cruising speed should result in an even more amazing top-speed. In view of this we'd like to extend an invitation to Mr. Kurtis on behalf of the S.C.T.A. The Association would be happy to time Mr. K's job at a future meet. S.C.T.A. is noted for their use of J. Otto Crocker's perfected timing device.

A new plate has been made available by Bob Stelling to adapt his gear box to the Ford 6 engine with a minimum of effort.

MAGNETOS
(*Continued from page 11*)

reversal in turn induces a high voltage in the secondary as shown in Figure 5.

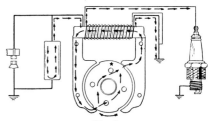

Fig. 5

This voltage becomes sufficiently high to overcome the resistance of the spark plug gap, resulting in a spark discharge, Figure 6. As soon as the flow of

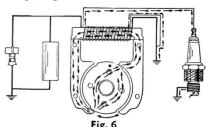

Fig. 6

current has been established across the gap, the resistance of the gap decreases and the secondary continues to discharge, the voltage oscillating downward, until there is insufficient voltage to maintain the flow of current across the spark gap. The flow of current in the secondary retards the flux change just as did the primary current, and it is the oscillating discharge of the secondary that causes the oscillating flux curve.

It should be remembered that the sequence of events depicted in Figures 4 through 6 occurs in a very small fraction of a second.

In Figure 7, the rotor has now turned

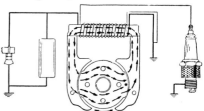

Fig. 7

180 degrees, and the flux is fully reestablished in the opposite direction from that shown in Figure 2.

This completes the first of the two spark-producing cycles which occur for each revolution of the rotor, and the rotor is in position for the start of the next cycle.

It should be realized that the entire cycle just described occurs 80 *times a second* when the magneto is operating at normal speed. From this it can readily be seen that extreme skill and quality workmanship are required in magneto design and manufacture.

QUESTIONS AND ANSWERS

Q. Do you have any maps or could you give me directions as to how to get to the lakes where the S.C.T.A. will hold their next trials?

M. KOJIMA
Pasadena, California

A. H.R.M. does not have a map of lakes directions, but a spectator has only to go to Palmdale between Friday night and Sunday on timing dates and follow the first roadster heading east.

Q. Where can I get a high compression head and a dual manifold for a Jeep engine?

KENNETH WELLS
Torrance, California

A. The Pacific Metal Products Co. at 4444 Sunset Blvd., Los Angeles, Calif., is at present the only company making this equipment. It will be awhile, though, before they will be able to supply the demand.

Q. Would it be possible to soup up a '39 Nash two-door that has a Nash 6-cylinder motor? If so, what could be done to it that would not be too expensive?

ROBERT HUDSON
Indianapolis, Indiana

A. It is possible to soup up a Nash, although it isn't done very often. Milling the head will give more compression, and, if possible, you could build a dual intake manifold. Porting and relieving might also help your performance. There are many other changes that may be effected but they would depend on the amount of money to be expended and on the skill of the builder.

Q. What is a suicide front end?

TOMMY HOLLAND
Los Angeles, Calif.

A. A suicide front end, as illustrated, is one having the spring suspended in front of the frame instead of directly under the cross member. The cross member is usually a piece of heavy pipe or angle iron with a flat piece of iron extending forward to bolt the axle to.

O. Does it help to keep a car from rolling by filling the left side of frame inside the channel with lead?

IVAN STEBBINS
Kansas City, Kansas

A. Filling the left side with lead will decrease the rolling tendency toward the right but by the same token will increase the roll toward the left. Also, skidding may result from the unbalance of the car. Weight is used by some builders to equalize weight distribution between the front and rear of the car.

Q. Is their any place for an airplane to land at the Lakes?

FRED RICHARD
Lompoc, Calif.

A. Yes, there is an airport at the southeast end of El Mirage. Many pilots utilize the level expanse of the lake bed to set in their ships. However, we don't recommend this to novice flyers.

Q. Who is the President of the S.C.T.A. and what is his address?

BOB DEMSON
Stanford University, Calif.

A. The President of the S.C.T.A. (as published in HRM, February, 1948) is Akton Miller and can be reached through S.C.T.A.'s new offices at 2380 S. Atlantic Blvd., Los Angeles 22, Calif.

Q. I am writing to ask for some information on my '32 V8 engine mounts. The body and frame are stock, but the engine is '46 Merc. I used the old '32 front engine mounts after cutting away to give the fan belt clearance . . . Had to cut off the later model mounts on the water pumps. This seems to be working out OK, but the lower hoses give me trouble because of the sharp kinks even though I'm using curved molded hose. Is there any other way to mount the engine by using the regular water pump mounting?

A. Most builders use the standard '46 engine mounts, changing the bases on the frame to give correct engine placement. A metal extension may be built on the radiator to bypass the sharp bends and provide a straight hose coupling.

Q. I would like to know when Russetta holds their time trials and if they time convertibles.

BRUCE BOUCHEA
San Bernardino, Calif.

A. Timing schedule is on page 19. Russetta times convertibles both as a coupe with the top up or as a roadster with the top down.

Q. I have heard that boring a Ford block to Mercury standard will not hold inserts. Is this true? Also, could you give me any information on gas injection?

JIM GESSFORD
Holdrege, Nebraska

A. Boring Ford blocks to Mercury standard is a common practice among roadster builders. This will not cause an appreciable amount of insert wear.

Gas injection has proven very successful in the speed world with Stuart Hilborn clocking 150.50 using his unit on a 1934 Ford block. This injection system is described in detail in HRM for April.

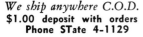

Built from a '41 Mercury by the Barris Custom Shop, this channelled convertible bears little resemblance to the original. The body hangs eight inches below the frame with the front fenders raised eleven inches on the body. Top of the car is only 4' 6" from the ground. Padded top and upholstery were made by Louis Chavis. Dash is constructed of chrome and clear lucite. Concealed push buttons operate the electric doors and truck compartment. Engine is full race '46 Merc. with Edelbrock heads, Weiand Manifold.

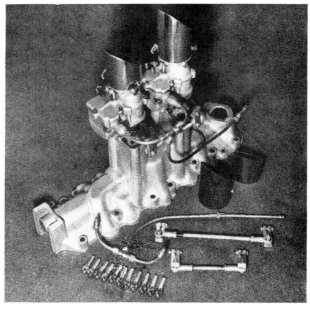

HOT ROD

Magazine

53

Dick Vineyard at Culver City   NOVEMBER, 1948   **25c**

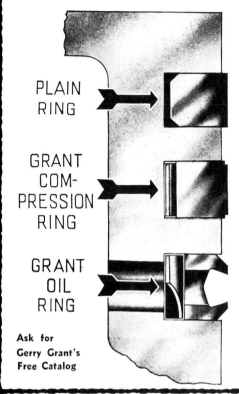

Editor's Column

With the coming of Winter, outdoor activities have slowed down in many parts of the country. At the same time clubs and associations have planned Winter programs which promise year 'round interest. A single example is the S.C.T.A. which is busy planning the 1949 Hot Rod Show to be held in Los Angeles in January. Out-of-town and out-of-state hot rod enthusiasts will find it worth their while to plan a trip to the coast for the show. Last year some 55,000 persons came to see the show. So many came, in fact, that some had to be turned away for safety reasons. The coming show, however, will run for a longer period of time with hopes of accommodating everyone. Some of the country's finest roadsters will be on display, along with the sleek streamliners which speed across California's dry lake beds. Make it a point to visit the Hot Rod Show between January 21 and 30.

November's cover car is Ed Walker's track job. The car has had a busy season winning races with the California Hot Rods, Inc. Rex Burnette has done a fine cutaway drawing on the Walker job. The drawing is on page 9 of this issue. Featured with the car is Driver Dick Vineyard of Los Angeles.

HRM wishes to welcome Walt Woron to its staff. Walt, who wrote the Front Drive Roadster article for the September issue, knows his hot rods throughout. Hundreds of readers have asked us to give them information on how to build a hot rod. That is just what Mr. Woron will do. He will start his series with a "strictly stock" job, building it up, bit by bit, into the quality roadster that is so popular today. His first article will concern itself to acquainting the reader with terms to be used throughout the series. This introductory story is on page 13 of this issue.

Alexis de Saknoffsky, famed industrial designer, contributes to this issue with his convictions about hot rods. His thought-provoking article entitled Automotive Design Trend appears on page 11.

Incidentally, in our October issue it was mentioned that Yam Oka held the one-lap record at Gilmore Stadium. Since then we have learned that the record was set by Bud Gregory in Larry Lunetta's track job. Later on, Oka equalled the mark made with Lunetta's car. Therefore, the record is still held by Gregory.

Keep those letters and snapshots coming in.—Ed.

HOT ROD Magazine

"World's Most Complete Hot Rod Coverage"

HOT ROD MAGAZINE, U.S. Copyright 1948 by the Hot Rod Publishing Company, 7164 Melrose Avenue, Los Angeles 46, California. Entered as second-class matter June 24, 1948 at the post office at Los Angeles, California, under the Act of March 3, 1879. SUBSCRIPTION PRICE: $3.00 per year throughout th eworld. Circulation: 40,000 monthly. On sale at newsstands, tracks and speed shops across the country. Phone: WEbster 3-4433.

Vol. 1   HRM—Published Monthly   No. 11

Associate Editors	R. E. Petersen, Robert R. Lindsay
Staff Writer	Walter A. Woron
Technical Adviser	Wally Parks
Art Director	Alice Van Norman
Diagramatic Art	Rex Burnette
Photography	Paul Schaeffer, Vick Drake, Al Moss, Terry Moore, Pete
Cartoons and Humor	Tom Medley
Reporters	Dick Robinson, Richard K. Martin, Pauline Bayer, J. Robert Seth, Melvin Dudley
Subscription Department	Marilyn Lord
Distribution	Gordon Behn

ON THE COVER: Dick Vineyard qualifies Ed Walker's No. 53 at Culver City Speedway, California. The asphalt track is banked to a high degree, being sixteen feet higher on the outside than on the pole. Vineyard won the California Hot Rods Championship Race at this track, completing the 100 laps ahead of a top field of roadster pilots.

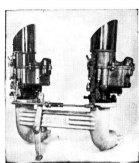

QUESTIONS AND ANSWERS

Q. In your July issue you pictured Bob Rufi's Chevy 4. I would like to know if this body was a belly tank or if he constructed it himself.

Bob Mattes
Throttle Thumpers
Chicago, Illinois

A. The old Rufi streamliner, now owned by Howard Markham, was built back in 1939 before there were belly tanks available. The car was designed and built in Rufi's garage, featuring aircraft-type construction with sheet aluminum covering a tubing frame. Bob, at one time, incorporated rear-wheel fairings and attained a one-direction speed of 143 mph. He also had a complete fire-control system in the engine compartment. Cockpit quarters were so close that Rufi had to have a removable steering wheel to facilitate getting in and out of the streamliner.

Q. I have a '31 Ford roadster that is stripped down. Could you possibly tell me where I could get insurance for it?

Dick Nolan
Laguna Beach, California

A. We understand that a legal roadster may be insured by filling out an assigned risk application at any insurance company. This form is sent to a state office that will assign the owner to an insurance company. The assigned company will handle the insurance at a 10% above normal rate. Records have proven that hot rods have a much lower accident rate than other vehicles due to quicker judgment and reaction of the younger drivers, as well as greater visibility of the cars. The practice of the press in calling any OLD car involved in an accident a hot rod has made insurance companies hot rod shy. Now, many roadster associations are working with civic groups to promote safety. The press, in turn, has taken a more favorable attitude and it may not be long before insurance companies inaugurate a new policy toward roadsters.

Q. I have a model A roadster ('29) with a '47 Mercury motor, column shift and a very unusual back deck which is molded in. Without channelling my frame, how can I lower the body? The car has model A fenders on it and, thus, makes it difficult to do so. If I put a drop center axle in front, my front tires will hit the fenders.

Doug Meyers
Oregon State College
Corvallis, Oregon

A. If you would like to use a dropped axle in the front without rubbing your tires, smaller tires might help. Long shackles and lowering blocks cannot be used on a model A. The rear spring directly over the axle prevents the builder from employing these lowering methods. The best way is to heat and bend the springs. Of course the most inexpensive method is to carry a large weight in the turtledeck.

Q. There is someone out there (L. A., we think) that alters press-on type metal cam gears by moving the timing mark slightly. We know he makes them for V-8 '60's. One of the midget owners in town had two of them not long ago that he ordered from out there. Unfortunately, he finds that he has lost the address. He says the improvement in performance on a full '60' was only slightly less than amazing. The midget owner-driver who used the second one is no less enthusiastic in his praise. So, we thought we would try one on a motor (V8 85) one of us is building.

Wilkie Talbert, Jr.
Byron Ward
Don Roof
Alburquerque Road Pilots
Alburquerque, New Mexico

A. Changing the timing mark on a cam gear is a practice employed by some builders. As with everything else pertaining to the speed field, there is no one setting that gives outstanding results. A setting that is perfect for one engine may not work for another. By moving the mark forward the intake valves will open sooner. The valves will open later than normal when the mark is moved in the opposite direction. It takes about a five degree change to make an appreciable difference in performance. Most speed shops have or can get a special timing gear for V8 85's that will take the place of a changeable cam gear mark. It will give a five degree change by merely moving the securing bolts. With this gear you try different combinations to determine the right one for your engine.

Q. Recently Reader Kenneth Wells of Torrance, California wrote this column seeking Jeep speed equipment (HRM, October). Another reader, David Carlson of Vancouver, Washington, has located a complete stock of Jeep equipment. It is carried by the R & R Manufacturing Company, Box 546, 1503 Nichol Avenue, Anderson, Indiana.

Q. How much does the average hot rod cost to build, especially a good-looking one like Bob McGee's? (HRM, October).

A. A roadster can be build for five hundred or five thousand dollars, depending on how elaborate the car is and how much of the work can be done by the builder. Bob McGee's car, considered above average, cost about three thousand dollars, plus long hours of work.

Q. I would like to know whether a model T frame would be too light for a V8 85 track roadster.

Roy Steiner
Sacramento, California

A. Quite a few track roadsters are running today with T frame rails. They have the advantage of lightness. Most California builders prefer '32 Ford rails, as their added strength helps to withstand the punishment received by a track roadster.

Bob Brown
Belmont, Massachusetts

It's in the Bag...

NEW CLUB IN DAYTON

Dear Sirs:

. . . We have started a club. . . hope to send you some pictures of the cars here in Dayton (Ohio). There are quite a few, some of which would stand up to California's (hotrods) any day. . .

JOHN PENNINGTON
Dayton, Ohio

We look forward to receiving pictures of your cars and club activities. "California style" hot rods are fast becoming popular throughout the nation and, in some cases, the world.—ED.

HOT RODS ON GUAM

Dear Sirs:

. . . At present, even here on Guam, there are several hot rods . . . I am in the process of just finishing one, a '32 V8 channeled job, with a new Merc ¼ stroker, hydraulics . . .

We have been trying to start a hot rod club here. . . .

DAVID L. WILLIAMS
Agana, Guam

SATISFIED READER

Hot Rod Magazine:

. . . The construction cutaway drawings included with the "Hot Rod of the Month" stories in the August and September issues are fine. Don't let up on this feature.

Tom Medley's pages in each issue are great. His cartoon, top of page 25, September issue, is terrific.

Congratulations also are in order on the fine job of reporting done on the "Front Drive Roadster" article in the September issue. Such a detailed report with clear illustrations is worth the subscription price alone.

I have enjoyed every issue so far and take pride in showing my collection of past issues to my friends who also receive a great deal of pleasure from them.

HAL C. KING
San Antonio, Texas

FASTEST HALF MILE

Dear Sirs:

. . . In your latest issue. . . it states that Dick Frazier of Mutual Racing Association set a world's record for one lap on the half mile dirt track there (Winchester, Indiana). It said he turned the lap in :21.37 in his roadster.

. . . Does this mean for big cars and roadsters only or does it include midgets also? . . When the midgets ran their first race at Gardena Bowl (now Carrell Speedway) Duke Nalon . . . set a new one lap record of :20.30. It was Sunday, November 10, 1946. . . Please send me a reply as I am curious about this.

REGGIE O'DONNELL
San Pedro, California

Records show that Duke Nalon, driving under United Racing Association sanction, turned one lap on that day in :21.30; not :20.30. Althought this time would still be faster than Frazier's :21.37, Nalon's record does not stand as a half mile time, for . . . at that time . . . Gardena Bowl was considerably short of a half mile in length.—ED.

WRONG CAPTION

Dear Sir:

. . . Bill (Otto) must have sent a photo of his cut down "T" in because you printed (it) . . . and wrote about the photo of '32 roadster with a '37 Caddie engine." That (caption) goes with my photo. . .

TOMMY GOSCH
Hollywood, California

The caption which was printed under Mr. Otto's car in the September issue was intended for a photo sent in by Mr. Gosch. This picture, along with its correct caption appears in this issue of HRM.—ED.

HOT ROD OF

Ed Walker, Dick Vineyard and No. 53 combine to make one of the hottest racing teams in the country today. Walker, veteran garage man, is owner and builder of the car. Vineyard, hot rod pilot since 1946, has driven the car to more "firsts" than any other CHR entry this season. No. 53 is one of the most unusual track jobs to appear in roadster racing.

Driver Vineyard was born in Los Angeles, California, where he attended Marshall High School. Back in 1940 Dick built his first hot rod, which he drove at Muroc Dry Lake as a member of the Outriders, an S.C.T.A. club.

In 1941, when he graduated from Marshall, Dick entered the U. S. Marine Corps, serving as a combat mechanic in the Pacific Theatre.

In December, 1946, Vineyard became a member of the newly-formed C.R.A., driving his first race at Bakersfield, California, in a roadster owned by Dick Benninger. In May of 1947 Dick built his own track job, No. 74, which he ran through Thanksgiving of that year, finishing 12th in C.R.A. point standings.

During the Spring of 1948 Vineyard joined the California Hot Rods, Inc., being appointed as a member of the Association's Board of Directors. The wheel of No. 74 was soon taken over by Bob Lindsey, another popular west coast driver, as Vineyard settled in the cockpit of Ed Walker's new job.

Interesting note about No. 53 is that the car has been running steadily since its bow into the CHR without any engine repair.

Dick capped CHR's summer racing season by winning the 1948 Championship title on September 24 at Culver City Speedway, California. He rode in stiff competition with other CHR speedsters for 100 hard-fought laps, winding up in the No. 1 spot for which he was favored.

Photos by Pete

TOP—A closeup of the chain drive shows a double-row chain connected directly to a sprocket on the rear axle of the car.

ABOVE—The frame is from '29 Chevy. Car has a Buick radiator, runs three Stromberg Chevy carbs on the GMC engine.

Dick Vineyard is right at home behind the wheel of No. 53. The car was built and is owned by Ed Walker (shown in inset). Dick is high-point man of the California Hot Rods. Walker operates a garage in Los Angeles.

Photos by Al Moss and Pete

Construction Cutaway

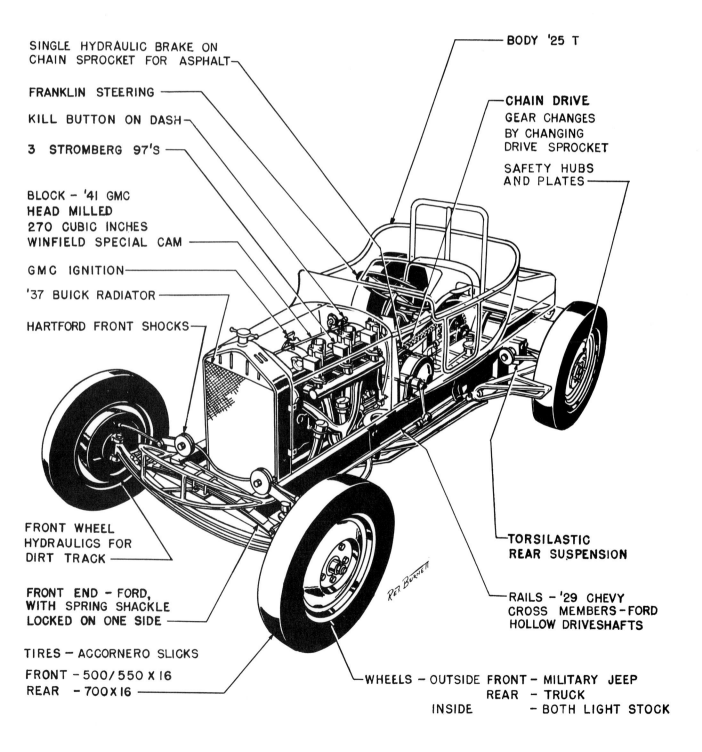

SINGLE HYDRAULIC BRAKE ON
CHAIN SPROCKET FOR ASPHALT

FRANKLIN STEERING

KILL BUTTON ON DASH

3 STROMBERG 97'S

BLOCK – '41 GMC
HEAD MILLED
270 CUBIC INCHES
WINFIELD SPECIAL CAM

GMC IGNITION

'37 BUICK RADIATOR

HARTFORD FRONT SHOCKS

FRONT WHEEL
HYDRAULICS FOR
DIRT TRACK

FRONT END – FORD,
WITH SPRING SHACKLE
LOCKED ON ONE SIDE

TIRES – ACCORNERO SLICKS

FRONT – 500/550 X 16
REAR – 700 X 16

BODY '25 T

CHAIN DRIVE
GEAR CHANGES
BY CHANGING
DRIVE SPROCKET

SAFETY HUBS
AND PLATES

TORSILASTIC
REAR SUSPENSION

RAILS – '29 CHEVY
CROSS MEMBERS – FORD
HOLLOW DRIVESHAFTS

WHEELS – OUTSIDE FRONT – MILITARY JEEP
REAR – TRUCK
INSIDE   – BOTH LIGHT STOCK

Rex Burnett

Northwest Championship Race

By RICHARD K. MARTIN

The second N. W. Championship one-hundred lap roadster race was held at the Aurora Stadium in Seattle, Washington, on Sunday, September 19th, 1948. This race was for both the R.R.A.O. and the R.R.A.W. with both associations having their own champions. Although both associations have their races together, they do not as yet have a common champion or point system.

This race was run off almost as any race, with a helmet dash, four heats, and a main event but no semi. The reason for this was that there were 24 cars in the main, and believe me, 24 cars on a quarter mile plant makes an interesting roadster race!

Len Sutton in car 27 had fast time of 16:11 with Pete Lovely 2nd in the 73 car and Max Humm 3rd in the 26 car. Max originally timed in the 73 car at 16:31 and then left it to drive the 26 car which he timed at 16:52. Pete Lovely, a Washington driver, and completely new to the car, then drove the 73 car end beat Max's own time by .11 second with a 16:20. All three cars were Oregon cars and drivers with the exception of Lovely. Sutton won the dash followed by Lovely and Humm.

The heats were inverted, and the first and slowest heat was won by Howard Osbourne in the 76 car (R.R.O.A.) who grabbed the lead from the start and by the fourth lap had a half lap on the second car so he just stroked on in with his lead.

The second heat was won by Russ Gilbertson in the 69 car (R.R.A.O.) who started in fifth spot and by the fourth lap had worked his way up to the front. For the following six laps, he was contested heavily by Phil Phobert in the 28 car (R.R.A.W.) but he never lost the lead and came home the winner.

The third heat was easily won by Kenny McBride in the 8 car (R.R.A.W.) as he grabbed the lead right after the start, and held it all of the way to the finish.

The fourth and fastest heat was won by Len Sutton in the 27 car (R.R.A.O.) who started last, was first on the fifth lap and when the checker fell on the tenth lap, he was stroking home a quarter of a lap ahead of Ernie Koch in the 72 car (R.R.A.O.). Bob Donkerin in the 5 car (R.R.A.W.) was

third, Pete Lovely in the 73 (R.R.A.O.) was fourth, followed by Max Humm in the 26 car (R.R.A.O.). John Gorman who had an early lead dropped out with a broken axle. That broken axle almost kept Gorman from winning this Northwest Championship Race. As the cars were lining up for the start. Gorman finally got his new axle in, and out on the track just in time to slip into his position before the starting flag fell.

The race was run straight-off and Sutton held his spot on the pole with Ernie Koch, in the 72 car, running second, and Bob Donker, in the 5 car, running third. At the 8th lap, Humm, who started in 5th place, had worked up to second spot but had to drop out at the 10th lap because of heating troubles.

At 23 laps Howard Osborne, who had started in the 19th position, in the 76 car, had moved up to 2nd spot with Koch third and Donker still following. Sutton still held his lead until the 35th lap when he blew his right front tire and pushed the 77 car into the outside fence in the 1st turn. This gave Osborne the lead with Koch second and Donker third.

After a 5 lap loss, changing a tire, Sutton was back on the track and making up plenty of time. Russ Gilbertson who started 13th in the 69 car worked his way clear up to 4th spot and then started dropping back. On the 70th lap looped out and could not get started again until the 73rd lap. On the next lap Sutton, who was again in about 6th place, looped out and lost two laps before getting back in.

Osborne who had been leading all this time, ran out of gas on the 89th lap and had to pull in for fuel. This left Ernie Koch in 1st position with John Gorman in second in the 1 car as he had finally passed Bob Donker in the 5 car while Donker switched from his main tank to his auxiliary tank.

(Continued on page 26)

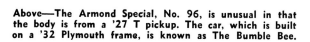

No. 37 went out of control during time trials, hit a retaining wall with throttle jammed open, turned infield where it burst into flames. Track crewmen put out the fire several times only to see it flare up again. The driver was not injured in the accident.

Above—The Armond Special, No. 96, is unusual in that the body is from a '27 T pickup. The car, which is built on a '32 Plymouth frame, is known as The Bumble Bee.

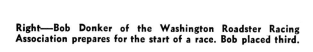

Right—Bob Donker of the Washington Roadster Racing Association prepares for the start of a race. Bob placed third.

Automotive Design Trend

DEMAND GROWS FOR PRECISION-BUILT AMERICAN SPORTSTER

by Alexis de Saknoffsky

Mr. Saknoffsky has had a widely-varied career which includes industrial engineering, auto, airplane and race boat design. He was born in Russia, schooled in Switzerland. For six years in a row he won the Grand Prix for body design at the Elegance Contest in Monte Carlo. It was this achievement that brought him to the attention of American automotive interests. His American accounts include Packard, Nash, Studebaker and Willys.—ED.

The notion that car driving is a sport will probably seem incongruous to a lot of Americans. Due to the tremendous development of the automobile industry, the average driver considers a car as a means of getting where he wants to go. Absorbed in his thoughts he automatically uses the controls of a car. As a result, the fine points of driving have become almost nonexistent.

Fine driving requires a special type of a car to show it off at its best. Fine driving, which, by the way, is vastly different from what you would call good driving, is a combination of: split-second judgment, judicious use of gears, and adequate use of brakes and horn. It is a smooth way of using everything the car engineer has put into the car. It does NOT mean racing from a stop light, nor stopping inches from a frightened pedestrian. It is a casual, poised use of a refined, mechanical product in your hands.

The reason fine driving is an almost extinct art is due to the fact that there is no such thing as a sports car in America. Anyway, it is not available through regularly established dealers and is confined to small groups of motor enthusiasts.

A sports car has to have: a delicate, high-geared steering, a lightning pick-up, oversized brakes, and a "hard" suspension. The smooth-running jobs, mass-produced here, have low-geared steering for easier parking, conventional pick-up for economy of operation and "soft" suspension, for which American cars are famous, but which is disastrous for fast cornering. These jobs have been carefully developed with an eye on the world markets. They are eminently suitable for the role they are expected to perform. They are, however, totally unsuitable for driving "connoisseurs."

These thoughts are a result of my twenty years of experience in designing cars and my recent study of the California "movement" known as "hot rods." I sincerely believe that we have in it something virile, dynamic and youthful, which, if properly channelled, could produce very worth-while national results. The sporty spirit which exists here, has prompted a number of enthusiasts to build their own vehicles. The fact that it has become an $8,000,000 industry proves that those enthusiasts are not isolated cases.

Thus far this "hot rod" movement has been strictly a hobby. Though SCTA claims that a certain number of engine developments and other improvements of recent date are traceable to early tests on "hot rods," the men who have put their time and money into these cars did not have the adoption of their ideas for mass production as a goal. I believe it will be vital and interesting to see what could be done in inspiring the sport-car minded California artisans to produce a prototype of a practical American sports car. With a suitable vehicle it is a foregone conclusion that the sport car interest will become as widely spread as the sport car movement in different countries of Europe.

The production of hot rods seems to me as highly important for several reasons. First—it is an excellent safety valve for the exuberance so natural in modern youth. It is a perfectly legitimate outlet for the craving for speed and thrilling performance, so characteristic of the present generation. Secondly—it encourages the development in our youngsters of the art of mechanical artisanship. This artisanship is seldom found in the auto-brotherhood. There is so much sloppy work performed in the great majority of garages that it becomes a rarity to see a mechanic who is proud of his work. Part of this is due to bosses who encourage speed in workmanship rather than quality. Much of it, however, is due to the most uninspiring finish and design of our mass-produced engines and parts.

All of us are sensitive to mechanical beauty. What can be more exciting than a beautifully finished racing engine? It has been a deep satisfaction to me to see some of the "hot rod" engines and parts produced in California, which compare most favorably to some of the most outstanding examples of European artisanship.

This, however, has not been true where body design and instrument boards are concerned. Few mechanical "artists" are also body stylists, which requires a very specialized training. The result is that there are altogether too many "hot rods" of bastard design, which combine, under the excuse of "functional design," magnificent engineering produced at the cost of thousands of dollars, with most unimaginative sheet metal and instrument grouping. True, there are a few "streamliners" around. But these are generally modified racing cars and totally unsuitable for all-around use. Whichever way you look at it, the "hot rods" should be taken out of the strictly hobby field and developed into a model, which is missing in the line-up of American cars.

What are my qualifications for speaking with authority about sports cars? Before landing in America in 1928, the writer raced for five years at European sport cars meetings. During those years he built up a reputation as a designer of sport car bodies.

Wealthy sportsmen from different countries trekked to the Van den Plas auto body works in Brussels, Belgium, which was famous for the lines and workmanship of its hand-built bodies. The writer was art director of this concern during the early twenties when the sport car was in its infancy and the industry was groping for a vehicle formula which would have the finish and the performance of a racing car and still be comfortable and weatherproof for every-day use.

Since 1933, on the monthly mechanical fashions pages of the Esquire magazine, the writer has been clamoring for an American sports car. However, up to now, he was unable to make U.S. production-minded manufacturers see the possibilities of a finely finished vehicle with an outstanding performance which would appeal to American sportsmen, who have to depend on costly imports or spend many thousands of dollars on hand-built custom jobs.

Our problem is to create the connecting link between this demand and the fertile pool of talent and imagination of our younger generation.

Lone Star Racing

T.R.R.A. WINDS UP ITS FIRST SEASON OF ROADSTER RACING

by PAULINE BAYER

Miss Bayer has acted as a reporter for HRM since June of this year, one month after the Texas Roadster Racing Association was formed. However, she has a busy schedule other than her reports to our readers. She owns two cars which she races in Texas circuits, operates a garage in Austin, handles programs for T.R.R.A., covers most midget races and all stock car races in the Texas area.—ED.

Three-fourths of the hot rods in the Texas Roadster Racing Association have been converted from the old body styles to the light T types. This marks a big advancement in Texas hot rod racing. In other words, these Texas entries are strictly race cars now, bringing forth faster and better shows. Car owners

RIGHT—B. C. Ryan (left) and Harry Elbel mix it up during racing at Pan American Speedway, San Antonio.

Photos by Terry Moore

R. L. Howland (P68) gets a shove from fellow T.R.R.A. driver A. M. Jarris during a race at Pan American Speedway in San Antonio, Texas. Rowland is running a Plymouth engine in his roadster. Jarris' car is powered by a V8. Rowland is from Mathis, Jarris from San Angelo.

topped off the conversion with new paint jobs and numbers.

In Texas roadster racing, the big duel is between the Corpus Christi boys and the San Antonio pilots. T.R.R.A. is still welcoming new memberships. A new entry from Houston is Leroy Ragsdale, who has a model B, the only one running in the circuit. It looks as if Leroy's car will offer great competition, if he can keep all four going. With the opening of the football season, Pan American Speedway in San Antonio changed its race night from Friday to Wednesday.

Pan American has proven to be an excellent roadster track. The midgets have used it for three years, now. PAS has two large grandstands which house 8000 spectators. The quarter-mile oval has a clay surface, is illuminated for night racing by a perfect lighting system. Entire track is bounded by a steel retaining wall.

George Carroll recently left the Association to try his hand at motor boating. The gang wishes him luck, at the same time hoping for an early return.

The Texas Championship race was held on October 9 at the C.C. Speedway in Corpus Christi. This race was sanctioned by the Texas Roadster Racing Association. Up to the date of this writing, Harry Elbel still holds the track records for both San Antonio and Corpus Christi. T.R.R.A. members and fans are looking forward to an exciting season of racing in the coming year.

George Carroll in No. 111 slips by Roger Berkhart, No. 1, and Henry Major, far right, as they tangle at Pan American Speedway. Carroll has a V8 engine in his roadster, Major—a Mercury, and Berkhart—a Chrysler.

Racing Jargon by WALTER A. WORON

Just got through porting and relieving my bent-eight."

"Yeah?" Thought you had a two-port Riley?"

"Did have, but had a chance to pick up an .080 over-bore, stroked-eight cheap, so traded off the four-barrel."

Confusing? Of course not—that is, if you've been around hot rods and the tracks long enough. But for newcomers to the game and to fans who have not been exposed to a great deal of such talk, it probably makes little, if any. sense.

Because of limited space, it is not possible to cover all of the various terms used in common racing talk; however, it is believed that the following resume covers those terms most generally used. To provide an easy reference, the terms are arranged in dictionary form and are grouped under the following categories: Engine, General; Engine Components and Accessories; Engine, Rebuilding; Frame and Body; Miscellaneous Car Terms; and General Terms.

Engine, General

Bent-Eight—Ford, Mercury, or Cadillac V-8 engine.

Four-Barrell—Four-cylinder engine.

Full-House—An engine with all racing accessories.

Mill—Any engine.

Engine Components & Accessories

Blower—A supercharger, which is used to increase the fuel-air charge inducted into an engine, and thereby increases the horsepower. The three types of blowers are: piston-cylinder type; positive rotary, Roots and vane types; and centrifugal types.

Blown Engine—An engine that incorporates a supercharger.

Crank—Abbreviated form of crankshaft.

D.O.—An engine equipped with dual-overhead valves.

Dual Set-Up—An engine using a dual intake manifold equipped with two carburetors. A dual set-up can be used on a four-cylinder, six-cylinder, or eight-cylinder engine.

Four-Port Job—A Model A or B block with a four-intake-port head (usually applies to a Riley head).

Header—Specially designed racing-type exhaust manifold, designed to prevent back-pressure in the manifold and permit better scavenging of the cylinders after each power stroke.

Jiggler—Rocker arm.
Jug—Carburetor.
Lid—Head.
Pot—Carburetor.

Shaft—Abbreviated name for engine crankshaft (same as Crank).

Single-stick—Single, overhead camshaft (see Stick).

Stacks—Short, individual exhaust stacks, with which no collector is used. Also could mean short "velocity" stacks used on top of carburetor.

Stick—Camshaft, used for opening and closing the intake and exhaust valves. Types of camshafts for hot rods consist of the following: stock, semi-race, ¾-race, super, and full-race.

Two-Port Job—A Model A or B block with a two-intake-port head (usually applies to a Riley head).

Engine Rebuilding

Over-Bore—An engine with the cylinders bored out oversize to increase the cubic inch displacement, or for the purpose of adding sleeves (if the same displacement is desired). Example: An .080 over-bore is an engine with the cylinders bored out .080-inch diameter oversize from the original diameter.

Porting—Consists of enlarging and polishing the valve ports (intake and/or exhaust) and adding oversized valves and stronger springs. This usually accompanies reboring, since the port diameter is fixed primarily by the cylinder bore—the larger the bore, the larger the ports.

Relieving—Consists of removing the ridge in the top of the block resulting from counterboring during manufacture for the valve seat. The removal of this ridge permits better "breathing" through the transfer passage. This refers, generally, to "L" head engines.

Stroker—An engine with a crankshaft stroked above normal (see Stroking).

Stroking—Consists of regrinding the crankpin in such a manner as to move its center further away from the center of the crankshaft, thereby increasing the stroke and swept volume of the cylinder. This results in a large increase in compression ratio plus an increase in piston displacement. To prevent the compression ratio from becoming abnormally high, stroked pistons are sometimes added, which are special pistons with the wrist pin located higher toward the crown. This results in a further increase in piston displacement. Stroked pistons, by themselves, could be used to increase the piston displacement, but would result in a decrease in compression ratio.

Frame and Body

Channel Job—A car with the floor cut out or "channeled," with the hangers moved up higher on the body structure, allowing the entire body to sit lower (with the floor below, or level with, the frame). The public has become more aware of this type of body styling (used on hot rods a number of years) with the advent of the new Hudson and its advertisement as, "the car you step *down* into."

Chopped Top—A hard or soft top that has been lowered by removing a section from the windshield posts, the windows, the doors, the top bows, etc.

Dropped Axle—Front axle with a sharp downward bend as it leaves the wheel, so that it is lower than ordinary, and consequently lowers the front end.

Filled Axle—A dropped axle that has both sides of the "I" beam section filled with metal at the bend to give added strength in that area.

Roll Bar—Steel bar welded to both longitudinal members of the frame and extending above and behind the driver to protect him in the event of a roll.

Sprung Weight—Also known as the sprung mass, it is that part of the car that is actually suspended and includes the weight of the body, engine and frame.

Stepped Frame—A frame altered in such a manner as to make a big step in the longitudinal members in order to fit over the axle, thereby lowering the frame and body.

Unsprung Weight—Also known as the unsprung mass, it is that part of a car that is not suspended by springs, including the axles, wheels and, in most cases, the brakes.

Miscellaneous Car Terms

Binders—Brakes.
Boots—Tires.

Dog Clutch—An in-out type clutch using a gear shift to engage the spline or dog gears of the engine crankshaft and the drive-shaft together. The shafts are not rotating at the time of gear engagement.

Locked Rear End—A straight-through drive system with the left and right rear axle shafts locked together with the ring gear and in which no differential action exists.

Quick Change Gear Box—A gear box so designed that the gears may be quickly removed and replaced. It can be used in conjunction with the dog clutch or as the rear end. The dog clutch is used to compensate for different wheel sizes, tires sizes, condition and length of track, and allows the car to deliver its maximum performance and to handle properly.

General Terms

Goat—Usually considered to be an old race car, generally used when speaking of a driver "herding his goat."

(Continued on Page 27)

PERSONALITIES By TOM MEDLEY

Jim LINDSLEY

POPULAR S.C.T.A. MEMBER!

JIM WAS BORN FEB, 13 1917 in SANTA MONICA CALIFORNIA. HE ATTENDED BELL HIGH SCHOOL BELL CALIF. GRADUATING in 1936 - HE JOINED THE BELL GEAR GRINDERS in 1940 and HAS BEEN ONE OF ITS MOST ACTIVE MEMBERS. JIM IS HIGH POINT MAN in THE GEAR GRINDERS SO FAR THIS SEASON!

BOY THESE LIGHTS ARE JUST LIKE DOWN TOWN!

JIM IS THE OFFICIAL RECORDER FOR THE S.C.T.A. HE IS ALSO RESPONSIBLE FOR THE SIGNAL LIGHT SET UP AT THE... S.C.T.A. LAKES! JIM BEING AN ELECTRICIAN BUILT THE ENTIRE SIGNAL SET UP SWITCHES and ALL. HE IS MARRIED AND HAS 3 BOYS!

JIM RUNS A "HOME MADE" STREAMLINER, TURNED 132.93 in THE "B" CLASS!

C.H.R. Championship Race

WEST COAST RACING GROUP HOLDS FIRST CHAMPIONSHIP EVENT

RIGHT — A tired Champion, Dick Vineyard, poses with the Hot Rod Magazine Trophy after 100 gruelling laps at Culver City Speedway in California.

Below—After many weeks of recuperating from his Gilmore Stadium accident, Yam Oka made his reappearance with a brand new "Eightball." The car was completely streamlined with all fixtures chromed. Yam placed Second in the race.

Grandstands of Culver City Speedway, California, were crowded to capacity on the evening of September 24. By the same token, the pits were lined with a maximum of entries. The reason: California Hot Rods, Inc. were holding their first Championship Race. Weather was excellent for the night race.

Culver City Speedway is a particularly hot track, what with a paved surface, banked 16 feet higher on the outside than on the pole, Racing fans have witnessed many an exciting show there. The scene was set for action, which is just what the roadster pilots gave their audience.

Dick Vineyard of Los Angeles was the man to beat, as he had taken more "firsts" than any other C.H.R. driver during their initial racing season. Dick and his mount, Ed Walker's No. 53, were set for all comers.

The evening's racing started with a trophy dash between Vineyard and Dick Benninger, another popular and hard driver. Benninger's entry, No. 5, is noted for being one of the loudest roadsters in the Association. The boys took the green flag at a hot pace. Vineyard nosed out his competitor for the three laps in :43.68.

Next event on the card was a match race held between Vineyard and Yam Oka. This was Oka's first race with his new car. Yam's old "Eightball" had been pretty well pushed in when he overturned during a race at Gilmore Stadium some weeks before. His new roadster really stood out with its bright red paint job, chromed front end and streamlined contour.

Oka gave Dick a close race for his money, especially for a first race in the new No. 8, but Dick edged him out in the event. Vineyard's four-lap

time was :56.90, a new record. Nine cars lined up for a 25 lap semi-main event. This feature was taken by Archie Tipton, with George Seegar in second spot and Mickey Davis winding up third. Incidentally, Davis had just returned from touring the midwest circuits. Tipton's time for the event, 4:49.42.

The final event of the night was the 100 lap Championship Race. Fourteen cars lined up for the start. The lineup included Joe De Hart, Stan Kross, Chuck Burness, Dick Vineyard, Yam Oka, Bud Van Mannen, Colby Scroggins and Vern Slankard, as well as other "name" drivers.

They took off to a good start and kept up a fast pace during the entire race. The hundred lapper was completed in 24:24.00, averaging faster than fifteen seconds per lap on the quarter mile oval. Taking his third event of the evening, Vineyard flashed across the

finish line ahead of Yam Oka and Chucl Burness, respectively. Dick then returned to the finish line to receive the Hot Rod Magazine Trophy, symbolic of the Association Championship spot.

All in all, it looked like Vineyard's show, with Dick taking honors in the Trophy Dash, the match race with Yam Oka and the featured Championship spinfest.

Earlier in the racing year, the car was not as hot as it is today. Owner Ed Walker had some trouble finding the right gear combination. Now that he has, there seems to be no stopping Dick Vineyard in Ed Walker's No. 53.

The week after the championship race, California Hot Rods switched over to Sunday afternoon racing for the remainder of the season at the 1/4 mile plant.

BELOW—Corvie Tullio (18) spins on the west turn. Vern Slankard in No. 26 barely misses Corvie as he tries to get by.

Photos by Al Moss

LEFT—Archie Tipton in No. 14 passes George Seegar on a turn in the semi. Archie is brother of Wayne Tipton, President of California Hot Rods, Inc. Both drivers have been up at the top of their association this year.

At S.C.T.A.'s September Meet

CLASS B ROADSTERS HOLD HARD FOUGHT BATTLE FOR FIRST SPOT

by WALLY PARKS

The S.C.T.A. ran its fifth meet of the 1948 series at El Mirage, September 25 and 26. Prevailing wind was from the west. Weather varied considerably between Saturday and Sunday. Some very good times were set during the first day's running. In the B Roadster Class lowest speed for points cars was 120.80. The C Roadster low-point mark was 124.65. Of the total points cars in each of the two classes the average speed was 128.097 (B Roadster) and 128.955 (C Roadster). There were 28 cars in the points in the BR Class and 24 in the CR Class.

The Spurgin-Giovanine entry had top score in the small engine Roadster Class. Doug Hartelt, last year's champ, took the B Roadster first spot. Paul Schiefer of San Diego was first in C Roadsters. He had the fastest roadster time of the meet. Ak Miller timed fastest in the D Roadster group with his rear-engine Cadillac. Second place in that class was Stan Jones in his V-16 Cadillac.

The most interesting competition of the meet was in the B Roadster Class, where the first spot changed hands several times during the running. Several record attempts were made in this class. Johnny Hartman's Chevy 6 turned 140.18 on Saturday and then made a new record in its class. This record held good for a few minutes, after which Hartelt boosted it a little and held it there. Two new cars showed up at the meet. They were Jack Avakian's rear-engine 24 T roadster and Bob Riese's 24 T tank-nose roadster. They both qualified for record runs, but failed to set records by a small margin. The Palm-Conkle entry also tried for a record but fell short of the mark.

Following Schiefer in the C Roadster Class were Harold Daigh and Barney Navarro, who had his blower job going. Two other San Diego cars followed Daigh and Navarro. They were Don McLean, turning 137.19, and Ed Stewart, turning 132.15 for the fastest '32 roadster time of the meet.

Alex Xydias took the A Streamliner Class with his Ford 60 tank at 132.93.

Marvin Lee got the top spot in the B Streamliners followed by Breene & Haller's Mercury drop-tank. Lee turned 146.81 and Breene reached 145.63. Path & Moore placed third at 142.18 with their tail job. The Burke-Francisco Class C tank turned 148.51 for high speed of the meet after having sheared a key in the pinion gear and being dismantled at the lake for repairs. Junior Rotter, having had a recent alignment on his tank, moved up into second spot with a time of 141.73. He was followed by Jack McDermott, who made 135.73. Two new records were attained at the meet. They were in the A & B Roadster Classes. The Spurgin-Giovanine A roadster set a record of 123.050, while Doug Hartelt's B roadster set a mark of 134.280.

This meet was a hotly contested affair with plenty of excitement amoung the clubs. With the coming meet being the last of the season, interesting competition is expected in all classes, with special attention being cast toward the B Roadster class.

TOP TO BOTTOM—

At the finish line Official Timer J. Otto Crocker records Junior Tucker's time between the two electric eyes.

A close contender for the B Roadster record, Jack Avakian's rear engine '24 T was built in thirteen nights by four men. These tank-nosed entries are becoming increasingly popular with S.C.T.A. membership.

Jerry Fairbanks' Cameraman Frank MacDonald and Director Arnold Wester were at the September meet to photograph a color movie for Popular Science Shorts.

TOP TO BOTTOM—
Assistant Timer Tommy Silvernail controls the instruments at the first trap.

A top contender in the A Class, Ray Brown's V8 '60' Eddie Meyer Special, turned 121.45. The roadster placed second in its class at this meet.

Unique feature of Bob Riese's B Roadster is the 3" tube frame that also serves as a radiator. This was the first dry lakes appearance for the roadster.

RIGHT—
Entrants make last minute checkups while awaiting their turn in starting line.

Comparative Timing

by J. ROBERT SETH

Editor's note — From Albuquerque, New Mexico, we have received some footnotes on the work of HRM Reporter Robert Seth. Mr. Seth organized the Roads Pilots club in Albuquerque. Since then there has been only one minor traffic offense in the club, that for illegal parking.

Recently a race was held at Gallup, N.M. (HRM, October, 1948). Mr. Seth reported the event for our readers. Untold, however, were some of the trials which beset Bob on that day. He made the trek to Gallup, with the Albuquerque supply trailer in tow. In the Fourth Heat (or Elimination) Bob placed second after losing a fuel pump mount and holding it in place with one hand, piloting the rod with the other. More than one reader in more than one state has written to HRM, praising the work of J. Robert Seth.

Many articles have been written about the speed and power that is developed by the rods at El Mirage, Harper, Mojave, etc. We all marveled at the speeds as they crept through the 140 mph range, and now the 150 mph mark has been passed. If times could be figured at an altitude handicap basis, these speeds would already be surpassed.

Recently it was reported that a rod near Denver, Colo. made a two-way run at 139.65 mph. That speed, considering the handicap he was driving under, is equivalent to about 164.32 mph at the standards of driving at such places as El Mirage. It is true though that if the car were taken to El Mirage it would act altogether different. It was built to run at about one mile altitude and like most rods it could not incorporate a device to compensate for altitude. Altitude is one of the greatest handicaps the hot-rodders in the midwest will be required to overcome. It hinders power and results in lower speeds and slower acceleration.

The 100 horsepower V8 engine will only develop 67.51 brake horsepower at 5,000 feet above sea level. This is due to the density of the air being lower, thereby containing less exygen per given weight. With less oxygen per cubic inch of displacement, there can only be so much gas mixed with the oxygen. Only so much power can be developed from a given amount of fuel. Due to less gas and air being used per stroke the power is cut down to a loss of 32.49% of the power that would be developed at sea level. It would be similar to running at 2/3 throttle.

What kind of results does this handicap bring? By comparative tests they are as follows:

Acceleration tests run over a half mile course, starting from a dead standing start and time over the course. The course consists of an asphalt strip, half mile in length, with a right angle turn to the left followed by a 400 ft. straight stretch and then a right angle turn to the right. Tests were run in California at about 400-ft. elevation and by the Albuquerque Road Pilots at about 5,800 ft. elevation.

Average in miles per hour to the nearest mile.

	400 feet	5,800 feet
Fastest car	72	50
Second	68	47
Third	67	47
Fourth	65	45
Fifth	63	44
Sixth	62	44

The cars were similar in both cases. The tests were first run in New Mexico and then similar cars, with as near as possible, identical equipment ran at 5,800 feet. All cars were V8 or Merc, with the exception of the sixth which were both four barrels. It is very noticeable that the speed ratio stayed quite close to 3 to 2. The deviation from this could be attributed to efficiency of the drivers.

By running similar tests at top speed the following comparative charts on speeds were prepared. The charts give the comparative speeds from sea level to the car being driven at 5,000 feet.

1	 90	119.2
2	.... 93.4*	123.75*
3	 100	132.40
4	.... 101*	133.62*
5	.... 101.6*	134.21*
6	 110	145.64
7	 120	149.72
8	.... 123.4*	149.19*
9	 130	158.27
10	 140	165.4
11	 150	169.43

*Speeds at which actual tests were run.

The speeds were taken from a graph and are fairly accurate by theory and practical tests. It is quite noticeable that speeds climb fast to the point of 120-149 point. After that point the ratio declines. The reason for this is beyond the knowledge of the author. The chart was supplemented by information gathered from aircraft books and data. The Aircraft and rod data compare very closely even to the point of the peak of engine performance.

CLUB NEWS

NEW MEXICO

By J. Robert Seth

Plans are being made for the Union of the Albuquerque Road Pilots and the Albuquerque Midget Racing Association to form the governing body of racing in the duke city. The association has its own track that was completed for the first midget race on October 17, 1948. The rod races are planned for the beginning of the 1949 racing season.

A recent comment of the press made a drastic change from the usual policy. They placed the blame of an accident which involved a California Hot Rod tourist on the local citizen that made a famous left hand turn from the right hand curb. It was a welcome surprise and was the first rod accident in this locality for this year.

Several of the top rod personnel have spent much time debating the merits of inverted starts. As the object of inverted starts is for the benefit of the paying patrons, it has not proven to be for the best. Some hotheads just won't play that way, others gauge their speeds so that they will still be in the front of the feature and walk away while the rest fight the handicaps. We talked over the possibilities of setting up a point system where the inverted starts could be paid off with the improvement of position. It would tend to equalize the guys that fake speeds to obtain choice positions as the square boys moving up through the handicaps would collect as much or a share of the dinero that makes the rods run.

I have heard that the midget drivers and owners are batting the same idea all along the coast circuits. I believe that such a point system would make the sport more interesting to the paying patrons and the drivers themselves. I think that this is food for thought for all of us.

Members of the Road Pilots have noticed the plans of the SCTA to run acceleration tests. They would like to see such tests run in several parts of the country under similar conditions on similar courses, so that comparative data could be made. Such tests could be run without too much expense and equipment and be fair comparative data. The Road Pilots would like to take credit for such tests, but I ran a similar test under the colors of The Glendale Wolf Pack way back in 1939.

(Continued on Page 27)

Parts With Appeal

◀◀◀

What could be more appropriate for the outdoors than the air cleaner so neatly displayed by Miss Shirley Buchanan? Just the thing for keeping road dust out of a high-speed engine, this cleaner is small enough to be used on a dual setup. After all, who wants to have a dirty engine?

There's bound to be more than one part in HRM's Parts With Appeal feature. In this case, the other item is blond and curvacious Miss Buchanan. Shirley is a popular Carolyn Leonetti model. She has graced the covers of U.S. Camera, Arrowhead, and Personal Romances, as well as many other publications.

Shirley was born in North Dakota. She was schooled at North Dakota State and the University of Illinois. She got the modeling bug by winning a local beauty contest. Later she applied herself as a stewardess with United Airlines and literally flew her way to California where she began her modeling career.

During the past year alone, Shirley has been Queen of the Orange Show, Miss Import & Export for World Trade Week, Queen of the Boat Show and Miss Richfield. With all this to keep her busy, Miss Buchanan still finds time to work on Children's Hospital Benefits with the Assistance League. Shirley also enjoys making her own clothes and adding to her teacup collection.

At present M-G-M is considering her for parts in "Neptune's Daughter" and "Annie Get Your Gun."

Photo by Pete

Photo by Pete

Fifth in a series of Harman & Collins Record Holders

148.02 m.p.h.

This speed was turned in a 1 way qualifying run at an SCTA meet by Paul Schiefer in his Mercury roadster using a HARMAN and COLLINS cam.

HARMAN & COLLINS, INC.

5552 ALHAMBRA AVENUE   LOS ANGELES 32, CALIF.

CApitol 4610

Special Race Gears

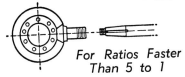

For Model "A"
"A" and "B" 1928-32

For Ratios Faster Than 5 to 1

Ratio	No. Teeth	Part No.
3.27	36-11	AJ111
3.78	34-9	AJ112
4.11	37-9	AJ113
*4.30	43-10	AJ114
4.56	41-9	AJ105
*4.62	37-8	AJ128
*4.88	39-8	AJ106

Stem Type Pinion

For Ratios Slower Than 5 to 1

*5.14	36-7	AJ107
*5.38	43-8	AJ108
*5.57	39-7	AJ109
*5.86	41-7	AJ110
*6.17	37-6	AJ116

V-8's 1933-48
V-8 10 Spl. 1933-34

Ratio	No. Teeth	Part No.
3.54	39-11	AJ121
4.11	37-9	AJ150
4.33	39-9	AJ152
*5.12	41-8	AJ127B

V-8 10-Spl 1935-37

3.54	39-11	AJ151
3.78	34-9	AJ122
4.11	37-9	AJ123
4.33	39-9	AJ124
*5.12	41-8	AJ127A

V-8 6-Spl 1938-47

3.54	39-11	AJ121A
3.78	34-9	AJ122A
4.11	37-9	AJ123A
4.44	40-9	AJ125
4.56	41-9	AJ126
*5.12	41-8	AJ127

(*) 5% Nickel

A. J. GETZ

4430 CARROLLTON AVENUE • **INDIANAPOLIS 5, INDIANA**

Southern California
Muffler Service

Mello-Tone Mufflers For All Cars 4.95 up	**DUAL MUFFLER SETS** 1935-48 V-8 & MERCURY—20.00 1949 V-8 & MERCURY—23.00	Exhaust Headers For All Fords 27.50 set & up

Free Illustrated Catalog

11142 Washington Place • VE 97038 • Culver City, Calif.

Drake Brothers Machine Shop
announce their new

FULL BALL-BEARING RACE CAR-TYPE LOCKED REAR ENDS WITH SAFEY HUBS FOR ROADSTERS

Also Prompt Service in

Cutting Drive Shafts, Milling and Redoming Heads
Punching Louvres in Steel or Aluminum Hoods
Novi-Governor Pistons

Phone LUcas 0748

3568 Fruitland Ave. • Open Saturdays • Maywood, Calif.

STATEMENT OF THE OWNERSHIP, MANAGEMENT, CIRCULATION, ETC., REQUIRED BY THE ACT OF CONGRESS OF AUGUST 24, 1912, AS AMENDED BY THE ACTS OF MARCH 3, 1933, AND JULY 2, 1946, of HOT ROD MAGAZINE, published monthly at Los Angeles, California, for October 1, 1948.

STATE OF CALIFORNIA }
COUNTY OF LOS ANGELES } ss.

Before me, a Notary Public in and for the State and county aforesaid, personally appeared ROBERT R. LINDSAY & ROBERT E. PETERSEN, who, having been duly sworn according to law, depose and say that they are the co-owners of the HOT ROD MAGAZINE, and that the following is, to the best of their knowledge and belief, a true statement of the ownership, management (and if a daily, weekly, semiweekly or triweekly newspaper, the circulation), etc., of the aforesaid publication for the date shown in the above caption, required by the act of August 24, 1912, as amended by the acts of March 3, 1933, and July 2, 1946, (section 537, Postal Laws and Regulations), printed on the reverse of this form, to wit:

1. That the names and addresses of the publisher, editor, managing editor, and business managers are: Publishers and Editors: Associates Robert R. Lindsay, 3517 Sawtelle Blvd., Los Angeles 34, Calif.; Robert E. Petersen, 7164 Melrose Avenue, Los Angeles 46, Calif.

2. That the owner is: (If owned by a corporation, its name and address must be stated and also immediately thereunder the names and addresses of stockholders owning or holding one percent or more of total amount of stock. If not owned by a corporation, the names and addresses of the individual owners must be given. If owned by a firm, company, or other unincorporated concern, its name and address, as well as those of each individual member, must be given.)

Hot Rod Publishing Company, 7164 Melrose Avenue, Los Angeles 46, Calif.

Robert R. Lindsay, 3517 Sawtelle Blvd., Los Angeles 34, Calif.

Robert E. Petersen, 7164 Melrose Avenue, Los Angeles 46, Calif.

3. That the known bondholders, mortgagees, and other security holders owning or holding 1 percent or more of total amount of bonds, mortgages, or other securities are: (If there are none, so state.) None.

4. That the two paragraphs next above, giving the names of the owners, stockholders, and security holders, if any, contain not only the list of stockholders and security holders as they appear upon the books of the company but also, in cases where the stockholder or security holder appears upon the books of the company as trustee or in any other fiduciary relation, the name of the person or corporation for whom such trustee is acting, is given; also that the said two paragraphs contain statements embracing affiant's full knowledge and belief as to the circumstances and conditions under which stockholders and security holders who do not appear upon the books of the company as trustees, hold stock and securities in a capacity other than that of a bona fide owner; and this affiant has no reason to believe that any other person, association, or corporation has any interest direct or indirect in the said stock, bonds, or other securities than as so stated by him.

5. That the average number of copies of each issue of this publication sold or distributed, through the mails or otherwise, to paid subscribers during the twelve months preceding the date shown above is: (This information is required from daily, weekly, semiweekly, and triweekly newspapers only.)

ROBERT R. LINDSAY,
ROBERT E. PETERSEN,
Publishers.

Sworn to and subscribed before me this 8th day of October, 1948.

RAY L. PARKER
[SEAL] (My commission expires Oct. 7, 1949.)

Laughs...from here and there

By TOM MEDLEY

Dorothy—"What's happened?" she asked her husband who had got out of the car to investigate the trouble.

Hal—"Puncture," he said briefly.

Dorothy—"You ought to have been on the lookout for this," was the helpful remark. "You remember the guide warned you there was a fork in the road."

Doctor (taking visitor around the asylum)—"This room is reserved for auto maniacs."

Visitor—"But the room is empty—are there no patients?"

Doctor—"Yes, but they are all under their beds, making repairs."

If you start on an automobile trip with the certainty of knowing where you are going—

If you don't have to stop every five minutes to look at your gas and oil—

If you stop at every signal and boulevard stop—

If you make every turn and detour correctly—

If you are driving along at just the right speed for safety and comfort—

Look around, brother: She's either asleep or she's fallen out somewhere!

Reckless Driver—"Hear those cylinders knocking?"

Timid Passenger—"It's not the cylinders, it's my knees."

The shortest perceptible unit of time is the difference between the moment the traffic light changes and that when the boob behind you honks his horn.

Policeman—(after collision) "You saw this lady driving toward you. Why didn't you give her the road?"

Motorist—I intended to, as soon as I could discover which half she wanted."

Policeman—"How did you knock him down?"

Los Angeles Motorist—"I didn't!" I stopped to let him go across and he fainted."

STROKER McGURK

HOT ROD HIJACKERS
STEPS TAKEN TO HALT SPEED EQUIPMENT THEFTS ON THE WEST COAST

In Southern California hot rodders and authorities have taken a grim outlook on the stolen goods situation. Many hot rods were reported stolen and, more recently, two large speed equipment houses were broken into and robbed. They were Bell Auto Parts of that city and Blair's Auto Parts of Pasadena. Bell lost about $1400 in goods and Blair reported over $2000 worth missing.

It's a pretty tough situation tracing stolen hot rods or parts thereof. Everyone is conscious of the easy changeability of a hot rod. The setup is comparable to the old stolen bicycle racket. A quick paint job, a couple of interchanged parts and they'd have a different bike . . . and a hard one to trace.

Two young hot rodders, both members of "The Dusters" club, reported their cars stolen sometime last May. They were George Christos and William Taylor of Los Angeles. Taylor's rod was parked in front of his house when it was stolen, while Christos' was in his own driveway. Months went by and the fellows had no word of their stolen autos. Meantime, George bought another car. On October 9 he went to the Department of Motor Vehicles in Hollywood to register the car. Two of his friends, Paul Bloome and Art Lord, went along for the ride. While standing in line, George struck up a conversation with William Hoffman who had just registered his hot rod.

As hot rodders will, the boys turned the conversation towards cars. Christos asked Hoffman what kind of car he had. Hoffman replied it was a '32. George then remarked his '32 had been stolen. Hoffman asked what kind of a setup he had on his car when it was stolen. George answered that he was running Navarro heads and an Ord manifold, whereon Hoffman got a "funny look" on his face. Christos and his friends became suspicious; so, they stepped outside to see if they could spot the car. They found it near-by. Close inspection showed that it was the car George's friend, William Taylor, had reported stolen. Everything on the car belonged to Taylor with the exception of the heads, windshield bracket, front tires and dashboard, all of which were Christos'.

At this point, George and his friends went inside the vehicle bureau, found Hoffman and took him to the near-by Hollywood Police Station where they explained the situation to detectives.

While Hoffman was undergoing questioning at the police station, George called his brother, Ted, and asked him to get in touch with Taylor. Ted, a member of the police motorcycle detail, then got Taylor over to the Hollywood station. While detectives talked to Hoffman, George asked him where he lived. He gave his address, whereon George and his friends started for that house. When they arrived, the trio went into the garage where they spotted a big loot, containing goods stolen from both Blair's and Bell Auto Parts. Further investigation showed that another garage in the same neighborhood held more stolen goods. Also recovered were 11 guns stolen from a Los Angeles sporting goods store.

Christos did not recover his roadster, although he understands the car was taken to Iowa for resale. Questioning of Hoffman, along with further investigations brought forth the names of a whole "ring" implicated in the thefts. George Christos deserves a good deal of thanks for making possible the apprehension of these persons.

On October 7 the roadster shown here

was stolen from Ned Cantillon and Paul Bousquet of Los Angeles. The '32 had no hood at the time of theft. Windshield was chopped to 6½", seats were of light blue leather. Dash had tachometer, 130 mph speedometer, vacuum gauge, amps and oil pressure dials.

Brake and clutch pedals were chromed as were arm-type shocks. The '41 Mercury engine ran Edelbrock heads and manifold. Readers are asked to be on the look-out for this car.

Most important is finding a remedy for these thefts, a means of stopping them before they happen.

In suggesting a remedy for thefts of hot rods and hot rod parts, Los Angeles police ask us to NUMBER all parts with metal hammer stamps and to make a list of these numbers. Other precautions can be taken, including building a lock on the steering apparatus of your car. This lock can be engaged while the car is not in use. If you value your equipment enough to want to hang onto it, you'll find it worth your while to take these steps towards keeping it.

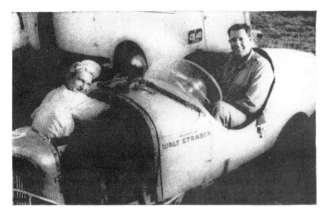

Owner Walt Straber and Driver Jim Morrison are well known in Indiana racing circles. Could Walt (Doctor of Motors) be performing an appendectomy?

Jack Reese in his Weber-equipped Four Barrel Flathead. This roadster may be seen around Visalia, California.

This long-hooded job belongs to John Wright of Dayton, Ohio, and houses '46 Ford 6. Original body was a sedan.

Joe Tashrio's '32 roadster runs a '37 Caddie engine. The scene is one of the palm-studded streets of Florida.

NORTHWEST CHAMPIONSHIPS
(Continued from Page 10)

On the 91st lap Russ Gilbertson finally went out for good with a severed ignition switch wire. Gorman then passed Koch on the 93rd lap to take over the lead which he held until the checkered flag. This was not Gorman's first win, as last season he was crowned Champion. This year, however, Bob Donker was high point man in the R.R.A.W. and Len Sutton became R.R. A.O. Champion.

The most amazing thing about this race was with 24 cars on a 1/4 mile track there was only one wreck and 19 out of the 24 cars finished.

Phil Phobert, last year's runner-up and a favorite, was unable to drive his fast car because of mechanical difficulties. He did drive a fine race and finished 9th in No. 28, a strange car to him.

Pete Lovely, a strong favorite in car 73 was forced to "stroke it" early in the race because of heating trouble.

The first twelve to finish are as follows:

1—John Gorman, No. 1—RRAW
2—Ernie Koch, No. 72—RRAO
3—Bob Donker, No. 5—RRAW
4—Howard Osborne, No. 76—RRAO
5—Verne Hansen, No. 81—RRAW
6—Ike Hanks, No. 888—RRAW
7—Bob Farr, No. 11—RRAW
8—Jerry Page, No. 30—RRAW
9—Phil Phobert, No. 28—RRAW
10—Len Sutton, No. 27—RRAO
11—Dan O'Heren, No. 42—RRAW
12—Dave Ware, No. 80—RRAO

During the time trials, car 37 hit the retaining wall in the 1st turn, jammed the throttle open, ran berserk thru the in-field and came to rest at the edge of the track on the second turn and burst into flames.

—Pan American World Airways Photo

ENGINEER BUILDS A HOT ROD: Judd Pickup (We're not kidding. That's his name.) Pan American Airways aeronautical engineer in San Francisco, California, built this roadster in his spare time. It has attracted more attention around the airline's base than the big planes that fly the Pacific. Judd is shown here with Toni Kibele, another PAA employee, in gay ninety getup. The car has a '29 A body, '34 V-8 rails. Engine is a big bore-big stroke '46 Mercury with Navarro heads and manifold. After the publicity picture was taken, Judd realized an ambition in leaving a little rubber on the airstrip.

CLUB NEWS

(*Continued from page 19*)

INDIANA

By MEL DUDLEY

Some time ago HRM received a letter asking why unsanitary conditions prevailed in the rest rooms of a certain Indiana race track. The question was forwarded to Mr. Dudley in that state.—ED.

In regard to the rest rooms at — —: They were very bad, but were much better this year. They were built new

from the ground up. I tried to get a picture but haven't yet. We have had to overcome many things like that. But for some reason beyond me tracks like that go better and hold up better than new and fancy plants.

The Mutual races have been going very smooth lately. Stover has his Hudson pretty sharp and has won a couple of features. Morrison's new motor is still buggy. Arnold has a new Mercury coming up any time now. Avery McAdams is trying to get a new Mercury going. Chuck Leighton is about tops when he runs but has been having a lot of tough luck. He is a hot little driver but needs a lot of polish yet. Beeson is coming along very nicely, but he has a lot of horses in that Chevrolet. He isn't exactly sure what to do with all of them yet.

The Triangle Association of Ohio has dropped everything except Shady Bowl at DeGraf, Ohio. These boys run with Mutual at Dayton on Saturday nights. That track is operated by Walt Scherer and his brother. Walt drives with us most of the time. He has promised me some pictures of some of the cars and drivers.

RACING JARGON

(*Continued from page 13*)

Herd—To herd (see Goat) means to drive.

Iron—A car, or engine.

Leadfoot—A driver who uses a heavy throttle, meaning that he is a fast driver.

Mount—A driver's car, or ride.

On His Head—A driver who has flipped, rolled or turned his car over.

On the Bubble—The pole position, or spot on the rail in the first row of cars in a race.

Rod—Abbreviation of hot rod, or roadster.

Tool—To drive, as "he sure *tools* that rod like an old-timer."

All readers interested in automotive design as a future are invited to a meeting to be held by Alexis de Saknoffsky at the California School of Art, November 15-16, 8:00 p.m.

Dry Lakes Results

S. C. T. A., Inc.
El Mirage Dry Lake
September 25-26

Place	Car	Entrant	Club	Speed	Points
A ROADSTER					
1	15	Spurgin & Giovanine	Albata	127.65	300*
2	36	Ray Brown	Road Runners	121.45	190
3	156	Don Parkinson	Low Flyers	116.42	180
4	157	Richard Fugle	Low Flyers	112.21	170
B ROADSTER					
1	1-R	Doug Hartelt	Lancers	140.62	300*
2	388	John Hartman	Pasadena Roadster	140.18	190
3	61	Jack Avakian	Road Runners	135.54	180
4	6	Palm & Conkle	Lancers	134.73	170
5	5	Bob Riese	Gear Grinders	133.13	160
5	33	Lloyd Kear	Mobilers	133.13	160
6	106	Starr & Alger	Lancers	129.68	150
6	149	Dick Finkle	Road Runners	129.68	150
6	299	Lehmann-Schwartzrock	Albata	129.68	150
7	393	Blinn & McCartney	Pasadena Roadster	129.49	140
8	146	Wilson & Knudsen	Road Runners	128.57	130
8	363	Vogel Bros.	Pasadena Roadster	128.57	130
9	470	Fred Oatman	Strokers	128.20	120
10	117	Guptill & Howard	Lancers	127.47	110
11	214	Carl Kaylor	Gear Grinders	127.11	100
11	321	Dan Busby	Dolphins	127.11	100
12	9	Tom Beatty	Stokers	126.93	90
13	132	Dean Batchelor	Road Runners	126.58	80
13	455	Arthur Tremaine	Strokers	126.58	80
14	436	Charles Clark	Clutchers	126.40	70
15	101	Don Olson	Lancers	124.48	60
16	307	Ernest Dewey	San Diego Roadster	124.13	50
17	27	Harvey Haller	Road Runners	123.28	40
18	318	Norm Lean	Dolphins	121.45	30
18	442	Jim Rawding	Clutchers	121.45	30
19	148	Donald Baker	Road Runners	120.96	20
20	453	Johnny Tracy	Strokers	120.80	10
20	477	George Kraycho	Strokers	120.80	10
C ROADSTER					
1	315	Paul Schiefer	San Diego Roadster	143.08	200
2	325	Harold Daigh	Dolphins	141.28	190
3	240	Barney Navarro	Glendale Stokers	139.75	180
4	305	Don McLean	San Diego Roadster	137.19	170
5	21	Ed Stewart	San Diego Roadster	132.15	160
6	47	Frank Leonard	Gophers	131.96	150
7	48	Bob Reemsnyder	Strokers	131.57	140
8	331	Doug Harrison	Dolphins	131.00	130
9	135	Peterman & Carrillo	Road Runners	130.43	120
10	30	Don Blair	Pasadena Roadster	130.05	110
11	104	Barber & Dolph	Lancers	129.12	100
12	200	Kenny Parks	Gaters	127.84	90
13	52	Frank Beagle	Strokers	127.29	80
13	140	John Harris	Road Runners	127.29	80
14	500	Jim Harber	Hornets	127.11	70
15	624	George Castera	Almega	126.93	60
16	55	C. W. Scott	Hornets	126.40	50
16	324	Dowell & Slawson	Dolphins	126.40	50
17	20	Harold Warnock	Lancers	126.05	40
17	461	Harold Osborn	Strokers	126.05	40
18	46	Bob Sykes	Lancers	125.17	30
18	59	Don Arnett	Clutchers	125.17	30
19	53	Coshow Bros.	Lancers	125.00	20
20	173	Don Lenk	Gophers	124.65	10
D ROADSTER					
1	34	Akton Miller	Road Runners	128.02	200
2	216	Stan Jones	Gear Grinders	127.11	190
3	463	Fred Woodward	Strokers	123.11	180
4	19	Burleigh Dolph	Lancers	122.11	170
A STREAMLINER					
1	555	Alex Xydias	Sidewinders	132.93	200
2	557	King & Hansen	Sidewinders	107.01	190
B STREAMLINER					
1	365	Marvin Lee	Pasadena Roadster	146.81	200
2	131	Breen & Haller	Road Runners	145.63	190
3	103	Path & Moore	Lancers	142.18	180
4	11	Stuart Hilborn	Low Flyers	136.36	170
5	222	Jim Lindsley	Gear Grinders	132.93	160
6	14	Phil Remington	Low Flyers	129.12	150
7	147	Fred Renøe	Road Runners	126.76	140
C STREAMLINER					
1	4	Burke & Francisco	Road Runners	148.51	200
2	319	Chuck Rotter	Dolphins	141.73	190
3	141	Jack McDermott	Road Runners	135.73	180
4	180	Hallman & Garrould	Gophers	126.22	170

(*—100 Points Added for New Record)

Pictured here is Conrad Curtis' dry lakes entry. Connie is editor of the Russetta Timing Association dry lakes program.

Bill Otto of Titusville, Florida, runs this roadster on the local tracks. The car is built on an A frame. Most of the body is constructed from a '42 Pontiac hood. The Mercury engine is Grancor equipped.

This '36 Ford runs Edelbrock heads, Thickston manifold, Harman & Collins cam with a '41 Mercury block. The car is owned by Leland Davis of Brookdale, California.

Belly-tank lakes entry turned 122.78 at Russetta meet. Dave Hunter, president of So. Pasadena Moles, owns the streamliner.

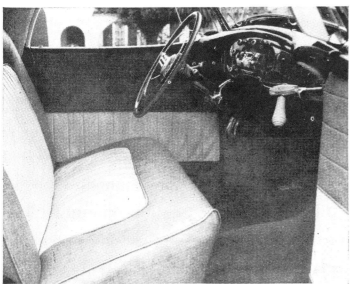

CUSTOM CAR

This sleek custom-built roadster belongs to Ray Giovannoni of Washington, D. C. Ray operates a speed shop in that city. He did much of the work on the car himself. Ray drove the car to the west coast to have a padded top fitted to it. The 1936 roadster has a '34 Ford V-8 engine, Eddie Meyer manifold, heads designed by Giovannoni, Harman & Collins cam. He runs Zephyr transmission cogs, Columbia rear end. Braking is full hydraulic. Column shift is from a '40 Ford. On the outside Ray has made many changes. Grill is from a Packard Clipper, running boards are removed, sides molded in. Seats, interior side panels and underside of the top are matching gray and white leather. The dashboard has been chopped and refinished in light brown. Ray's roadster caused much comment on its recent trip to the west coast. There is little wonder, trim job that it is.

LEWIE SHELL

HOT ROD
Magazine

Daigh's Record Roadster

DECEMBER, 1948 **25c**

PUT GERRY GRANT'S "140 M P H" KICK IN YOUR IRON

MY RACING COMBINATION
Built to eliminate DRAG

GRANT COMPRESSION RING

1. This ring keeps film of oil on cyl. walls.
2. It allows much freer running engine. Quick break-in.
3. Prevents blowby and power loss.
4. Gives upper ring lubrication.

GRANT OIL RING

1. My slanting grooves carry off only excess oil.
2. No spring used in back of oil ring in racing set-ups.
3. Is self-flushing on up and down strokes.

DEAR RODDERS:

I get a whale of a kick out of helping you put that "140 m.p.h. kick" in your iron. (More than one Grant user qualifies this).

. . . Thanks for all your swell cards and letters about my GRANT PISTON RINGS.

Keep me in mind next time you set up your job; and tell your competitors to send for my FREE catalog if they want more speed.

Gerry Grant

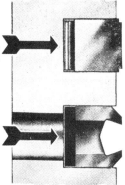

Get my Grant Micro-Finish Piston Pins

Get my Grant Inserts and Mains for your Fords and Mercurys.

Grant
MOTOR PARTS

Ask for Gerry Grant's Free Catalog
GRANT & GRANT, 241 N. Westmoreland Ave.
Los Angeles 4, California   FEderal 2185

Editor's Column

Here is the twelfth issue of HRM. A full year has passed since the first copy was placed on sale in Southern California and other spots. It hardly seems that long when you stop to think that Regg Schlemmer's amazing Mercury roadster was on the cover for setting an even more amazing 136.05 mph mark at S.C.T.A.'s last 1947 meet.

Once again a Schlemmer job comes to the front, this time under the handling of Roy Prosser in the C.R.A. Invitational Championship Race. Regg's No. 8 went for the checkered flag in the 20-lap championship runoff on October 31 at Carrell Speedway, Gardena, California. Complete coverage of the race is related by Dorothy Sloane on pages 14 and 15. There are excellent photos to illustrate Dorothy's accurate story.

Our cover car and driver are Harold Daigh of Paramount, California, and his Class C Roadster. The car, built by Harold and his brother, Chuck, was timed at 143.19 average during the final S.C.T.A. lakes meet of this year. Pictures, cutaway drawing and story appear on pages 16 and 17 of this issue.

More news and action from the Mutual Racing Association are presented by Mel Dudley on page 10.

Report on the October 30-31 meet of the S.C.T.A. may be found on pages 8 and 9, where some unusual lakes entries are featured. This meet was the last of the '48 season.

Walt Woron continues his BUILDING A HOT ROD series on pages 12 and 13. This, the second article in the series gives readers an idea of the different types of cars which can be built, suggestions on what to look for when purchasing the original model, etc.

Tom Medley's PERSONALITIES feature focuses on Red Renner, popular frackle-faced Indiana driver. The drawing and footnotes are on page 19.

The November issue of HRM carried a story on Comparative Timing by our able New Mexico Representative, J. Robert Seth. The article has caused quite a bit of controversy, some of which is offered in friendly rebutal on page 28 of the December issue.

We, the editors, the staff and our many representatives take this opportunity to thank our readers for their continued support and interest throughout 1948.

We also want to wish you all a MERRY CHRISTMAS and a HAPPY NEW YEAR.—ED.

"World's Most Complete Hot Rod Coverage"

TABLE OF CONTENTS

HOT ROD MAGAZINE, U.S. Copyright 1948 by the Hot Rod Publishing Company, 7164 Melrose Avenue, Los Angeles 46, California. Entered as second-class matter June 24, 1948, at the post office at Los Angeles, California, under the Act of March 3, 1879. SUBSCRIPTION PRICE: $3.00 per year throughout the world. Single copy—$.25. Circulation: 40,000 monthly. On sale at newsstands, tracks and speed shops across the country. Phone: WEbster 3-4433.

Vol. 1   *HRM—Published Monthly*   No. 12
Associate Editors...R. E. Petersen,
                                                     Robert R. Lindsay
Technical Advisers...........................Walt Woron, Wally Parks
Art Director..Alice Van Norman
Diagramatic Art ....Rex Burnette
Photography ....Paul Schaeffer, Vic Dreka,
                               Gene Vix, Dyson Smith, Pete
                               Lee Blaisdell, Howdy Williams
Cartoons and Humor..Tom Medley
Reporters.........................Dick Robinson, Richard K. Martin,
                            Pauline Bayer, J. Robert Seth,
                            Melvin Dudley, Howdy Williams
Subscription Department......................................Marilyn Lord
Distribution ....Gordon Behn

ON THE COVER: Harold Daigh "hot foots" it away from the starting line at S.C.T.A.'s October meet. The full belly pan Mercury holds the Class C Roadster record with an average of 143.19 mph. The car has been in constant S.C.T.A. competition during the 1948 season.

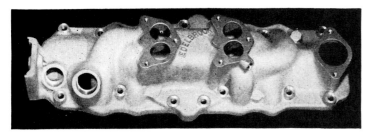

QUESTIONS
AND
ANSWERS

Q. I have a '32 Ford coupe. I am
putting a full race 100 H.P. Mercury
block in it. I would like to know if this
motor is too hot for such a small light
car. Should I have hydraulic brakes or
are mechanicals safe enough?

> Stuart Hartman
> Downey, California

A. Mercury engines are often used in
'32 frames with excellent results. Hydraulic brakes are suggested, but not necessary.

Q. I am in the process of building a
hot rod using a 1930 model A Ford coupe.
I am using 1946 Ford wheels on the rear,
but find that the lugs will only turn about
twice. How can I correct this unhealthy
situation?

> George Hough
> Evanston, Illinois

A. The best solution is to take the car
to a machinist and have the drums (not
the wheels) machined where the lugs fit.

Q. I am running a stock '48 Ford
with heads and manifold . . . No. 51 jets
(carburetor). My mileage is poor and pickup is fair. What do you suggest?

> Charles Insinger, Jr.
> Philadelphia, Pa.

A. Get a Keller carburetor kit from
your Ford dealer and have it installed. If
this doesn't bring the desired change, go
down on your jet sizes.

Q. I would like to know where I could
get information regarding specifications,
limitations, etc., of Class A, B and C rods.
Is it legal to use superchargers on A, B
or C rods, or do they belong in the unlimited class?

> Richard A. De Wolfe
> Rosamond, Calif.

A. The dry lakes class requirements
for both S.C.T.A. and Russetta Timing are
given in the article called Building a Hot
Rod, printed on pages 12 and 13 of this
issue. In S.C.T.A. superchargers shove the
entry up a class, except in cases where
the blower is stock equipment on the
American made engine being used. Blown
engines are moved up a class in the Russetta Timing Association also.

Q. Will the '49 Merc. crankshaft with
the 4-inch stroke fit in an older model
block or can it be made to fit, and how?
What type of rods and pistons must be
used if it will fit?

> Mack Christy
> Flagstaff, Arizona

A. The '49 Merc. crank will fit older
models. Of course, the longer stroke demands some attention. Get Mercury rods,
pins and pistons and you will have a perfect fit.

(Continued on page 26)

It's in the Bag...

HELPFUL TO AMATEUR MECHANIC
Dear Sirs:

I have been reading your magazine for quite a few months and have found it to be very interesting.

Although auto mechanics is not my type of work, I like to play around with my car whenever I get a chance . . . I can see where your magazine will really help a fellow a lot.

> Al Steiger,
> Philadelphia, Pa.

SUBSCRIPTION LIST JUMPS
Hot Rod Magazine:

Please enter my subscription to HRM starting with the November issue.

> Cpl. Chilton L. Culbertson,
> U.S. Army Paratroops,
> Fort Bragg, North Carolina

HRM PROVES ITS WORTH
Dear HRM:

We are way out here in Wyoming, but not too far to write and let you know what a wonderful break for the newly organized "Wyoming Auto Racing Club."

We are fortunate to have found a magazine which has proven its worth to all its enthusiastic readers and members of our club.

> Freddy Blume,
> Cheyenne, Wyoming

READER'S REQUEST
Gentlemen:

. . . I have a rather unusual request to make of you. However, it occurs to me that some of your other subscribers are in a similar position. In addition to your magazine I also subscribe to Road and Track Magazine, published in Burbank. . . . I have not received copies of this magazine for three months. Two letters (one registered) which I

sent these people to inquire about the delay, have been apparently delivered; but neither letter has been answered. I would appreciate your investigation of the Road and Track publishers' condition. In short, if you can ascertain that they are out of business or that publication has been delayed, and publish this information in your magazine . . . it will do me quite a service. I feel sure that others of your subscribers will also benefit. . . .

> Major Frank M. Newman
> Austin, Texas

Affiliated sources have given us the following information: For several months Road and Track has been subject to internal difficulties. At present there has been no release date given.— ED.

JARGON CORRECTIONS
Gentlemen:

. . . . Have just received the November issue, and wish to offer a couple of corrections to the article entitled "Racing Jargon".

First, the term "D.O." refers to dual overhead camshafts, not dual overhead valves. . . .

Second, under the heading of "Engine Rebuilding," and the paragraph on Stroking, Mr. Woron states that moving the piston pin toward the crown of the piston will result in increased piston displacement. Since the piston displacement is the product of the area of the piston, or cylinder and length of stroke, and the number of cylinders, the placing of the piston pin with relation to the head of the piston can in no way increase the cubic inch displacement of the engine. I agree that compression changes do occur with changing this relationship, but the piston displacement must remain the same for a given bore and stroke, regardless of changes in piston or connecting rod dimensions.

> J. R. Ackermann
> Dearborn Speed Shop
> Dearborn, Michigan

Reader Ackermann is correct on both counts.—ED.

FINAL MEET OF

OCTOBER 30-31 AT EL MIRAGE

After a week's postponement as a result of heavy rains which flooded the dry lake bed, the S.C.T.A. held its final meet of the 1948 season on October 30 and 31 at El Mirage. More than half of the lake surface was still under water and it was necessary to set up two separate courses for running the two days' events. Both courses were considerably shorter on the approach to the timed quarter mile than those which have formerly been used, thus making the speeds a little slower than usual.

In spite of the short course distances, three new records in the Roadster classes were established. In Class 'C', engines with 250 to 350 cubic inch displacement, Harold Daigh of the Dolphins Club raised his own record average of 140.955 mph. to 143.195 mph. Daigh also set the meet's fastest roadster qualifying time of 145.63 mph. which was also second fastest time of the entire meet.

In the 'B' Roadster class of competition Bob Riese's new No. 5 stepped out to win the top place in its class with a qualifying run of 137.61 mph. and then set a new record average of 137.190. The former records in this class have been held continuously by last year's champion Doug Hartlet whose last record stood at 134.280 mph. Doug made a determined attempt to hold onto the class record but the little Riese machine, with its super tank-nosed streamlining and advanced engineering set the pace too high.

As was expected, the veteran team of Spurgin & Giovanine once again raised their own record in class 'A' when their 1925 Chevrolet 4 cyl. roadster toured the two-way runs in an average of 123.655 mph., after having qualified at 125.52 earlier in the day. This gave them a perfect score in S.C.T.A. class competition since they succeeded in placing first and setting a new record in their class at every scheduled meet of the season. This feat brought them a total of 1800 points and won them the title of Season's Champions for 1948.

TOP—One of the many "Burke-built" entries, the Lodes Brothers' streamliner, leaves the starting line in a cloud of dust. This small-sized tank (50 gallons) timed 105.88 mph in A streamliner class.

ABOVE—Ed "Axle" Stewart in his unchanneled Ford set the fastest '32 roadster time at the meet. His time was 126.05 mph. Ed is a member of the San Diego Roadster Club. His car, one of the few unchanneled roadsters running, has a Mercury block.   Photos by Pete

TOP TO BOTTOM—

The Breene and Haller rear engine Mercury placed first in the B streamliner class. The car made a top speed of 140.40 mph.

Fred Renoe's "One-half Fast" car runs in the B streamliner class because of the chopped rear. Fred is the son of Richard Renoe, president of the Road Runners Club. Engine is a 249 cubic inch 1946 Ford.

Norm Lean brought out this razor-nosed roadster at the final meet. The roadster timed 125.17 mph in B class competition.

When Jim Woods wants to get at the engine of his Ford 6, he loosens two bolts on the body and props it up on its axle . . . rear, that is. This setup is convenient as the engine sets well back toward the firewall.

S.C.T.A. SEASON

Fastest time of the meet was again set by the Burke & Francisco Class 'C' wing-tank Streamliner with a time of 150.75 mph. This was the well-known "Sweet Sixteen" car that was on display at last year's Hot Rod Show in Los Angeles. As well as holding the present 'C' Streamliner record, the Burke-Francisco car holds the S.C.T.A. fastest one-way speed time of 153.32 mph., which was set at the August meet at El Mirage.

In other Streamliner classes of competition, Alex Xydias, So-Cal Speed Shop Spl. placed first with his 'A' Class Ford V8-60 tank job at 127.29 mph., and the Breene & Haller Mercury tank was first in Class 'B' with a qualifying speed of 140.40 mph. Stuart Hilborn's fuel-injection Streamliner, which has been a consistent winner in the 'B' Class, ran into transmission difficulties and placed second at 134.93 mph. and was closely followed by the Path & Moore tail-job which turned 133.72 mph.

Other noteworthy times made in the Roadster classes were Paul Schiefer's 'C' class speed of 139.53, Frank Leonard's 'C' class speed of 138.46, John Hartman's Class 'B' time of 137.19 made with a Wayne-equipped Chevrolet six, and Doug Hartelt's 135.13 class 'B' time. Only car to earn points in

the big engine 'D' Roadster class was Jot Horne's Duesenberg '32 roadster which qualified at 124.48 mph. In the small engine 'A' class Ray Brown's Meyer-equipped rear-engine Ford-60 'T' roadster took second at 121.95 while Dick Fugle's tank-nosed Ford-60 'T' placed third at 101.91 mph.

During the Saturday running, Marvin Lee's sensational Chevy-six rear-engine streamliner ran into difficulty and sheared a rear wheel, causing it to flip into the air and roll eight times. Since Marv's car is an outstanding example of safe and sound construction he emerged from the ride with only minor

(Continued on page 29)

INDIANA WINDS UP '48 RACING SEASON

MUTUAL PLANS WINTER MEETINGS AT CLOSE OF BIGGEST YEAR

By MEL DUDLEY

The annual association trophy banquet is set for Sunday afternoon, December 5, at the Hotel Roberts in Muncie. Members will start right in on the election of officers and the rules meetings. The rules committee, consisting of Dick Frazier and Owners Ermal McCormick (No. 62) and Joe Walls (Nos. 16 and 61) are busy drafting the proposed regulations which will be put up to the members for adoption. We also have some more social events coming up. Everyone is very much interested. Forty-nine will be the tenth season for the Mutual and, from all indications, will be the biggest yet by far.

Full Schedule for '49

It is probable that there will be about five races a week next year. There are some new cars under construction which look very good. These, along with those built this Fall, will make it pretty rough for anyone next season.

Closing Race at Sun Valley

This season's racing was completed on November 7 with a program at Sun Valley. Hurricane was represented at the race by the Erickson Brothers' Mercury driven by Bill Walker of Anderson. Little Baldy Metsker of Goshen, Harold Mowell of Springfield, Ohio, and

This unusual shot shows Cecil Simmons of Muncie (No. 15) giving the "bounce" to an Ohio entry (No. 26). Neither of the drivers lost control in this freak accident.

Jackie Johnson, midget driver of Indianapolis, were also visitors. There were plenty of thrills in the race, but no serious accidents. Avery McAdams hit the gate when his throttle stuck leaving the track. The car, which belongs to Leo Stohler, was out for the rest of the day, but Avery was unhurt.

The feature race was a thriller from start to finish. Renner and Frazier, starting in eighth and tenth respectively,

came through the pack. On the eighth lap Frazier pulled in line with Red. For three laps they were wheel to wheel. Then Frazier pulled away for a good lead. Renner was running with a broken shock which made it impossible for him to hold it on the turns. The last few laps saw Renner, Stover and Skinner fighting for second and they finished three abreast.

The new Mercury owned by Ermal McCormick of Markleville was given its baptism by Johnny Arnold. He won the fourth heat but tangled with No. 4 in the feature. Neither Arnold nor Junior Fort in No. 4 were hurt, but both cars were out. These two new cars will be heard from next year.

Frazier on Top

Dick Frazier and his No. 32 are still the undisputed champions although Renner and Stover were able to make him fight the limit when they got going at the last of the season.

Here are the standings at the end of the '48 season:

Driver Standings

1—Dick Frazier (Muncie)	1799
2—Ralph "Smokie" Stover (Muncie)	1501
3—Jimmy Morrison (Muncie)	1314
4—Johnny Arnold (Muncie)	1224
5—Sam Skinner (Muncie)	1144
6—Red Renner (Woodburn)	1074
7—Bobby Beeson (Shirley)	1006
8—Gene Pyle (Dunkirk)	829
9—Buzzie Henline (Kokomo)	621
10—Jr. Fort (Markleville)	447
11—Joe Nestor (Fairview)	421
12—Ed Ball (Calif.)	411
13—Wayne Alspaugh (Newcastle)	374
14—Harold Mowell (Dayton)	353
15—Mickey Potter (Ft. Wayne)	324
16—Everett Burton (Wheeling)	272
17—Paul Fleet (Anderson)	268
18—HIG Hillegas (Huntington)	230
19—Ray Erickson (Chicago)	186
20—Bob King (Muncie)	169

TOP—At Sun Valley (Anderson, Indiana) fans, drivers and crews stand during the traditional playing of the Star Spangled Banner. Driver Bobby Beeson (inset) sits at the wheel of Maurice Mutersbaugh's roadster. Maurice stands at right. Bobby is the "Racing Farmer" of Mutual. BELOW—A couple of the Mutual boys hit the throttle during a race at Sun Valley.

Photos by Wayside Studio

B Class Coupe Record holder Lou Baney with his 123 mph V8.

Frank Leonard drove his channeled T to top place in the B class.

Three New Records At Russetta Meet

The last Russetta Timing meet of 1948 was held on November 7 with new records being set in several classes.

Fastest coupe time of the day was Lou Baney's '32 V-8 turning 119.84 and 123.11 for a 121.475 average. This established a new record in Class B coupes.

In the A coupe competition Bob Pierson timed 120.32 while B. Subkoski timed 110.56, neither of them approaching Don Brown's record of 123.12.

Fran Hernandez came close to Brown's C class record of 120.80 in his fenderless coupe. His time: 119.20 mph.

Topping the other B roadster contestants by ten mph, Frank Leonard averaged 139.22 with one-way time of 135.13 and 143.31.

A new C roadster record of 134.00 was set by Bob Riese of the Drifters. However, his record was not official as all Drifter entries' times were voided because the club shirked its assigned lakes duties. Many association members felt that this punishment hardly seemed fair, contending that the speeds attained should stand and punishment be given in another manner. As the records now stand, Ak Miller now holds the C roadster record with a 123.11 average.

Hutters entry Bob Reemsnyder drove the fastest A roadster entry for a time of 122.95. Class record is held by Jim Guptill at 125.51.

In the streamliner classes Bob Tattersfield made record runs, timing 137.19 and 135.95 for a 136.57 average in his V8 belly tank.

Dave Hunter in the Moles belly tank took the B class record with a 126.51 mph average after Drifter Frank Breene's average of 141.96 was disqualified.

Next year promises to be a bigger year for Russetta Timing with revisions in rules, organization and car classifications now under way. In one season of running as an incorporated body Russetta Timing Association has done much to prove that coupes have a definite place in timing competition.

A Coupes

		Qualifying Time
1.	Bob Pierson	120.32
2.	B. Subkoski	110.56
3.	Walt Redman	104.04
*	A. S. Collinsworth	99.77
*	Dick Thomas	97.82
4.	K. C. Moore	93.65
5.	Holbert & Jackson	92.02
6.	Lou Baney	85.06
7.	Frank Jennings	80.50

B Coupes

1.	Lou Baney	123.11
2.	Don Towle	116.58
3.	Marion Thompson	111.32
*	Willie Faughnder	107.39
4.	Jim Sherman	104.40
5.	D. L. Morgan	103.44
6.	Willie Werder	100.00
7.	Lynn Yaket	99.77

C Coupes

1.	Fran Hernandez	119.20
*	Jack Colori	114.50
2.	Robert Cantley	112.50
3.	Carl Nickoloff	105.35
*	Chas. DeWitt	100.55
4.	Chas. Townsen	99.82
5.	Carl Taylor	99.77
6.	Eugene Husting	97.82
7.	Jay Henry	95.23

A Roadsters

1.	Bob Reemsnyder	122.95
2.	Jackson & Holbert	119.68
3.	Roland Mays	119.52
4.	Bruce Robinson	118.42
5.	Fred Norton	113.78
6.	George LaRue	111.80
*	John Sundin	105.26
*	Jim Lindsley	105.01
7.	Cliff Crane	99.44

B Roadsters

1.	Frank Leonard	143.31
*	Doug Hartelt	128.57
*	Harvey Haller	123.62
2.	Dick Jones	117.03
3.	Dean Moon	116.12
4.	Phil Weiand	102.11
5.	Leroy Scheel	100.22
6.	Don West	90.90

C Roadsters

*	Bob Riese	138.88
1.	Earl Keithly	120.96
2.	Ken Arnold	117.03
3.	George LaRue	115.08
4.	Rulon McGregor	114.35
5.	Gerald Butler	112.21
6.	Joe Warner	110.42
7.	Bob Mahen	110.02

A Streamliners

1.	Bob Tattersfield	137.19
*	Jim Lindsley	123.96
2.	S. C. Davidson	115.53

B Streamliners

*	Frank Breene	146.10
*	Akton Miller	131.57
1.	Dave Hunter	128.38
2.	Frank Wilkson	112.21
3.	Tom Koulan	106.25
4.	Don Ricks	74.43

*Drifters times were disqualified.

RECORDS

A Coupe		
Don B. Brown		123.12
B Coupe		
Lou Baney		121.47
C Coupe		
Don Brown		120.80
A Roadsters		
Jim Guptill		125.51
B Roadsters		
Frank Leonard		139.22
C Roadsters		
Akton Miller		123.11
Streamliners		
A—Bob Tatterfield		136.37
B—Dave Hunter		126.51

RIGHT—A full pan extends from the nose to the rear of Bob Cantley's 36 coupe. He placed 2nd in Class C at 112.50 mph.

BELOW—Addition of a tail to the familiar drop tank gives the Tattersfield entry a weird appearance. With a borrowed engine the car clocked 136.57 mph for a new record.   Photo by Pete

BUILDING A HOT ROD
By WALTER A. WORON

Classification and Selection

When the average person begins to build a hot rod, he is somewhat at a loss as where to start, and what points should be emphasized. Naturally, this depends mainly on the use the car is to be put to: whether it is for track or dry lakes use, or whether it is for use as a custom street job.

If a track job is desired, probably the most economical and practical method is to start from scratch. That is, pick up a frame, axles, wheels, etc., from a junkyard, buy an engine and accessories and build up from there.

If a strictly lakes hot rod is desired, probably the same procedure can apply, whereas if a combination street-and-lakes job, or just street rod is wanted, this can begin with a stock car, stripped down, and then built up from there.

Before delving into construction details, however, it is advisable to consider future possibilities of the car. For example, a street job may be built up and later developments might arise that would make it advisable to enter the car in track or dry lakes competition. For this reason, the more important points of the basic types are listed, which should be kept in mind during the construction of a particular type of car.

Track Job

A hot rod for track use is, generally, a standard size, stock roadster body of unaltered contour, powered by an American Automotive Production engine of 300 cubic inch displacement unblown, or less.

More specifically, the most important limitations and restrictions on track hot rods, as set up by the California Roadster Association (and used quite generally by the majority of hot rod racing associations), are as follows:

The body must be so suspended that the road clearance at the rear of the car is between 17 and 26 inches, with steel or tubular bumpers (stock not allowed) installed to within 17 to 23 inches of the ground. The car, of a wheelbase not less than 99 inches nor more than 115 inches, must not weigh less than 1200 pounds nor more than 2600 pounds. The tread should be between 50 and 58 inches.

Unlike a street hot rod, glass cannot be used for the windshield. Instead, an acrylic plastic, such as Plexiglas, Lucite, or Pyrolin, should be used. In addition, all headlights and/or tail lights must be removed or recessed. The doors must be welded or securely fastened and all exterior accessories must be removed. Fenders and fender braces are not permitted, and the car must be equipped with a full hood and radiator shell.

Engines equipped with overhead cams are not allowed and, if the engine is blown, it must be under 183 cubic inches displacement. The car must have a positive-neutral clutch and a fireproof firewall between the engine and cab.

Wheels used on the hot rod cannot be over 20 inches in diameter, nor under 15 inches, and double-acting shocks must be installed at all four wheels. Suitable brakes must be installed.

Every rod must be equipped with a cut-off ignition switch and a fuel shut-off valve, both within easy reach of the driver.

Four-wheel-drive cars are not allowed.

Most racing and timing associations require safety belts.

Lakes Car

Before building up a hot rod for lakes use, first consider the class to be entered, for there are various classes and several types of body designs that are specified for lake meets. In the SCTA, for example, there are two body groups, with these two groups being broken down into four further divisions of varying cubic inch displacement. However, since late rule changes may alter these class divisions somewhat, it is always advisable to check with the association before the actual hot rod build-up.

One of the two SCTA classes is known as the roadsters, taking in cars that are equipped with American Production Roadster bodies of unaltered height, width and contour. Streamlining of the chassis and of the grille is the only allowable change in contour. (This is now a subject of much controversy.) Any streamlining aft of the firewall automatically bans the car from the roadster class. Minimum wheelbase in the roadster class is 95 inches. A pick-up body may be run in the roadster class, provided that the cargo bed is 36 inches or longer and is of standard width and height.

Any car that cannot make the roadster class due to streamlining or change in body contour is placed in the streamliner class. This class does not allow stock bodies, coupes or sedans, however, and the minimum wheelbase is set at 85 inches.

Engines for both the streamliner and roadster classes must be of American Automotive Production manufacture, with the car being classified according to engine displacement. If the engine is equipped with a supercharger or double overhead cams, it is placed in the next higher engine class.

The four class divisions of roadsters and streamliners are as follows:

Class A—0 to 183 cubic inches.
Class B—183 to 250 cubic inches.
Class C—250 to 300 cubic inches.
Class D—300 cubic inches and over.

Some stock engines and their respective classes in accordance with the above, are as follows:

Class A—Ford V-8 60, Chevy 4, and Ford Model T; Class B—Ford A's and B's, Chevy 6, Ford V-8, Ford 6, Merc; Class C—Oldsmobile 8, Lincoln Zephyr ('35-'41) and Cord V-8; and Class D—Lincoln Zephyr ('42-'47), La Salle V-8, Cadillac V-8, on up to the Marmon V-16, which has 490.8 cubic inches of displacement.

This is typical of a roadster adaptable for both street and lakes use. Here the car is rigged for lakes use. A few additions and changes will qualify it as a street job.
Photo by Pete

The track roadster generally looks similar to this job. Most track cars are strictly for racing, cannot be driven in traffic.   Lee Blaisdell Photo

Technical regulations governing the cars are, in general, the same as those set down by the CRA for track roadsters, with the exception that dimensional limits, outside of minimum wheelbase, are not set forth. Glass cannot be used for the windshield, exhaust outlets must be so arranged that they are directed away from the driver, fuel tank and tires; metal engine hoods must be used, although hood side panels are not required; either floorboards or belly pans must be provided; full metal firewalls must be installed; fire extinguishers must be attached in the car within easy reach of the driver; and all construction details of the car must be of the highest workmanship.

Most street roadsters can be designed in such a manner that they would be eligible to enter dry lakes competition in the SCTA; however, if the car is such that it cannot be quickly converted to meet the entry requirements of one of the two body classes, it can possibly be entered in Russetta Timing Association meets.

The RTA, although having practically the same standards to meet as the SCTA, permits a wider variety of entries, by allowing coupes and sedans to enter competition. The classes are as follows:

Coupe A: Must have stock fenders; the body may be cut or channeled, but not both.

Super Coupe B: Fenders not required; may have reduced frontal area; may be cut, channeled or have a belly pan.

Coupe Unlimited C: Takes in coupes of above two classes that use dual overhead cams and/or engines that have over 300 cubic inches displacement.

Roadster A: Fenders not required, but body must sit on top of frame; frontal area cannot be reduced; belly pans are not permitted.

Super Roadster B: May have reduced frontal area, may be channeled and have a belly pan.

Roadster Unlimited C: Takes in coupes

of above two classes that use dual overhead cams and/or engines that have over 300 cubic inches displacement.

Streamliners: No limitations on body design, except that if the engine has dual overhead cams or is over 300 cubic inch displacement, it moves up into the next classifications, which is Streamliners, Unlimited.

Note: If the engine is blown, the car moves up one class. For example, a Coupe A that has a blower moves up into the Super Coupe B class.

The car must be equipped with good brakes; the headlights must be removed or be taped; a metal firewall must be installed; the car must have a windshield or the driver must wear goggles; the car must have either a floorboard or belly pan; drivers must wear crash helmets; if the car has springs, it must have shocks; the exhaust outlet must be aft of the firewall; and the turtle deck must be secured.

Street Job

It will be assumed, for the purposes of this discussion, that the average reader is primarily concerned with the intricacies of building up a street hot rod; however, since there are no requirements set up by any organization (ex-

cept those dictated by common sense) there will be, naturally, many controversial points. An example of these might be any one of the following: the best grind cam, the best compression ratio, the manifold best suited to a V-8, etc.

When taking one of the several methods of beginning the build-up of a hot rod — that of buying a car in fair shape and proceeding from there—the important point to consider at first is the frame, and not the engine. In considering high speeds, the reason for this will be evident, for, in order to attain the best performance it will be necessary to thoroughly rework the engine. In addition, if the frame is in good condition, the time and labor that would be spent on this part of the car can be spent, instead, on the most vital part of a hot rod—the mill, or engine.

A rough check of frame alignment can be made by sighting down each of the rear wheels to see if the car "tracks." If the body is in good condition, as indicated by a close examination of the doors in relation to the body framework, this will also save time that can be devoted to more important details.

The majority of other items are not too important if a great deal of conversion work is to be done, and can be based on an evaluation of their condition as versus the cost. For example, the front axle will probably be replaced with a dropped axle, new springs and shocks will be installed, the engine will be rebored, ported and relieved, engine accessories, such as high-compression heads, special intake manifold, high-lift cam, etc., will be added, and the interior will be redecorated.

In building up any hot rod, regardless of the type, it should be remembered that the product can be no better than its producer. The greater the amount of time and effort that is expended in the construction of a hot rod, the better the result will be.

In the streamliner class, the most popular type has a body constructed from an airplane belly tank. The streamlining effect gives the car a great advantage over conventional contour jobs.   Lee Blaisdell Photo

CRA Holds Championship

54 ENTRIES TURN OUT FOR FINAL RACE OF THE YEAR

TOP—Roy Prosser, 1948 Champion, is shown at the wheel of Regg Schlemmer's powerful roadster. Roy's handling of the car proved worth seeing. Unlike the usual run of car-driver combinations, Roy seemed to have complete control of the car even on the fast turns.

ABOVE—Allen Heath piloted Duke Randall's No. 95 during the day's program. Shown here during the 20 lap runoff, Allen tries to hold back Troy Ruttman. The couple had been thrown together in a special match race earlier. The event turned out to be a dud; however, they made it up during the runoff where the big money lies.
Photos by Pete

The California Roadster Association gave the race-minded public their money's worth when they put on their annual National Championship Race at Carrell Speedway, Gardena, on Oct. 31st.

A fine turnout of 54 cars filled the pits with plenty of excitement as the owners and mechanics made last-minute changes in an effort to qualify for one of the positions that made up the show.

There were 156 laps of racing. Each of the four heat races was made up of eight instead of the usual six cars. This made two sets of sixteen cars for the twin 50 lappers. The top five finishers of each main went into the 20-lap runoff to determine who would take home the beautiful trophy which was presented by Hot Rod Magazine. A twelve-car consolation race gave some of the slower boys a chance to at least break even on expenses.

Roy Prosser, dapper little flyweight, almost cleaned the field for the day, winning everything he ran but the trophy dash, which he finished a close second to Jim Rathman.

Both of these boys have been east for the '48 season, Jim with his own car and Roy driving Regg Schlemmer's Number 20 for the first part of the season and finishing in big cars.

Roy has been one of C.R.A.'s top drivers and, with three months away from base, was still in sixth spot in point standings.

Schlemmer sold his roadster after only four races

BELOW—The Trophy Dash featured the four fastest cars instead of the usual two. They were Jim Rigsby in No. 1 position on the pole, Troy Ruttman on the front row outside, Roy Prosser—pole position, second row, and Jim Rathman in the fourth starting spot. Rathman (hidden behind Rigsby) worked his way up to get and hold the lead in the dash. Prosser placed second.
Photo by Dyson Smith

ABOVE—Jim Rathman (X) and Jim Rigsby (77) battle it out during one of the heat races.
Photo by Pete

National Race At Gardena

LEFT—Roy Prosser is shown receiving the Hot Rod Magazine Trophy from Monti Mae Figaro.

BELOW—Roy also received other awards for placing first in the 1948 championship race.

Photos by Pete

By DOROTHY SLOANE

and Roy went into big cars where he drove 35 races from South Dakota to Florida, competing in 12 state fairs and never finishing lower than fifth.

The car Roy drove in the C.R.A. National Championship race was also Schlemmer's. Regg is building up a big car for Roy to drive in the coming A.A.A. races.

Rathman spent the whole season in the east driving the beautiful bronze job that C.R.A. had on display in their booth at the last Hot Rod Show. He cleaned up on racing and then sold his car before coming home and will begin all over to get ready for next year.

The boys' experiences must have taught them plenty as they were without doubt the fastest and hardest cars to catch on the track.

They started side by side in ninth and tenth spot in the first 50-lapper and finished one and two with Roy taking the lead in the second lap and holding it all the way to finish a good half a lap ahead of everyone.

Duke Randall was on hand after a long absence during which he completely rebuilt his number 95. He had Allen Heath, one of the top notch midget drivers for U.R.A., at the wheel. Allen and Troy Ruttman, who started his racing career with the roadsters but has moved up into the midget field with Heath, continued their famous fued when they qualified for the second 5-lap event.

Heath sat in the pole position in the line-up while Troy was way back in eleventh spot. Heath took the lead and held it for 25 laps. Troy had moved up into second place by the 17th lap and took the lead in the 26th, lost it to Heath in the 33rd, but regained it in the 41st and held it to finish first. Heath still held second and Lou Figaro came in third.

For the run-off Prosser started on the pole in the last row with Rathman right in front of him and Troy Ruttman beside him in tenth position. Heath was in eighth spot directly in front of Troy.

(Continued on Page 23)

BELOW—Joe James (R4) passes safely as Chuck Leighton cracks into the crash wall on the south turn. This action in the first 50-lap main event was due to a blown tire.

LOWER LEFT—Shortly after the start of the first 50 lapper Dick Vineyard (57) and Bob Scott in No. 48 make their bids for first spot. Joe James in No. R4 is close behind them.

The power plant of Harold Daigh's record-holding Class C roadster is a bored and stroked '40 Merc of 268 cubic inch displacement. The bore is 3 5/16 inches, while the crank has been stroked 1/8-inch by Miller. The engine is electronically balanced and uses Navarro 9 1/4:1 heads.

The engine was originally set up to run on gasoline, but was later switched to alcohol, and now can use either gas or alcohol for fuel. In order to use gasoline, the jet sizes in the twin Stromberg carburetors (used in conjunction with a Navarro dual manifold) are changed from 89 mains and 50 wells to 63 mains and 48 wells. An aircraft-type hand pump is used to pressurize the fuel tank.

Additional engine accessories inclued a Smith & Jones 272 cam, a Filcoolator oil cleaner, twin Wico mags, and Douglas exhaust headers.

The transmission uses a straight high gear and a 3.27:1 gear in place of the 3.54 gear used originally in the '32 ball bearing locked rear end.

The chassis and body are conventional, consisting of an A frame and a '27 T body. The radius rods are from a Model A, while a '32 dropped axle is used in the front. Torsional suspension is featured in the front, with a transverse leaf spring and friction shocks installed in the rear.

The wheels for the roadster were made for Daigh by the Motor Rim and Wheel Company and are used in conjunction with Ward 5.00:16 tires in front and Firestone 7.50:16 tires in the rear. Hydraulic brakes are installed on the rear wheels only.

Daigh has actually had coparatively little trouble with the car since late last season, when he, his father, and brother jointly built up the car. (At the last lakes meet of the '47 season—the first time out—he used his brother's engine in the car.) Since that time, he has installed the '40 Merc in the car and has made minor changes, such as a change in exhaust valve angle and the replacement of the original ignition with the twin Wico mags. This latter change, however, was made after the October SCTA meet in which Daigh set the existing Class C Roadster record of 143.195 m.p.h.

Providing he can find a sponsor for his car, Daigh will enter his car in track hot rod races during the '49 season, and, from present indications, he is sure to provide stiff competition to all comers.

(Continued on next page)

Construction Cutaway

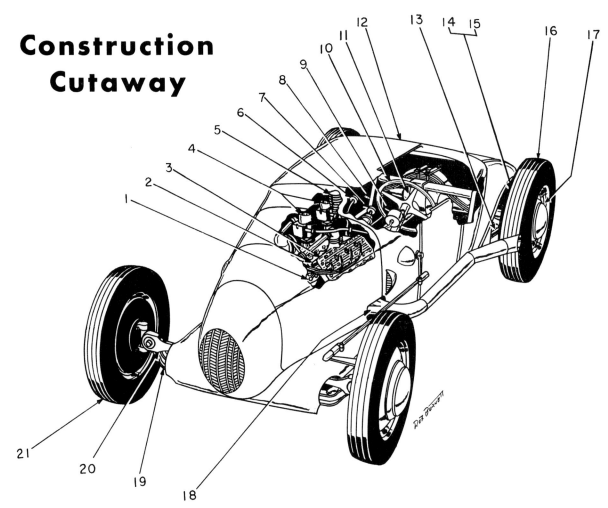

1. Wico mags on Barker V-Drive
2. '40 Mercury engine
   268 cubic inches
   Electronically balanced
   Smith and Jones cam
3. Navarro heads and manifold
4. Stromberg 97's
5. Filcoolater oil cleaner
6. Transmission—straight high gear
7. Aircraft hand pump
8. '29 A frame
9. Sun Tachometer
10. Franklin steering
11. 3.27 rear end
12. '27 T body
13. A radius rods
14. Rear hydraulic brakes
15. Friction shocks on rear
16. 750x18 Firestones on rear
17. Motor Rim & Wheel built wheels
18. Douglass headers
19. '32 dropped axle
20. Torsion type front suspension
21. 500x16 Wards on front

Wishbone is split with drag link passing through the eye. Note axle fairing which helps to cut down the overall drag on the roaster.   Photos by Pete.

Engine is set deep in the body for better balance. During dry lakes competition an extra "hood" covers the two carburetors to allow for free flow of air. The engine gets its spark from two Wico magnetos. The $\frac{1}{8}$" bore and $\frac{1}{8}$" stroke add up to a Class "C" displacement of 268 cubic inches.   Photos by Pete.

Foot pedal is on far right and pressure pump is easily accessible. The right side of the cockpit is covered with a tarp to cut down wind resistance.

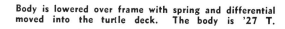

Body is lowered over frame with spring and differential moved into the turtle deck. The body is '27 T.

The Daigh Brothers with Harold's record-holding roadster.

HOT ROD OF THE MONTH

(Continued from Page 17)

When a roadster gets into the 145-mile-an-hour bracket, that's news! An official S.C.T.A time of 145.63 m.p.h. was set by Harold Daigh on the fast leg of a record run at El Mirage. That was on Saturday, October 30. The return run averaged out at 143.19 m.p.h.

Brothers Harold and Chuck Daigh have worked on Harold's roadster since 1947. The car was first run, using the engine and other equipment from Chuck's own car, at S.C.T.A.'s final meet of the '47 season. It was timed at 123 mph at that meet. Since then, Harold has been busy making improvements on the Navarro equipped roadster. At the second S.C.T.A. meet of this year, he reached 135 mph. Chuck, on the other hand, has busied himself with his own entry.

Harold was born in Ontario, California. The Daighs now live in Paramount, formerly known as Hynes, also in California.

Harold is president of both the Coupes Club, a member of the Russetta Timing Association, and The Drones, an independent Southern California outfit. His S.C.T.A. membership is with the Dolphins.

For the future, Harold has hopes of building a streamliner. That is, "If the S.C.T.A. can get a good strip for timing." He feels that the times being reached at El Mirage today are about as fast as they will go under present conditions. He is a member of the California Roadster Association and so far has worked with the group as a mechanic. However, he feels that he is somewhat qualified as a driver, having put in two seasons of Sunday racing in '60' midgets while stationed in the Florida area during the war.

As of the final dry lakes timing meet of S.C.T.A.'s 1948 season, Harold Daigh had piled up a total of 1150 points in his white Class C roadster. This total places him in about sixth spot in the S.C.T.A. points standings for 1948.

PERSONALITIES By TOM MEDLEY

- RED - RENNER

POPULAR INDIANA RDSTR DRIVER. RED, WHO HAILS FROM WOODBURN INDIANA, IS 21 YRS. OLD and HAS BEEN DRIVING SINCE LATE '46. HE HELD THE RECORD at WINCHESTER IN A FORD "6" AT :23.68 — TILL FRAZIER BROKE IT THIS YEAR!

ALL THESE NUMBERS CONFUSE ME!

BOY THESE CALIFORNIA CARS REALLY HAVE THE OATS!

RED HOLDS THE RECORD FOR TELEPHONE NUMBERS in THE CIRCUIT!

HIS HARD DRIVING and GOOD DISPOSITION ARE WELL KNOWN ON THE MID-WEST TRACKS

RED DRIVES NO. 20, THE CALIFORNIA BUILT RDSTR THAT HELD THE DRY LAKES RECORD OF 148:27 M.P.H.!

TOM MEDLEY -48-

Parts With Appeal

◀◀◀

When it comes to hot rod equipment, who would want to be without their dash mount hand air pressure pump? A polished and ready to install unit, this hand pump is similar to the race car side mount pump. It has a flange mounting for fitting in the roadster instrument panel. The pump is made of 24 ST Dural with heat treated cast alloy ends. And, of course, it features the efficient check valve used in the race car pump.

It is not often that a pressure pump is seen in such interesting surroundings. Pretty Billie Jeanne Eberhart graces the December Parts With Appeal feature. Billie was born in Laramie, Wyoming, nineteen years ago. She was schooled there until her sophomore year, when she moved with her family to the West Coast. Settling in the famed San Fernando Valley, she graduated from North Hollywood High School.

Miss Eberhart has proved herself artically inclined in several ways. Since the age of five she has been a singer and dancer. In recent years she has appeared in many plays and stage performances as well as a number of motion pictures. Billie majored in liberal arts in school. She is accomplished at oil painting, specializing in still life. Next year she plans to continue her schooling with a college course. As yet, she has not decided on a school. Her final artistic interest is her modeling career. In this field she works under the guidance of the Dorothy Preble Agency. Favorite sports include skiing and horseback riding. Other specifications: 110 lbs., 5' 6", brown hair and brown eyes. Hand pressure pump manufacturers are expecting a great boom in sales after seeing Billie Jeanne Eberhart with their product. It is generally agreed that, during December of 1948, the hand pressure pump is certainly a "Part With Appeal."

Photo by Pete

Photo by Kent Hitchcock

Sixth in a series of Harman & Collins Record Holders

92.54 m.p.h.

L. O. Turner's "Green Hornet" set a world record in the 225 cu. in. Div. II hydroplane class at the Salton Sea on Oct. 18, 1948, using a HARMAN & COLLINS cam.

HARMAN & COLLINS, INC.

5552 ALHAMBRA AVENUE - LOS ANGELES 32, CALIF.

CApitol 4610

S.C.T.A. DRY LAKES RESULTS
OCTOBER 30, 31, 1948

A ROADSTER

Place	Car	Entrant	Club	Speed	Points
1	15	Spurgin & Giovanine	Albata	125.52	300*
2	36	Ray Brown	Road Runners	121.95	190
3	157	Richard Fugle	Low Flyers	101.91	180
4	628	Ted Lapadakis	Almega	94.73	170

*New Record—123.655 mph. average

B ROADSTER

Place	Car	Entrant	Club	Speed	Points
1	5	Bob Riese	Gear Grinders	137.61	300*
2	388	John Hartman	Pasadena Rdstr Club	137.19	190
3	1	Doug Hartelt	Lancers	135.13	180
4	61	Jack Avakian	Road Runners	134.32	170
5	9	Tom Beatty	Glendale Stokers	132.35	160
6	6	Jim Palm & Conkle	Lancers	127.29	150
7	299	Lehmann & Schwartzrock	Albata	126.58	140
8	318	Norm Lean	Dolphins	125.17	130
9	121	Fred Hadley	Lancers	124.82	120
10	27	Harvey Haller	Road Runners	123.96	110
11	149	Dick Finkle	Road Runners	123.79	100
	214	Carl Kaylor	Gear Grinders	123.79	100
12	33	Lloyd Kear	Mobilers	123.62	90
13	307	Ernest Dewey	San Diego Rd. Club	123.45	80
14	106	Starr & Alger	Lancers	122.44	70
15	470	Fred Oatman	Strokers	121.95	60
16	38	Bob Wenz	Low Flyers	121.13	50
17	177	Don Neary	L. A. Gophers	120.32	40
18	227	Bailey & Bingham	Gear Grinders	120.00	30
19	330	Taylor & Peterson	Dolphins	119.52	20
	866	Robert Clews	Oilers	119.52	20
20	393	Blinn & McCartney	Pasadena Rd. Club	119.36	10

*New Record—143.195 mph. average

C ROADSTER

Place	Car	Entrant	Club	Speed	Points
1	325	Harold Daigh	Dolphins	145.63	300*
2	315	Paul Schiefer	San Diego Rd. Club	139.53	190
3	47	Frank Leonard	L. A. Gophers	138.46	180
4	104	Barber & Dolph	Lancers	133.92	170
5	324	Dowell & Sullivan	Dolphins	131.38	160
6	48	Bob Reemsnyder	Strokers	129.68	150
7	135	Peterman & Carillo	Road Runners	127.11	140
	305	Don McLean	San Riego Rd. Club	127.11	140
8	200	Kenny Parks	Gaters	126.22	130
9	21	Ed Stewart	San Diego Rd. Club	126.05	120
10	55	C. W. 'Scotty' Scott	Hornets	125.52	110
	624	George Castera	Almega	125.52	110
11	53	Coshow Brothers	Lancers	123.45	100
12	331	Doug Harrison	Dolphins	123.28	90
13	541	Tommy Tompkins	Sidewinders	122.78	80
14	505	LeRoy Holmes	Hornets	121.95	70
15	65	Bub Marcia	Road Runners	121.29	60
	461	Harold Osborn	Strokers	121.29	60
	736	Dahm, Dent, & Cass	Pasadena Pacers	121.29	60
16	24	Dick Kraft	Lancers	120.96	50
	450	Alva Voegtly	Clutchers	120.96	50
17	240	Barney Navarro	Glendale Stokers	120.80	40
18	17	Ludvig Solberg Jr.	L. A. Gophers	120.64	30
19	208	Roger Sale	Gear Grinders	120.32	20
20	821	Nick Christos	Dusters	120.16	10

*New Record—143.195 mph. average

D ROADSTER

Place	Car	Entrant	Club	Speed	Points
1	238	Jot Horne	Gear Grinders	124.48	200

A STREAMLINER

Place	Car	Entrant	Club	Speed	Points
1	555	Alex Xydias	Sidewinders	127.29	200
2	557	King & Hansen	Sidewinders	112.92	190
3	71	Lodes Brothers	Road Runners	105.88	180

B STREAMLINER

Place	Car	Entrant	Club	Speed	Points
1	131	Breene & Haller	Road Runners	140.40	200
2	11	Stuart Hilborn	Low Flyers	134.93	190
3	103	Path & Moore	Lancers	133.72	180
4	147	Fred Renoe	Road Runners	124.30	170
5	222	Jim Lindsley	Gear Grinders	120.48	160

C STREAMLINER

Place	Car	Entrant	Club	Speed	Points
1	4	Burke & Francisco	Road Runners	150.75	200
2	159	Nairn & Remington	Low Flyers	132.54	190
3	310	Junior Rotter	Dolphins	127.84	180
4	141	Jack McDermott	Road Runners	126.22	170

Club Points Standings

		Total	Prev.	October
1	Road Runners	8680	6990	1690
2	Lancers	6880	5860	1020
3	Low Flyers	4910	4300	610
4	Dolphins	3890	3010	880
5	San Diego Rd. Club	3620	3090	530
6	Strokers	3260	2990	270
7	Gear Grinders	2930	2120	810
8	Albata	2370	1930	440
9	Sidewinders	2320	1850	470
10	Pasadena Rd. Club	1870	1670	200
11	L. A. Gophers	1850	1600	250
12	Glendale Stokers	1380	1180	200
13	Gaters	1150	1020	130
14	Mobilers	1110	1020	90
15	Almega	740	460	280
16	Hornets	610	430	180
17	Clutchers	600	550	—
18	Throttlers	550	550	—
19	Quarter Milers	190	190	—
20	Pasadena Pacers	60	—	60
21	Roadmasters	50	50	—
22	Oilers	20	—	20
23	Dusters	10	—	10

CRA CHAMPIONSHIPS

(Continued from Page 15)

At the fifth lap Troy was in the lead with Prosser crowding close at his heels. Rathman was running third in the sixth. It was a close packed race until Rathman broke a wheel in the ninth lap and hit the wall.

Heath got stuck in traffic and finished fourth, with Ken Stansberry taking third.

Prosser took over the lead in the 12th lap and held in all the way to win the Championship title for 1948.

There was plenty of passing in the heat laps and with a close paced field of eight cars. Roy Prosser in the second heat and Jim Rigsby in the fourth proved that it doesn't mean a thing where you start when they came all the way from last spot to win.

Rigsby got a break in the last lap of the heat when Lou Figaro made one last try to get past Dempsey Wilson who was in the lead. They both slipped out and Rigsby, running third, slid through the hole and crossed the finish line to win by less than a car length.

The newly paved half-mile track gave the boys quite a little tire trouble. Lou Figaro lost his right rear tread just as he came out of the last turn in the final lap of the second 50. Andy Linden was not so lucky. The same thing happened to him in the first 50 but early enough in the race that he dropped from second to eighth before he got the checkered flag.

Chuck Leighton blew a right front tire and hit the fence after completing 49 and one-half laps in the first 50 lapper. Luck rode with him, too, and he was able to hold his position in third because of his lead over the cars behind.

The C.R.A. gave an unexpected demonstration of the value of one of its rigid restrictions when Red Amic driving a car equipped with safety plates broke a wheel. The safety plate held the wheel on and Red was able to finish the race.

The one jarring note of the whole afternoon came when the supposedly deadly rivals, Troy Ruttman and Allen Heath, were prevailed upon by the management to stage a three lap grudge race before the main events.

Whether the boys were saving their cars or just weren't mad on such a beautiful day is not certain. But certain it is that the race looked more like a love match than a grudge race with each driver practically riding the binders to keep from passing the other one.

Other than this one sour note in an otherwise perfect day of racing, everyone agreed that the C.R.A. Invitational Championship provided plenty of good roadster racing.

CLUB NEWS

MOJAVE TIMING

By R. J. BUTLER

The second annual meeting for all members of the organization was held on the evening of November 21, 1948.

Thirteen trophies were presented to the various winners for MTA's 1948 season, which came to a close on October 31.

Bill Bartlett, Bud Hand and Bob De-Shields won trophies for being the three top point winners. Jim Nelson, De-Shields and Hand received trophies for their records at the end of the season. Arnold Birner, Nelson, Bartlett and DeShields received awards for being high point men at the individual meets. Bert Howman received the Perpetual Four Cylinder Roadster Trophy (for the fastest four cylinder roadster of the season) from Gus Sommerfeld, the 1947 winner.

New officers were elected. Ric Howard of the Rumblers was elected President, Gus Sommerfeld, also a Rumbler, Vice President, and BH Club member Bob Larson was made Secretary-Treasurer. These men will take over their offices on January 1, 1949.

MUTUAL RACING

By MEL DUDLEY

The Mutual is settling down to the winter's work. There will be association meetings in addition to the usual election and rules meetings. H.E. Messler, owner of No. 5, was host at a smoker at Huntington on Saturday night, November 5. Tom Cherry has invited all of the boys to the opening of his new speed shop in "Gasoline Alley," Muncie, Indiana. Here are the car standings at the end of the 1948 season:

No.	Owner—Make	Points
32	Hack Winninger, Merc.	1832
16	Joe Walls, Hudson 6	1444
62	Ermal McCormick, Ford 6	1287
39	Walt Straber, Ford 6	1286
7-11	Maurice Mutersbaugh, Chev	1076
26	Amos Potter, Ford 6	996
33	Art Rhonemous, Ford 6	838
61	Joe Walls, Hudson 6	680
93	Carlos McDonald, Ford 6	508
49	Bill Penrod, Ford 6	508
49	Bill Penrod, Ford 6	506
23	Heuer Bros. (Gimball) Fd. 6	421
10	Jonie Van Dyke, Ford 6	367
4	Chas. Holloway, Ford 6	291
88	David Robinson, Olds 6	274
85	Julius Zimmerman, Chry. 6	257

A total of 97 drivers and 91 cars competed in Mutual events this year.

S.C.T.A.

Plans are under way to produce the SCTA's first annual Year Book which will include news and pictorial interest for all of the clubs in the organization.

NEW MEXICO

By J. ROBERT SETH

Due to the first snow falls in the state and the general coolness of the weather, there has been very little activity with hot rods. The final agreement for next summer's racing in Albuquerque has not been settled, but progress is being made.

The ALBUQUERQUE ROAD PILOTS became members of the Bernilille County Safety Council. It is another step in the club's list of public spirited activities. The showing of the Green Cross on the roadsters is bringing the awakening to several "die-hard" anti-hot rodders.

The organization of a club in Sante Fe is in progress. There has been talk among the group of naming it the Santa Fe Road Pilots to become a state organization rather than a local group. It has its possibilities. I have been appointed to approach the A.R.P. on the subject.

I was wondering if there weren't other groups or individuals that would be interested in such an organization. If so, I would be glad to answer any letters and would like to receive others' views on the subject. I can be reached by writing: 322 South Arno Street in Albuquerque or 654 Granada Place in Santa Fe.

C.R.A.

Carrell Speedway's (Gardena, Calif.) biggest gate of the 1948 season was at the CRA 500 lapper on May 30. The crowd for the roadster race total 18,247. There was a $7680 purse, plus $240 in qualifying money.

Laughs... *from here and there*

By TOM MEDLEY

STOP, LOOK, LISTEN — The reflective man stopped to read the railway warning.

"Those 3 words illustrate the whole scheme of life," said he.

"How?"

"You see a pretty girl . . . you *stop*, you *look*, after you are married you *listen*."

———

The only thing in the way of the automobile these days is the pedestrians.

———

Saleman—"What kind of car would you like, madam, four, six or eight cylinders?"

Timid Customer—"Couldn't I begin with one?"

———

It was their first quarrel and the sordid subject was money.

"Before we were married," she cried bitterly, "you told me you were well off."

"I was," he snarled, "But I didn't know it."

———

Even a judge can turn to his own mental resources, if circumstances are against him.

A bedraggled individual denied that he was intoxicated when the police officer testified that he found the prisoner lying in the street.

"Very well then," said the versatile judge. "You're fined $5.00 for parking more than 6 inches from the curb."

"WOW! LOOK AT THAT VACUUM READING!"

A little girl asked her mother if there were any men in heaven.

"Mama," she said, "I never saw a picture of an angel with a beard or a moustache. Do men ever go to heaven?"

"Oh, yes," replied her mother, "men go to heaven, but it is by a close shave."

———

"No," said the man behind the wheel, "I can't say I have even had to complain of back seat driving. In fifteen years, I have never had a word from behind."

"What kind of a car do you drive?"

"A hearse!"

An automobile collided with a milk wagon and sent the milk splashing on the pavement; soon a crowd gathered.

"Goodness," exclaimed the man, "what an awful waste!"

A very stout lady turned and glared at him, "Just mind your own business."

———

"Your doctor's out here with a flat tire."

"Diagnose the case as flatulency of the perimeter and charge him accordingly," ordered the garage man, "That's the way he does."

STROKER McGURK

NEW QUICK-RELEASE SAFETY BELT

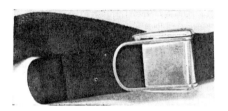

Pacific Airmotive Corporation of Burbank, California, has a new safety belt for roadsters, midgets and big cars. The belt is featured as having the 50% greater strength recommended by the National Aircraft Standards Committee. The buckle has a new, non-jamming design that can be opened with a maximum pull of 45 pounds, even when a weight of 500 pounds is hanging on the belt.

Webbing is of 2-inch width, is flameproof and mildew-resistant. The webbing is available in six colors.

Dick Bair of Akron, Ohio, owns this convertible sedan. Car has a '46 Merc. engine, running Weiand dual manifold, Offenhauser heads and a Winfield cam.

This '29 A coupe belongs to Ed Ulrich of Seymour, Connecticut. It is powered by a Mercury engine with a Winfield cam.

Drivers Speed Hull and John Robinette are shown coming out of the south turn at Columbus, Indiana Speedway. Roadster racing at this track is sanctioned by the Southern Indiana Racing Association.

Bob Hart's '32 roadster was built in 1938-39 in Nassau, New York. It has a full 1946 Mercury motor, hydraulic brakes.

Comparative Timing

To all car owners who regularly run in competition, Mr. Seth's article in November Hot Rod was indeed interesting and presented ideas which may be new to many of us. However, lest some readers gain incorrect ideas from his story, some investigation of his theories seem justified.

His statement concerning a loss of power in a stock 100 HP engine of 32.49% at a 5000-foot elevation can only be referring to such an engine with no correction of jet sizes to maintain mixture ratio. The above figures give a loss in power 6.5% for every 1000 feet in altitude increase. Actually, the figure is closer to 3% loss per 1000 feet, if corrections in carburetor mixture are made to maintain proper mixture ratio. This is the simplest correction for altitude although the 3% power loss still occurs.

Another factor influencing engine output is "Volumetric efficiency." This simply means the percentage of engine displacement that is taken in during a complete cycle. High altitudes, with the consequent reduction in atmospheric pressure, reduce this V. E. the same 3% as mentioned above. Therefore, in order to regain this lost volumetric efficiency, larger valves, cleaner ports, longer intake valve openings or any of the other steps which increase engine output, must be taken. We all know that higher compression heads must be used at altitude. Few realize that an engine built to gain maximum B.H.P. at 5000 feet or more would perform unsatisfactorily or fail at sea level.

Other factor which can be utilized to regain sea level performance are gear ratio and tire sizes used. To allow the engine to run at higher RPM (or less load) higher ratios and smaller tires are indicated. The engine must turn more RPM in order to burn the same amount of mixture per minute at altitude as at sea level. This amount of mixture per minute is simply another expression of H.P. The engine is a pump and, if it pumps less mixture per stroke at altitude, it must make more pumping strokes (RPM) to pump the same weight of fuel. Weight of fuel burned determines the H.P. developed.

Three favorable factors of altitude have been neglected in Mr. Seth's discourse. These are decreased average intake air temperature, less air resistance (drag) and decreased exhaust back pressure. Lower air temperatures tend to improve volumetric efficiency. Less drag at altitude, due to low air densities, reduces air resistance. For example, a jet plane must take in air, compress it and burn fuel with it to develop thrust (H.P.). Yet, in spite of the decreasing thrust (H.P.) at altitude, the plane flies faster because of less drag.

Finally, it is not conclusive to compare performances under conditions as widely differing as Mr. Seth mentions without making all of the adjustments which will allow the engine to develop its maximum H.P. at that altitude.

The mistake was made by running cars with "identical equipment" at 400 feet in California and at 5800 feet in New Mexico. El Mirage is at an elevation of 2400 feet. By that token engines run there are subject to a loss in H.P. of 37.1% of the loss suffered at 5800 feet. Mr. Seth's 100 H.P. V8 should develop nearly 82.6 H.P. at 5800 feet (with all adjustments) and 93.3 H.P. at El Mirage. When the favorable factors mentioned above are utilized at altitude, the difference in performance is much less than he theorizes.

This can easily be proven by the New Mexico delegation if they wish to time their best LOW ALTITUDE car at a meet of either major timing association at El Mirage next season. All concerned would be satisfied if it would clock better than 139 mph, not to mention 164.32 mph!

C. E. CAMP
R.T.A.

Gentlemen:

We read with interest the fine article in your last issue on Comparative Timing by J. Robert Seth, and found his deductions to be interesting and enlightening. We are inclined to differ with some of his expressed views regarding the conditions under which time trials are run at El Mirage Dry Lake. In the first place, El Mirage is located at an altitude of about 2500 feet above sea level. Second, the humidity and atmospheric conditions are far from favorable for producing ideal engine output. Third, and possibly post important, is the fact that the surface over which our time runs are made is loose and dusty, which not only allows unwanted slippage but actually creates a physical resistance.

In a test with a low-powered automobile we found that there was a definite decrease in maximum obtainable speed on the lake bed as compared to runs made on an adjacent black-top road at the same altitude. Our car was capable of towing a roadster at 65 mph on the roadway and dropped to 52 mph on the lake bed with no load in tow.

It is the sincere conviction of the members of our club that in ten years running at the lakes, members of the

S.C.T.A. have been able to develop some of the fastest "hot rods" in America. We are inclined to doubt the accuracy of the 139.65 two-way run speed of the "rod" near Denver, Colorado. As to the possibility of their attaining a speed anywhere near 164 mph at El Mirage, THAT we'd like to see! We would also like to know who made the "sea level" test run of 149.19 as stated in the article.

We're all in favor of comparison tests, but let's check car against car under similar conditions and leave the theorizing to the aircraft books and charts. We would like to see some friendly competition matches between the Road Pilots, their neighbor organizations and our Southern California group. We believe a suitable location could be arranged which would be equally convenient for both factions.

With all due respect to Mr. Seth, let us point out that we enjoy reading his articles and appreciate his sincere interest in the sport, but we also believe that the S.C.T.A. boys are still a few jumps ahead and would like further opportunities to prove it to our skeptical neighbors from other areas.

RICHARD R. RENOE, President
ROAD RUNNER CLUB of
Southern California.

S. C. T. A.

(Continued from Page 9)

scratches. This instance gave definite proof to the advantages of having a securely fastened safety belt and protective helmet, as are required in all S.C.T.A. competition.

In running over a shortened course at this last meet, the S.C.T.A. has proven to itself that more lengthy runs are not necessary, and has further simplified its goal for obtaining a paved strip over which to conduct these events. Whereas they have previously searched for a five-mile-long location, they have now reduced that distance to a total of two and one-quarter miles, which should make the project much more easily attained. Members are confident that with a smooth paved surface over which to run they would be able to move their present day speeds into the high 160 mph. bracket and are hopefully looking forward to the realization of their planned straightaways.

Members of the organization are already planning for newer super-creations with which to boost the records next season. With thirty-six clubs from as far north as Oakland and ranging south to San Diego and El Centro, the SCTA is continuing its drive toward stabilizing the so-called "Hot Rodders" into safety-conscious groups through the sponsoring of their "World's Safest Automotive Speed Trials."

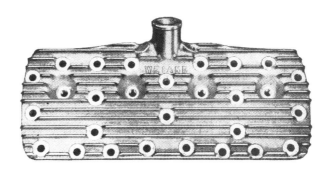
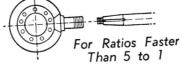
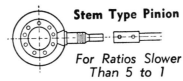

CUSTOM CAR

Take eight parts Ford, one part Studebaker, one part Nash, one part Buick, and one part speedboat . . . pound well . . . and come up with an automobile as individual as a tailor-made suit!

By using that formula and utilizing virtually every spare hour away from his duties as a Mid-Continent Airlines pilot, Captain Sam Giberson, Kansas City, Kansas, has turned a boyhood dream of a "personal" custom-built roadster into reality—just one year and $2600 after starting work on the idea.

Finding that used car parts were almost as difficult to obtain as new cars, Giberson had to make many substitutions, but the finished product bears a strong resemblance to the original sketch.

His first purchase was a 1934 Ford V8 panel truck, all of which was promptly discarded except the frame, rear end and transmission. The body was a 1934 Ford roadster, shortened ten inches and lowered five inches . . . the front fenders from a 1940 Studebaker . . . the front grill from a 1940 Nash . . . the hood from a Buick Roadmaster . . . and the dashboard once was part of a speedboat. The one brand-new part of the car is the engine itself . . . which is a 1947 super-charged Mercury.

Photos by Howdy Williams

350

Index